Improbable Fiction

*"If this were played upon a stage now,
I could condemn it as an improbable fiction."*
—*Shakespeare*, Twelfth Night

IMPROBABLE FICTION The Life of Mary Roberts Rinehart

JAN COHN

UNIVERSITY OF PITTSBURGH PRESS

Published by the University of Pittsburgh Press, Pittsburgh, Pa. 15260
Manufactured in the United States of America
First paperback edition, 2006
10 9 8 7 6 5 4 3 2 1
ISBN 0-8229-5912-7

Grateful acknowledgment is made to Frederick R. Rinehart for permission to reprint material from Mary Roberts Rinehart, *My Story* (New York: Farrar and Rinehart, 1931; rev. ed., New York: Rinehart, 1948) and from manuscript materials in the Rinehart collection, Hillman Library, University of Pittsburgh.

Acknowledgment is made to the heirs of the following individuals for permission to reprint excerpts from their letters: Newton D. Baker, Cyrus Curtis, Josephus Daniels, George H. Doran, Howard Mumford Jones, George Horace Lorimer, Adelaide W. Neall, and Kenneth Parker. Correspondence to and from Roger Scaife is located in The Houghton Library, Harvard University, and is used by permission of the library. Special thanks goes to Frederick R. Rinehart for permission to use letters written by Mary Roberts Rinehart, Stanley M. Rinehart, and Stanley M. Rinehart, Jr., as well as his own.

Picture Credits: cover and frontispiece, Historical Pictures Service, Inc., Chicago; p. 11, from 1977 "Mystery and Suspense Engagement Calendar" compiled by The Main Street Press, Clinton, N.J.; pp. 12 and 226, from *My Story* by Mary Roberts Rinehart, by permission of Frederick R. Rinehart (p. 226, photo by Hal Phyfe); p. 18, photo courtesy of Shadyside Hospital; pp. 33, 86, 102, from the Rinehart collection, Hillman Library, University of Pittsburgh, by permission of Frederick R. Rinehart; p. 41, R. W. Johnston's Studios; p. 62, Jack Sussman; p. 139, Melbourne Spurr, by permission of Mildred Spurr; p. 155, Lenore Kent; p. 176, Clinedinst; p. 190, Ben Pinchot, N.Y.; p. 214, Tom Kelley; p. 217, reprinted from *The Saturday Evening Post* © 1936 The Curtis Publishing Company; p. 220, *Ladies Home Journal* (May 1931). Other photos by permission of Frederick R. Rinehart.

This book is dedicated

—encyclopedically—

to

Bill

my parents

Cathy and David

and

to all our good friends in Pittsburgh.

Contents

Illustrations

Acknowledgments

THE PREPARATION OF THIS BOOK began in libraries; accordingly, my thanks begin with the archivists, curators, and librarians who have been so helpful to me, most especially Charles Aston and Jean Blanco of Special Collections, Hillman Library, at the University of Pittsburgh, who have become colleagues in Rinehartiana. Special thanks are due, as well, to Marilyn Albright and Dorothea Thompson of the Hunt Library, Carnegie-Mellon University, for locating particularly elusive references and copies of hard-to-get early Rinehart stories. Saundra Taylor, Curator of Manuscripts at the Lilly Library at the University of Indiana, turned up a draft of the Bobbs-Merrill promotional literature for *The Circular Staircase;* and Peter Parker, Chief of Manuscripts at the Historical Society of Pennsylvania, made available to me some early correspondence between Rinehart and George H. Lorimer. The Houghton Library at Harvard University was kind enough to send me copies of Rinehart's correspondence with Roger Scaife from its Houghton-Mifflin collection. Betty Quinette of Allegheny High School found Mary Ella Roberts's high school transcript.

A number of people have provided me with information not found in libraries. Barbara Reid of the Mary Roberts Rinehart Foundation has been extremely helpful, particularly in copying the original file cards on which Rinehart had her publication records kept. Linda and Gary Otto, who now own the Beech Street house where the Rineharts lived from 1907 to 1911, let me see their house both before and after renovation. Mrs. Robert W. McKnight cordially invited me to her home in Sewickley and shared her memories of the Rinehart family. William Hackett's letters have been rich in background information about Rinehart publishing, as have been conversations with Fred Cushing. Dr. Sidney Kaufman examined Rinehart's medical record with me and helped a layman understand it. My parents, Beatrice and Allan Kadetsky, took on the wearisome task of searching out early and obscure Rinehart stories in the Boston Public Library. The award for research, however, goes to David Solomon, who, being sent on a near-hopeless quest to search all Pittsburgh newspaper files on microfilm for two stories written by Mary Roberts in 1892 or 1893, found them!

The manuscript for this book was read and criticized in several stages by colleagues and friends. Mary Briscoe of the University of Pittsburgh provided helpful suggestions and moral support. David Walton of Carnegie-Mellon University read two versions, critiqued them thoroughly, and provided expert and sensitive editorial help with the second. My husband Bill not only read all the versions from first draft to page proof, but assumed the unrewarding job of telling me that certain sections (the bad ones) were bad. My editor, Louise Craft, has, while kindly respecting my wishes, made excellent changes and judicious cuts.

My deepest gratitude goes to members of the Rinehart family. Ted and Betty Rinehart in New York and Alan and Ernestine Rinehart in New Orleans have been generous with hospitality, information, family letters, and photographs. They have always encouraged this book and they have never attempted to shape its ideas or censor its content. Rinehart's grandson George and his wife Sharon Rinehart, and Rinehart's niece Virginia and her husband Sillman Wallace have also graciously extended hospitality and shared reminiscences. Another grandson, Stanley Marshall Rinehart III, spent an afternoon talking with me about his grandmother. Rinehart's longtime secretary, William Sladen, has my special thanks as well. Blessed with a remarkable memory, he gave me a morning of invaluable conversation, checked my bibliography, read and checked the manuscript, and continued in correspondence to answer my questions.

A part of the research for this book was done under a Falk Grant from Carnegie-Mellon University.

Introduction

"THERE IS NO TRULY HONEST AUTOBIOGRAPHY," Mary Roberts Rinehart wrote in the opening pages of her own autobiography, *My Story,* published in 1931. The truth about one's own life is blurred and altered, she explained, through conscious acts of tact and unconscious defenses of memory. Beyond that, for a storyteller, for one whose gifts lay in the ability to shape human experience to fit the molds of fiction, the act of autobiography became in part an act of fiction-making. *My Story* is almost an autobiographical novel.

I first learned the name of Mary Roberts Rinehart when my parents attempted to explain to me that visits to the local library were more fruitful for children who learned the names of the authors whose books they liked. Grudgingly I gave up the hunt for intriguing titles and settled down to a youth largely misspent in the reading of mystery novels, among them those by Mary Roberts Rinehart.

The name, however, was all I ever learned. So, it came as a great surprise to me, many years later, to learn that Mary Roberts Rinehart had been born in Allegheny, right across the river from Pittsburgh where I was then living. Moreover, she had lived in Pittsburgh's suburbs for half her long life, and after her death her sons had given her papers to the Hillman Library at the University of Pittsburgh—a ten-minute walk from my office at Carnegie-Mellon University.

The habits of that misspent youth had pursued me into adulthood, and I thought I might very much like to write the biography of a mystery novelist. But it did not turn out that way. Thousands of letters and scores of books later, I learned that my "mystery novelist" was someone considerably more prodigious: a writer of novels and plays and stories and articles, a war correspondent, a traveler to remote and exotic places, a wife and a mother, and—in that strikingly American way—a public person, a celebrity.

Still, the character I was learning about was distanced; she came to me secondhand, sometimes filtered through others' memories, sometimes through the personae she assumed. The evidences of another person's existence—her books and letters, photographs and portraits, a fountain pen or a Queen Anne desk—and the living witnesses, her children, are material enough but in their very substantiality interpose themselves between biographer and subject.

Immediacy came accidentally and, at first, through trivia: a scrap of paper, mistakenly filed among some *Saturday Evening Post* correspondence, with a scribbled recipe for cheese dip; a 1947 grocer's bill for gifts of food sent to old friends in postwar London. Then, one afternoon, while I was working at the Hillman Library, a metal strongbox was brought to my desk. It had not been opened; indeed, the box was locked and the key missing. But that day a carpenter broke the lock so that I could examine the contents of the box. It was crammed with papers—folded up, rolled up, some torn. Under the papers were souvenirs. The box held Rinehart's mementoes of her days as a correspondent at the Front during World War I: diaries, notes, photographs, passports, *cartes de séjour,* hotel bills, shipboard programs. And more bizarre trophies, among them, wrapped in a piece of stained surgical gauze, a bit of shrapnel removed from the head of a Belgian soldier; Rinehart had watched that operation being performed.

Working on that box of souvenirs, reading the war diaries, I found that Mary Roberts Rinehart was becoming material, firsthand, for me, and that these pieces of evidence, of materiality, were now taking shape, forming patterns. But when I returned to *My Story,* to test my patterns, I found them to be slightly askew, different from those in the autobiography. The idiosyncratic weighting of events in that book puzzled me. And the character there was different, too, a smoother, more tranquil figure than mine.

A partial answer to that puzzle lay in a sheaf of papers I found late in my research. At close to eighty, Mary Roberts Rinehart decided to write another, more intimate version of her life story, something for her sons to read. As it turned out, she distributed only three or four pages to her family. She left a hundred more pages, some revised in her cut-and-pin fashion, among her papers. I read those pages wondering why a woman who burned drafts and notes and preserved no diaries save those from the Great War had not discarded this. Whatever the reason, I was grateful, for nowhere did her voice come through clearer. The storyteller's shaping, the celebrity's posture, disappear, and in her bold hand, only slightly weakened by age, Rinehart wrote about the confusions and the frustrations of her adolescence and her early marriage and her consequent need to become someone, to achieve something.

But brought up as she had been, the daughter of a proper Victorian household, Rinehart distrusted that ambition. Out of the central disharmony of her life, the profound ambivalence with which she enacted her roles as writer and as wife and mother, she constructed an apologia, explaining her career to her audience, her family—even to herself. She needed a structure that justified ambition and hard work and success, and she found that structure in what I call the Rinehart myth: the successful writer born out of financial need, family responsibility, and pure chance.

Those are the patterns of *My Story,* so successfully woven that it becomes Rinehart's dominant fiction, and—as she warned her readers almost half a century ago—not "truly honest." And if like autobiography, biography, too, fails to be "truly honest," it is because in its own way biography is an act of fiction, shaped out of the imagination of the biographer, where the act of discovery continually threatens to become an act of creation.

Improbable Fiction

1

The Street

1876–1895

IT WAS NOT PRECISELY A STORY of rags to riches. Arch Street, where Mary Ella Roberts lived as a child, was a respectable neighborhood, if far from a wealthy one—by no means a slum. Riches, on the other hand, were to come, as well as fame and the friendship of powerful men. Unlike other American women of the time who found their way to wealth and position in brilliant marriages, Mary Roberts Rinehart made her own success. Her life story, the ambition and the hard work that made possible her progress from genteel poverty to what some have called "tycoon-hood," may qualify her as America's first female Horatio Alger.

Rinehart's life story began in America's centennial year. The well-to-do made their way to Philadephia and the great Exposition. The Roberts family, at the western end of the state, were not among those well-heeled visitors. Tom Roberts, a young man with a new wife, worked as a clerk. His small salary could not support a house and, as was customary in those days, he brought his bride to live with his mother. Even after Mary Ella was born on August 12, 1876, the Tom Robertses stayed on at 6 West Diamond Street with Grandmother Roberts, Uncle John and his wife Sade, and three young aunts.[1]

It was a household accustomed to hard work and few luxuries. James William Roberts, Mary's grandfather, had been born in 1817 in rural Washington County, south of the growing industrial city of Pittsburgh. He came from a family of Seceder Presbyterians who had emigrated from Northern Ireland to America in the middle of the eighteenth century and moved to western Pennsylvania before 1800. The Roberts men were ministers and teachers; the women, wives of ministers and teachers. James's father, Abram (Mary's great-grandfather), had taught arithmetic, but unlike the rest of the family, James had no profession. Seeking work, he moved north to Allegheny, across the river from Pittsburgh, sometime before 1850, when Thomas, his first child, was born. He and his wife Margaret lived on Beaver

3

Street and he supported his growing family as a carpenter and a watchman until his death in 1863, at the age of forty-six.

When Roberts died, his widow, Margaret Mawhinney Roberts, left with five surviving children and no money, "turned to her needle," in the contemporary phrase. The boys, Thomas and John, were thirteen and ten then; the three girls were younger: Letitia, eight; Anna Margaret, five; and Matilda, an infant under a year old. From her house in Allegheny the Widow Roberts built something of a little business, hiring sewing girls to help her with her orders. They worked in a back room, "badly lighted and cluttered with sewing machines," as Rinehart recalled years later in her autobiography, *My Story*.[2]

Allegheny was Pittsburgh's smaller sister city in the 1860s. At the beginning of the Civil War it had 25,000 inhabitants, half as many as Pittsburgh. The ratio remained the same through the next two decades; by 1880 Allegheny's population was 78,000 compared with Pittsburgh's 156,000. After 1880, however, the great influx of immigrant labor swelled Pittsburgh to half a million, while Allegheny had, by 1890, grown to only 100,000. In fact, the two cities were developing very differently in the latter part of the nineteenth century. As Pittsburgh became a great industrial city, its central area, where the three rivers meet, changed from a place where small brick houses shared city blocks with factories, warehouses, stores, and markets, in the older American manner, to a modern downtown. By the 1870s, well-to-do Pittsburghers were moving to newly fashionable neighborhoods, among them Allegheny. Allegheny itself had been made up of small manufacturies, business establishments, stores, markets, and houses—a smaller replica of Pittsburgh across the river. Slowly the manufacturing moved out of Allegheny and more of the area was given up to private residences. Some were the grand new houses on Ridge Avenue; more were the old two- and three-story brick houses in which families like the Robertses lived on Diamond Street.

While Mrs. Roberts provided money for the family from her dressmaking business, the boys picked up what jobs they could, at first as errand boys, later as clerks. Thomas Roberts was twenty-five and working as a clerk when he married Cornelia Gilleland. She, too, came of Seceder Presbyterian people from Northern Ireland. She was brought up on the family farm in Valencia, about twenty miles north of Pittsburgh. Her mother had died, probably when Cornelia was in her teens, and her father had remarried. Disliking her new stepmother, Cornelia, with her sister Ella, left the farm and moved to Allegheny.

Not long after, at the age of twenty-two, she married Thomas Roberts and a year later their first child, Mary Ella, was born. Mary, or Mamie as she was called as a child, lived in her grandmother's house for four years. Her parents occupied the front room on the second floor and above them, on the third floor, lived Uncle John and his wife Sade. Sade, whose neurasthenic "delicacy" fascinated young Mamie, and John, her loving and generous uncle, would become central figures in Rinehart's life and imagination.

In 1880, when Mamie's sister Olive was born, Tom Roberts moved his family to their own home on Arch Street. The two-story brick row house was not large but it was "solid and substantial."[3] On the first floor were a parlor, a dining room, and a kitchen. Behind the kitchen a shed housed the hydrant from which Cornelia Roberts drew water. Across the alley at the end of the yard rose the gray walls of the penitentiary. On the second floor were three bedrooms and, at the top of the stairs, a back room, for a maid—when times were good—for storage in leaner times. That house, like the street on which it stood, deeply impressed itself on Mary's imagination and reappeared frequently in her fiction.

> Under an old ailanthus tree, was the house . . . a small brick, with shallow wooden steps and—curious architecture of the Middle West sixties—a wooden cellar door beside the steps.
>
> In some curious way it preserved an air of distinction among its more pretentious neighbors, much as a very old lady may now and then lend tone to a smart gathering. On either side of it, the taller houses had an appearance of protection rather than of patronage. It was a matter of self-respect, perhaps. No windows on the Street were so spotlessly curtained, no doormat so accurately placed, no "yard" in the rear so tidy with morning-glory vines over the whitewashed fence.[4]

The house was Cornelia's province. She was hard-working, a farmer's daughter, and she scrubbed away at the ceaseless Pittsburgh grime, and cooked and baked and marketed and sewed her daughters' clothes. "Nothing was ever so immaculate as her house, so white as the oilcloth on the kitchen table, so red as the legs of those tables, so smooth as her beds."[5]

> The parlor was seldom used. It was furnished with rosewood upholstered in black horsehair, and on each chairback was a carved rose surrounded by leaves. There was an old square piano [Cornelia's Hardman upright, bought on the installment plan], also, and between the two windows a long gilt mirror, with a marble slab a foot or so from the floor.[6]

The house was part of a row of four. Next door lived a deaf and dumb professor with his spinster sister and beside them, the Millers. Clem Miller was a veteran of the Civil War and a survivor of Andersonville Prison. Bessie Miller was Mamie's playmate. Together they created a house for their dolls in Cornelia's shed—except on the days when the washerwoman came to work and shooed the girls away. Mamie lost her friend in 1884; at seven Bessie died of scarlet fever. The last family in the row had pretensions and steadfastly ignored their neighbors. Around the corner were John and Sade, expressing a new prosperity with a stable at the end of their lot, and close by was Grandmother Roberts, who now took in roomers. Matilda (Mary's favorite Aunt Tillie) helped with her mother's house. The other daughters were also kept busy. Letitia (Aunt Tish) was sent to a seminary to be trained as a teacher, but Tish, "the great lady of the family,"[7] never worked as a teacher. Anna Margaret (Maggie), destined to become the spinster sister, eventually took a job in a department store.

Tom Roberts, meanwhile, was doing well. The year he rented the house, he became a sewing machine agent; the year after, the manager of a sewing machine agency. By 1882, with whatever know-how he had picked up from his mother's dressmaking establishment, he was managing the Domestic Sewing Machine Company near the corner of Sixth Street in Pittsburgh. The next year the agency had changed its name, becoming T. B. Roberts and Co. At that time, in the middle 1880s, Roberts left his house each day in the morning coat and high silk hat that marked him as a solid man of business. He walked with other men of affairs down Federal Street, the main street of Allegheny, and across the Sixth Street Bridge. Only a few yards along Sixth Street was Roberts's office. There was horse-car service as well, and sometimes Mamie paid the nickel fare and took the car to her father's office, where "two or three women sat at sewing machines, demonstrating what sewing machines could do, and the window was filled with examples of this work, puffings and ruffings."[8] Roberts sat at his desk at the back of the establishment; he spent less time selling than hoping to sell machines and most of his time dreaming up ideas for new patents.

The life of the Street was to provide a rich source of memories for Mary Roberts Rinehart, representing both the security and warmth of family life and the trap, the narrowness, of middle-class mores. But for Mamie Roberts in the mid-1880s, the Street was the whole world. The milkman came daily to fill a quart pitcher for five cents; cream, a luxury, cost twenty cents a quart. The butcher was a German, with a shop in the Old Market on Federal Street; he sold the Rineharts their Sunday roast for fifteen cents a pound. Country people brought vegetables and fruit, chickens and eggs and butter to the Old Market. The center aisle was given over to women selling dairy products, and Cornelia bought her eggs and butter from distant Gilleland relatives. Cornelia fed her family on nine dollars a week, and they ate well. On Tuesday,

Thursday, and Saturday, her daughters in tow, she did her marketing. Mamie loved to watch oysters being "ladled out of a great hollow marble bowl."[9] The grocer had a telephone, introduced to Pittsburgh in 1877 and improved in 1879 with a new switchboard to serve its 777 subscribers. When Mamie Roberts was a child, the grocer's telephone was used only for emergencies like summoning the doctor, as when Olive fell desperately ill of typhoid fever. Years later she would use the butcher's telephone to hear her husband read her a publisher's letter accepting the manuscript of *The Circular Staircase*, her first published book.

The market, an occasional car ride to her father's office, and the Street —Allegheny was a narrow but comfortable world. Horses and carts rode over the cobblestone streets, cattle were driven through on their way to the slaughterhouse, cows grazed on the Common. But changes came. Gas lights were installed. The Common became a park. In the winter Mary and Olive skated there on the frozen lake and in the summer Cornelia sometimes made them sandwiches to take on picnics. And there was the Second Ward School where Mary, a chubby "little girl with a round face, blue eyes, almost black hair, and a snub nose,"[10] began her education. The very first thing she learned there was the necessity of becoming right-handed; a smart rap over the knuckles of her left hand, gripping a pencil, enforced that lesson.

Saturdays brought the weekly bath. Cornelia pumped up the water from the hydrant and heated it in the boiler on the stove. Then Mamie and Olive were thoroughly scrubbed in the tin tub on the kitchen floor. They were ready now to suffer another Presbyterian sabbath, another day of prohibitions. Although Tom Roberts did not attend church, the rest of the family did. After morning services came the heavy Sunday dinner and then the long, long day of sabbath quiet, broken by Sunday school in the afternoon. Olive recalled sitting quietly on the front stoop, hands folded;[11] Mary remembered that the piano could be played—but only for hymns. In the silence and inactivity, she could brood about salvation and about the change of heart necessary for conversion. God was a grim judge; salvation seemed doubtful.

Many years later from the incalculably different world of 1954, Rinehart remembered her childhood as contented but not particularly joyful. There were few recreations for children and many restrictions. Tom and Cornelia were not demonstrative, not to one another nor to their daughters. Misbehavior was treated severely. "[My parents] believed in corporal punishment, and my mother kept a small whip for that purpose." Sometimes there was "trouble" between Mamie's parents, particularly if Tom stopped on his way home for a drink or two; his wife had no tolerance for his "weakness."[12]

Cornelia was not, however, so rigid as her mother-in-law, for she did attend the theater. Once, in the mid-eighties, she and Tom went to Pittsburgh to see *The Black Crook,* a scandalous affair in which the leading lady appeared in black tights. That same evening, Aunt Ella, Cornelia's sister, treated Mamie to a visit to the exposition grounds. While the two were examining pianos, exhibited on a balcony above the main hall, the balcony gave way. Mamie fell onto an iron fence, her cheek impaled and her thigh broken. Grandmother Roberts interpreted this "as a penalty" for Tom and Cornelia's playgoing.[13]

An even more frightening episode occurred for Mamie when she was about five. A woman applying for a domestic job lured her away from the house, taking her a considerable distance. Mamie slowly became alarmed and when she began to cry, the woman took her "into a courtyard filled with wagons and there shut me in an outbuilding." She took a pin and ring that Mamie wore and warned her to be quiet.[14] Much later, Mamie emerged from the courtyard and was found by a policeman. She was safe, but the frightening memory lingered for many years.

There was violence, too, on the Street. The butcher's daughter murdered her mother with an axe. In the new steam laundry next to the four row houses, a young laundress caught her hand between the hot rollers of the mangle, and Mamie long remembered her horrible screams. There were, too, the periodic floods and "resignedly the families in the district prepared for them." In February 1884 the waters crested at 36.5 feet and low-lying Allegheny was inundated. Tom Roberts is recalled "rowing his family through his Sixth Street office," silk hat on his head.[15] Five years later Mary stood with her mother and watched dead bodies carried by on the rivers swollen with the waters of the Johnstown Flood. Still, Mamie Roberts was growing up in a fairly protected world, far from the strikes, violence, poverty, and typhoid epidemics of industrial Pittsburgh. Not until she entered the hospital as a nurse-in-training would she encounter that world.

The model Cornelia Roberts provided for her daughter Mamie was a conventional one but as things turned out a puzzling one. The industrious Cornelia cared for her house, her daughters, and her husband—ironing each morning the splendid silk hat Tom sported on his way down Federal Street to the office. But the reward for this model existence was not forthcoming, and Cornelia Roberts faced a series of savage blows in the years ahead.

In contrast was the model provided by Cornelia's sister-in-law Sade, the "delicate" one. Sade spent much of her time in ill health, often confined to her room. As an older woman, Rinehart recognized the neurotic nature of Sade's indisposition, understanding that ill health was real enough to her but at the same time provided an escape—an escape from childbearing,

Rinehart later thought, and she observed how "the club of [Sade's] delicacy was held over all our heads. She must never be worried, never do any labor." She died, many years later, of cancer; until then "she sat in her immaculate house, her beautiful hands folded, her little shawls about her shoulders, and I looked at her with admiration and with awe."[16] Unlike Cornelia, Sade was protected, for Uncle John prospered and in his prosperity lavished care upon his wife. By 1890 John and Sade moved to elite Sewickley up the Ohio River —a move Mary herself would make some twenty years in the future.

The contrasting examples of Cornelia and Sade were to become deeply impressed on Mary Roberts Rinehart's mind. She would always endeavor to live up to her mother's exact example as wife, mother, and housekeeper. On the other hand, she had learned from Sade the attractions of escape from domestic and maternal responsibilities: "In writing I was seeking escape, as Aunt Sade had sought it in her delicacy."[17] In fact, she could imitate Aunt Sade more exactly, and sometimes she, too, used ill health as an escape from her own furious energy.

For the Thomas Roberts family prosperity did not last long. Financial problems began in the late 1880s; by 1887 Roberts had lost his sewing machine franchise, and the Domestic Sewing Machine Company had found a new manager. By 1888 he was on the road as a traveling salesman. Then, in 1890, Mamie's first year in high school, the family left Arch Street for Poplar, farther north in Allegheny and farther away from the Common, center of genteel houses and family life.

For Mamie, hard times first became apparent when the maid was let go and piano lessons ceased. Clearer evidence was to come. One day Mamie found that she had been moved into Olive's room, for there were to be roomers in hers. "With the innate snobbishness of children I hated having 'roomers.' The girls I knew were of well-to-do families. Practically all of them were infinitely better off than we were. They gave little sub-deb parties . . . with real dance programs with tiny pencils tied to them, and with a man at the piano and sometimes a violinist also." Although roomers were not so demeaning as boarders, who had to be provided with meals, the change was humiliating for a sixteen year old. Mamie and Olive, moreover, had to help their mother with the housework; with or without a maid Cornelia Roberts maintained her immaculate house and middle-class ways, undergoing what Rinehart later called "that agonizing strain to keep up appearances which is the real tragedy of the impoverished genteel family."[18]

In high school Mamie elected the "English Course," more academic than the practical "Normal Course" or "Commercial Course"; she also edited and wrote for the school paper and was a member of the debating society. There were fifty-nine students who completed high school in Mamie's class, eighteen in the English course. In her first year she did her best work, attaining an average of 81.7. She took six courses: rhetoric, history, literature, physical geography, algebra, and Latin, in which she progressed over the next years through Caesar and Vergil. Her average fell a bit in her second year—most notably through a descent in her history grade, from 83 to 71. Her senior year showed a further decline, to a 76.2 average, probably reflecting her distress and self-consciousness about the family situation in the early nineties. She took only four courses that year: literature, geometry, natural philosophy, and rhetoric.[19]

The courses in which Mamie did consistently well were rhetoric and literature. She had done a great deal of reading from the time when she discovered that the mayor's office housed not only the city jail but a library as well. She read "with amazing rapidity" but in a hit or miss fashion that took her through the great English novelists of the nineteenth century and on to the more morally dubious Dumas, Balzac, and Zola. She read, however, "for the stories alone and with no comprehension whatever of the human relations involved." By 1890 Mamie could borrow books from the splendid new Free Library in Allegheny, Andrew Carnegie's gift to the city.[20]

There was another source of books as well, books of a less high-minded cast. In the summers Mamie spent some weeks in the country, visiting Gilleland aunts and uncles in Valencia. One day she stumbled upon a cache of dime novels, stashed under the hinged cover of a kitchen bench. Foxe's *Book of Martyrs*, with its lurid descriptions of men burned at the stake, was on top; underneath were such treasures as *Deadwood Dick* and *Red Hand, the Avenger*. This was not, or so Mary Roberts Rinehart recalled in 1909, the reading matter of the Gilleland relatives, but of that stock-farm character of the nineteenth century, the hired man, "pale-eyed, pale-haired, melancholy."[21]

Although Mamie had no burning desire for self-expression, she did like, as Rinehart recalled, "to sit down with a clean sheet of paper and put words on it." In 1892, her imagination filled with romantic fiction and her practical side with the determination to supplement the diminished family income, she published her first piece of fiction. In September 1891 the *Pittsburgh Press* had announced a monthly contest open to "Our Amateur Contributors." The *Press* would print the best stories (600-word limit) in the Sunday paper and, each month, award the writer of the best story two five-dollar gold pieces. On March 27, 1892, M. E. Roberts' story, "Lord Ainsleigh's Heir," appeared in the *Pittsburgh Press*. It was followed, on April 17, by "A Double Tragedy," by M. E. R. The *Press* did not award pieces of gold for either of these works.[22]

"Lord Ainsleigh's Heir" is a story of a young American's discovery of his true parentage. The pleasure that Charlie Gilbert takes in learning that he is the son of a titled Englishman is blighted, however; for it appears he is (as a consequence) the brother of his fiancée. But in the end this difficulty is resolved when Charlie's betrothed finds that she, too, has been misled about her real parents. The story closes with Charlie and Belle married and, as Lord and Lady Ainsleigh, established "in their beautiful London home, among all the paintings of ancestors." While it is incautious to look too deeply into an adolescent story, particularly one so filled with the stereotypes of sentimental and sensational Victorian fiction, it is curious to find that a couple of the recurrent, though often buried, themes in Rinehart's fiction do appear in it. One is the disguising of a young man's or woman's real parentage. The other is the threat of incest, in later stories implied through extremely complex chains of relationships.

"A Double Tragedy" is a story of revenge and remorse, too complicated even to summarize, featuring Mary Roberts Rinehart's first detective —Richards, known as "The Shadower." Rinehart, years later, had "no recollection of those early efforts, except that they must have been terrible, but I do remember that my Uncle John read one of them, and said there was enough plot in it to make a book!"[23] Uncle John was right, whichever of the stories he read.

As an adult, Mary Roberts Rinehart saw two distinct sides of her character, reflecting the different qualities of her parents: "I inherited from my mother a sort of fierce driving energy and a practical outlook on life which have been most helpful. But such invention as I have, such dreams as I have

A cartoonist's view (1920) of Mary Roberts finding the "hired man's" reading matter.

dreamed have come from [my father]. And quite early by unconscious imitation I assumed his viewpoint." In Rinehart's 1914 novel *"K,"* young Sidney Page, who like Mamie lives in a house where women earn money by doing needlework and taking in roomers, sits on her porch, looking at the darkening street, and the author tells us that "with that dreamer's part of her that she had inherited from her dead and gone father, she was quietly worshiping the night. But her busy brain was working, too—the practical brain that she had got from her mother's side."[24]

Tom Roberts, in his life and, even more powerfully in his death, was the central figure of Mamie Roberts's childhood. He was, like his brother John, a very handsome man. A portrait photograph of the two brothers shows young men as similar as twins, with oval faces, regular features, and striking dark eyes, John seated in a casual pose, Tom beside him, wearing his tall silk hat.[25]

Tom Roberts (standing)
with Uncle John.

In the early 1890s, when hard times settled over the whole country, Tom Roberts's financial situation worsened. He tried selling insurance, selling wallpaper on the road for his brother John, and promoting the new cash register—but those business ventures met with no more success than his previous attempts. Suffering continual frustration, Roberts apparently began to drink more heavily.

Financial hardship only exacerbated Roberts's more generalized sense of frustration. His ambition lay in inventing and he developed some kind of rotary shuttle for sewing machines. When the patent expired, he did not have the money to renew it. It was a particularly bitter pill, for he had once turned down, so Rinehart recalled, an offer of $10,000 for the rights. He attempted to make other innovations as well: an insulation material for telegraph wires, a scheme for making cement out of the slag from Pittsburgh mills —a feat of alchemy for the slag that sat in great ugly mountains along Pittsburgh's riverbanks. Rinehart recalled her father working at his drawings in his Sixth Street office and at home, with his close friend, D. F. Patterson, an attorney who lived nearby on North Avenue. Patterson and Roberts schemed together, at one time working on an idea for a new washing machine. Patterson was to supply the capital, Roberts the know-how. "Together they would go into the dining room, where the table was large, and spread out their drawings and blue-prints. They dreamed and talked in low voices and high figures, and in their dreams they were incredibly rich, incredibly successful."[26]

Only in his dreams, however, did Tom Roberts ride the wave of American prosperity. Cornelia, more practical and saddled with roomers, "did not approve." In his dreamy ambition, perhaps also in his growing frustration, Roberts lived somewhat apart from the domestic realities of the household. When his lawyer-friend was not with him, he read. Olive recalled that her responsibility was to fetch two books a day from the library for her father.[27] "He loved us all, I am sure," Rinehart remembered, "but we were curiously detached from his inner life." The judgment is generous. Mary Roberts Rinehart had learned to cope with the memories of her father, but for young Mamie Roberts there was confusion and resentment. She was helping with the housework; her room had gone to the roomers. Her resentment echoes in a curious story she told about the death of her little bird. "But his death alone was not the tragedy. It was that his death had been unnecessary. We had gone into the country, and my father was to look after the bird. But he and his friend the dreamer had had some new and magnificent idea. They went away to talk it over, and Dicky had died of starvation."[28] As she learned from the roles played by Cornelia and Aunt Sade, Mamie learned from her father's example as well. What she learned was never to fall a passive victim to poverty.

Even as a child Mary Roberts was ambitious and independent. Her progressive parents allowed her a bicycle, freeing her at once from the immediate vicinity of the Street and from the innumerable restrictions on the life of a young girl growing up in a still-Victorian world. The neighbors protested; bicycle riding was "unfeminine and immodest. It would make me bold." With boys as playfellows, Mamie could ride out to the country on a Saturday, carrying her box of lunch. It was freedom and exercise, and it was also a way in which boys were removed "from the unpleasant world of ugly whispers into the open air of good fellowship."[29]

It was, though, still a morally stifling world. Mamie was taught not to see the evidences of sin. There were girls who cut and curled their hair and who painted their faces. "But," Rinehart remembered, "you never looked at them. You looked away quickly, as though they were not there." She was trained, as well, not to look at saloons or at billiard halls. Divorce was possible but, with respectable people, it was met with ostracism. No "spirits" were kept, at least openly, in the house. Mamie did enjoy the chaste romances appropriate to a girl of her time. She once adventured out to lunch and a matinee with her high school Latin teacher. And at about the same time, when Mamie was fifteen or sixteen, she "even became engaged . . . to a tall blonde boy," who gave her "a ring set with a sardonyx." Engagements were official enough to permit an embrace every now and then, but Rinehart noted that "nothing more passionless can be imagined."[30]

The conventional expectation for young girls was marriage. Those who wanted or needed to support themselves until marriage might work. New kinds of jobs were opening for young women—they could become clerks in the department stores that were replacing the older dry-goods establishments or office workers, perhaps "typewriters"—but these were not jobs appropriate to young women of good family. Teaching, of course, remained respectable work for women, and it would have been suitable for Mamie, like her younger sister, to prepare through the high school "Normal Course" for a position as a teacher. In any event, she was beginning to recognize that she should prepare herself for a career, for even as a child Mamie had seen the plight of dependent single women, living with relatives, their position "always humiliating and often actually wretched."

> Economically, they were almost helpless. Unmarried women of good family had practically no resources. They could, like my grandmother, resort to the needle, or open their houses to paying guests; or if sufficiently trained they could "teach school." Also in dire emergency they could go into shops as saleswomen. This last, however, implied a loss in social status.[31]

A new career possibility for Mamie Roberts appeared one day in the person of a female doctor. C. Jane Vincent, M.D., moved onto the Street. As Rinehart recalled, the Street did not give her any trouble; they simply did not patronize her. Mamie announced to her amused family and her derisive school friends that she would become a doctor, and she continued to cherish that idea when the time came for her to graduate from high school.

Mamie was graduated in June 1893, the year of the panic and the beginning of the severe depression that followed it. Hard times came with particular viciousness to industrial Pittsburgh. Many workers had not yet recovered from the suffering that came with the Homestead Strike the previous summer. So serious was the situation that in a period before welfare and in a city where management, and the "respectable people," had come to hate and fear the factory workers—especially the immigrant factory workers—on whom the economy now relied, it became essential to provide relief. In the winter of 1893–1894, the city gave over $130,000 to needy workers and their families. Private charities, spurred by Andrew Carnegie and working through the mills, provided another quarter of a million. (Some of that money, as it turned out, was subsequently deducted from the workers' paychecks as better times returned.)[32]

For Mamie Roberts hard times meant the end of any college plans. But Uncle John made a generous offer; he would send her to medical college. Unfortunately though, Mamie was too young, at sixteen, to enter, and she came up with the alternative idea of going to nursing school. In 1884 the Homeopathic Medical and Surgical Hospital and Dispensary had begun to train nurses, the first school for nurses between the Allegheny Mountains and Chicago. Although Rinehart did not recall how the idea of nursing had occurred to her, perhaps she had been intrigued by stories about this new profession for women.

One such story, curiously enough, appeared in the *Pittsburgh Press* right beside M. E. Roberts's first published story, "Lord Ainsleigh's Heir." "TRAINED NURSES," the headline read, "Graduating Exercises at the Allegheny General Hospital. ELEVEN WILL GET DIPLOMAS." The article was illustrated with drawings of two nurses, Miss Tildlesley and Miss Perkins, and informed interested readers that

> there is not a more attractive commencement service at any educational hall than the white-capped nurses hold at the presentation of the hard won diploma, that appears so innocent a roll, with a blue ribbon knotted around it, but means so much labor, courage, watchfullness and so thorough a learning of the healing in the soft, deft touch of a woman's hand in the sick room.

And, if that were not sufficiently appealing to a young girl, the article went on to describe the "frock" of the new nurses, "of a delicate blue-gray chambray, with large white apron and half sleeves of the finest linen, and white cap." Such a costume had "much of the picturesqueness of the winsome attire of the nun added to in effect by the silver chain hung from the waist, with scissors, a little cushion for often-needed pins, and such necessaries."[33] That was an article the fifteen-year-old Mamie had to have read.

Her enthusiasm was not shared. Mrs. Roberts was appalled. Not only would her daughter be working, but the kind of work, the exposure to what Rinehart would come to call "life in the raw," was something to which Cornelia was fundamentally opposed. Mamie, with the determination that already marked her character, went to see the family doctor about arrangements. The doctor was on vacation and his practice was being overseen by "a very dark young man, black hair, small black mustache, black eyes behind *pince-nez.*"[34] He was Dr. Stanley Marshall Rinehart.

Dr. Rinehart, at twenty-four, was a very young doctor, but in relation to the sixteen-year-old girl who came to his office, he was the voice of maturity and professionalism. He accused her of believing that nursing was a romantic career but finally agreed to take her through the hospital. He was very proprietary, very tough: "I know every rat hole in it," he asserted. Mamie toured the hospital and, altogether undiscouraged, made application to the superintendent of nurses—lying a bit about her age, which she claimed was seventeen. Then, "Late in the afternoon of August eighteenth, 1893, my father took me to the great gloomy red brick building which was to be my home for two years. . . . He gave my bag to a smiling colored doorman, and went away."[35] Mamie had left the Street, entering the Pittsburgh Training School for Nurses as Miss Roberts, probationer.

Despite Dr. Rinehart's warning that a nurse's life was not all a matter of smoothing pillows (a comment repeated to young Katie Walters in *The Doctor* [1935]), Mary was not prepared for the life she would meet at Homeopathic. "I had had no preparation for it, nor for the human wreckage I was to encounter. I had no knowledge whatever of brutality, or cruelty, or starvation." Genteel poverty had represented, after all, a sheltered life. Now Mary would learn not only about sickness and mutilation, about work and fatigue, but about the laboring men of Pittsburgh and their families, and about the prostitutes, the toughs, the police. Like Sidney Page, the student nurse in *"K,"* she had "outgrown the Street,"[36] but she had not yet learned about the world.

Much of what Mary Roberts saw in the hospital reappeared in the works of Mary Roberts Rinehart. Occasionally the stories were comic. Rinehart's wonderful spinster Tish would be laid up with a bruised knee in Mary's hospital in "The Amazing Adventures of Letitia Carberry" (1911). More often, hospital situations were sentimentalized in comic romances like "Jane" and "In the Pavilion" (both 1912) or in stories of unwed mothers like "The Miracle" (1912) and "God's Fool" (1913). Nurses figure frequently in Rinehart's fiction, sometimes as minor characters, occasionally in a central role, the best known being Hilda Adams, the nurse-detective "Miss Pinkerton." Most significant are Rinehart's two long novels about hospital life, *"K"* and *The Doctor,* in which young women enter nurse's training, providing Rinehart the opportunity to recall and reexamine her own early experiences.

Mary Roberts was introduced to the medical world in E Ward, where the women typhoid victims were sent. In August 1893 the ward was overcrowded, five cots added to the customary fifteen beds, for typhoid came to Pittsburgh every summer. Like other probationers, Mary was set to the most menial tasks, revolting to stomach and pride, but somehow she began to fit into hospital life. What had seemed confusion became routine. At first, however, there was only chaos—for Mary and for Sidney Page in *"K"*:

> There were uniformed young women coming and going, efficient, cool-eyed, low of voice. There were medicine-closets with orderly rows of labeled bottles, linen-rooms with great stacks of sheets and towels, long vistas of shining floors and lines of beds. There were brisk internes with duck clothes and brass buttons, who eyed her with friendly, patronizing glances. There were bandages and dressings, and great white screens behind which were played little or big dramas, baths or deaths, as the case might be. And over all brooded the mysterious authority of the superintendent of the training-school, dubbed the Head, for short.

Mary worked a twelve-hour day, bathing patients, changing beds, carrying food trays, feeding the more critically ill. More than anything else, Mary cleaned. Her second day in the hospital she was sent to clean up in the operating room. In those days operations "were untidy things," wet and bloody, so that "an operating room after a series of operations looked like a shambles."[37] Mary was told to carry a pail out of the room and to her revulsion found that the pail contained a human foot.

As a probationer she was the lowliest of creatures. The hospital was made up of juniors and seniors. The staff, the doctors themselves—awesome figures—were divided into medical and surgical men, and each category had its junior and senior members. The internes, too, came as juniors and seniors. At the top of the ladder was the hospital supervisor, and he had an assistant supervisor. The nurses were ruled by a superintendent, she too with an assistant. Mary grew to admire and love the superintendent, Marguerite Wright, "a great lady, cultivated and of fine family. She had been a pioneer in her profession, graduating in one of the very first classes from Bellevue Hospital in New York." Like the other probationers and student nurses, Mary was, of course, in terror of Miss Wright, but years later she would paint a deeply affectionate portrait of her as Miss Nettie Simpson in *The Doctor,* dedicated to service and "ruling her school with a rod of iron."[38]

After her probationary period, Mary Roberts was accepted as a student nurse. Until then, she had worn washable dresses of her own, covered with an apron; now she had striped uniforms with white collars and little white ties. The caps were "of stiff tulle, pleated into a narrow band," and worn on the top of the head. At her side she carried a black bag for her surgical scissors, forceps, and thermometer. Junior nurses, moreover, were salaried; they received eight dollars a month, but they had to replace their own thermometers.[39]

Student nurses, unlike probationers, were given night duty—twelve hours of grueling work. The hospital had one hundred and fifty beds, plus its emergency and operating rooms. The nursing staff consisted entirely of thirty student nurses. On night duty they not only carried the responsibility of the

The 1896 graduating class of nurses from the Pittsburgh Training School for Nurses at Homeopathic Hospital. Nurse Roberts is fourth from the left in the second row.

wards and the private patients, but also handled the cases brought into emergency—the sick or injured, sometimes men who had been fished out of the river "dazed with drugs, writhing with poison." The drug cases had to be kept awake. One interne would beat them with wet, knotted towels while he and an orderly walked them up and down the emergency room. On night duty there were also deaths—expected deaths in the wards, sudden and violent deaths in the emergency room. And there was delirium, particularly the delirium that came with typhoid. One night a delirious patient escaped; he had freed himself from the long roller towel used to tie him to his bed. He accosted Mary in the linen room, "eyes blazing with fever," and then turned and ran.⁴⁰ That man with his roller towel found his way into "The Amazing Adventures of Letitia Carberry" and in that benign atmosphere became a good deal less frightening. In another version, in *"K,"* he races down a fire escape only to be chased and apprehended by a heroic Sidney Page.

It was not only the moments of violence, the sickness, and the death that made the hospital seem to Mary "life in the raw." Even the obstetrics ward was a shock to her, for she knew practically nothing about human sexuality and childbirth. At the end of the nineteenth century there was seldom any anesthesia used, and the ward cases very rarely went through childbirth with any pain-killing drugs. The ward housed expectant mothers, new mothers, and newborn infants. Close by were the delivery rooms. The wards, moreover, held a mixed population—black and white, immigrant and native-born, married and unwed. Although the first labor she assisted at struck Mary with horror, she trained herself to see "something of beauty . . . [in] these distorted women, going heavily about in their blue wrappers." They listened to the screams of other women in labor with dignity and calm, "accepting the common lot of women without complaint." Katie, in *The Doctor,* never sees that "something of beauty," and Rinehart uses that fact as evidence for the hardness in her character. Katie "hated the sight of women in their loose wrappers waiting in the ward for their hour to come, and sitting and rocking placidly their grotesque and distorted bodies." When Katie, the nurse who "loathed their swollen faces, their swollen legs and feet," marries a doctor herself, she refuses to bear a child.⁴¹

The obstetrics ward also brought Mary Roberts into contact with unwed mothers and prostitutes—those females with the short, curled hair and painted faces she had been brought up not to see. Those in the maternity ward Mary came to see with great sympathy, claiming that their illegitimate children, "love children" in the language of the day, were more beautiful than others. But there were prostitutes in other wards as well, some ill, some drunk or on drugs, some suicidal. One night two women from "disorderly houses" were brought in; "they had quarreled, and slashed each other badly with razors."[42] Mary was struck by the fact that they harbored no bitterness toward one another, merely blaming the episode on drink.

Another side of life to which the hospital exposed Mary Roberts was that of the Pittsburgh working class. She saw them first in the typhoid wards and in wards filled by the destitution of the winter of 1893–1894, later in the operating room, to which "came the accidents from the great steel mills, many railroad and street car cases." Mary learned that these men, and those sick from starvation and exposure, were the victims of a system in which "the employer still bought his labor as a commodity in a highly competitive market." The workers had no individual value to the mill owners, for "when a man was hurt another automatically took his place."

> The men were injured, were brought in and forgotten. Practically always the hospital cared for them without compensation, although here and there was one who either paid himself, or was paid for, the six dollars a week which entitled him to a napkin on his tray. The burden of this care was passed on to the community, which bore it for many of the great industries which were reaping fortunes.

Mary Roberts Rinehart was never a radical thinker, but her pity and her sense of social justice were aroused. Without unions, pensions, or profit-sharing and with no money for lawyers, these men taught Mary that something "was wrong, rottenly wrong." Even a policeman, still recovering from a bullet wound received during the Homestead Strike, told her that the men "got plenty of trouble," and, as Mary said, his heart was with the workers. At times, their suffering grew almost more than she could stand. One night she watched the too-long death of a man who had been caught in a flywheel "and whose body felt like jelly."[43] But she did go on.

Recalling her hospital days in *My Story*, Rinehart talks of how she wanted to write about life as she was seeing it in the wards. What she was seeing all about her was creating "a gulf" between her and her family, "the unbridgeable gulf of differing interests." Even with Uncle John, when Mary spent a day with him and Sade riding horses at their Sewickley house, the young nurse found there was much she could no longer talk about. She was, she realized, still a little girl in their eyes, and it would have horrified her aunt and uncle to hear what she had been encountering in her work. She found out, however, that she was not able to write about the real drama of the hospital either, "about the injustices and kindnesses and violence of that life"; instead, she turned the material into comedy and romance. Stories about the realities of life, as Mary had discovered them in the wards of Homeopathic, were beyond her. In one section of her autobiography, Rinehart concedes that such writing had always been beyond her, perhaps because she felt it too deeply. "I wanted escape from remembering,"[44] she wrote, for remembering frightened her.

The painful experiences at Homeopathic dulled Mary's appetite for studying medicine, and the half-formed expectation of going on to medical college slowly faded. In fact, by March 1894 she had altogether altered her plans; ironically the change involved Dr. Stanley Marshall Rinehart again. In the early days of her training, Mary saw the young doctor only occasionally. He was a junior member of the surgical staff, a gruff perfectionist with a fierce temper, and Miss Roberts was as intimidated by him as were the other nurses. After a time they met elsewhere than the operating room; when Mary saw him with his young patients in the children's ward, she was struck by his warmth and playfulness.

Dr. Rinehart came from a family that had moved to Pittsburgh in 1811 when his father, William, was five years old. Later, William and a brother ran a tobacco warehouse, manufacturing and dealing in "all kinds of tobacco, snuff and segars."[45] William Rinehart married three times, and Stan was the son of his third wife, Louise Gillespie. William was sixty-one when Stan was born and he died, in 1881, when his son was only fourteen. Subsequently, Stan was brought up by two of his half brothers, T. C. and Fred Rinehart, with whom he lived on Western Avenue in Allegheny.

A bequest from another half brother provided money to send Stan to Adrian College in Michigan, but he also worked during the summers to help with the expenses and he found employment as a pickle counter for the young Heinz Company. After college he went on to medical school at Hahnemann Hospital in Philadelphia. Stan returned to Pittsburgh in 1891 for his internship at Homeopathic Hospital. By 1893, when Mamie Roberts first met him, he had an office on Second Street, was affiliated with Homeopathic, and was still living on Western Avenue with his half brothers.[46]

Friendships were not encouraged between doctors and nurses; romances were forbidden. Therefore, it was a bold young nurse who told a surgeon on the staff of the hospital that she wanted to study German. Stan lent her a German book and occasionally Mary went to his house "and in his office he gave me a lesson." As Rinehart confesses, the German was very hard for her, "and soon the lessons were the most barefaced of excuses." If the German did not progress, the romance did, and in May 1894 Mary and Stan became engaged. The engagement was, of course, kept secret, and Mary wore her ring on a ribbon around her neck. But the secret was soon discovered and Dr. Rinehart was called before a meeting of the board. If the board hoped to cow the young surgeon, it was mistaken. Mary, eavesdropping from a nearby staircase, heard Stan "in a shockingly loud voice . . . announce that he meant to marry me."[47] The board acquiesced but insisted there be no announcement. Mary continued her training, for Stan was as yet in no position to support a wife, and in 1894 a young man did not marry until he was financially established. At the same time, a young lady did not marry and undertake a career. Mary's training continued, but she knew that she would not become a nurse.

By the fall of 1894, in her second year in training, Mary was occasionally sent out on private cases, charity cases, and she had her first exposure to the slums of industrial Pittsburgh. Her first assignment took her to a filthy house in a remote part of the city to nurse a typhoid patient. Never before had she seen the slums of industrial Pittsburgh—wooden row houses, overcrowded, filthy, and rat infested. Other private-duty assignments were less sordid; once she was sent to a sanatorium in the mountains to nurse a paranoid patient. While there, she received news that her grandmother had died. Margaret Mawhinney Roberts had been living with Aunt Tillie, her youngest daughter, who had married Joe Aikens. As she was going down the cellar stairs, her foot caught in the trailing hem of her wrapper, and she broke her neck in the fall. Not long after, Tillie's daughter was run down by a railroad train, and "a cloud seemed to have settled down" on the family.[48] But worse lay ahead.

Tom Roberts's economic situation had been serious enough before the panic of 1893. The depression that followed increased his difficulties. Although he maintained his one-room insurance office, he sold little or no insurance. He continued to draw his plans, devise his inventions, and apply for his patents. He had told his daughter, when he left her at Homeopathic to begin her training, that soon he would be able to take proper care of her: "His ship would come in, somebody would buy a patent, and I would go home again."[49] Mary had long since ceased believing in that magical windfall. And she saw little of him now, for he was on the road, carrying one product after another to the small towns of Pennsylvania and Ohio. There was little money in these towns and even if a sale was made, it was sure to be a small one. The work was exhausting and discouraging, and Roberts was drinking heavily.

On October 23, 1895, Tom Roberts arrived in Buffalo, New York, and checked into the Tremont House. Although he was traveling for a Pittsburgh-based soft-drink firm called the Nux-Phospho Company, he apparently went to Buffalo to see about a position there and to consider settling in that city. Some days after his arrival, Roberts received a letter from Nux-Phospho dismissing him for his drinking and consequent negligence of business. If he had felt a brief spurt of optimism at a new chance in Buffalo, that gave way to despair. Roberts lingered on at Buffalo for three weeks; then, shortly after dinner time on November 14, he returned to his hotel room, took a large dose of chloroform, and shot himself through the heart.[50]

Mary was on a private case, caring for a pathetic woman who was dying of cancer. The woman had an illegitimate child and was consequently abandoned by her family, shunned by her neighbors. On the night of November 14, Mary received a telegram at that bleak house. Roberts's friend, the lawyer, wired to tell her that her father had died. On the morning of the fifteenth, Mary took a train back to Pittsburgh. She read the morning paper on her way and only then learned that her father's death was self-inflicted. His suicide was treated in the sensational manner of the day. "CRAZED BY REVERSES" read the *Press* headline. A detailed story described Roberts's financial and drinking problems, quoting the letter from Nux-Phospho and one from "a daughter, who signed herself 'Mary.'" That letter, the reporter confided to his readers, "bore a touch of pathos, and was a model of penmanship and composition." Besides the letters, Roberts's effects included two or three insurance policies, a silver watch, and thirty-seven cents.[51]

Mary had left the Street two and a half years before, feeling she had outgrown it, hoping to evade the trap of the ordinary. Now she had come back to wait, with her mother and Olive, for the train carrying her father's body back to Pittsburgh. The funeral took place at home, on Poplar Street, on Sunday, November 17. Like Sidney Page, Mary learned that November day that "the Street *is* life: the world is only many streets."[52]

2

The Doctor's Wife

1896–1907

DURING THE WINTER of 1895–1896, Mary completed her nurse's training and graduated, with fourteen other young women, from Homeopathic. And she prepared for her wedding. Whatever pathetic or sordid coloration recent events had cast over Mary's life, the wedding would reflect a new start. It would be a fine, respectable wedding initiating a fine, respectable marriage. Uncle John, generous as always, gave Mary a hundred dollars for a wedding dress, and for the first time in her life she went to a dressmaker to have her gown made. Cornelia sewed, preparing lingerie and linens for the trousseau. Mary and Stan saw to some changes in the Western Avenue house that was now to be their home, as Stan's brothers had moved.

The Rineharts were married at seven o'clock, Tuesday evening, April 21, 1896, in the Second United Presbyterian Church in Allegheny, with the Rev. W. H. McMillan officiating and the Rev. C. E. Wilbur assisting. Olive was Mary's maid of honor, dressed in white organdie over white satin. Stan had six ushers, including two of his half brothers. Mary was splendid in her turn-of-the-century bridal dress. As one newspaper reported in a column headed "A Wedding in Allegheny of More Than Ordinary Interest," she was "handsomely gowned in ivory white satin, bodice high and skirt trained." She had a veil of tulle held with a "bandeau of white ribbon and ostrich tip," called a "bird of paradise." She and Olive both carried white roses and the church was decorated with Easter lilies.[1]

Uncle John gave the bride away. There were friends from Allegheny and from the hospital. The paper noted, "The Homeopathic Hospital took care of itself for an hour last evening"; even the superintendent came with his family, as well as the medical and surgical staff and "almost the entire training school for nurses." The bride and groom, "popular members of the hospital corps," were entertained after the ceremony at Cornelia's residence, and then Mary and Stan left for New York, "shortly to sail to the Bermudas for their honeymoon trip."[2]

It was Mary's first trip to New York, her first occasion to take the train

24

to New Jersey and, with the New York skyline rising ahead, to cross by ferry to Manhattan. She could never have imagined how familiar that trip would become ten or a dozen years later. The sailing trip to Bermuda was also a new experience, one that would in later years seem tame enough to a woman who crossed the Atlantic in wartime, traveled through the deserts of Egypt and Iran, and climbed the Rocky Mountains on horseback. But in 1896, to the new wife of Dr. Rinehart, it was apparently too much excitement, for Mary was not well in Bermuda. In 1932, when their son Alan was in Bermuda, Stan wrote to him, recalling the honeymoon thirty-six years before.

> Your being in Bermuda certainly brings me back to the days of our wedding trip. I'll not bother you with a recital except to tell you how much I wish I were with you, and we could together go back to Walsingham Caves, Thomas Moore's old stamping ground and visit the coral reefs and become acquainted again with the monsters of Devil's Hole. We had an old gray mare that took us about the country in a buggy. They were halcyon days but I am afraid I got the halcyon because Mud [the boys' name for MRR] was sick practically all the time, as I think you know. There were times when I had to give her a hypo of morphia before we went out to become intimate with nature.[3]

The pain and illness Mary experienced in Bermuda were the beginning of a considerable period of poor health. Mary attributed the breakdown in her health in part to the grueling work in the hospital. To some extent, too, the emotional shock of the previous winter was taking its toll.

The Rineharts returned to Allegheny and the house on Western Avenue, "the brick house on the corner," where Mary "was enormously proud of my status as a wife." Her world consisted primarily of housewifely duties, to be performed as Cornelia had taught her. Bread was baked in the house and Mary made her own jellies, pickles, and jams. She did her shopping in the old Allegheny market, patronizing some of the same men and women her mother did. The country people, in town with their chickens and butter, still called her Mamie. It was, all in all, a comfortable and thoroughly conventional life. In addition, Stan's offices were in the house and among Mary's responsibilities was making out and sending off the quarterly bills. Fees were low. "Office prescriptions were one dollar, visits were two. Babies ranged from ten dollars to fifty, depending on who bore them."[4]

By December, Mary was pregnant. Whatever she had seen in the hospital of the difficulties of pregnancy and the terrors of labor must have been intensified by her own illness. "I was very ill before each child came, for the entire period. I had the pernicious vomiting of pregnancy, and there would be consultations about terminating it." Mary never tolerated heat well, and she dragged herself through the last two months of her pregnancy in the hot, sticky Pittsburgh summer. She was driven one particularly bad day in August to a rocking chair in the damp, cooler cellar—"next to the coal bin"—where she drank glasses of ice water to refresh herself.[5]

The day after, August 18, 1897, Stanley Marshall Rinehart, Jr., was born. Despite Mary's own sickness (she weighed only ninety-six pounds), the nine-pound baby was fine and healthy. Mary and Stan now began what she later described as a change "from a pair of happy children into a family group." The world that Mary now moved through was "a small place, smaller than ever."[6] Rinehart recalled that between Stan's practice and the baby (and the two more soon to come), they did not dine out for ten years, nor did she sleep anywhere but at home for seven.

The following year the Rineharts moved to a different house on Western Avenue, a little west of the Commons. It was a solid, three-story, two-family brick. The doctor's offices—waiting room, consulting room, dispensary—were on the first floor, the family living rooms on the second, and the nursery on the third. They had two maids now and, sometimes, a young black boy—called a "buttons"—to answer the door. In that house the Rineharts' other two sons were born: Alan Gillespie, on November 18, 1900; Frederick Roberts, called Ted, on September 14, 1902. A busy household—children, patients, family pets. Then in 1903 Cornelia came to live for a time with Mary and Stan, for Olive had married Lowrie Barton and moved to Butler, Pennsylvania, about thirty miles away.

During this time Mary was often unwell. She had at least two operations—perhaps as many as four—in a five- or six-year period.[7] She was sick with diphtheria as well, caught while nursing Stanley, Jr. She sometimes felt "the old itch to write" but there was little time. She did manage to write a series of home-nursing articles in 1898 or 1899 and she sent them to *The Ladies' Home Journal*, which promptly returned them. Home-nursing was, in fact, something at which Mary was gaining considerable experience. When Stan was absent from the office, she sometimes tended neighbors with bruises or cuts. And one summer, at Aunt Tillie's place on Lake Erie, she helped Stan with an emergency operation on one of the boys. First she sterilized the kitchen table for the operation; then she administered the anaesthetic.[8]

The boys' sicknesses terrified Mary; she had seen too much in the hospital to remain sanguine in the presence of accident or illness. Ted, the baby, raised the greatest fears. At six months he had whooping cough and went into convulsions. Doctors whom they called in saw no hope and one night Stan told Mary that the baby would die. Miraculously he survived. But then, probably before he was two, Ted escaped his oldest brother's supervision and wandered into his father's office. There he found and swallowed a bottle of carbolic acid. Somehow he survived that too. In Butler, Olive was not so lucky. Her baby daughter, playing on the floor while the family unpacked in their new house, got hold of a bottle of cascara pills and died while Olive was running with her to the doctor across the street.[9]

Rinehart's published recollections of these early years emphasize her role as a mother, painting herself as a woman awash in children, nearly shipwrecked occasionally by their accidents and illnesses. Of her role as a wife she says relatively little; that, she asserted, was a private matter: "Nor does that wedding journey, nor the life that commenced in the brick house on the corner belong in this narrative. That is my own, and my husband's."[10] The Rinehart myth, as Mary Roberts Rinehart created it, insisted on the primacy of Mary's role as wife and mother. Its corollary was her long-time refusal to provide for her public details about her personal, domestic life.

About the early years of her marriage, Rinehart built a wall of secrecy, partly no doubt out of a sense of decorum and partly because she preferred not to relive in her imagination a period that had been, despite her advertised role as wife and mother, one of considerable unhappiness. Late in life, however, when she was close to eighty, Rinehart did write about those years in an unpublished autobiographical fragment. There Mary wrote about the time Stan proposed, recalling: "The great thing then was that a member of the hospital staff wanted to marry me, and I remember that it was almost too wonderful to believe. But I do not remember any great ecstasy." Her next words reveal the constant censorship of Victorian propriety Mary never quite escaped: "How frank should I be here?" And she was altogether unprepared for sexuality. All she had learned of it had come from "the hospital and the prostitutes I knew there . . . and in the worst possible way."[11]

At first Mary found herself "contented in my marriage but not ecstatic," but hard work, long hours, and little money had an erosive effect even on contentment. Housework and child care were not Mary's only tasks; besides making out the bills for Stan, she assisted him occasionally in minor surgery in his home office and answered the door for his patients, looking she said "like the household drudge I was." So intensely did she envy those patients, "their ease, their leisure, and most of all their clothes," that she could recall after more than half a century one "blue tailor-made suit with white collar and cuffs." When she had earned some money of her own, she bought one too.[12]

Only once did she entirely lose her composure, shedding the training that had made her so careful not to worry her husband. The incident was born of frustration and disappointment. The young Rineharts never went out in the evening; there was little money and less free time. And then a friend gave them tickets to the Metropolitan Opera, on tour in Pittsburgh.

Mary dressed in what finery she had and waited for Stan to come home. Hours passed and it was not until 9:30 that he returned. Furious, Mary demanded an explanation, but Stan said only, "Let it go, can't you." Mary picked up his silk hat and flung it at him, and then the two assumed a sullen silence. Not until days later would Stan tell her that, exhausted, he had fallen asleep on the streetcar and woke to find himself miles out in the suburbs of Pittsburgh.[13]

Mary found her way out of that life by writing; her writing was, before anything else, a means of self-preservation. In her published autobiographical writing Rinehart grafted onto the laconic accounts of her early married life occasional, but contradictory, comments about writing. She felt the "old itch" to write, she says, explaining, however, that she had no time. Elsewhere she asserts that the world she knew, the world of the hospital, was not a world she could write about; that reality was not what people wanted to read. Or she demurs about her abilities, her inferior education, especially compared with her college-educated husband. Moreover, she knew no one who wrote and had no idea of how to go about selecting subjects or marketing stories. And sometimes she declared that she did not even care to write; her family came first: "Who could write? Who wanted to write? All that mattered was the family, to keep it together, to hold it intact."[14]

Nevertheless, by 1904 Rinehart was writing abundantly and selling her writing. It is important to understand how that happened, how Mrs. Stanley Marshall Rinehart began to permit herself such independence and ambition, for her upbringing, the culture in which she lived, said no to those impulses in women. Certainly, she was bright, ambitious, and just a little unconventional. She had been the little girl with the bicycle—the second girl's bicycle in Pittsburgh. She had wanted to be a doctor. She had successfully undertaken nurse's training. On the other hand, she believed passionately in the family, her family. She wanted her husband to be strong and successful as her father had never been, and she wanted her sons to survive. It was the question of the Street again. On the one hand there was convention and security; on the other hand there was the world.

Looking back on those years when she began to write, Rinehart restructured events, finding causes to explain and even vindicate her success. She created, in fact, something of a myth—the Mary Roberts Rinehart myth. In part, the myth denigrated her writing. It was, first of all, explained as a mere invalid's pastime. For example, Rinehart attributed the beginning of her literary career to the suggestion of a nurse who was caring for her during her convalescence from diphtheria. The nurse found an ad for verse in *Munsey's Magazine* and suggested to her patient that verse-writing might amuse her— or so the story goes.

It is much more likely that Mary had already written a fair amount of poetry by that time. Early in 1904 the first piece to be published under the name of Mary Roberts Rinehart appeared in the *Pittsburgh Sunday Gazette*. The piece was a poem and it was, as well, a compromise between the two sides of her nature—the mother and the writer. "The Toy Railroad" appeared in the paper ornamented with line drawings of two little boys playing with their train and then of the same boys asleep in their beds.

> I know of a railroad that's managed and run
>   By a dear little curly-haired boy.
> He's engineer, fireman, conductor in one
>   With a small brother in his employ.[15]

The *Gazette* paid Mary Roberts Rinehart two dollars for the poem.

The nurse to whom Rinehart attributed the start of her literary career probably did no more than suggest a market for Mary's verse. *Munsey's Magazine* turned out to be the right market, for in May 1904 it printed a comic poem by Rinehart and paid her ten dollars. The poem was called "The Detective Story," and it is a spoof of the modern detective, the genius popularized by Conan Doyle.

> A murder is committed, and that page is full of gore,
> Of smashed and broken furniture, and blood-stains on the floor.
> A livid, ghastly corpse is quite essential to the tale,
> And people standing round with trembling knees and faces pale.

The local police are dolts, missing the plainest clues; therefore, they "Bring in the great detective with the shrewd and kindly face." The detective detects. He finds a thumbprint on a cake of soap and "human cuticle" on a towel. On the floor a bit of ash brings more enlightenment: " 'Aha!' he says at length. 'The villain smoked a Henry Clay!' " Scratches on the floor are measured to reveal "his shoes are B, size eight, / And by the length of stride he's five feet nine when standing straight." The thread of a suit and a single hair stuck to the chandelier complete the description, and looking out the window the detective sees the murderer walking down the street. Case closed:

ENVOY
Ah, thanks to British Conan Doyle, to French Gaboriau,
And also many thanks to our own Edgar Allan Poe.
To them we owe a debt of gratitude that's hard to pay,
For teaching us to frustrate crime in such an easy way.

Mary had apparently been keeping up with the crime novel since the days of *Deadwood Dick.*

Rinehart's first poem in a national magazine had poked fun at the fictional form she would become most famous for. Her second poem, "Modern Drama," published in *Munsey's* the next month (and worth twelve dollars) ridiculed the theater, where she would make her greatest financial successes. Other satiric poems from 1904 poked fun at advertising or at competing schools of medicine (allopathy versus homeopathy versus hydropathy).[16] More frequently, though, her interest lay in children's verse. Probably in 1904, though it may have been a year earlier, she wrote a series of sentimental and comic poems for children, mostly about animals made coyly human. Then, setting off for the second time in her life for New York, Mary tried to find a publisher. She had no success, and the typescript of the poems still remains folded up with her few other unpublished pieces. She did, however, meet a Mr. Curtis of Bobbs-Merrill and he was, if not encouraging, at least friendly. Mary took the ferry back to New Jersey and the train to Pittsburgh, and she decided to give up writing. Considering that almost all she had written was children's verse, the explanation Rinehart gives for her discouragement is baffling: "[the public] wanted romance, adventure, to sublimate their drab lives, to escape gloriously for a few hours at least into Utopia."[17] Of course, Rinehart did not abandon her writing in 1904; what she did was to turn from verse to fiction and, thereby, inaugurate her real career.

In narrating the story of her early attempts at fiction, Rinehart developed a second element of the myth. Here, too, she debased her real talent, her real desire to become a storyteller, for as she explained it the impetus behind her writing was financial necessity. Stan and Mary planned a trip to New York in 1904; Cornelia, who had moved back with Olive, would come to take care of the children. The vacation was an index to the relative prosperity of the Rineharts, and it was also a rest for Mary before another operation. Stan celebrated with a present, a small diamond pin. In New York they visited the stock exchange and, while they were there, a panic developed on the floor, wiping out their stock market investments and putting them in debt for the considerable sum of $12,000. "And then, quite literally," says Rinehart, "I was forced to write."[18] Writing in the interest of the family exchequer was a worthwhile activity, not so dubious an undertaking as writing for the sake of one's own ambition. It was 1892 and the *Pittsburgh Press* all over again.

The Rinehart myth, built up over a quarter of a century of interviews and essays and expressed most fully in *My Story,* is of crucial importance in understanding Mary Roberts Rinehart. Only within the protective structure of that myth, only as a wife and mother whose writing was undertaken for the good of the family, could Mary defy the Victorian culture into which she had been born. Without a doubt she felt enormous guilt; ambition and energy overrode that guilt most of the time, but only under the protective cloak the myth provided.

Mary's ambivalence toward her writing was matched, although to a lesser degree, by uncertainties about the marriage state. Apparently she undertook the responsibilities of motherhood wholeheartedly, but the role of wife was sometimes chafing; sometimes she wanted to be free. Later in life she explored these feelings both in her fiction and in her unpublished autobiographical writings. Although in 1904 and 1905 these emotions were, for the most part, suppressed, Mary still experienced frustration and confusion. And for Stan, like Mary brought up in a Victorian world, an ambitious, independent, successful wife was an uncomfortable anomaly.

Something of Stan's discomfort can be seen in two anecdotes from those years. On one occasion he took a story of Mary's to some reporter friends of his for their evaluation. He came home with their judgment: Tell her to stick to her housework; she has no literary ability. Mary also took a good deal of not-very-funny ribbing from the Rineharts' men friends. In 1909, when she had achieved considerable success, she described what she was willing to accept as comic deflation. According to a newspaper interview, "when Mrs. Rinehart began to write, she used to read her 'copy' aloud to her husband, another young physician and a lawyer who gathered for a weekly bridge game, and they all stood on their chairs and talked at the tops of their voices, so that she could not possibly be heard."[19]

Such incidents help us understand how important the explanation of "necessity" was for Mary when she began to write fiction in a rush of extraordinary—and typical—energy. The New York trip over and her operation successfully completed, she set about trimming household expenses. She let the servants go, all but one girl. She answered the phone and the door for the doctor and took care of the house. Stan and Mary alternated nights caring for the children, for Ted still needed to be fed every two hours. And in the evenings or in whatever corners of time she could find during the day, she wrote stories. Success—at least publication—came quickly. In December 1904 *Munsey's* published a story.

Rinehart always remembered the *Munsey's* story as her first published fiction, but in fact it was preceded not only by her two juvenile pieces in the *Pittsburgh Press*, but also by a one-column story, "Harmony in the House," in the *Associated Sunday Magazines* in October 1904. The story in *Munsey's*, while still only three pages long, was a much more serious endeavor. Mary called it "The Alter Ego," but the magazine changed the title to the less intellectual "His Other Self" and, taking no chances, provided a subtitle: "The Strange Story of the Man Who Was Two Men." The story came from one of

Stan's cases. A man had hurt his head trying to catch a lighted lamp his children had upset and, regaining consciousness, knew neither wife nor children. It turned out that, years before, he had sustained a head injury in a train wreck. Now, thoroughly unstrung, the man ran off; as Rinehart moralized: "I regret to say that he abandoned his family and disappeared."[20] But the incident fascinated her and she wrote the story the night Stan told it to her and sent it to *Munsey's* the next day.

"His Other Self" opens as Joe Kelly regains consciousness after an operation to relieve a pressure in his brain. A woman he does not recognize brings him broth and talks about their children. At first he is sure that "the woman's story is preposterous," but then he sees his calloused hands and feels his heavy beard. This makes no sense to him at all. His name is Franklin Elbert Martin, a graduate of Yale, 1876. He had come to work, about a year later, in the Rochester Ammunition Factory. Hearing this story, the doctor is horror-struck, for the factory had blown up in July 1877. It is now 1902. Left alone, Martin broods; his working-class surroundings are repugnant to him—his "wife" with "her none too tidy hair," the room in which he lies, his own hands—and his despair increases.

He spies a gun on the mantel and, weak as he is, drags himself out of bed toward it. With the weapon in his hand, he is uncertain, until he sees himself in the mirror, "the face of a man past middle life, roughened with exposure," and he cannot bear it. He pulls the trigger, but in his weakness manages only to injure himself. As the story closes, the wife enters again, and the man on the bed says, "Well, Marthy . . . where's the baby?"

"His Other Self" reveals how carefully Rinehart would work to avoid offending popular morality—the hero of Mary's story does not run off and abandon his family. It reveals, too, themes that would reappear in much of her fiction: the idea of lost identity, of restoration (however brief it may be here) to a higher social class, and the theme of suicide, the moment of weakness and despair that is irresistibly powerful. There is, as well, a curious personal trick of Rinehart's—the use of a date significant to herself. Martin graduated from Yale in 1876, the year Mary was born. He is temporarily reborn as Frank Martin in 1902, the year of Ted's birth.

Munsey's paid Rinehart thirty-four dollars for "His Other Self." As she had with "Harmony in the House" and her nine published poems, Mary cut the pages out of the magazine and carefully pasted them in a small brown scrapbook. By the middle of 1905 she had filled the brown book with twenty-one pieces, eleven poems and ten stories. In a bankbook she kept a careful financial record of each piece she sold: the name of the piece, the magazine or newspaper that bought it, the price paid.[21] The stories and poems in the brown book brought in anywhere from two dollars for "The

Toy Railroad," to sixty dollars for "An Anonymous Guest," again in *Munsey's*. But she had found other magazines too. *All-Story*, another of Frank Munsey's publications, bought two; *Era* (paying a miserable six dollars), *Argosy*, and *Smith's Magazine* each bought one.

By 1905 Mary was working with extraordinary energy and speed. She wrote in long hand, after one abortive attempt with a typewriter. A young girl in the neighborhood typed the stories and Mary folded them to fit into regular business envelopes and mailed them off. Soon she needed a second scrapbook, and she began to fill a red-bound volume with the stories she had published. *Munsey's* and the affiliated *All-Story* remained her best markets, but other magazines accepted a story now and then. *The American Illustrated Magazine* paid her eighty dollars for "An Experiment in Poverty"; *The Woman's Home Companion*, fifty dollars for "An Episode of the City." After eleven more stories were clipped and pasted in the red book, Mary could no longer keep up. She continued to clip the stories, but there was no time to paste them neatly in a scrapbook.

A page from Mary's bankbook listing stories, magazines, and prices received. *The Circular Staircase* (second from the top) brought $500.00.

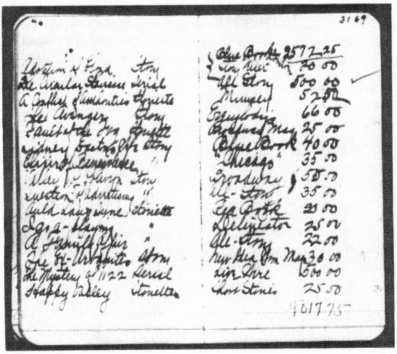

Mary Roberts Rinehart's first stories, like her juvenile stories published in the *Press,* are heavy with plot—as she recalled, "weird and often horrible" plots.[22] Each moves with amazing speed through the convulsions of plot, so that there is the air of anecdote about much of this early work. The characters are shadowy, imitations of the stereotyped characters in most magazine fiction of the day. The writing, on the other hand, is unaffected, clear, without much heavy-handedness or sentimentality.

She tried everything. There were comic stories about men forced by overprotective wives or pompous young doctors to give up alcohol or tobacco, comic romances like "An Anonymous Guest" or "The Artist and the Elephant," in which an independent young girl, sketching camels at the zoo, bribes the guards to let her stay after closing. She ends up on the back of an elephant who has broken loose and her fiancé, come to find her, is hoisted up there with her. A fire then breaks out and the narrow escape of the two lovers reconfirms the girl's need for her young man.

Among the "weird and horrible" plots are a number that bring the situation to a desperate point and then to a quick, and not very convincing, resolution. "Through the Gap" finds a young man, dazed after a train wreck, sure his wife and baby have been killed. To a stranger he pours out his fears and his confession: he had been in flight, discovered in an act of forgery. His wife and baby appear and the stranger, moved by the scene, tears up the warrant he was carrying for the young man's arrest. "The Doctor's Visitor," like a number of other stories, creates suspense and terror, only to dissipate them with a comical ending. The doctor, alone in the middle of the night with a strange young patient, is led to believe that the man is an escaped homicidal lunatic. The timely arrival of the police aborts a jujitsu competition between them. Only afterwards does the doctor discover he has caused the apprehension of a young minister, nervous from overwork on his Pentateuch lectures.

"The Mystery of the Clay Balls" and "His Father's Son" reveal that Mary was continually working out ways of thinking about her father's suicide, of trying to understand the relationship of children to fathers who have done something amiss. For Mary Roberts the scars of the suicide were deep. For years she could not talk of it at all. She did, however, write about it in one way or another almost from the beginning. Sometimes she wrote about fathers who disappear and return; sometimes about fathers whose acts of violence or shame are recapitulated by their children. Often, as in her first juvenile story, she wrote about men and women who discover they are not what they appear to be and whose real parents and background are uncovered during the story. Such stories, at first crude and later sophisticated, echo the universal childish belief that each of us is, in fact, the secret and abandoned child of some king or prince, not of the ordinary and imperfect adults with whom we live. Tom Roberts's suicide reactivated that fantasy in his daughter and she wove and rewove it into her fiction.

A particularly bizarre reworking of the suicide theme appears in "The Mystery of the Clay Balls." It tells the story of Ellis, a young man attempting to work a silver mine his father bought years before. His father had disappeared, leaving his wife and small son alone. Now the young man and his Indian laborers are troubled by attacks made on them; someone hurls clay balls at them, each filled with a nugget of silver. Finally, Ellis discovers the attacker; they struggle in the dark mine and Ellis, wounded himself, kills the other. When light is brought, Ellis sees his assailant: "From head to foot the creature was covered with a growth of long, fine hair, even the face, except the eyes, being thus hidden, while the nails were long and claw-like." Then a ring taken from the wild man yields an inscription: the creature was Ellis's father.

Jim, the young factory worker hero of "His Father's Son," is furious when his mother tells him that his father is coming home from fifteen years in jail for manslaughter. Jim recalls how he had suffered as a child from the taunts of his friends: "All the wrongs of the last years, all the shame, all the covert malice of his associates, all the burning humiliations, came over him in a tidal wave of resentment." Wandering about, Jim meets a fellow worker who jeers at him for his jailbird father. Overcome with rage, Jim strikes the man and leaves him for dead. He spends the night in the attic, awaiting the police, but the man he had hit has not died. Chastened, his lesson learned, "his father's son" goes down to the kitchen and the story closes with the words, "Welcome home, father."

The pages of the bankbook were filling and at the bottom of each Mary figured the cumulative total. By February 1905 she had published fifteen pieces and earned $206.50; by the end of the year, fifteen more to a total of $675.50. In the first half of 1906, another fifteen nearly tripled the total, $1,842.50. The major contribution to that sum came from Mary's first serial, sold to *All-Story* for $400. It was *The Man in Lower 10*.

To anyone who has read the earliest short stories of Mary Roberts Rinehart, *The Man in Lower 10* is nothing short of miraculous. Characters, plotting, pacing, tone, all come under control. Mary had been writing for no more than a year and a half, perhaps for less, when she undertook her first book-length fiction. Somehow in that frantic apprenticeship she had learned almost all she needed to know.

The Man in Lower 10 takes the lavish plotting of the early stories and spreads it out over a full-length fiction. The dead body found in the lower berth of a train en route from Pittsburgh to Washington, a train wreck, mysterious lights at the vacant house next door to the hero's home, a midnight carriage ride to a deserted country mansion, and a generous supply of curious clues make the mystery rich in incident. There are a good number of interesting characters as well: an aged steel magnate; his beautiful young granddaughter, Alison West; the evil woman who has her weak-spirited and already-married brother, Sullivan, pursue, compromise, and elope with Miss West. The malefactors also include a forger, Bronson, and his vicious common-law wife. The hero-narrator, Lawrence Blakely, has gone to Pittsburgh to procure evidence of Bronson's forgery. When Blakely returns to Washington on the train, his papers are stolen, a dead body is discovered, and the train is wrecked. In the midst of all this, he discovers a beautiful young girl who turns out to be Alison West, his law partner's fiancée. While the pursuit of the stolen bonds is carried on, what Rinehart would come to call the "buried story"[23] of Alison's relationship to Sullivan gradually emerges. At the same time Rinehart enriches the texture of the novel with a love story, and in the end Blakely and Alison are united.

With two sets of crimes (the forgery and the stolen bonds on the one hand; the plot to have Sullivan commit bigamy to marry the rich Alison West on the other) and a distinct set of clues and motivations to go with each, Rinehart had established the basic elements for all her mystery novels. Almost always there would be a series of criminal acts undertaken for gain. Of more importance was the "buried story"—hidden marriages, elicit love affairs— from which erupt acts of violence. And always Rinehart would weave through these complex plots a romantic story of love between two young people.

The Man in Lower 10 has two other Rinehart trademarks. One is an atmosphere of suspense and horror that gives the reader the creeps. Mysterious hands appear through trapdoors; eyes glow out of the darkness of an unfamiliar room. The other trademark is humor. Rinehart learned to employ comic incidents and characters in all her mysteries, but there is an unusual element of comedy in *The Man in Lower 10*. Here she chose to satirize the detective novel as she wrote one. Rinehart later recalled that she had written *The Circular Staircase* as a satire, but it was in fact *The Man in Lower 10* that, like her poem "The Detective Story," poked fun at Poe, Conan Doyle, and Gaboriau. The vehicle for the satire is a little man named Wilson Budd Hotchkiss, who carries around a notebook, searches for clues, tails suspects, and comes up with astonishing inductions. He introduces himself to Blakely with the announcement, "I use the inductive method originated by Poe and followed since with such success by Conan Doyle." His culminating act of detection comes late in the novel when he boasts of having discovered the missing Sullivan and sent the police to apprehend him, " 'It's a great day for modern detective methods,' he chirruped. 'While the police have been guarding houses and standing with their mouths open waiting for clues to fall in and choke them, we have pieced together, bit by bit, a fabric—'" He is interrupted by the arrival of the police and their captive. Alas, Hotchkiss has not been tailing Sullivan but Blakely's own confidential clerk.[24]

Mary wrote *The Man in Lower 10* during the summer of 1905, in a house they had rented for the season in a suburban neighborhood a few miles up the Allegheny River. Rinehart credited Robert H. Davis of *Munsey's* with encouraging her to write a longer work than she had previously done and with suggesting, perhaps half ironically, that a love story be added to a mystery. Mary must have been ready to attempt longer pieces by this time, for she wrote the novel in three or four weeks. With the same astonishing speed she completed two other long fictions in the next few months. *Tom Watson's* ("The Magazine with a Heart") bought a serial called *The Doctor's Story* for $225, and *All-Story* took "The Sutherland Tragedy," a novella, for $75.00.

In 1904 or 1905 Mary also began to try her hand at drama. For her first attempt she planned a big scene featuring an automobile race: "A panorama at the back [of the stage] was to revolve" so that two racing cars "appeared to be going at full speed." Only after working out the technology did Mary settle down to construct a plot to fit the race scene, using a starch box for a stage and appropriating her sons' lead soldiers, each tagged with a name and pushed about the starch box as the plot was worked out. In two weeks she had written her play and, at a dinner party where a theatrical manager was one of the guests, Mary read the thing aloud. It was, she shuddered to remember, "supremely and terribly dreadful."[25]

Mary may have been shamefaced but she was not discouraged. The theater fascinated her. It was one thing to write fiction, in her own home and in the time she could salvage from domestic responsibilities. It was quite another to work in the theater, attend rehearsals, go with the company on the road before the New York opening. It was "an excursion into a new [world]."[26] Obviously, play-writing meant as well a further bid for freedom from a conventional life. Finally, as the glossy magazines of the day attested, it was in writing for the theater that real fortunes could be made.

Mary wrote a second play, to be called *The Double Life*. Provincial, naïve, and, by theatrical standards, absolutely conventional, Mary took it to New York and, in an act of astonishing innocence, left it at the stage door of the Belasco Theater with instructions that it be given to Mr. Belasco. Then she went to her hotel room to wait by the telephone for his call. David Belasco was at that time the great man of the American theater, and he was currently engaged in the production of one of his most successful and important plays, *The Girl of the Golden West*. It was ridiculous to assume he would even glance at a one-act play written by an unknown Pittsburgh housewife. Astonishingly, he telephoned the next evening. Mary later recalled: "I was not at all surprised to hear Mr. Belasco speaking, but I was truly shocked when he suggested that I meet him in Mr. Frank Keenan's dressing room on Monday night. I flatly refused to do it!"[27] With whatever incredulity, Belasco sent Mrs. Frank Keenan, as a chaperone, to fetch Mrs. Rinehart.

Belasco thought the play was promising but he wanted it rewritten into three acts. Mary went home to work on the revision and extension of the play, returning to New York during the summer for conferences with Belasco, who was charmed with his protégée, earnest and naïve in her homemade dresses. Often she sat with him in his box in the theater, learning stagecraft from *The Girl of the Golden West*; after each performance Belasco "catechized" her on it. "What did I see? What had I learned?" And she began to meet the men and women of the New York theatrical world, who fascinated her. She was—at least part way—into the Bohemian and glamorous world of the theater, far from Allegheny, the nursery, and the doctor's office, eating late suppers with Forbes Robertson, Billie Burke, E. H. Sothern, and Julia Marlowe. She smoked her first cigarette; she began to act "New Yorky." And then, after a day or two, the ferry to New Jersey and the train ride back to Pittsburgh, "my real world . . . [for] I was with the theater not of it." How could she be? The lives of the actors and producers she met were centered altogether on the theater: "Religion, politics, even the usual responsibilities of family ties hardly existed for them. . . . They were free."[28]

If Belasco was playing Pygmalion, his Galatea soon gave him a cruel surprise. Returning to New York, she showed Belasco's contract to an actor who told her she needed an agent and suggested Beatrice deMille (the mother of Cecil B. De Mille), at that time a theatrical manager in New York. Mary took the contract to deMille, who condemned it as "wicked." With distance, Rinehart commented, "I daresay it was, but while I had worked hard, [Belasco] had worked harder." But that summer, with deMille's encouragement, Mary faced Belasco with her opinion of the contract. "The result was catastrophe. He was furious. He refused even to see me."[29] Looking back, Rinehart tried not to blame deMille, but she had learned a hard lesson, particularly when the production of *The Double Life*, in the hands of producer L. S. Sire, failed miserably.

The Double Life, as its title suggests, was a reworking of "His Other Self," Mary's early amnesia story. Rehearsals began in the fall of 1906 and the company went on the road in late November or early December. Mary went on the road with the company but she was not in New York for the opening at the Bijou Theater on Christmas Eve. Christmas Eve was for the family. Perhaps it was just as well, for there would have been little acclamation for the author "Rinehart Roberts," a name chosen to disguise from prejudicial critics the sex of the playwright. The play closed after twelve performances.

A richly circumstantial account of Mary's emotional response to her experience with the stage appears in the form of a short story, "The Night of the Play," published in *Argosy* in April of 1907. The narrator, Marcia Barr, has like Mary worked with a wooden box and lead soldiers to construct a play. And like Mary she is married, the mother of three small sons. Marcia's husband Philip is sympathetic; "if there had been times in the last year when he had missed their quiet evenings together, he had been unselfish enough to conceal his loneliness."

Marcia receives a letter from New York provisionally accepting for production her play *The Second Wife*—another echo of the amnesia story. When another play folds, *The Second Wife* is rushed into and through rehearsal. Needed in New York, Marcia prepares to leave, suffering deep ambivalence. Saying good-bye to the children, "she was quite speechless with the lump in her throat." Yet success meant money for the family, a vacation for her husband, and Florida in the winter for her ailing child. Marcia's guilt, like Mary's, is assuaged by the Rinehart myth.

In New York, Marcia is seduced by the world of the theater. A drama critic even suggests she move to New York and Marcia is tempted until "she remembered how impossible such a course would be, with Philip and the babies." Taken up by the theater crowd, none of whom "seemed to have homes or the responsibilities that accompany them," Marcia grows more attractive; "she had time for personal adornment, there were no nagging household worries."

Having given her heroine the same divided mind that she herself is suffering with, Rinehart goes on to provide a double-barreled happy ending. Marcia is finally to be rewarded both domestically and professionally, but not until each world is threatened. The play opens and the audience acclaims it; the author is called before the curtain. But the next morning the critics are merciless. Wounded, Marcia packs and sets off for home, but to her surprise Philip is not at the station to meet her. Uneasy, she arrives at the house to see a light on in the nursery. Philip, white-faced and unshaven, is up with a dangerously sick child. The Barrs share a forty-eight hour vigil, while Marcia suffers "remorse, the feeling that she had offered up her loved ones on the altar of ambition." When the child recovers, Philip brings a clipping. The critics were wrong and the play is expected to be a big success. "And then," the story closes, "the playwright who had written the greatest success of the New York season dropped on her knees beside a little iron bed and burst into tears."

Five years later, in 1912, Rinehart again wrote about her early work in the theater. Although she had by that time produced the successful play,

Seven Days, earning enough money to assure herself that there would be no roomers at the Rineharts, she remained haunted by ambivalence. In writing "Up and Down with the Drama," an anonymous, biographical essay, for *The Saturday Evening Post,* Rinehart takes a much more assertive tone than she had in "The Night of the Play," blaming the failure of her first play on the leading man. She repeats the story of the starch box and toy soldiers, the meeting with Belasco (although refraining from using his name), and the difficulties she encountered in the production of her first play, moving on to the crisis—her quarrel with the leading man who wishes to change some lines in the play. Defiantly, Mary leaves the road company and returns to Pittsburgh: "I would not mother my mutilated, emasculated, sick and tortured brain-child as it went before the public." The fiasco, it is clear, is not her fault.

Self-assured as Rinehart is in this piece, she takes the time to answer, still anonymously, the criticism she has been facing; she notes that magazine readers, for example, write to ask if she thinks it is possible to be a literary woman without neglecting her family. "I get plenty of these letters," she writes, "for I am pretty well known." And her answer in 1912 was typical of what she continued to assert about married women and careers: "It is quite possible [to have a literary career] if one is willing to work twice as hard as the ordinary woman. I do four times as much as any woman I know." And then Rinehart turns to the issue of the rewards for that hard work, the money she has earned. At one and the same time she wants it known both that she has earned a very substantial amount of money and that, with a husband to support her, she really does not need to earn money at all. The result is curious:

> I write and make a little money. I was not compelled to. My husband is a professional man who resents my desire to earn money for myself when it is unnecessary. But why should I not? I've made as high as fifty thousand dollars a year when I had successful plays on. And eight years ago I had never earned a dollar.[30]

Writing that began, as the myth recounts, out of financial necessity was seen in 1912 as merely supplementing an otherwise substantial family income. It was at once merely "a little money" and $50,000 a year.

Of course, the money was in one way absolutely necessary. In the beginning Mary had used what her stories brought in for minor luxuries, "an oriental rug or two, and uniforms for the maid," a coveted dining-room set, a handsome tailor-made suit. But as Rinehart's earning power rose so did her standard of living.[31] In 1907 the Rineharts left the house on Western Avenue for a more substantial home on the corner of Beech Street. This was a single-family dwelling, large and square with a porch across the front. Three fine rooms opened off the entry hall; an elegant staircase mounted half a flight and then turned and rose the other half to a spacious second-floor hall. There were large bedrooms on this floor and smaller ones on the third. Across the street was the Methodist church; across the back yard, the Presbyterian. It was the finest home that Mary had ever lived in, and while the Rineharts did not purchase but rented the house, it represented at least a modest increase in their standard of living, from sixty to eighty dollars a month in rent. Moreover, by the next year, 1908, Stan had moved his office to Diamond Street. The family residence was no longer the doctor's office as well.

While Mary continued her writing, now in a second-floor study, and Stan his medical practice, the boys were immersed in their own world. Stan, Jr., was nine, Alan seven, and Ted, the baby, four. Many years later, when Stan, Jr., was a father himself, he recalled that he and his brothers "lived quite remote from our parents," representing a kind of "closed corporation which took the blessings and strictures of parental control much as the rail-

After three novels and the stage success of *Seven Days*, Mary in 1909 remains for the photographer part of a Victorian family in its Victorian parlor on Beech Street.

roads regard the I.C.C. If you could get away with it, good. If not, well, it was worth trying anyway."[32]

The boys, certainly the older two, were self-styled inventors, in the tradition of their grandfather. Their inventions must have made for some powerful interruptions in Mary's concentration. They found a new use for illuminating gas when they employed it for blowing bubbles. Hitching a rubber hose to the gas pipe, they turned on the jet and produced enormous bubbles. "It was only when we thought of lighting them with a match that the ceiling got burnt," Stan, Jr., explained. Another complex scheme involved a way to shoot the pigeons in the steeple of the church across the street. Silence, at least comparative silence, was essential; so they selected a C.B. .22 calibre cartridge over the noisier BB cartridge. The next technological problem had to do with the policeman on the beat. With optimal timing they could shoot a pigeon at the right moment to have it drop at his feet. In the midst of this engrossing activity, the boys were called to pose for a formal photograph with their mother, one representing "the author at home." The picture appears in *My Story* and in it, Stan, Jr., explains, "The look of self-satisfaction on our faces has nothing to do with 'the author at home' but with our solution of a difficult technical shooting problem." That evening the boys presented two dead pigeons to their parents and, shortly after dinner, the policeman appeared at the door to give Dr. Rinehart his unsolicited opinion: "[The pigeons] are either shot from that open window or the curse of God's on them. And I'd hate to think that even if it's a Protestant church they're living in."[33]

Amid exploding gas and plummeting pigeons, Mary continued to write at a remarkable pace. From her second-floor study stories went out, still to the faithful *All-Story* and *Munsey's*, but now as well to *Everybody's, Red Book, Lippincott's, Scribner's,* and *Harper's Bazaar.* If the theater experience had been temporarily discouraging, Mary's fiction was providing considerable gratification. Again she tried her hand at long mystery stories, and *All-Story* accepted another, to begin in its November 1907 issue. That was *The Circular Staircase,* and it brought $500, a hundred more than *The Man in Lower 10.* In February 1908 *Live Wire* began to run *The Mystery of 1122* (later renamed *The Window at the White Cat*), for which they paid $500. Mary's bankbook total now reached $4,017.75.

By January 1908 another $900 had been entered, in two installments. On December 15 Mary received $400 and on January 16, $500. The entries were labeled "Advance on Circular Staircase" and, in parentheses, the single word "book." With that, the bankbook ends, and the doctor's wife who wrote magazine stories became Mary Roberts Rinehart, the famous novelist.

3

Successes

1908–1911

WITH THE PUBLICATION of *The Circular Staircase* Mary Roberts Rinehart became a success. It altered everything. No longer was it possible for Mary to see herself as a housewife and mother who scribbled stories in her spare time to earn a subsidiary income for her family. She had begun, whether she liked it or not, a career; she had become a professional. The story of the publication of *The Circular Staircase* is the story of the turning point in Rinehart's life. It is, then, not surprising to find that she gradually shaped this episode to fit the structure of the Rinehart myth.

In *My Story* Rinehart emphasizes her awareness of the magnitude of the step she was taking. With some timidity she asked Stan what he thought of her trying to publish a book; Stan's "literary standards were high, and while he had regarded my writing leniently, it was also with a certain indulgence."[1] Another insight into Mary's ambivalent view of herself as a writer comes when she retells this incident in the second (1948) edition of the autobiography; there Rinehart recalls her hesitation and attributes it to her father: "My father's literary taste had been impeccable."[2] These accounts, written after years of success and wealth and fame, reflect with bitter accuracy the self-effacement of the Victorian woman. On the edge of the decision to move from the modesty of magazine publication to the assertion of book publication, Rinehart recalled and subscribed to the idea of the intellectual superiority of her father and her husband. Only the encouragement of another important man, Uncle John, made possible her boldness.

Necessity had initiated her career; now accident became the catalyst that pushed her to success and fame. The story is that Uncle John, visiting from Cincinnati, asked for something of his niece's to read and spent one morning with "the battered old carbon copy" of *The Circular Staircase*. He rushed through his lunch to return to the manuscript, and "when he had finished he came to me. 'That's a book, Mary. You ought to have it published.'" She demurred, "'It isn't good enough for a book.'"[3] Books, after all, were the creations of real writers, different in kind from the casual and fugitive productions that appeared in magazines. In the final entry in her bankbook, in January 1908, Mary had written that single and magical word, "book." In this version of her success story, Rinehart has Uncle John speak that word first.

The vagaries of chance continue to dominate the episode. Naïve and somewhat abashed, and with no knowledge of publishers, Mary picked a book at random from the shelf of their library. Since the book, a novel by Anna Katherine Green, bore the Bobbs-Merrill imprint, Mary sent the manuscript to Bobbs-Merrill. She had had, of course, an earlier contact with the publisher. When she carried her collection of children's poems to New York, it was a Mr. Curtis of Bobbs-Merrill who had been kind to her. At any rate, she took the carbon to a printer, had the edges trimmed and the pages bound, and mailed the manuscript to Indianapolis.

The Bobbs-Merrill Company was delighted with the manuscript. Editor Hewitt Howland wrote that they wanted to publish the book and that he wished to come to Pittsburgh to talk about the possibility of other books. Waiting for Howland's visit, Mary went into a frenzy of domestic activity. Stan "was interested but still rather amused," and the boys, watching their mother bake a cake, anticipated a birthday party. Mary also sewed new curtains and a new valance for the bed in the guest room. Howland arrived, ate the cake, sang songs around the piano with the family, and bought two other manuscripts, *The Man in Lower 10* and *The Mystery of 1122*.[4]

The Circular Staircase had not, as Rinehart's description of "the battered old carbon copy" suggests, been lying for months or years in a drawer in her desk. The first advance payment from Bobbs-Merrill was made in December 1907, a month after serialization in *All-Story* began. Mary probably wrote the story that summer, and while *All-Story* was running it, Mary was revising for book publication. Bobbs-Merrill was setting type when the last magazine installment appeared in March 1908.

Shrewdly, Howland chose to bring out *The Circular Staircase* first, for in it Rinehart improved upon *The Man in Lower 10* in every way. The plot is more complex, and the characters more fully developed. The setting, a large country house rented for the summer, provides a rich source of mystery and terror, and it has the added advantage of confining the action to a single location—a half-isolated, rambling old country house, something Rinehart would exploit over and over in her mystery stories. The humor of *The Man in Lower 10* appears in the new mystery, without the satiric element, and it is enriched by incident and character. But the single major achievement of *The Circular Staircase* is Rinehart's creation of the narrator, Miss Rachel Innes, a spinster of middle years.

The spinster was a staple of popular American fiction in the latter part of the nineteenth century. By reason of her advanced age, she was no longer restricted to the conventional behavior demanded of single women and, without the responsibilities of a married woman, she enjoyed relative freedom. She might earn a living or run her own farm. She could be strong, both physically and intellectually, and she could exhibit wit, strength of will, and any number of interesting eccentricities. As Rinehart knew, most single women were in fact none of these things; rather, they were dependent women forced onto the charity of their relatives. But in fiction such handicaps were nonexistent.

Rachel Innes is the descendant of the independent and eccentric spinsters of that fiction. Her level-headed intelligence is apparent at once and it is played off against the nervous, fearful character of her maid Liddy. In any emergency Liddy goes to pieces; by the middle of the novel she has "given up all pretense of bravery," and sleeps "with a prayer-book and a game knife from the kitchen under her pillow, thus preparing for both the natural and the supernatural."⁵ Miss Rachel, on the other hand, participates gamely in a midnight disinterment in a splendidly creepy graveyard.

One element of the humor of the *The Circular Staircase* comes from the elegant and somewhat stilted language in which Miss Rachel recounts her adventures. The voice we hear from the beginning of the novel is genteel, brisk, and self-aware: "This is the story of how a middle-aged spinster lost her mind, deserted her domestic gods in the city, took a furnished house for the summer out of town, and found herself involved in one of those mysterious crimes that keep our newspapers and detective agencies happy and prosperous." The close of the novel finds Miss Rachel restless, with nothing but the customary quarrels with Liddy to occupy her. As she says, "To be perfectly frank, I never really lived till that summer."⁶

The more comical aspects of Rachel Innes's character, her old-fashioned ideas, for example, are highlighted in her relationship with her young niece and nephew, Gertrude and Halsey. Miss Rachel inherited her family when her brother died and has been working ever since to "perfect the profession of motherhood." By the time that Gertrude is old enough to go to dances and Halsey is a college man with a car, Miss Rachel can say, "The additions to my education made me a properly equipped maiden aunt." One component of that education comes with Halsey's car: "I learned how to tie over my bonnet a gray baize veil, and, after a time, never to stop to look at the dogs one has run down. People are apt to be so unpleasant about their dogs."⁷

Probably the most endearing characteristic of Rachel Innes is her delight in adventure. She is not a shrinking violet nor a fainting gentlewoman. She is, in fact, somewhat sorry when the adventure of the summer has come to an end. The events at Sunnyside have taught her "that somehow, somewhere, from perhaps a half-civilized ancestor who wore a sheepskin garment and tailed his food or his prey, I have in me the instincts of the chase." If she were a man, Miss Rachel reflects, she could trap criminals, "but being an unmarried woman, with the handicap of my sex, my first acquaintance with crime will probably be my last."[8]

The reviewers loved Rachel Innes. The *New York Times* said that "it would not be possible to invent a more pleasantly diverting character than the lady (it would be a pleasure to call her young, but she confesses to gray hairs) who is at the centre of the mystery and who herself narrates it."[9] The reviewer hoped for another Rachel Innes story in the near future, but he was to be disappointed. Miss Rachel never appeared again, at least not under that name, but as we shall see, this adventuresome spinster bears a strong resemblance to Rinehart's, and America's, sublime and ultimate spinster, Tish.

Bobbs-Merrill, too, was delighted with Rachel Innes. A promotional piece called her "the sardonic spinster who tells the story . . . a genuine achievement, a real creation." She was unlike any previous detectives; "she is unique and a joy forever." After a paragraph lauding "this gentle old maid of Spartan possibilities," the house writer turned to other delights of the novel: "Now, don't think *that!* Of course, Gladys, there are young people in it, and love-making." As in *The Man in Lower 10,* Rinehart had put together comedy, mystery, and romance, and increased the amount of each. Again, Bobbs-Merrill: "Have you ever before found humor in the midst of mystery? Well, I guess not." But in *The Circular Staircase,* "at the moment when the excitement is getting too tense and your hair is rising too straight, relief comes in a good hearty laugh."[10]

The promotional literature by Bobbs-Merrill produced Rinehart's first biographical sketch. "Pittsburgh has an author!" it shouts. "A real live popular author." To ask who this author is is "to argue yourself unknown." " 'It' is Mary Roberts Rinehart. That is the way she is styles [*sic*] on the title page. But on her card she is Mrs. Stanley Marshall Rinehart, of 954 Beech Avenue. There's a doctor's plate on the door." The reader is told that Rinehart was born and educated in Pittsburgh and that she "commenced [as an] author at fifteen by contributing the evening short stories to Pittsburgh newspapers."[11] This translation of two stories submitted to a contest into what sounds like a steady job as a newspaper contributor proves that Madison Avenue is neither the product of the second half of the century nor confined to New York City.

While some enthusiastic huckster was grinding out that bit of advertising, Mary underwent a severe attack of cold feet. The whole concept of book publication, and the anticipation of book reviews, sent her off to the country with the three boys. In Harmony, Pennsylvania, some twenty-five miles north of Pittsburgh, Mary found a farm owned by Ferd Bame, whose wife took in boarders. There she cowered, fearing the worst. Mary's attack of cold feet did not come solely from her anticipation of bad reviews. *The Circular Staircase,* as a mystery novel, was lowbrow literature; "the people I knew did not read this type of literature." Stan, especially, did not read "this type of literature," and he "had not even read the manuscript." "In fact," Mary recalled, "I am not sure he ever read it, for he disliked and avoided both mystery and crime." In self-exile at the Bame's, Mary received a visit from her mother, who came to hear all about the book. "Listen, Mama," said Mary, "I came here to forget it. It's what papa would call trash, and you know it!" [12]

The Circular Staircase, with its unique combination of mystery and comedy, outran Mary's wildest expectations. The success of her first book changed almost everything in her life. For one thing, the Rineharts enjoyed a new affluence. They would soon have an automobile, a fine Premier touring car. There were additional servants hired at the Beech Street house and the boys were enrolled in private schools. Rinehart recalled that she "had fallen into the way of spending my own money," as well as the money the doctor earned. Stan, to be sure, wanted to support his family himself, but Mary was secure in the knowledge that all the losses suffered in 1903 had been paid off and was pleased with her ability to purchase new luxuries. [13]

There were changes as well in Rinehart's writing habits. No longer was she writing and publishing dozens of hastily written short stories every year. In 1908 she published about a dozen stories, the serialized version of *The Circular Staircase,* and *The Mystery of 1122.* In 1909 only five stories, and six in 1910. It was not that she was working less diligently; rather she was working on longer pieces and revising the work she did with a good deal of care. Once, during the earliest period of her writing, Rinehart met Willa Cather who had lived for a few years in Pittsburgh, writing and teaching school. Cather told Rinehart that she put away the completed draft of a short story, returning to it after a number of weeks or months in order to revise it thoroughly. Rinehart was not prepared to follow that advice at first. But after about four years she did a thorough revision of a story that had been returned by a dozen magazines. To her delight, the revision was accepted by *Scribner's,* and "Those That Wait," appeared in that fine magazine in January 1910. It was a lesson Rinehart learned; from then on all her work was completely rewritten three times or more.

There were also important changes in Rinehart's concept of herself. She could write a book, have it published, and see that book succeed not only with a popular audience but with a reviewer in that citadel of eastern respectability, the *New York Times.* She had been a young and provincial protégée of Belasco's at those dinners in New York. Now she was invited to Indianapolis to meet the Bobbs-Merrill people and attend the Indianapolis 500. There she met Booth Tarkington, George Ade, and James Whitcomb Riley, sharing a box at the races with them. A little shy still in the midst of the famous, Mary was asked to dinner at Tarkington's house. Although Mary Roberts Rinehart would never find herself at home among writers, nor would she spend much of her time with either the literary establishment or the literary bohemia of America, she was fast becoming a public figure to be reckoned with.

The success of *The Circular Staircase* encouraged Bobbs-Merrill to bring out two Rinehart books in 1909, *The Man in Lower 10* and *When a Man Marries. The Man in Lower 10,* published first, made the best-seller list, in fourth place for the year, the first American mystery novel to be a best-seller.[14] It was not, however, so good a book as *The Circular Staircase,* as the *Times* reviewer noted. While he liked the plot, with all its complexities, he felt that "the sense of humor which pervades the story does not seem exactly suited to the character through whom [Mrs. Rinehart] speaks."[15] In fact, the reviewer missed Rachel Innes.

When a Man Marries was also a best-seller, tenth on the list for 1910. *When a Man Marries* had begun its career as a novella published in *Lippincott's,* in December 1908, under the title *Seven Days.* It was Rinehart's first piece of fiction to be placed in a high quality magazine, and *Lippincott's* paid her the very good price of $300. The idea for *Seven Days* came from an experience at Homeopathic Hospital. In the winter of 1894–1895, smallpox broke out in the hospital. Convalescent patients were sent away, some patients were moved to the Municipal Hospital, and Homeopathic was put under a quarantine. Although Mary recalled some difficulties during this period, with mutinous patients eager to break out, in fact, it was something of a holiday. In retrospect, the idea of a quarantine was an engaging one for a fiction writer, depending, naturally, on which people were to be locked up together for a week.

Rinehart made the most of the idea. Her heroine, Kit McNair, feels compassion for an old pal, Tubby McGirk, whose wife Belle has left him. She gets their crowd of young socialites together for a dinner at Tubby's and, just when the party seems to get going, Tubby's Aunt Selina arrives. Aunt Selina is the repository of all virtue—and of all the money Tubby hopes to inherit. She has not been told of Belle's departure, nor would she tolerate it. Tubby talks Kit into playing Belle's role. Shortly after Kit has acquiesced and been introduced to Aunt Selina as her niece-in-law, Belle turns up for a surprise visit. In the midst of these confusions, Tubby's Japanese butler faints; he appears to have an infectious disease. All the other servants decamp, someone informs the health authorities, and the house is quarantined. The helpless rich must care for themselves. A further twist occurs when some jewels are stolen, and there is, of course, a love story for Kit.

Like *The Circular Staircase, Seven Days* is a generous work, giving the reader mystery, romance, and comedy in one package. Moreover, with its limited setting—mostly the dining room and the roof garden of Tubby's house—and its comedy of crossed identities, *Seven Days* was obviously the stuff from which plays are made. Mary had not dropped her interest in the theater; over the past couple of years she had made some money as a play reader and play "doctor" for Beatrice deMille. She probably sent *Seven Days* to deMille who showed it to Wagenhals and Kemper, up-and-coming theater managers of the day.

Lincoln Wagenhals and Collin Kemper were young would-be actors from Ohio when they met in New York in 1892. Seeing a brighter future in management, they joined forces and in 1893 took over Stone's Opera House in Binghamton, New York. There they opened a stock company, Wagenhals handling the business end and Kemper directing the plays. The operation was at best marginal, and Wagenhals took a company on the road to earn some needed capital. He returned with the funds, but from an unexpected source. In an Ohio town he was shot by a holdup man and received $5,000 in insurance. With that money the two went back to New York City and by 1906 had promoted the building of the Astor Theatre on Broadway. W&K eventually made a great deal of money, no little part from their long-term relationship with Mary Roberts Rinehart, beginning with the production of *Seven Days.*

W&K wanted to buy the property outright. Rinehart turned that offer down, subsequently agreeing to have a young playwright named Avery Hopwood write a script from her story. Hop, as his friends called him, came from Ohio too. He was twenty-seven, still fresh from his first play, *Clothes,* produced in 1906. He later became a successful dramatist, writing such plays as *The Gold Diggers, Fair and Warmer,* and *Getting Gertie's Garter.* When he died in 1928, he left an estate of a million dollars,[16] a good part of which came from the collaboration of Hopwood and Rinehart.

The adapting of *Seven Days* did not go smoothly at first. Hopwood brought the completed script to Pittsburgh and Rinehart was distinctly disappointed: he had turned her farce into a comedy. The decision was finally made to work together—and to write a farce. Hopwood stayed on in Pittsburgh, and the two worked out a method for their collaboration based on the strengths of each. Rinehart had great facility with dialogue. She walked about the room talking the play while Hop wrote down what she said. His talents lay in structure, in discovering and repairing faulty places in the script. He was also witty, able as Rinehart said to "take a line of mine, twist it about, and make it into a laugh."[17]

Hopwood and Rinehart went on the road with the company, revising and improving the play for the New York opening, November 10, 1909, at the Astor, where it was an immediate success. The critic for *Theatre Maga-*

zine agreed that it was clever although he thought some of its laughs were gained by "extortion."[18] Extortion or not, *Seven Days* ran for 397 performances, with Georgia O'Ramey in the role of Kit McNair and Herbert Corthell as the romantic male lead. At the end of its first season (1909–1910), *Seven Days* was already the fifth longest-running play in New York, in a season that included *The Chocolate Soldier*, *The Passing of the Third Floor Back*, and *The Melting Pot*.

The success of *Seven Days* encouraged Wagenhals and Kemper to prepare touring companies, and by the late spring of 1910 five road companies were being readied to set off around the country in August and September. Financially, *Seven Days* far outstripped any of Rinehart's early work, for major theatrical successes paid a great deal more handsomely than did either books or magazine stories. In an interview with the *Pittsburgh Post* in 1913, Rinehart stated that she had earned $100,000 on her novels "and fully as much in royalties on her plays during the last few years."[19] *Seven Days* was, however, the only successful play she had written at that time (a 1912 effort called *Cheer Up* closed after twenty-four performances), and it brought Rinehart $50,000 a year in 1910 and 1911.

One effect of Mary's growing income was the possibility of more interesting and fashionable summer holidays for the family. Now it was no longer necessary to find a suburban house to rent or to visit Aunt Tillie and her family, the Aikenses, at Lake Erie. Instead, the Rineharts joined a good many other well-to-do Pittsburghers on their way to Bemus Point on the eastern shore of Lake Chautauqua, where they rented a cottage and took their meals at the large hotel. Chautauqua provided, among other attractions, a spiritualist camp across the lake, and at least once during the summer the Rineharts went to Lily Dale for their first encounter with spirits and mediums.

The most important result of the Chautauqua summers had its seeds in a trivial enough event. Mary and her family were amused to watch three fellow visitors, a trio of spinsters, in their anguished and futile attempts to deal with a stray dog. Out of those spinsters Rinehart created Tish and her two cohorts, Lizzie and Aggie, and in 1910 *The Saturday Evening Post* published Rinehart's first Tish story, "That Awful Night." Letitia Carberry is Rachel Innes intensified. Where Rachel is courageous, Tish is foolhardy, undaunted. Where Rachel is genteel, Tish is a tartar about modern vices, particularly swearing and drinking intoxicating beverages other than her own blackberry wine. But unlike Rachel, dragged unwilling into the twentieth century by her niece and nephew, Tish embraces every new fad and each new technology —from health foods to airplanes, from golf to blimps, from camping out and trapping her own food to fixing automobile races. Tish is supported in her activities by Lizzie, who narrates the stories, and Aggie, lamenting all her life for her dead fiancé—the roofer who took one too many steps backward.

"That Awful Night" was published on March 5, 1910, in the *Post*, which would remain Tish's exclusive home for nearly thirty years. Like almost all the Tish stories, "That Awful Night" mixes wildly improbable adventures and misadventures with a love story. Here a young man has abducted the girl he is convinced wants to marry him, despite her protests. He has carried her away in a motorboat, which runs out of gas; the recalcitrant girl thereupon throws the oars overboard. Swimming to shore to steal some gas, the young man comes upon a rowboat under the confused captaincy of Tish. The three women are trying to get rid of a dog someone has thrown onto their property. They loathe dogs (for Tish's uncle was once bitten and from that point on his family found bones in his washstand drawer). They have attempted to chloroform this one in order to abandon him on a nearby island. The rowboat has been "borrowed" for this purpose in the dead of night, and when the young man finds them, Tish is rowing facing forward, to see where she is going, with Lizzie helping by rowing facing backward, to avoid being splashed by Tish's inexpert oars.

The first Tish story lacks some refinements that would come later. Characters like nephew Charlie, Hannah the maid, and the minister Ostermaier and his wife are not yet part of Tish's world. Furthermore, in the light of future episodes, a stolen boat and a little mayhem are pretty pale stuff. But one thing Rinehart established from the very beginning was Lizzie's mode of narration. Lizzie tells each story for the sole purpose of exonerating Tish from the malicious misunderstanding that follows each escapade. Thus, the stories open with a sampling of absurdities listed in Lizzie's upright and proper voice, and this voice is heard right from the beginning of "That Awful Night."

> Nothing would have induced me to tell the scandalous story had it not been for Letitia's green kimono. But when it was found at the Watermelon Camp, two miles from our cottage, hanging to the branch of a tree instead of the corduroy trousers and blue flannel shirt that one of the campers said he had hung there overnight, it seemed to require explanation.

With "Three Pirates of Penzance," published in August 1910, Rinehart moved into high gear with Tish. As the story opens, Tish drives her car onto a ferry, across the ferry, and—the bar being down—off the ferry and into the lake. Rescue arrives in the form of a young man, the love interest of the story, who takes the ladies to a local hotel and makes an announcement: "He was going to order supper for us all, and three Martinis. Tish said it was all right, although she didn't see why we needed guns. It looked like a safe place." Presented with drinks, but assured that they contained no whiskey, the threesome drink with pleasure. As a result, Lizzie can assert: "Never did I eat so delightful a meal. . . . I recall distinctly shaking hands with Tish and agreeing to come to the hotel to live." Later, in their hotel room, they are horrified to find the bureau moving; it turns out to be the hiding place of the young man, sworn to unravel the machinations of the local politicians. Tish is by no means abashed at a moving bureau; she tells it to put up its hands and warns it that they are armed.

The *Three Pirates of Penzance* is a wonderfully comic story, Tish at her best. From that point on the editors at the *Post* would plead for more Tish stories from Rinehart. And more would come.

On Beech Street, Mary had established a routine for her busy life. With the boys off to school and the doctor downtown at his office, she spent the day writing in her second-floor study. It was her deep conviction that she could separate the parts of her life; efficiency and hard work were all that were needed. "While the boys were in school and my husband out, I wrote; when the front door slammed I stopped writing." There was adequate domestic help to take the household burdens off her hands. She gave the household orders in the morning, worked all day, devoted her evenings to her family. "Life was a simple matter, even life and work, if one organized it."[20]

That, at any rate, was the plan. But writing is not so easily picked up and dropped, not even with Mary Rinehart's concentration and energy. And, there were additional responsibilities now: files to be kept and financial records, with weekly checks, royalties on *Seven Days,* and quarterly checks from Bobbs-Merrill arriving at the house. There would soon be inquiries from international agents and from that new industry, motion pictures. There were interruptions in the ideal household routine. Visitors came from Indianapolis to talk about the publishing of her books and from Philadelphia, where the *Post* was published. Hop was at the house, reworking scenes of a play and revising dialogue in the second-floor study—not at all eager to stop at the slam of a door. And then, too, Mary was often away, in New York with a play or at an Author's League Dinner.

"Whether I had wanted it or not," Rinehart wrote, "I now found myself with a profession; a profession and a problem." The true artist, as Rinehart understood him or her, was someone with freedom, someone who "lived and expressed herself only in her art." But Rinehart had "never known freedom, so it did not occur to me that I had bartered it for a family." A few women had emerged from the home but "almost all had failed to make the compromise between marriage and a career." Mary wanted her career, but like many other married women with professions, she insisted on fulfilling the roles of wife and mother without stint. The solution was simply that she "must carry a double burden, that was all."[21]

In 1908, however, Rinehart's burden was increased. At the same time that *The Circular Staircase* was published, her mother suffered a paralytic stroke. Cornelia survived the stroke but she could not talk; moreover, she had lost the memory of how to perform the simplest acts. Some tasks, like eating with a spoon, were taught her, but speech never returned. Fortunately, the Rineharts could afford a nurse-companion for Cornelia, for she could not be left alone. As some recovery was made from the effects of the stroke, a form of epilepsy set in and even greater watchfulness was required. Saddest of all were the futile efforts Cornelia made to communicate with the family, but the best that was worked out was a system of questions to which Cornelia would reply with a shake or a nod of the head.

There was another problem too. Dr. Rinehart, now the head of surgery at Homeopathic, developed a painful condition of his hands, perhaps akin to arthritis. In those more careless days he treated himself with morphine, which masked the pain but caused tremors, an unsteadiness of the hand. It became clear that he could not go on with surgery. He could continue his career as a general practitioner, but medicine was changing in 1910 and "the general practitioners had been fighting a losing battle against the specialists."[22] Medicine was becoming more scientific and more technological. The X ray had come into use, laboratory analyses were becoming common, and bright young doctors were prepared to work with these advances—and to work as specialists.

In "The Medical Quick-Lunch Counter," a seriocomic article for the *Post* (July 26, 1913), Rinehart describes the situation of the old GP, the family physician who "drove up in the professional buggy and treated everybody in the house, from blowing out Johnny's ear to healing the finger father shut in the drawer." But for a young doctor the current situation is catastrophic.

> After a year or so of general practice, with the net result of having acquired a list of charity families that are trying to solve their problems in division of income by multiplication, and one call to the rich family of the neighborhood—to kill a goat that had been kicked by a horse—the young doctor begins to realize that when Johnny gets the earache these days he is hied off uptown . . . to an ear man, who blows out his ears, with due attention to the asepsis of the nasal mucous membranes and naso-pharynx, according to Politzer of Vienna.

So, after a year in a corner office, this young doctor finds that Johnny's father has called him only twice, once to request him to sign a vaccination certificate (no charge) and "once to ask him about the disposal of a dead cat in the back alley." All this is witty enough, suitable for the *Post* audience. As the situation affected Stan, however, and as Mary watched her husband's growing frustration, it was a good deal less lighthearted an experience.

For Dr. Rinehart it must have been a confusing and troubled time. He was forty-three years old in 1910 and his career was coming to an untimely end. The solution lay in retraining. A good number of American doctors were going off to Europe, particularly to Vienna, to study a specialty. The Rineharts had money now, and that meant that the whole family could spend a year abroad. If Stan objected to using Mary's money, she was adamant: "We pooled our resources, at my insistence. . . . Now and then I find a woman who regards her earnings as her own, to use as she likes while her husband bears the family burdens unassisted."[23] Rinehart had no patience with such women. Nor did she want the family separated. Stan needed the work in Vienna, and she had the money; they would all go together.

In May 1910 Stan left for a couple of weeks to begin some refresher work back at Hahnemann in Philadelphia. This was probably the first separation that left Mary at home while Stan was away and she was very lonely. The plan was for her to join him at the end of the second week for a brief vacation, probably in Atlantic City (where all good Pittsburghers went to die, in the contemporary saying), but only a day or two after Stan's departure, Mary was considering traveling to Philadelphia the first weekend.

Better judgment prevailed; the trip, Mary decided, was an unnecessary expense since they needed money not only for Vienna but for their summer holiday. Mary wrote to Stan debating the relative merits of the shore and Chautauqua. Chautauqua won out, for it was less expensive and Mary knew from experience that she could work well in the lakefront cottage. The letters from Mary to Stan over those two weeks in May tell a good deal about the complicated texture of her life. There were the children to see to: the two older boys had gone to the east side to visit the Aikens cousins in Wilkinsburg; Ted, at home, was busy learning to ride a bicycle; the circus was in town, and all three boys and John Aikens were going with Mary. And one of the maids, Elizabeth, was causing a commotion, as Mary mentioned to Stan. Stan, Jr., wrote more circumstantially to his father about Elizabeth, as man to man: "This is confidential. Mother received Elizabeth and somehow mother and Elizabeth were in the cellar and Elizabeth would have struck ma but ma had a croquet mallet."[24] Furthermore, Olive was ill and Mary traveled to Butler to find her violently nauseated and probably pregnant.

At the same time, proof sheets had arrived for the second printing of *The Window at the White Cat*, as *The Mystery of 1122* had been retitled. On May 24 Hewitt Howland came through Pittsburgh and stopped to see Mary.

Bobbs-Merrill was planning a second printing of 30,000 copies and he promised her at least $5,000 in royalties for the summer. Along with the proof sheets Mary was working over an idea for a play, apparently one she and Stan were collaborating on, but nothing seems to have come of that idea.

A minor responsibility, but a persistent one, was a young Syrian named Tufik. Tufik more or less materialized in the Rineharts' life in 1907 or 1908, but once there he clung like a burr. He sold kimonos in gaudy colors, and lace doilies, antimacassars, and bureau covers. When Mary bought something from him, she had, as she was to discover, purchased a long-term commitment as well. In 1910 she was still straining to maintain her good cheer in the face of Tufik's steadfastness, for Tufik, in Rinehart's words, had made her "his good lady, his mother, his sister and his aunt." Each time she sent him out with some money to find employment, he returned, throwing himself on her charity and compassion. He eyed the preparation for the Rineharts' departure for Europe with understandable anxiety: "He wept and tore his hair." So the Rineharts bought him a ticket for Syria and, despite some mishaps, at last "saw him go."[25] Like many of Rinehart's more absurd experiences, the story of Tufik is retold as a Tish story, "Like a Wolf on the Fold." When Tish and Aggie and Lizzie return from a trip to Panama and find Tufik on their doorstep, there is nothing else for them but to duck down in the taxi, hide out overnight in a hotel, and leave the next day for Europe.

Mary was also concerned, while Stan was away, lest the work he did at Hahnemann be inadequate. Perhaps he should go down to Johns Hopkins for a few days or, if necessary, there was the possibility of spending a couple of weeks at Harvard during the summer. When Stan wrote that the work was really going better than he had at first thought, he also told her the alarming news that he was becoming interested in tuberculosis. "Ah, my dear," she wrote back, "I wish it wasn't tuberculosis. I'm becoming afraid. Couldn't you use an antiseptic spray of some kind? So much depends on you, including the boys, and Your loving Mary."[26]

Final arrangements were made after the summer holiday at Bemus Point; Cornelia was taken to live with Olive for the time and the house was closed. The five Rineharts piled into their Premier automobile and set off for New York. Mary and Stan sat in the open front of the car, Stan, the driver, on the right, Mary on the left swathed in the veils and dustcoat of the day. In the back sat three identically dressed boys, ages thirteen, ten, and eight, who amused themselves en route by tying strings to their straw hats and allowing the hats to blow off. When some kind villager shouted after them that their hats were lost, the boys jerked the strings and towed the hats back to the Premier—astonishing the local populace. In New York they planned to stay with Stan's half brother, Edward Rinehart; however, in the middle of the night one of his children was stricken with infantile paralysis. The Rineharts decamped before dawn and stayed at Monmouth Beach till their boat sailed.

The Rineharts sailed on October 8, 1910, moving out on the river as the band played "The Star Spangled Banner." Fruit and flowers awaited them in their cabin. The trip was uneventful, at least insofar as it was recorded by thirteen-year-old Stan, Jr., who had been "requested by [his] parents" to keep a diary of the trip.[27] On the sixteenth they passed the Isle of Wight and the cliffs of Dover, and the family was in England. Once cleared at customs, they made a mad dash for the London train and, at last, a compartment, and tea—provided in a basket.

The family spent almost a week in London, visiting the British Museum, Saint Paul's, Madame Toussaud's, and Westminster Abbey. On the twenty-second they took the channel boat from Folkestone to Boulogne for a week of shopping and sightseeing in Paris. Mary's high-school French was, apparently, inadequate for the shopping.

> She went to a store and asked where she could get a hat or chapeau. A woman showed her a building. Mother went in and went up to a door and walked in. She was in a barber shop. She backed out and went into another room where they did manicuring. She said "chapeau" and pointed to her head. The woman said "yes; yes" and showed mother into a shampoo parlor. At last she got to the right room but she was nearly worn out.[28]

They left France for Zurich and Innsbruck on the twenty-ninth and, finally, on November 1, they boarded the early morning train for Vienna.

Viennese hotels were something of a shock for the American family, enormous rooms, an abundance of mirrors and gilt and bronze, but only small beds tucked insignificantly into the corners. *Pensions* were even more foreign. Vienna was a city of flats, old buildings, endless flights of cold stone stairs, apartments above street-floor shops. Some *pensions* came with *Frühstück,* a scanty European breakfast of coffee and rolls; others provided full board.

Stan set off at once to see about his work, and Mary spent the next couple of days hunting for suitable quarters and acclimating the children, principally by visiting toy stores. She found a *pension* called The Elite that they could move into on Monday, November 7. They decided to spend the weekend at Semmering in the Tyrolean Alps, but when Stan went back to Vienna ahead of the others, he found The Elite "terrible." Mary and the boys remained in Semmering for another week while Stan located both a *pension* and a governess for the boys. Fraulein Reif, the new governess, rode up to

Semmering to meet her charges on the sixteenth and returned to Vienna and the Columbia Pension with the family. By Alan's birthday on the eighteenth, they were settled enough for a birthday party.

In their three rooms at Frau Gallitzenstein's Columbia Pension, the Rineharts established their routines. Stan attended lectures and clinics and took brushup lessons on his German. Mary and the boys studied some German as well, the boys with Fraulein Reif. Lessons, walks, and the attractions of model airplanes and trains kept the boys busy, leaving Mary some time to write. The rooms, however, were cold and dark. The dampness and mist of the Viennese climate intensified the winter darkness that settled in the rooms as early as three in the afternoon. The elegant, highly decorated porcelain stoves, despite the improvident number of briquettes Mary fed them, did not dispel the chill or the damp.

Details of Viennese life were impressing themselves on Mary's memory and imagination. The porter was particularly striking, his moustache bound in a bandage to keep the ends curled. He chained the entrance to their *pension* at ten at night and charged each resident who wished to enter or leave the building after that hour. Also at ten he turned out all the hall lights, and for those returning later he provided himself as a guide up the dark stairs, holding a tiny candle. Like the service at the door, the light of the candle cost five *Hellers,* or a penny, for each person.

The *pension* rooms themselves struck Mary with their odors, their stale air, their remembrance of former dinners. Onions were always in the air, fried, boiled, whatever, "shades of dead-and-gone onions." Fresh air was thought dangerous, and it was kept out by double windows "with red cushions between to make assurance more sure." To Frau Gallitzenstein's horror the Rineharts unfastened those windows before they went to sleep.[29]

The meals, except for the meager breakfast, were good, but the hours were strange. At two in the afternoon dinner was served, consisting of "soup, meat, salad, and dessert." At seven-thirty in the evening, the guests had "cold meat, compote or stewed fruit, cakes and tea, with Swiss cheese."[30] Much more festive was eating and drinking in the bars and coffee houses or in elegant tea shops like Demel's.

Vienna in 1910 was in the final period of its splendor. Whatever contrasts of rich and poor Pittsburgh provided were as nothing compared with the imperial splendor and the absolute destitution visible in the Austrian capital. The pleasures of Pittsburgh, some music and some theater—for the Rineharts, most typically, a game of bridge or dinner with their friends—did not prepare them for the night life of Vienna. After the opera there were the coffee houses until midnight, and after midnight "little theaters where two or three mildly shocking farce skits make up the program . . . dance houses like the Tabarin . . . with mad Hungarian orchestras, a program of Apache dancers from Paris, darkies from the States who sing and clog, Spanish dancers, and Russian Cossack dancers."[31]

In the daytime there was the Prater or the Ringstrasse. One could stroll, looking at the Viennese women, said to be the most beautiful in the world. In the Prater there were band concerts and Strauss waltzes. After ice-skating in the winter, there was tea at Demel's, where aristocratic men and women met and flirted and gossiped in a dialect of German that left Stan and Mary baffled and uncomprehending.

Into this scene, very like a play by Schnitzler, came thousands of American doctors prepared to study specialties under the medical men of Austria. As Rinehart explains it in "The Medical Quick-Lunch Counter," a system had been worked out in perfect understanding: "The Americans control the market, but they pay the best prices. What they do is merely to insist that goods come up to specifications." Small groups of American doctors, under the leadership of the American Medical Association of Vienna (established in 1903), selected the docent with whom they wished to study some specialty and each student paid about sixty dollars a month for lectures and clinics. The Austrian experience repaid the Americans with advanced medical training —and with prestige. "It sounds a lot better to say you took ophthalmoscopy and practical refraction from Fuchs, in Vienna, than the same thing from somebody in Sioux City, Iowa."

Stan settled on heart and lung medicine, attending clinics at the Allgemeiner Krankenhaus, where about 50,000 patients a year were admitted and another 200,000 received treatment as outpatients. Postmortems, routinely conducted, provided excellent diagnostic training. Although he was working hard, Stan occasionally attended lectures by well-known professors in other fields of medicine. One such lecture was given by Sigmund Freud, but Dr. Freud's views on infant sexuality deeply offended Dr. Rinehart's Victorian principles.

For Mary impressions of imperial Vienna began to blend with Stan's descriptions of his hospital work; in time they would together provide the material for *The Street of Seven Stars* (1914). Now she stored away images of the cold *pensions,* the porter, the dazzling courtesans, colorfully uniformed soldiers, Hungarian musicians, Slavic dancers, the aristocrats at tea, and the destitute in the hospital wards. It was the sense of contrasts that remained most vivid for Rinehart and affected her social and political sympathies. Mary became aware that the quasi-radical sympathies she had developed in her own hospital work had given way in the "comfortable happy domesticity" of marriage. Vienna taught her that there was danger in "the bourgeois point of view, the comfortable acceptance of things as they were, the emphasis on possessions, on comfort, on peace at any price."[32] Throughout her stay Mary brooded on the poverty of Vienna and on the smug satisfaction of the Austrian bourgeoisie. In *The Street of Seven Stars* it is Peter Byrne, the American doctor studying at the Allgemeiner Krankenhaus, who reflects on "the contempt for human life of overpopulated cities, coupled with the extreme poverty and helplessness of the masses [which] combined to form that tragic part of the world which dies that others may live." Peter is also aware of the incongruous mix of life on the streets of the capital:

> of gray women of the night hugging gratings for warmth and accosting passers-by with loathsome gestures, of smug civilians hiding sensuous mouths under great mustaches, of dapper soldiers to whom the young girl unattended was potential prey . . . this night city of terror, the day city of frightful contrasts, ermine rubbing elbows with frost-nipped flesh, destitution sauntering along the fashionable Prater for lack of shelter, gilt wheels of royalty and yellow wheels of courtesans—[33]

The Rineharts left Vienna on the morning of February 25, 1911, riding away from the Columbia Pension in the rain in two horse-drawn cabs piled high with their luggage. They spent a week in Munich, enjoying the pre-Lenten celebration, including a parade and a good deal of civic disorder on the twenty-eighth. By March 4 they were in Berlin. On March 10 the Rineharts took the train to Cologne and another to Brussels, and on the eleventh they crossed from Calais to Dover. In London the doctor spent two weeks at Guy's Hospital and, with Mary, visited with Dr. Sydney MacDonald, a British physician with whom they had become close friends in Vienna. The family sailed for home on the *Baltic,* from Liverpool on March 25, reaching New York on April 2. A few days later they arrived back on Beech Street and Stan, Jr., closed his diary: "We are content to reside here in content, Ich habe die Ehre! Adieu!"[34]

Mary looked around with new eyes at Pittsburgh, "powerful, rather untidy in the morning light," and at herself as she might have been seen by "any early rising neighbor . . . a youngish woman, in a long and tight Bond Street, tailor-made suit," marching up the steps of her house to confront "a figure on the porch, a cringing figure with limpid brown eyes and a tentative smile. . . . It was Tufik, brazenly back again from Syria."[35]

4

Sewickley
1911–1914

THE RINEHARTS RETURNED from Vienna in the spring of 1911 to an America living through the final years of what seems in retrospect a period of extraordinary pleasure and charm. The strictures and confinements of the Victorian period were gradually easing. The rich and the well-to-do young were driving automobiles. Motion pictures provided a new form of entertainment —morally dubious, in some eyes, but engaging. Some men were flying airplanes. Still, as Rinehart looked back on those years, evidences of an older world remained: "Women were still wearing skirts to the ground, high choker collars, huge hats with spotted veils, whalebone corsets, pinched in at the waist. The average parlor of the day was in bright red mahogany, done in some contrasting brilliant velvet, with a figured carpet, heavy lace curtains and walls papered and cluttered with design."[1]

Recalling those days, Rinehart observed that "the mania for slenderness had never been thought of,"[2] and mature women were expected, in the language of the day, to put on flesh. Like other matrons in their thirties Mary, who had weighed under a hundred pounds when Stan, Jr., was born, had attained the dignity of flesh. But she was an attractive woman, looking, in her photographs, younger than her years despite the seriousness with which she characteristically faced the camera. In her magazine portraits she gazes steadily out at the reader, her blue eyes fine and dark. Under a mass of dark hair, her face is at once serious and feminine, its oval softness strengthened by a broad forehead and a square chin.

Mary Roberts Rinehart passed those years before the First World War in an idyllic atmosphere. With the considerable money she was earning from royalties and the increased prices her new work commanded, Mary determined to leave Beech Street and Allegheny, for Sewickley, a few miles down the Ohio River from Pittsburgh. A rural area originally, Sewickley had become a suburban refuge for wealthy Pittsburghers late in the nineteenth century; it was, in the words of *Munsey's Magazine,* the "highest of all Pittsburgh heavens."[3] It had long represented business success and social grace to Mary.

60

Uncle John and Aunt Sade had moved there during the years when the Tom Robertses were forced to leave their Arch Street house, and Mary and Olive had often visited them there, enjoying the gentility of their home and riding Uncle John's horses.

Mary was, as she often admitted, much better at making money than at keeping it. She had already made a couple of unfortunate investments in get-rich-quick schemes; she bought one-sixteenth of a gold mine and, "long enough after that for me to have known better," gave an ex-aviator $10,000 for what proved to be a nonexistent oil development. "I could earn money, but I could not keep it," Rinehart wrote. "And this leads directly to the story of the house which I bought, almost immediately after our return [from Vienna]. . . . I wanted that home fiercely. It spelled peace, security. There was behind that desire, I think, all the insecurity of my girlhood, even my father's tragic and unnecessary death. I wanted safety and permanence, a sanctuary for me and mine."[4] Moreover, to spend her money for her family blurred the edge of ambition, turned personal success into family good fortune.

What Mary found in Sewickley was a large old house built at the end of the Civil War by the railroad magnate, George W. Cass. "Cassella" was "a vast ruin," but grand, sturdy, on a high bluff overlooking the Ohio River. At first "Cassella" looked like another of Mary's gold mines or oil wells, for extensive repairs and remodeling had to be undertaken. The initial cost of the house was about doubled by those repairs. As Mary said, "I had put every dollar I possessed into the original purchase," but there was nowhere near enough to meet the eventual cost of $90,000. The bemused doctor, estimating the financial burden his wife had assumed, suggested they name the house The Bluff, for, as he put it, "That's what we're putting up!"[5]

By the time the Rineharts moved into the remodeled and redecorated house, in the winter of 1911–1912, Mary felt "rather like Cinderella at the ball," so far was Sewickley from "the little brick house on its quiet street." The small parlor of Arch Street had grown into "a long Georgian drawing room"; the small fenced yard, into a full-scale garden.[6]

Behind the house was a ravine, an enticing spot for the adventurous boys as well as a place to keep whatever animals were not, like the dogs, allowed the freedom of the house. There were pheasants and rabbits; Ted kept guinea pigs. Alan, still the inventor if not by now the mad scientist, devoted himself to experimentation. He was intrigued by the railroad torpedo and, having learned how it was made, produced one of his own. He tested the product by slamming an iron dumbbell against it. "A stupendous explosion resulted, and I rushed to the window to see a small boy, singed as to eyebrows and hair, totter out of a cloud of smoke, and dazed, sit down on the drive."[7]

For the young Rineharts and their friends the Sewickley house was a

The house in Sewickley.

comfortable place, with more delights than restrictions. Some advantages were unexpected. A small girl, visiting the Rinehart boys, was marched into the doctor's presence to have a loose tooth extracted. Olive's young daughter, Virginia, was a frequent visitor, trailing after her three handsome older cousins, marveling at the immense icebox with doors on two sides so that it could be opened for fruit or other delicacies without a visit to the kitchen. Maggie the cook permitted the children this privilege and was, accordingly, a favorite. Sometimes Mary allowed the children at her afternoon teas and parties, served in the summer on the veranda, where Mary sat in the clouds of soft white material that made up the afternoon dresses of that day.[8]

Life in Sewickley was gracious. In the morning the men took the train to town; in those days transportation between the suburb and the city was efficient and trains ran frequently. Stan left from the station at Glen Osburne, the village next to Sewickley, and the two older boys commuted as well, to Shadyside Academy on Pittsburgh's east side. On Saturday the Sewickley women rode to Allegheny and, in the same old market where Cornelia had shopped, did their marketing, to be met on their return by hired hacks prepared to carry market baskets back to the house. There was a country club, which the Rineharts joined, and sometimes formal, sometimes casual visiting. Mary wrote some years later, "To this day I look back on the years [in Sewickley] as the happiest I have ever known."[9]

The purchase and remodeling of the Sewickley house overextended Rinehart financially and once again she was driven to writing to support "this new scale of living." As before, financial need was a positive stimulant, and "I wrote madly, anything, everything. I could not stop."[10] Rinehart would never again publish the mass of short fiction she had in her first years of writing; she had learned to revise too carefully for that. But the years from 1912 to 1914 saw a prodigious amount of work. In 1912 she published one serialized novel, nine short stories, and one article; in 1913 another serialized novel and eight stories. In 1914 three novels ran in magazines and seven short stories appeared. Four of the five novels were immediately issued in book form, so that by the summer of 1915, seven years after the appearance of *The Circular Staircase*, Rinehart had published ten books. At the same time she was still working on material for the stage, both revising plays for deMille and working on *Otto IX*, a play based on Viennese materials.

At first Mary wrote at home. She established order in the house, explaining to the servants that her ability to produce fiction—and to pay their wages—depended on their ability to keep things running smoothly. But working at home did not prove satisfactory. Cornelia was unable to understand the need to leave her daughter uninterrupted. "She felt that if she entered my study very quietly, and touched me only lightly on the arm, she

Far from Victorian taste, Mary expresses a new stylishness in her Sewickley drawing room.

would not disturb me!"[11] It did not take many of these heart-stopping experiences to send Mary in search of some other work place. Dr. Rinehart had set up an office in Pittsburgh, in the Jenkins Arcade. On the street floor shops surrounded a central walkway and on the upper floors were offices set around a central court. Stan provided an office for Mary there. It was a room designed for taking X rays and, as a result, the walls and ceiling were painted black. She moved in with a table and a chair, and a great stack of the yellow paper on which she wrote her drafts in long hand. After a couple of years Mary moved to a larger, more comfortable office in the Arcade.

The room in the Jenkins Arcade was more than a writer's study; it was also a business office. Financial matters continued to grow more complicated. There was also a great deal of correspondence—from deMille, from theatrical producers, from readers, and from magazines, including almost daily letters from *The Saturday Evening Post*. Mary hired Helen Mayall to handle the correspondence and the financial books and to type the finished manuscripts from her longhand drafts of stories and novels. An efficient woman, Mayall was soon able to answer a good deal of the business correspondence herself. Within a few years, when the boys were off at school and college, she took over some of Mary's correspondence with them as well, sending them notes, forwarding their allowances, and frequently reminding them that their bank accounts were overdrawn.

With her downtown office Mary came into contact with unmarried women working in offices and stores, and she was pleased to see them freeing themselves from "their vicarious lives in grudging households." Some of the women she saw were married, "beginning now to carry the double burden of home and profession, or of home and earning." Watching these women, Mary came to the conclusion that "the busy business man was largely a creation of his own imagining. It was the women who were doing the drudgery, the uninteresting detail, in those offices." The drudgery, however, was worth it, for it allowed women to surrender the "factitious value" that had been placed on household occupations in order to maintain their self-respect. It was a new world for women, Rinehart believed, and she herself had been "a pioneer."[12]

In 1912 Rinehart published a new mystery novel, *The Case of Jennie Brice,* serialized in *Everybody's* and brought out in book form by Bobbs-Merrill in 1913. Rinehart drew on her own early memories for the setting in Pittsburgh and Allegheny and for details of the devastating Johnstown flood. The narrator of *Jennie Brice* is a middle-aged widow who supports herself by taking in boarders. But Rinehart was working again with the fantasy of aristocratic birth, and in reality the narrator was "born on Penn Avenue, when that was the best part of town," the daughter of a wealthy old Pittsburgh family who cut her off when she eloped. In the course of the mystery she befriends her sister's daughter but never reveals her identity, not even at her niece's wedding, where she resists the powerful temptation "to run out and claim her, my own blood, my more than child."[13]

The After House, serialized by *McClure's* in 1913 and published by Houghton Mifflin in 1914, is based on a true account of a series of brutal axe murders committed aboard a lumber schooner, the *Herbert Fuller,* in the 1890s. The mate, Bram, had been convicted. A lawyer friend told Mary the story one afternoon at the country club; it intrigued her and she asked the lawyer to get her the court records. After reading the material, Mary found herself on the side of those who believed the mate innocent. There was an alternative suspect, a Scandinavian crew member, who had by this time, with a knife attack on a nurse, proven himself a homicidal maniac.

Rinehart altered the real story of the *Herbert Fuller* murders in *The After House.* She changed the lumber schooner to a private yacht, introduced upper-class characters, and created a narrator, a doctor just out of medical school who, in need of summer work, signs on for the cruise and falls in love with a member of the party. With the narrator's pleasant wit and the love interest, Rinehart had changed the unrelievedly grim murder story into a novel that could be subtitled *A Story of Love, Mystery, and a Private Yacht.* The murders, however, are gruesome, and with that ironic pleasure she always found in recording significant dates in her fiction, Rinehart set the killings on the night of August 12, her birthday.

When *The After House* was published, Bram had spent seventeen years in an Atlanta jail, protesting his innocence. Rinehart set about demonstrating in the novel that certain evidence given at the trial was concocted. At issue was what could or could not be seen from a certain position on the deck of the *Herbert Fuller.* Rinehart researched the problem and checked her findings with the Kearsage Association of Naval Veterans. The witness who testified to having seen Bram's actions on deck had to have been perjuring himself. Rinehart incorporated the new evidence into her novel.

The After House created interest in Bram and led to the reopening of the case. Even while *McClure's* was running the novel, Bram received a parole. In January 1914 he wrote to Roger L. Scaife, Rinehart's editor at her new publisher, Houghton Mifflin, thanking him for the good work the book had done and asking him for help in his pardon appeal to the president and the attorney general. Mary heard from him, too, shortly after his release on parole: "Permit me to say to you, in the presence of Almighty God, that I never committed the crime for which I have unjustly suffered more than seventeen years behind prison bars."[14] Real life was even better than fiction, and

Rinehart's role in seeing justice done the falsely convicted mate was an even better story than the novel itself. Decades later, in 1957, television exploited that story in a play written for the Bell Telephone Hour, with Claudette Colbert playing the part of Mary Roberts Rinehart.

Some of the work Rinehart produced before the war represented an attempt to go beyond her previous writing, to move from mystery and farce to more serious fiction. Almost from the beginning she discovered how difficult it was to bid for serious attention. The critics had her pigeonholed: She wrote first-rate and innovative mysteries; why should she do anything different? But part of the difficulty lay in the developing Rinehart myth. Mary continued to justify her career, particularly the outset of that career, in terms of the family's financial needs. But the myth, in this context, proved a double-edged sword, and financial success began to tar her writing with the brush of commercialism.

Mary exacerbated the problem. For example, an interview with the *Pittsburgh Post*, in February 1913, was headlined "Mrs. Rinehart's Royalties." The reporter found Rinehart happy to talk of her financial success: "Literature is more a business than a passion with me." But she discovered that there were costs to her own self-esteem in that assertion. Some years later, commenting on the fact that her rental of a downtown office gave her "an entirely undeserved reputation for commercialism," Mary defensively asserted that she was, by that time, writing only partly for the money.[15]

Another problem lay in the changing subject matter and treatment of major fiction in the early twentieth century. Rinehart wanted to write serious novels, but she was unwilling or unable to follow the path of realism. Realism came to mean for Mary Roberts Rinehart the exploitation of the violent and immoral, especially the sexually immoral, in fiction. Rinehart returned frequently to the question of realism: "Realism had at last achieved distinction in the writing world, but now I had my children to consider. They read what I wrote, not always but often, and I would not depress them. Nor would I write a line that they could not read."[16] Her serious novels, therefore, tended to present real social problems, but in their outcomes they almost invariably retreated into romance—the conventionalized happy ending.

The preference for the conventional was not always Rinehart's alone. As she became a more and more successful popular writer, the mass magazines who bid for her stories and novels made demands of their own. Nowhere was this more apparent than in Rinehart's relations with *The Saturday Evening Post*, and by 1912 she had become one of the *Post*'s major contributors.

For the first thirty years of the century, *The Saturday Evening Post* was America's foremost popular magazine. Before movies, radio, and television assumed the task of informing and entertaining the nation, the *Post* provided news, commentary, and fiction for a vast audience. By 1913 it had a weekly circulation of two million copies and an audience, conservatively estimated, of ten million readers, about 10 percent of the population. The *Post* was owned by the powerful Curtis Publishing Company of Philadelphia. Cyrus Curtis demonstrated his publishing genius in his selection of editors: Edward Bok for *The Ladies' Home Journal* and for the *Post* George Horace Lorimer.

Lorimer was called the Boss and he earned the title. Editor of the *Post* from 1899 to 1936, he turned an insignificant weekly into America's most powerful magazine. Politically, socially, economically, and morally, he knew what his audience should read, and he made sure the *Post* provided it. In 1912 he gave his audience six stories by Mary Roberts Rinehart; nevertheless, he turned down with a shudder of horror "The Miracle," Mary's sentimental story of an unwed mother in Homeopathic Hospital. With a keen eye on the *Post*'s family audience, he flatly refused to print such material. Lorimer needed his top writers—but only on his terms. He never contracted for work he had not seen. He never paid what he considered exorbitant sums in an effort to outbid the competition. What he offered his writers was a prompt editorial decision, full payment on acceptance, and the largest audience in America.

In 1913 Rinehart sold her first serious—nonmystery—novel to the *Post*. *The Street of Seven Stars* appeared early in 1914, and its conventional solution to somewhat unconventional problems is representative of how cautious both Rinehart and Lorimer were with the moral issues of the day. Set in Vienna, it is the story of Dr. Peter Byrne and a young American violin student named Harmony Wells. Both Harmony and Peter are very poor and for both it is difficult even to remain in Vienna for their studies. But Peter is committed to his profession and Harmony, it is made clear, is an exceptionally gifted musician.

In a rather daring excursion into bohemian morals, Rinehart soon sets the two young people up in housekeeping together but provides a chaperone in the person of Dr. Anna Gates. Anna enhances the conflict between marriage and a career for Harmony, for she is the exponent of women's independence, offering "an incredible liberty in the name of the freedom of the individual." Rinehart, however, undercuts Anna's bravado; early in the novel she confesses, "I think I have my own little tragedy, because I have to go through the rest of life alone, when taken in time I'd have been a good wife and mother."[17]

Anna Gates does not come off without her moments of triumph, but she is not the heroine of the novel, and it is Harmony who must choose between her music and her love for Peter Byrne—she cannot have both. In the final pages of the novel, Harmony learns that "there is only one thing worth while—the love of a good man." Harmony goes to Peter who is packing to return to America and declares her love. When Peter asks her about her career, she answers, " 'Career? I shall have a career. Yours!' "[18]

The *Post* editors were delighted with the novel. Churchill ("Churchy") Williams, an editor who worked closely with Rinehart for many years, wrote congratulations on *Seven Stars* and added the gratifying comment, "I believe you've got your feet on a new path." Even before he had seen the whole manuscript, Churchy was writing, "[This serial] will, I am sure, do more for you than all your other stories in The Post or elsewhere." Moreover, Lorimer had confirmed that he would pay her ten cents a word; he sent Mary the news that he liked it, but with his typical gruff humor assured her, "I didn't cry."[19]

When Houghton Mifflin brought out *The Street of Seven Stars* in the early fall of 1914, the reviews were overwhelmingly positive. The *Times* found it "delightful," and *Outlook* pronounced it "wholesome," adding that it "ought to be put in the hands of many American parents who send their daughters abroad under the impression, apparently, that cities like Vienna, Paris and Berlin are as safe for young girls as American villages." Churchy's convictions were echoed by *Publishers Weekly,* which called the novel the best thing Mary Roberts Rinehart had done, and by the *Springfield Republican,* writing that "the author seems to have found her true role."[20] Such general critical approval for Rinehart's serious fiction would be short-lived, but in these innocent prewar years it looked, for at least a brief period, as if Mary Roberts Rinehart's serious novels, heavy with the freight of Victorian values, could attain both popular and critical success.

It seemed as well that she might become part of the literary establishment. In 1912 she had, to her own astonishment, received an invitation to the great literary event of the year, the seventy-fifth birthday party for William Dean Howells—the grand old man of American literature. As the author of some best-selling mysteries and one very popular farce, Mary was "astounded to receive an invitation."[21] Under the circumstances a dress from Paris designer Worth seemed *de rigueur.*

The dinner took place on Saturday night, March 2, at the elegant New York restaurant Sherry's. It was reported the next day on the front page of the *New York Times* under the headline, "TAFT JOINS IN PRAISE OF W. D. HOWELLS." Four hundred guests were present, making up "such a gathering of distinguished men . . . as few occasions in the past have called together in the city." In the ballroom "was practically every literary celebrity of the country." The guest list, on an inside page, is indeed impressive. Among the literary elite represented were George Ade, James Branch Cabell, Abraham Cahan (whose *Rise of David Levinsky* was modeled on Howells's *Rise of Silas Lapham*), Willa Cather, the American Winston Churchill, Thomas Dixon (whose *Clansman* would soon be made into Griffith's great film *The Birth of a Nation*), Ellen Glasgow, Zane Grey, Mark De Wolfe Howe, Edwin Markham, and Albert Paine (Twain's literary executor and biographer). There were important editors and publishers like Bok of *The Ladies' Home Journal,* Adolphe Ochs of the *Times,* and Ellery Sedgwick of the *Atlantic Monthly.* Muckrakers were represented by Jacob Riis and Ida Tarbell, journalists by William Allen White. Critics Charles A. Eastman and James G. Huneker were present, as well as Wellesley's poet-teacher Carolyn Wells and America's leading arbiter of manners and morals, Emily Post.[22]

It was a dazzling occasion. After dinner and speeches there was coffee and then Howells's formal reception of each of the guests. But for Mary and Stan it was a glimpse into a world they simply did not inhabit. The *Times* reported that "nearly everyone in the hall knew every one else," and after shaking hands with the Dean of American Letters, the guests "strolled about chatting with their acquaintances." But Mary and Stan had precious few acquaintances in Sherry's ballroom. Perhaps George Ade was pleased to revive memories of the Indianapolis 500. Willa Cather might have remembered the young woman to whom she had given advice nearly a decade earlier in Pittsburgh. And a disturbing moment for Rinehart may have come when Winston Churchill, speaking as the representative of American novelists, paid homage to Howells: "Perhaps not the least of the debts which literature owes him is that he has kept himself clean against pollution of American letters by the muddy tide of commercialism, of materialism, which has swept over our country, and which is leaving its stain on other dignified professions besides our own."[23]

A new impetus to the commercialism Winston Churchill deplored was, in 1912, just beginning to dangle its monetary charms before the eyes of American writers. In November 1912 Beatrice deMille wrote Mary that "Cecil and Lasky and one big backer are all three going into the moving picture business."[24] It was still to be several months before Cecil B. De Mille, Jesse Lasky, and the "big backer," Samuel Goldfish, would take the train west. Meanwhile, Lasky and Goldfish provided the money for De Mille's production of a new Rinehart farce called *Cheer Up.* Despite the well-known Walter Hampden in the lead, *Cheer Up* was a flop, closing after twenty-four performances. Beatrice, however, retained her confidence in Mary's work and asked whether she might not let Cecil and his two associates have *The Circular Staircase* and *The Man in Lower 10* for their new company.

Nothing apparently came of that idea, for Rinehart's first movie sale did not come until about a year later, when she sold a number of short stories for seventy-five dollars to a film company. By 1914 Rinehart looked like a valuable source of story material to at least four new companies: Famous Players-Lasky (made up of De Mille, Lasky, and Goldfish—who later changed his name to Goldwyn when he went into business with theatrical producer Edgar Selwyn), Vitagraph, Selig's Polyscope, and Essanay Film Manufacturing Company of Chicago. Vitagraph bought an early story, "What Happened to Father" (*Lippincott's*, 1909) and released it as a film in November 1915. That same year Selig released *The Circular Staircase*; he had also bought *The Man in Lower 10* but, failing to make a picture, forfeited the rights. The Essanay Company, unable to get hold of *The Circular Staircase*, simply produced a film called *The Circular Path* and released it in competition with the Selig film.

Surviving correspondence between Rinehart and Fred Wagner of Essanay gives us a glimpse into the business end of movies in the early days. In February 1914 Wagner acknowledged receipt of four Rinehart works—*Where There's a Will, The After House,* and two short pieces including an early Miss Pinkerton story. Two days later Wagner wrote again, asking for two more stories, one a two-reeler and the other a three-reeler, or so they estimated. He noted that their usual payment was twenty-five dollars a reel, but conceded, "On account of your reputation as an author and the superior quality of the stories, we are willing to offer $500.00 for these two short stories."[25]

That letter goes on to extol the virtues of the Essanay Company. Wagner explained how solid and energetic his company had become, producing "Interesting and Educational Events in Motion Pictures." They had offices in Niles, California, and a distribution agency, the General Film Company of New York, with thirty-six offices. Through their distributor they furnished one film subject every day in the week to eight hundred theaters, thus, Wagner estimated, reaching ten million viewers a day! The company's unique scheme, outlined in a March letter, was to arrange for simultaneous story publication and film release, for they needed only six to eight weeks to adapt a story and film it. They also needed, to be sure, the cooperation of the magazines, and, hoping that Rinehart would put in a good word for him, Wagner fatuously urged the advantage of such a scheme for the *Post*.[26]

In March, Mary sold Essanay two comic stories for $100 each. A month later she was offered a more permanent deal (like the one Essanay had worked out with George Ade) to provide a story a week, not in completed form but in a 500-word synopsis. Mary turned that proposition down, but continued to negotiate with the company for individual short stories. In July, Essanay wrote again, asking the price for *The Amazing Adventures of Letitia Carberry*. That letter, nearly the last in the file, was signed by the young editor of scenarios for Essanay—Louella O. Parsons.[27]

The business Rinehart conducted with the infant film industry was brisk if not particularly lucrative. Business with the theater, however, was hopelessly bogged down. In the fall of 1913, Rinehart sent Beatrice deMille a one-act play called *Otto IX*. Exploiting the more *gemütlich* aspects of Vienna, *Otto* appeared to have just about everything a play producer would want: a charming ten-year-old prince as hero, a romance between a young soldier and a princess of the kingdom of Livonia (threatened by the spectre of an arranged marriage to Karl of Karnia), international intrigue, threats of revolution, a misanthropic duchess, a devoted chancellor, a superannuated one-legged soldier, and a collection of vicious insurgents.

DeMille sent the play to producer Winthrop Ames and everyone was optimistic about a 1914 production. But Mary was not well during the spring of 1914; her general condition had begun to deteriorate early in 1913 and overwork had not helped the situation. Exhaustion, ill health, and a guilty feeling that she had not, after all, been devoting much of herself to her family brought Mary to the determination that they all should take another trip abroad in the summer of 1913. After that trip, spent motoring in England, Mary underwent an operation and early in 1914 she suffered diphtheria. Not until late in the spring of 1914 did she resume work on *Otto*, now planned as a full three-act play. Ames wrote that he had found a perfect boy for the title role, a thirteen-year-old English actor, Reggie Sheffield, and he was sure that the play could be mounted at the beginning of 1915. But by late in September he was not so sanguine, criticizing one of Mary's ideas for the second act. Apparently feelings were ruffled on both sides and it was not until March 1915 that Ames wrote asking what they should do about *Otto*. Mary sent back a cool reply informing him that she had sent it to a couple of other producers. But to no purpose. Belasco would not touch anything with a child star and Holbrook Blinn did not like the revisions Mary had done on the original.[28]

At about this point Mary decided to give up the idea of a play and turn the story into a novel. Roger Scaife of Houghton Mifflin was encouraging, seeing it as "an excellent cross between Little Lord Fauntleroy and The Prisoner of Zenda." As a book for a juvenile audience, rather like Twain's *The Prince and the Pauper,* with which there are obvious parallels, the novel could sell for years.[29] But in 1915, with the European war nearly a year old, the title was a problem, for "Otto" was no longer an endearing name. The manuscript was renamed *Long Live the King* and published in 1917. Negotiations for theater production did continue halfheartedly until, in March 1917, Ames found himself without a male lead; so long had *Otto* hung fire that Reggie Sheffield had grown up. The play was never produced but ten years after Mary had sent the script to deMille, it became a considerable success as a movie starring Jackie Coogan.

In the summer of 1914, when the archduke was assassinated in Sarajevo and the European nations began to mobilize for war, Mary Rinehart was at work on a new novel, scheduled to begin serialization in *McClure's* in October. *"K"* would be one of Rinehart's most popular books. Published by Houghton Mifflin in August 1915, it sold more than 100,000 copies by December. Serial rights were arranged in other countries as well, under what would become a long-term arrangement with agent Curtis Brown of London. In 1918 Jewel Productions brought out a film version called *The Doctor and the Woman*, and in 1924 Universal made *K—the Unknown*, paying Rinehart $3,500 for the rights.

"K" was an important book as well. It was, in the first place, a serious novel, without recourse to mystery or farce. Certainly, the favorable reception of *The Street of Seven Stars* provided encouragement for this new venture. But *"K"* was a good deal more challenging to Mary than was the Viennese novel, for it was a re-creation of the Street, of the life Mary had known as a child and a young woman in Allegheny. In Sidney Page, Rinehart created her first autobiographical character. When we meet her, Sidney is just eighteen; she lives with her mother and her Aunt Harriet (who sews for a living) in the boarding house her mother runs. Sidney's father, like Mary's, is dead, the father who had willed her "that dreamer's part"[30] of herself; and, like Mary, Sidney is about to enter nurse's training.

From the beginning of the book, Rinehart strikes the theme of freedom. Sidney yearns to be free of the Street, to do something with her life—if not something big, then something useful. Rinehart tells us, however, that "nothing, that early summer night, seemed more unlikely than that Sidney would ever be free to live her own life."[31] She is hemmed in by the Street, trapped in her responsibility to her mother. Sidney's ambition is indeed far-fetched, but not because of the Street. In *"K,"* as in *The Street of Seven Stars,* Rinehart has her heroine give up her freedom in exchange for love.

Into the Page's house moves K. le Moyne, a new boarder. As the novel unfolds we discover that K. has concealed his real identity; he is, in fact, the great surgeon Edwardes. After studying in Berlin, he had returned to America and built his own hospital. Success with an operating procedure he had developed led to a great deal of renown and brought many people to his clinic. With the money he made, Edwardes opened a free ward, and that was his undoing. The compassion that led to his charity work backfired when, in the course of a few months, three charity patients died. Despite Edwardes's careful operating system a sponge had been left in each of those patients. (We learn eventually that the sponges were the work of a jealous enemy.) Despairing, Edwardes abandons his profession and his name. In "K" Rinehart recounts the story of his renewal of faith in himself; by the end of the novel he returns to his own name and his work.

Sidney enters the hospital as a trainee and falls in love with the attractive, but unworthy Dr. Max, the star of the hospital, called "The Little Tin God" by the internes but worshiped by the nurses. Max courts Sidney, but at the same time he carries on an affair with Carlotta Harrison, a nurse of shadowy past and dubious morals. Sidney slowly matures into self-understanding, finally learning that she cares not for Dr. Max but for the idol she has created. Now the way is clear for Sidney to recognize her love for K. She has only one more lesson to learn—that love is greater than personal freedom.

> She felt as if she had been wandering, and had come home to the arms that were about her. She would be married, and take the risk that all women took, with her eyes open. She would go through the valley of the shadow, as other women did; but K. would be with her. . . .
> Where before she had felt the clutch of inexorable destiny, the woman's fate, now she felt only his arms about her, her cheek on his shabby coat.

For a woman, then, there was the love of a man and the bearing of his children; for a man, "work, and faith to do it, and a good woman's hand in the dark, a Providence that made things right in the end."[32]

Never before had Rinehart worked so intimately with materials from her own life. Even the story of the sponges came from an experience of Stan's, although it was not that kind of factualism that made the writing of "K" so difficult. Much more arduous were the task of bringing forward her own complex and contradictory desires and the risk in examining her own half-buried memories of those crucial years at the end of the nineteenth century from her father's suicide to her own engagement and marriage. While Mary was writing "K" she was often ill, and it seems clear that her illness was at least in part a result of the disturbing personal memories she was reviving. Her hand cramped severely; halfway through the novel it gave out completely. She tried soaking and massaging it, but in the end she had to dictate much of the novel. When the dictated portions proved unsatisfactory, she discarded them and "painfully recommenced by hand."[33]

Rinehart recalled: "I had no faith in the story itself. The very fact that I liked it myself discouraged me." And certainly she suffered anxiety about its deeply autobiographical cast. She gave Stan the completed first half of the novel to read, telling him that she planned to burn it.

> He took it into town with him, and in agony of mind I walked the floor and waited. At last the telephone rang, and I was trembling so that I could hardly answer it.
> "Go ahead," he said. "It's fine. It's far and away the best thing you've ever done."

Stan must certainly have recognized in "K" echoes of his wife's own experiences. He must have known as well that, given the subject matter of "K," his encouragement had more than literary significance. That encouragement came and it came at a crucial point for Rinehart, allaying both her anxiety and the pains in her hand. "The next day I was at work, and with a pen."[34]

The critics' reception of "K" prefigured the future response to Rinehart's nonmystery novels. *The Street of Seven Stars* had enjoyed almost uniformly positive reviews, but "K," a much more interesting novel, met with mixed evaluations. *The Literary Digest* admired the plot construction and the new sureness of technique, claiming that "Mrs. Rinehart [had] never written a more engrossing story." Conversely, most reviewers found fault with the handling of the plot. Even when, like *Publishers Weekly*, they were sympathetic to the book as a whole, finding in it the embodiment "of the real salt of the earth, the milk of human kindness," reviewers spoke of its shortcomings. *Dial*, pleased to see doctors and nurses treated with "patient and scrupulous fidelity," thought the narrative "somewhat jerky" and objected to the "foregone conclusion." The *Boston Transcript*, after a fairly measured evaluation of the characters and plot construction, ended up on the negative side: "Mrs. Rinehart's book is a bad novel."[35]

The review most wounding to Rinehart's ambitions as a serious novelist appeared in the Sunday *New York Times*. "The dominant sentiment in one's mind upon finishing "K" is wonder as to why Mrs. Rinehart has cast aside her first form of expression, the novel of mystery and detection of crime." The reviewer goes on to ask why, having written first-rate mysteries, does she want to have her adventure in "the more aristocratic pastures of the pleasure-seeking reader." He then tries to answer his own question:

> Was she, perhaps, moved by that mild contempt, most undeserved, which so many fiction writers feel for the novel of plot and incident, of mystery, adventure, solution of criminal problems? For they are prone to think, the people who can write these novels surpassingly well, that

they want to do something better, something more intellectual, something of a "higher class."[36]

The problem with *"K"* does not lie in Rinehart's inability to write nonmystery fiction. Nor does it lie essentially in the construction of plot or the handling of the conclusion. *"K,"* like Rinehart's other serious novels, suffers from a failure to carry out its premises. Sidney's story is more important than K.'s story, and Sidney's story probes the issue of a woman's freedom. Rinehart understood that issue, lived with it, felt it deeply. In the earlier parts of *"K"* she treated it with honesty and intensity, but she could not carry out in her story the full implications of the theme. As a result she placed increasing weight on the shallow mystery of K.'s past and left Sidney with the foregone conclusion of sacrificing freedom in the interest of love.

In short, while Rinehart was willing to raise the question of women's freedom over and over in her stories and novels, she was not willing to resolve that question in any way other than that familiar to the conventions of popular fiction. The only story of a woman's successful struggle for personal independence that Mary Roberts Rinehart ever wrote was her own autobiography.

5

The Great Adventure
Summer 1914–Spring 1915

JUNE 28, 1914. The Archduke Francis Ferdinand, heir to Austria's throne, drove in an open car through Sarajevo in Bosnia, parading the power of empire in the face of insurgent Serbian nationalists. Gavrilio Princip waited with a pistol behind a house on Franz Josef-Strasse, where the archduke's chauffeur, having turned by error, stopped the car to turn around. Princip leaped onto the car, firing at the archduke and his consort. The "dastardly act," in the words of the *New York Times*, seemed the work of a conspiracy, and the *Vienna Reichspost* lamented that "with bleeding hearts we have to announce that the murderer belongs to that race which has ever enjoyed the especial attention and greatest good-will of our reigning house."[1] The First World War was only weeks away.

While ministers of state met late into the night and armies were mobilized across Europe, the Rinehart family was vacationing at French River in Canada. At their isolated fishing camp they were all but cut off from the outside world, except for a "daily steamboat which brought down the river our provisions, boxes of fishing worms from Toronto, and the newspapers." Rowing out to meet the steamboat, the Rineharts learned of the European war: "The Germans swarming across Belgium, and our little boat tied to a stake while we cast for bass."[2]

To most Americans in the summer of 1914, war was unthinkable. Europe, locked in complex alliances and corrupted by old suspicions, had blundered into armed conflict. America—the New World—was free of Old World intrigues; America wanted no part of the barbarous effects of European historical entanglements. On his editorial page in *The Saturday Evening Post*, George Horace Lorimer made those feelings plain, adding that the alliances formed by this war were in themselves adequate demonstration of its irrationality. Certainly, Lorimer argued, France and Germany, nations that "lead the van of civilization," should be allied against "Cossack Russia and Bourbon Austria," both retrograde autocracies. The actual alliances of

1914 show, he reasoned, "how completely detached from real human interests this whole statecraft stuff of war and diplomacy is."[3]

But at night in the fishing camp in Canada, her family sleeping "the sleep of neutrality," Mary Roberts Rinehart lay awake. "Already I knew that I wanted to go to the war."[4] The idea was extraordinary, preposterous. Mary was thirty-eight years old, married, the mother of three children. She had, to be sure, broken away from Victorian conventions sufficiently to make a career for herself. But to leave her family for an indefinite time, to cross the Atlantic, to expose herself to the dangers of war—the proposition was outrageous.

None of that mattered. Mary's restlessness, her desire for adventure, her deep preference for real life over fiction drove her to the war. It would be the great moment of her life and, somehow, she knew it. "All my suppressed sense of adventure, my desire to discover what physical courage I had, my instincts as a writer, had been aroused," she wrote some years later. And in the persona of Tish she asserted, "I do not intend to let the biggest thing in my life go by without having been a part of it."[5]

Mary's passport to the Front was *The Saturday Evening Post.* Lorimer may have thought the war in Europe barbarous and irrational, but he knew a good story when he saw one. By the end of the first week in August, he had sent Irwin S. Cobb and Samuel G. Blythe, two of his most experienced writers, to Europe. Blythe's assignment was to cover the capital cities. Cobb was to get to the Front; he could however, visit only the German Front, for the Allies had closed their lines to correspondents. Isolated in Canada, Mary did not know any of this, and she wrote as soon as possible to Lorimer asking him to send her to Belgium for the *Post.* Lorimer replied on August 18: "Cobb and Blythe are already on the other side and if you really mean business, I shall be glad to talk with you at any time, with a view to sending you to the front. When would you be ready to start?"[6]

Mary was probably ready to start the next day, but her enthusiasm was not shared by Stan. While Lorimer continued to make plans for Mary's trip, sending Churchy Williams to Pittsburgh on September 14, the doctor continued to make objections. By the end of the month Stan had prevailed. Perhaps Mary wrote to Lorimer to tell him, or perhaps Stan got in touch with the Boss himself and told him to forget it. In any event, when Lorimer wrote to Mary on the twenty-fifth, it was to console her with the idea that public interest in the war would soon wane, adding, however, "The European mess was as big a temptation for me as it was for you."[7]

Things appeared to rest at this point for the next couple of months. Family life resumed its normal course for the Rineharts except that in the fall Stan, Jr., left for the Morristown School in New Jersey. Mary returned to revisions of the ill-fated *Otto,* first in Sewickley and then in French Lick, Indiana. While away she complained of feeling ill and tired and lonely, and Stan replied with affectionate humor: "Poor child, alone in a great hotel, with no mother to guide her." He sent along a list of things not to do—no correspondence, no writing—and as an afterthought wrote across the upper corner of the page, "This letter contains many valuable *Don'ts* for authors and other lunatics." In November she took the play to New York where rehearsals were supposed to begin, but there were more delays. Mary decided to stay on for a day or two anyway, visiting Beatrice deMille. Again the doctor was solicitous: "If you care to, why not stay with Mrs. DeMille a week—in New York or Atlantic City? Do whatever you think best about coming or remaining."[8]

Under the appearance of carrying on her work, Mary was building up a head of steam. Certainly, her trips away from home in Indiana and New York produced warning signals that Stan's good-natured acquiescence only muted. Reading her weekly issue of the *Post* that carried reports from Cobb and Blythe, Mary brooded on the war. In November the stories of a third correspondent were added to their war coverage, and it did not ease Mary's state of mind to find that this reporter was a woman, Corra Harris, the widow of a circuit-riding preacher and the author of popular novels.

All the Rineharts were together in Sewickley for Christmas. It was "much like other Christmases," Rinehart recalled. "But there was a difference." In a piece of remarkable compression and understatement, she added, "There had been a grave conference with my husband, and I was leaving at once for the war."[9]

Mary wired Lorimer that she was ready to go, adding the persuasive information that she was planning a trip to England in any event, for the not-very-convincing purpose of seeing the English production of *Seven Days* through rehearsals. Would the *Post* pay her way and would Lorimer provide her with the necessary letters of introduction? Lorimer wired his reply on December 29: "YES IF YOU WILL WORK EXCLUSIVELY FOR THE SATURDAY EVENING POST IF THIS MEETS WITH YOUR IDEA LET ME KNOW WHEN YOU CAN SEE ME EITHER HERE OR IN NEW YORK TO TALK OVER DETAILS WILL GET YOU ALL THE LETTERS IN THE WORLD." In a follow-up letter on December 31, Lorimer agreed that the *Post* would pay Mary's expenses, if she would agree not to be "too blamed expensive," and $1,000 for each article, as long as she worked exclusively for the *Post*. Then a newly avuncular Lorimer added:

I am only making this proposition to you with the understanding that you are planning to go abroad anyway. Frankly, I do not care to take the responsibility of sending any one over there except old maids, widows and our real rough boys like Cobb and Blythe. Personally, I should urge you not to take the risk, though I understand the appeal that it makes to every writer, man or woman, with red blook [*sic*].

Lorimer closed, "I am strongly tempted to throw up my job and go myself."[10]

In the rush and excitement of the few days before she sailed, Mary had little time to explore her complicated emotions. She had made her bid for extraordinary freedom and she had won it. She had put herself in a position to accomplish things women had not previously accomplished. Moreover, in her weeks at the Front, she would manage to do things that no men had done, affording her a very distinct pleasure. At the same time she was aware both of the possible danger she might face and of the way in which she had bolted her duties as a wife and mother, had, like some especially perverse heroine of a new *Doll's House,* slammed the door on the Victorian world in which she had been raised. In some ways, after all, Stan was right, and no one knew that better than his wife. But stronger than all these feelings, sweeping them away with its power, was the excitement that came with releasing her previously guarded sense of adventure.

Mary left Sewickley on January 8, 1915. Movie photographers were present taking pictures of the car as it backed out of the garage. Mary wore flowers, the gift of the maids and William the gardener. In tears, Maggie the cook gave Mary a holy charm to keep under her pillow. Mary took with her photographs of Stan and the boys in a folding frame and several reporter's notebooks. Having set out to do the unimaginable, Mary planned to record every moment of her adventure. In spite of her lifelong habit of discarding what she had finished with, Rinehart set about collecting the documents and souvenirs that would preserve that adventure. Among the documents, later laid away in a strongbox, is a diary of the weeks Rinehart spent at the Front. It is her only extant diary.

Mary sailed from New York, Janary 9, 1915, on the *Franconia.* Once aboard ship and out of the harbor, she wrote to Alan and Ted—a mother's letter, not a war correspondent's. She told them that the sea was rough and the weather wet and cold and that the ship had been refitted for wartime. "At night the lights go out on the decks. Inside thick cardboards are fitted against the ports so no ray of light can escape. And while we pick up wireless messages we send none." In her cabin were flowers from friends, "two big steamer baskets," as well as letters and wires. There were presents from the family, too, including a basket of grapes. "Everytime I feel a little gone and homesick I run to my cabin and eat an English hot-house grape." Referring to the boys' special gift, she promised, "The chewing gum I shall keep for a very rough day!" Messages for the servants followed and then assurances that she was fine. Certainly, the boys were kept in the dark (at least officially) about the real nature of this trip, for their mother assured them that she intended "to come back rested and not nervous." Mary concluded:

God bless you both. Be good boys. There may be a time when you will not hear from me, but do not worry. I shall come back safely, like Jock [the family dog]. Be careful of trains and automobiles, and don't forget your

Loving and devoted mother
Mary Roberts Rinehart[11]

Mary cabled Stan on her arrival in London on the nineteenth of January and immediately set about meeting useful persons to whom Lorimer had given her letters of introduction. The most important connection Lorimer had provided was Lord Northcliffe, the powerful publisher of the *London Times*. She met Northcliffe for lunch on the twentieth, and afterwards they went to the *Times* office where Northcliffe dictated letters introducing Rinehart to the commander of the Belgian army and to the Belgian premier, part of the exiled government in London.

Northcliffe was not merely accommodating. Official policy had established a powerful censorship, and in accordance with that policy the Allies had banned correspondents from the Front. Northcliffe opposed government policy, arguing for the necessity to counteract German propaganda by informing Americans about Allied advances. Thus, he was eager to give Mary information about places to visit and people to meet. He even suggested that she ask to be presented to the Belgian king and queen at La Panne, where they had set up a temporary headquarters. Rinehart, seeing a chance for an even better scoop, countered by asking to interview Queen Mary of England. Northcliffe was at first "aghast" at the idea of a reporter interviewing British royalty, but on second thought he became "keen on it."[12]

Northcliffe's cooperation notwithstanding, Mary had to face the fact that getting from England to the war zone was still just about impossible. Due to the ban on correspondents at the Front, there were hundreds of reporters in London, all trying to cross the Channel and none of them succeeding. Mary's ploy was her nurse's training; she was qualified to visit and accurately report on the war hospitals. The evening of the twentieth she went to the Savoy Hotel to meet Dr. Depage, the head of the Belgian Red Cross and physician to the queen of Belgium. She argued her case to Depage, explaining how much good she could do by informing America about conditions in Belgium. She must have been very convincing, for the next day she wrote in her diary that plans had been made for her to leave England on Monday, the twenty-fifth. It was arranged for Depage to meet her in Calais, where he would put a car at her disposal. Mary closed that diary entry: "I am to go to the firing line. No woman has been there yet."[13]

She spent the next days making preparations. Dr. Sydney MacDonald, the Rineharts' old friend from their months in Vienna, gave her a typhoid shot and she did some shopping—a warm dressing gown, a rain cape, and "a plain black silk dress . . . in case I see the Queen of Belgium." Meeting with Northcliffe again, she expressed some nervousness about traveling to Calais, where no civilians were allowed to land. Northcliffe, with his evidence to date of what this American woman was capable of accomplishing, simply assured her: "You'll go. That's all. You'll go."[14]

On the night of the twenty-fourth Mary made her last entry in the first diary notebook. That portion of her journal was to go, sealed, to MacDonald. "The only thing I fear about this trip is pneumonia or influenza. But in the remote contingency of my not returning in four weeks, he will send it [the diary] on to Stan. For a few days, then—"[15] She left on the train for Folkestone the next morning appearing oddly festive in a black taffeta dress and a fur coat, wearing roses. With her were her notebooks, a mess kit, and one of the four official cards of the Belgian Red Cross. That card, she later said, got her out of England.

Mary's anxiety about landing in France was intensified when the boat for Calais docked instead in Boulogne. Depage was waiting for her in Calais and somehow she had to get there to meet him. In London, Mary had heard a number of unpleasant stories about what had happened to correspondents discovered in France or Belgium and visions of foreign jails unsettled her. But there was no trouble. She simply walked over to the train station and bought a ticket for Calais. It was at the station in Boulogne that Mary saw her first hospital train. As she stared at the wounded men lying on stretchers on the station platform, her sense of adventure began to give way to horror.

She spent that night in a cold hotel room in Calais, the thermometer registering only eight degrees centigrade, and arrived the next day at La Panne, the site of L'Ambulance Océan, Dr. Depage's hospital. La Panne had been a seaside resort, built on sand dunes. The beach was now studded with guns, and soldiers drilled along the edge of the ocean. Rinehart described the large hotel where Depage had established his hospital: "Paint its many windows white, with a red cross in the centre of each one. Imagine its corridors filled with wounded men, its courtyard crowded with ambulances, its parlours occupied by convalescents who are blind or hopelessly maimed, its card room a chapel trimmed with the panoply of death."[16] In six nearby villas were housed King Albert, Queen Elisabeth, and the remaining court and government of Belgium.

Mary was given a room at the hospital. That night she lay awake listening to the guns and to the wounded men in adjacent rooms. "A man in the next room has started to moan and shriek. My God, this dreadful war! . . . The delirious man in the next room is singing Tipperary!"[17]

On the twenty-ninth, under the guidance of General Melis of the Belgian army, Mary began a tour of several kinds of war hospitals: surgical, typhoid, and one made from a converted channel steamer. She had met Melis at the Hôtel des Arcades in Dunkirk the day before, and there she had had her first experience of modern warfare when the Germans bombarded the city. The bombing began at dinner time and an alarm bell rang to warn the diners. The only woman in a dining room full of officers, Mary asked the maître d' where she should go. He explained that she was safe enough where she was but could certainly go to the cellar. "I wanted to go to the cellar or to crawl into the office safe. But I felt that, as the only woman and the only American about, I held the reputation of America and my sex in my hands."[18] More to the point, Mary saw that the officers remained in the dining room; only some of the waiters took refuge below. She stayed where she was—and ordered coffee.

Whatever good humor Rinehart brought to the situation in her writing about it, the fact remained that she was struck with horror at the bombardment—the helplessness of the civilian population, of "family groups, noncombatants, folks who ask only the right to work and love and live [who must] sit and wait with blanched faces." The bombing continued until three in the morning and every so often Mary—by that time in her hotel room—went out into the corridor to ask assurance of Mr. Singleton, her occasional escort and special attaché to the Belgian Ministry of War. Singleton spent the night on a sofa outside Mary's room, as both guard and solace. The zeppelin and its bombs did relatively little damage that night, but it brought Mary Rinehart her second lesson in war: "It is a curious thought that the fulminate of mercury detonators in all these bombs are possibly made by Jack Semple, at home!"[19]

On the twenty-ninth Melis showed Mary the ruins of Ypres. "No woman had been there before, and everyone stared." She was saddened by the "wanton destruction" of all the old and beautiful buildings, the Cloth Hall and the Cathedral, each half a millennium old. In Ypres she met M. le Commandant Delaunois, who gave her some souvenirs: a German cap taken during a recent attack on Ypres, a postcard from the pocket of a dead German, a *Feldgesangbuch* (a book of songs and hymns prepared for soldiers in the field), and, "best of all," the envelope from a letter written by "the gallant defender of Liège," General Leman, then a German prisoner.[20]

Such memorabilia fascinated Mary. She had the German postcard translated and kept it and the translation in the strongbox. The card is, in its very banality, affecting; Hedwig asks her husband, Otto, if he has received her packages and the photographs of the children. The closing caught at the pathos Mary was coming more and more to see in the war, the disruption of commonplace lives: "This week I have been busy with the children's clothing. I wanted also to write you a letter but must wait until tomorrow to get some writing paper. We think of you, dear Otto, and write to me. Greetings from your Hedwig and children." Rinehart kept the card in an envelope marked "the greatest human document of the war."[21]

Mary's diary recorded not only events and sights but the people she met. Many of those people would appear in *The Amazing Interlude*, Rinehart's 1918 novel about Sara Lee Kennedy, a girl who leaves her fiancé to run a soup kitchen near the Front and who falls in love with Henri, the brave and mysterious Belgian aristocrat. Among the people who provided material for *The Amazing Interlude* was Glory Hancock, known as "Morning Glory," a pretty young American nurse whose work with wounded soldiers had received some publicity. Sara Lee Kennedy would be created, in part, from Morning Glory. Henri has his source in a man Mary met in Belgium, a man she recalled a number of years later: "[He] remains today as mysterious a figure as he was then. I do not even know if he survived the war, that quiet man, so curiously powerful to effect the impossible, so cultivated and yet so obscure. What was he really . . . ? What was his power, that he could have me moved about at will?"[22] The diary, curiously, tells us nothing about him; perhaps he was M. le Commandant Delaunois who told Mary about the destruction of Ypres, explained its historic buildings, by then rubble, and presented her with memorabilia she was to cherish. The idea for Sara Lee's soup kitchen came early the next week when Mary visited a British Naval Air Station to see the airship Beta. There she learned about two English women (one of them a novelist) who ran a soup kitchen near the front lines, serving food to wounded French soldiers.

Soup kitchens, hospitals, and air stations faded into insignificance by the middle of the week. Adventure had come to Mary in full measure—she was to be taken to the Front and into No Man's Land between the Allied and the German lines. Mary's triumph was a little tarnished when she learned that half a dozen reporters had been allowed into Belgium to go on this expedition. Still, she had the edge on them, for she was in possession of an official *carte de séjour*, while they were permitted to stay in Belgium for only twenty-four hours.

> I was not, I think, greatly popular. It annoyed them to realize that I was there for an indefinite stay, and I did not blame them.

"How long have you been up here?" [Journalist] Ward Price inquired.

"Three weeks," I said cheerfully.[23]

The party of reporters and military guides went first to Oudstuyvenskerke, where they were briefed on the German advance, and then on to the headquarters of the third Division of the Belgian Army. Rinehart noted "the church full of straw and sleeping men. The game of poker under the image of the virgin." Setting out again, Mary reminded herself to use no names, only initials, and then observed: "The German lines are very close now. . . . The barbed wire barrier tears my clothes. The wind is howling fiercely."[24]

They stop to meet Colonel Jaques, "the hero of the Congo," and to eat biscuits and cheese with chocolate or wine. After that "we start on the perilous part of the trip," driving to a position just behind the advance trenches, where they leave the cars. It is sleeting and ahead of them No Man's Land lies flooded, like lakes—but full of dead bodies. "Here the stench begins." Occasionally the moon emerges, giving the scene an eerie beauty but increasing the danger. "We are in full view of the German trenches." Dressed in khaki, Mary fears she glows in the moonlight: "I shine like a star. I feel that a thousand rifles are picking me out."

At this point the men solicitously assure Mary that she need go no farther. There has been, however, no firing from the enemy lines and, having a "strong curiosity, . . . I begin to presume on my luck." They make their way along a fascine road, a makeshift path of wood and straw set across the flooded field separating the Belgian from the German lines. Some four hundred yards away they come to an "outpost, a destroyed village, shining white in the moonlight."

Their destination, two hundred yards from the German lines, is a ruined church. The church tower, with only three of its walls still standing, is the post from which a Capuchin monk, formerly an army officer and now a volunteer, observes the German trenches and reports back to the Belgian lines. Mary can imagine "no more truly heroic deed"; there is not even the "contagion of courage" for the monk.

The return along the fascine path is a letdown, and Mary grows aware of the rain and her own physical discomfort. "My heavy boots chafe my heel, and I limp. But I limp rapidly. I do not care to be shot in the back." She is heady with triumph, but that does not diminish her ironic self-awareness. "I have done what no woman has done before, and I am alive. But my heel hurts. That annoys me. Instead of being grateful, I am pettish!"[25] Back in her hotel room at 4:30 A.M., Mary stays awake to record the adventure.

The following day she spent in bed, sick, but by Thursday, Rinehart to present too much of a target. And cross the railroad. The road is obstructed with a barb-wire labyrinth. One threads it with caution. The moon has come out, very clear. The lowlands are lakes with streaks of silver, with rippling wars. We are ahead of the trenches now. And a sentry challenges us every few feet. Here the stench begins, for the silver lakes are full of dead & rotting bodies. Here too we are in full view of the German trenches, and are to remain so ~~for the balance~~ until we return to the "barrier." I begin to regret my khaki suit. It seems to me that khaki is no color for moonlight. ~~It glimmer.~~ I shine like a star. I feel that a thousand rifles are picking me out.

A page from Rinehart's World War I diary describing the midnight trip across No Man's Land.

was a correspondent again, as she watched Dr. Depage operate. Depage successfully removed a piece of shrapnel from a soldier's brain, but he could not save from permanent paralysis a man with a bullet in his spine. Depage gave Rinehart the piece of shrapnel, wrapped in gauze, and it too found its way into the box of memorabilia. Later that same day, "a stately general" called on Mary to tell her that King Albert of Belgium would receive her the next day at his villa. In her diary she wrote, "I am very nervous."[26]

Preparing for her interview, Mary Roberts Rinehart turned from fearless reporter to self-conscious woman. She had to buy shoe buttons, find white gloves, have her hair washed. Considerably nervous when she arrived at the villa, Mary was not put at ease by another general who explained that she was not to speak before the king spoke, nor to stand closer than six feet to the royal presence.

The interview began awkwardly; for the first few moments King Albert said nothing at all. With "the usual American horror of a complete silence," Mary finally reminded him of the protocol she had just learned: "You know, sire, you are supposed to speak first." "Oh, am I?" the King replied. "Well then, suppose we sit down."[27] But even sitting down was not so simple; the king held out a chair for her, but Mary's instructions had been to sit only after his majesty had been seated.

Mary had been led to expect about ten minutes of conversation with the king, but Albert turned out to be an easy, informal man and the two of them talked together for an hour. She wrote up the interview the next day and left it to be checked by the king. When she received her copy back from the royal secretary with the word "Approved" written across the top of the first page, she was greatly excited: "I had in my hand the first authorized statement made by the king about the war, a document of real political significance. They said, 'You are making history, Madam.' For there are no precedents. It has never been done before."[28]

An interview with the queen followed shortly, on Tuesday, February 9. "I was very calm," Mary recorded. The interview was informal and Mary was very much taken with young Queen Elisabeth. The two women smoked cigarettes, small, brown ones with gold tips, and Mary found it "very interesting that [the queen] lighted my cigarette herself."[29] That night Rinehart left Belgium, crossing to England on an Admiralty boat.

In London, Mary waited for Northcliffe to complete the details for her meeting with Queen Mary and in addition to arrange an interview with Winston Churchill. On her own Rinehart was trying to "pull wires"[30] to be sent to the British and French lines. By February 17 all the arrangements were made. The Churchill interview was set for that evening and the meeting with the queen for the next afternoon. Moreover, Paul Cambon, the French ambassador, had met with Mary and promised to provide her with passes and letters to the French army. On the nineteenth she would cross the Channel again.

The Churchill interview interested Mary very little. After a brief talk, she left him with a list of prepared questions and somewhat vague plans for a future meeting. It was hard to keep her attention even on the first lord of the Admiralty; after all, the next day she was to meet the queen of England—certainly the most royal of all royalty to an American. "I am to courtesy [*sic*]," Mary wrote, rehearsing her instructions, "And to say 'Your Majesty' the first time. After that, 'Madame.'"[31]

In her diary, "for the benefit of posterity," Mary noted precisely what she wore: "a black velvet skirt and black brocaded coat, trimmed with skunk fur. A smart black turban with black aigrettes, white gloves, white topped shoes, a white crepe blouse, and my ermine stole and muff." The ladies-in-waiting told her she looked very smart. The queen's somewhat more subdued ensemble was recorded too: "a plain green broadcloth suit, a black hat with feathers, and fox furs." She wore diamond and emerald jewelry, and her hair, of which Mary noted there was a great deal, "carefully marcelled," forced her to "wear her hats too high."[32]

Rinehart was enchanted with the queen. "I have seen the Queen of England. I have done much more. I have talked to her for almost an hour. She is charming—the most surprising person, considering what I expected. Full of fun, beaming with kindliness, and so much handsomer than her photographs."[33] They met at St. James's, rather informally, and the queen—in a playful mood—rummaged through a pile of knitted slippers ready to be sent to the Front. Amused at some very large ones, the queen slipped them on and slopped around the room. Mary's democratic heart was melted. It was wonderful and it was another first, for the queen had never before been interviewed for the American press.

Mary was now ready to leave London again, taking with her the letters Cambon had given her for Generals Foch and Castelnau and a pass through French customs. The pass was overwhelmingly official looking; an engraved card, a foot wide and seven inches long, it instructed the customs official to examine the bearer's luggage with "tous les égards et tous les ménagements qui peuvent se concilier avec l'exécution des règlements."[34] Mary closed the second volume of her diary, a record that was

at the beginning, about a lonely American woman suddenly thrust among the exalted ones of the earth, among war and battle and royalties, divided between timidity and ambition, feeling much of the time much too small for the thing she had undertaken, sitting huddled behind fierce military chauffeurs, or beside genial but imposing generals.[35]

Then she left for Folkestone and a newly dangerous Channel crossing; the German blockade had begun on the eighteenth.

The second Channel crossing presented unexpected difficulties, but by this time Mary was more than up to meeting them. When she arrived at the pier in Folkestone, there were two Channel boats. She had planned to travel to Calais but the Calais boat was not—mysteriously and authoritatively—carrying any passengers save soldiers that night. She was directed to take the Boulogne boat. But since Mary's last Channel crossing in January, the train between Boulogne and Calais had been discontinued, and it was in Calais that a military car was awaiting her. Mary was unable to make any impression on the officialdom at Folkestone for all her papers from Cambon, and there she seethed on the wharf, "hideously disappointed." As it grew late, Mary grew more frustrated. She moved away from the center of activity at the pier and back into the shadows. She allowed herself to be forgotten. And then she acted. "It seemed best to take a chance, so, armed with my Belgian Red Cross card, my passport, etc. I ran up the dock. It was dark and raining. . . . I found the Calais boat and wheedled the officer to let me sail on it. He agreed at last, which was a good thing, for the Boulogne boat had gone."[36]

When the boat docked in Calais early the next morning, Mary simply disembarked, crossed the square to the Hôtel Terminus, and engaged a room. There she ordered a boiled egg and coffee, nursed a worsening cold, and waited for Singleton to provide a car. He did so by the next day and Mary moved back to Dunkirk and the Hôtel des Arcades, where a number of letters from home awaited her. The letters, with commonplace news from the family, proved unnerving. Alan sent a recent Latin test and an illustration of their new toboggan path. He was busy "trying to temper copper." "The tempering of copper," he lectured, "is a lost art." Ted explained that, too late for Sunday school, he was using the time to write her "a short epistle." Mary wrote in her diary, "Shall try to see Churchill Friday and sail Saturday."[37]

On Tuesday, Mary began her tour of the French and English lines. It proved to be much more formal and much less exciting than her weeks in Belgium, a change signaled by the appearance of a Miss Bostwick, an Englishwoman who served as companion and interpreter. They stopped first to spend a number of hours with General Foch, credited with stopping the first German drive across the Marne to Paris. He invited Mary "to déjeuner . . . minced meat and cabbage, and mutton cutlets, fried potatoes, strawberry jam and small cakes. Red wine. Cheese and coffee." She and Foch talked at length about American ignorance of the actual situation at the Front, and Foch expressed his hope that Rinehart could help America learn what was really happening. After their talk there was dinner ("soup, roast, soufflé"), when Foch asked about "the influence of the German press" on public opinion in America. That evening Mary went to her "bleak and cheerless" hotel room at Cassel, the stove cold, the candles burned out, artillery thundering far off.[38]

Before she left the next morning, Rinehart was given a list of deeds of heroism by French soldiers as part of Foch's campaign to enlist American sympathy. Then she left by car for Saint-Omer and British headquarters. She sent her letters of introduction to General Huguet, liaison officer between the French and British armies, and he "called at once" to ask her to lunch at Staff Headquarters. Unfortunately, neither the Prince of Wales nor Field Marshal Sir John French was present at the time, but Mary did meet French the following day. On Thursday, Mary was driven along the British lines, stopping to lunch with Viscount Haldane. Mary, perhaps replete with army food, commented that he "had a boil on his neck, but invited me to lunch most hospitably"—this time it was beef stew.[39] Haldane, allowing Mary to take his photograph (in defiance of French's orders), observed that she was the only woman who had even been inside the British lines.

The tour of the French and British lines was informational but, subtly, disappointing, or so the diary suggests. The excitement and immediacy of Rinehart's notes at the Belgian Front give way to a sober reportorial account of people, places, and menus. She was, apparently, eager to go home. For one thing, the family letters awaiting her at Dunkirk had been unsettling. Perhaps, too, freedom and adventure had taken her too far, arousing carefully repressed frustration and even hostility about marriage itself. Between the entries of February 24 and 25 in the war diary are several blank pages. On one of them is written in a neat and careful hand, over and over, "Mrs. Mrs. Mrs. . . . ." Then those words were overwritten in a wordless pencil scrawl.[40]

The final notes in the war diary are marked, "1 A. M. Friday [February 26]. Have just run the blockade again." The handwriting is shaky for Mary was undoubtedly on the train for London: "This is early Friday. Tomorrow I sail for home!"[41]

Rinehart's war articles and their subsequent publication as *Kings, Queens and Pawns* were a great success. Lorimer, who kept cautioning Mary against giving any of the material away in articles or interviews before it appeared in the *Post*, did agree that the *London Times* could run the entire series after the *Post* publication. In May he sent her a copy of a wire from Northcliffe, who was delighted with the pieces now appearing in London:

"Three rousing cheers for Mary Reg." A month later Lorimer wrote to tell Mary that there had been an increase of 50,000 in the weekly circulation of the *Post*: "Your articles have been fine and have helped a lot." By the end of 1915, Northcliffe wrote again, this time to Mary, calling *Kings, Queen and Pawns* "the best of the war books" and asked Mary for some copies to give to royalty.[42]

Kings, Queens and Pawns retraces Rinehart's steps at the front lines and in the hospitals, but it is not a narrative of her experiences so much as a report, personal and affecting, of the war, of the men who were fighting it, of the men who were lying in the hospitals. The next to last chapter, "How Americans Can Help," is a detailed and moving account of the condition of the hospitals and the men in them, and a series of anecdotes about the sacrifices being made for the wounded soldiers by the French and Belgian people, by the peasants. There are stories of courageous medical personnel as well; one tells of a surgeon who had an X ray machine at his disposal but no gloves or lead screen for his own protection. "He worked on, using the deadly rays to locate pieces of shell, bullets and shrapnel, and knowing all the time what would happen. He has lost both hands." Rinehart urges all "Americans willing to take their own cars, and willing to go to work," to go to France where they will find "plenty to do."[43] For those who must stay at home, there is work too—sending supplies, providing money for supplies, even rolling bandages.

At the close of the book, Rinehart tells her readers that war is brutal, that it reveals "that civilisation is a shirt over a coat of mail," but shows as well "that hatred and love are kindred emotions, boon companions, friends." In the final words of the volume, Rinehart paints a description of war; it is not a description of battle.

> War is not two great armies meeting in the clash and frenzy of battle. War is a boy carried on a stretcher, looking up at God's blue sky with bewildered eyes that are soon to close; war is a woman carrying a child that has been injured by a shell; war is spirited horses tied in burning buildings and waiting for death; war is the flower of a race, battered, hungry, bleeding, up to its knees in filthy water; war is an old woman burning a candle before the Mater Dolorosa for the son she has given.
>
> For King and Country![44]

6

A Public Person

1915–1917

MARY HAD GONE to the war to satisfy her need for real-life adventure. When the articles she wrote about that adventure appeared, they had an effect she could not possibly have anticipated. With their publication Mary Roberts Rinehart became that curiously American phenomenon—a celebrity. And as a celebrity, a public person, Rinehart found that real life and the opportunity for adventure came to her. And always she would be "newsworthy."[1] Reporters and interviewers sought her out. Editors and the public were eager to learn her opinions about almost any subject: the moral dangers of the movies, America's responsibility toward nations engaged in the Great War, the most efficient way to shop for clothes, America's economy. As a figure of interest in her own right, Rinehart could now publish not only fiction but articles. The subjects themselves—travel, Cuban hoteliers, army training camps—mattered less than did Mary Roberts Rinehart's expression of opinion on those subjects.

Writing the war articles proved taxing for Mary. There was, in the first place, the pressure of time. The earliest piece, the interview with King Albert, was published on April 3, 1915, barely a month after Mary's return from Europe. Ten more war articles appeared between April 10 and July 31. Another difficulty lay in the fact that special care was necessary in preparing the articles. The royal interviews needed formal approval. Caution was necessary in all the pieces, for Rinehart had to take pains "to reveal nothing which was valuable for the enemy."[2] Particularly trying was the need to shape the essays to fit America's formal position of strict neutrality; Rinehart had evidence for facts that had to be deleted, dismissed as untrue, since they conflicted with the official attitude of balanced and disinterested observation. She felt that her articles has been "emasculated," as when her references to poison gas were disallowed. "I was met . . . by instant incredulity as to chlorine gas. Apparently no public reports had yet been made as to the use of poison gas by the Germans, and it is my recollection that I was obliged to cut out all reference to it in my war articles. Yet I had sat by men dying of it, their lungs seared with it."[3]

From 1915 on it was Rinehart's unshakeable belief that America would enter the war, that America had a moral responsibility to fight alongside the Allies. The sinking of the *Lusitania* in May only deepened that conviction. The ship's loss brought private as well as public grief for Mary; Mme. Depage, the wife of the Belgian surgeon, had gone down with the liner, on her way back to Europe after a visit in America to help the cause of Belgian relief. Mary, too, was raising money for Belgium and for the Red Cross, and the two women had sometimes worked together. Contributions were generous—the wealthy Pittsburgh Mellons sent a railroad carload of supplies—but charity was not belligerency and even the *Lusitania* incident did not bring most Americans to Mary's point of view.

The *Post* was, as always, a bellwether. By the summer of 1915 Lorimer was printing a minimum of war-related material, but with the sinking of the *Lusitania* came a strong response in the *Post* from former President Taft and an even stronger prowar piece, "The Pentecost of Calamity," from novelist Owen Wister. On the other hand, Lorimer still argued against war on his editorial page: It was war that had turned the German people into barbarians— the *Lusitania* was evidence. America's geography saved the country from war: "That is our inestimable advantage. . . . That deep reaction from the bloody and heathen barbarism of war is the finest prize of our culture and our highest justification."[4]

By late spring Mary was "tired and dispirited," "was growing morbid."[5] In fact, she was suffering a considerable letdown after her weeks at the Front. The prospect of a summer of fiction-writing with a vacation back at French River did little to raise her spirits; it was as if nothing had changed. And then celebrityhood bestowed its first gift—Howard Eaton came to Pittsburgh and proposed that Mary join his party in a trip through Glacier Park.

Howard Eaton was born in Pittsburgh, the oldest of the three Eaton brothers. In 1879 he went west, first to the Bad Lands and later to the Big Horn Mountains. Early in the twentieth century he had established a ranch in Wolf, Wyoming. For years he had taken his friends with him on hunting trips through the mountains, and now, in 1915, he was planning to guide his first party through newly opened Glacier National Park. He wanted the expedition recorded and who would serve better than the now famous Mary Roberts Rinehart? Mary was tired, she had work to do, she had her family to consider and her mother, and she "hesitated."[6]

But not for long. A new kind of adventure was simply too tempting and the possibility of writing articles about the West, still largely unknown, was attractive. She approached Lorimer with the idea, but he was not particularly fond of travel pieces and suggested she use the summer material for some Tish stories. In time, Tish would find herself in Glacier Park, having convinced her sidekicks that they should join her in seeing America first. But *Collier's* did accept Rinehart's proposal and published the account of the trip with Eaton in April 1916; Houghton Mifflin subsequently brought out the book *Through Glacier Park*.

Mary was not altogether unprepared for the rigors of travel through the mountains, for she rode horseback and had camping experiences from the previous summer. Still, an expedition of three hundred miles, over six mountain passes, was a major undertaking. On July 11 she left Pittsburgh for Chicago and from there took the Great Northern Railway to Glacier Park Station, to be met by Eaton and old Chief Three Bears of the Blackfeet Indians. The next morning the party of forty-two set off on horseback to cross the Rocky Mountains. There were eastern men and "timorous women," cowboys, photographers, a college boy or two, and Eaton, "at the head of the procession . . . sitting on his big horse silhouetted against the sky."[7]

The first day they did twelve miles, mountain miles, sometimes riding and sometimes leading their horses along trails covered with slippery shale. Lunch on the trail and then, at night, setting up camp and sleeping in tents. Mary was exhausted but exhilarated. "My starved romanticism flourished there. . . . I forgot the war, and that over the mountains where the sun came up men were killing each other." Her articles glowed with excitement and the sense of "achievement; of conquering the unconquerable; of pitting human wits against giants and winning—a sporting chance."[8]

Each morning "Uncle Howard" awakened the camp: "Time to get up! Five o'clock and a fine morning." Mary washed in the icy water and met the day in the modest costume of the time, "a gray riding suit, consisting of a long divided skirt and a long coat." The skirts were divided during the ride but when the women alighted they would "retire at once behind their animals, and there hurriedly button together the skirts so that they presented an unbroken front to the casual eye."[9]

But if the costumes were dandified, the trip was not for dudes. In the pleasantly comic tone she adopted for her travel pieces, Rinehart describes a pass. "A pass is a bloodcurdling spot up which one's horse climbs like a goat and down the other side of which it slides as you lead it, trampling ever and anon on a tender part of your foot. . . . A pass is a thing which you try to forget at the time and which you boast about when you get back home." Although she felt sure that Gold Dollar, her buckskin, had taken an instant and permanent dislike to her, Mary admired his sanity: "On a switchback he was well-behaved. He hugged the inside of the trail, and never tried to reach over the edge, with a half-mile drop below, to crop grass." The trip demanded stamina as well as nervelessness. One day the party rode thirty-five miles through rains that turned the trail into a "black swamp" through which the horses struggled while the riders were continuously rocked back and forth in the saddle.[10]

All the dangers and the inconvenience of Mary's trip are elaborated in "My Country Tish of Thee." Tish is magnificent. Before she leaves home she learns to ride and to use a lasso. Other research prepares her not only for trapping squirrels but even for such exigencies as snaring a mountain lion in the squirrel trap. She brains the beast with a rock and makes a broth of it—having read that mountain lion tastes like veal. As for the question of divided skirts or breeches, Tish opts for breeches. "I've felt for a long time that I'd be glad to discard skirts. Skirts . . . are badges of servitude, survivals of the harem, reminders of a time when nothing was expected of women but parasitic leisure," says Tish, always on the same side as Mary, though perhaps a little more advanced.[11]

In Glacier Park, Mary first learned of the plight of the American Indian. The Blackfeet of Montana were traditionally hunters, but the U.S. government had moved them to a reservation and tried to turn them into farmers. Their crops, such as they were, failed. The Indian agent then ordered them to "drive their great tribal beef herd to the east side of the reservation" and to leave them there. The herd then "had been driven off by cattle rustlers." Thus the winter of 1914–1915 had been, Mary learned, "one of starvation, and the old chiefs with tears in their eyes told me of the deaths of their children from famine."[12]

The Blackfeet saw in the "warrior woman," who had crossed the ocean and seen the Great War, a spokesperson for their cause. In a fine ceremony they initiated Mary into the tribe. An aged warrior and Chief Tail Feathers Coming over the Hill presided over the ceremony. Assisting were braves with exotic names: Two Guns White Calf, Eagle Child, Big Spring, Black Bull, Yellow Wolf, and Stab by Mistake. Mary was renamed Pitamakan, or Running Eagle, and received a number of presents, including an old buffalo hide, a paint pouch, and a dagger sheath. Subsequently, Chief Three Bears named a waterfall for Mary, "Pitamakan Falls."

The initiation delighted Mary's sense of romance; at the same time she realized that it was wonderful publicity. Houghton Mifflin was to release *"K"* on August 8, and on July 22 Mary wired the details of the ceremony to Roger Scaife: "ADOPTED INTO PIEGAN OR BLACKFEET INDIAN TRIBE LAST NIGHT IN POWWOW HELD AT CUTBANK CANYON GLACIER PARK GIVEN NAME "RUNNING EAGLE" (PITAMAKAN) AFTER FAMOUS WARRIOR WOMAN OF THE TRIBE."[13]

Rinehart was, however, absolutely sincere about helping the Blackfeet, promising them to go to Washington on their behalf. Soon after her return she met with Franklin Lane, secretary of the interior, and told him of the conditions she had seen—Indians starving, ill, going blind from trachoma. Her plea had its effect, as did her celebrity. That afternoon Lane promised an investigation and started food on its way to the reservation. The next year, in April, Mary continued her work for the Indians, at that time with a delegation of Blackfeet. She was, she admitted, a little self-conscious to be seen at Washington's elegant Shoreham Hotel with eight full-blooded Indians, "with earrings and long braids of black hair, in which was twisted red flannel by way of ornamentation."[14]

So much had Mary loved the weeks with Eaton, that she planned two expeditions to the West with her family in 1916: one through the western part of Glacier Park and the other through the Cascades. Such trips were not for tenderfeet. Stan "had always been a camper and out-of-doors man." Mary "had had the previous summer's experience. But to the boys it was new."[15] All the Rineharts trained by spending two weeks with Eaton on the eastern side of the park. Then they left Eaton to ride through the relatively unknown western side and to shoot the rapids of the Flathead River. Finally, they planned to "cross the Cascades over totally unknown country to Puget Sound."[16]

The trips are recorded in *Tenting Tonight* (1917) and they were clearly much more arduous, at times foolhardy, undertakings than Mary's first trip. The party was made up of the family, a movie photographer, guides, packers, and a cook. Thirty-one horses carried people, provisions, and the two boats in which they were to run the Flathead. "Before us was the Big Adventure." Riding through the western side of Glacier Park was arduous but not particularly hazardous, although the two big riverboats created problems. By the time the party reached the Flathead, however, Mary was beginning to have second thoughts. The sight of the river was not encouraging: "The North Fork of the Flathead River is a riotous, debauched, and highly erratic stream," that appeared to be running at "about ninety miles an hour." She began to harbor a secret hope that the boats would be smashed as they were lowered down the cliff into the water. The ropes held, the boats were in the water, and with the assurance that it would "make a good story," Mary was in one of the boats. For the next four days she traveled down the Flathead, along with one or another of her menfolk, who took turns at sharing Mary's adventure. Mary was triumphant: "I do not know, but I am very confident that no other woman has ever taken this trip. I am fairly confident that no other man has ever taken it."[17]

The river trip was breathtaking—beautiful and frightening. At first the shallow water appeared quiet, but the current was rapid and to Mary it

MRR as "Running Eagle," with the Blackfeet Indians in Wyoming.

By a western stream Mary enjoys a favorite sport.

seemed like riding an infinite toboggan slide. Farther on were rocks—boulders that created small whirlpools—and always the fear of an uncharted waterfall. By the third day they had reached an even more treacherous part of the Flathead where, "racing at mad speed," the boatmen needed all their strength and skill to elude the rock-created eddies. At one stretch, too dangerous to attempt, the boats were roped down the river. Another wild passage through a narrow canyon and they reached the final and easiest stage; "The river became almost a smiling stream."[18]

Mary celebrated her fortieth birthday on the Flathead. Stan had secretly arranged to have food and a special cook sent ahead to their projected camp. When the boats were drawn up to shore and Mary walked to the campsite, she found candles set out on the ground cloth that served for their table. After days of "canned salmon and fried trout," there was fried chicken and fresh bread, cheeses and cake and candy, and—incredible Stan—champagne, drunk out of tin cups.[19]

Nineteen people, including a naturalist-photographer, a chief guide, and a woodsman-hunter, made up the party for the second part of the journey, across the Cascades. This expedition, too, would make a good story, for it had never before been done. It proved to be exceptionally difficult and hazardous from the start and it grew more so when they reached Cascade Pass and found it closed by snow, necessitating a detour to the nearly inaccessible Doubtful Lake. Rinehart described the detour in a chapter called "Doing the Impossible." They rode at first along "an overgrown trail, mountain walls so close on each side that the valley lay in shadow."[20] After a while they reached a rock slide—three miles, up hill, over jagged, slipping rocks. After the rocks came the real climb.

The switchback trail to Doubtful Lake was the worst climb Mary had ever made. The narrow trail, winding back and forth against the mountainside, was strewn with rocks, sometimes covered with snow. They could not go back, for the trail was too narrow for the horses to be turned around. Two pack horses slipped and fell; only with the "infinite labor" of the packers were they roped down to the ledge below and saved. At one point the trail became a path of broken ice as they crossed the top of a waterfall. They climbed three thousand feet to Doubtful Lake where they camped, but there was no feed for the horses and no grass.

The next morning they climbed eight hundred feet to the top of the pass. The party split up, some taking the route over a snowfield; the others climbed through slippery mountain heather. Then the descent began. They rode little, more often leading their horses. There was a good deal more snow than they had anticipated, and there were rock slides across the trail, at that point only a rocky ledge, thousands of feet above the valley. Even below the timberline the descent remained arduous, with fallen trees and thick vegetation. Sixteen miles from the top of the pass they made camp, amid cypress trees thirty-six feet in diameter. The horses still had not eaten, but the next day was the journey's last. They were exhausted but jubilant. Miraculously, they had not lost a single horse, and they had crossed the Cascades.

Never again would Mary make such a trip through the Rockies. Although she returned for many years to Eaton's Ranch and from there took short trips into the Big Horns, there was never another expedition of such length or such difficulty. Why, indeed, did she attempt it at all? For one thing, Mary had fallen in love with the West. It had seemed at first empty and strange and hostile; it later became a second home. For another, the trips through the mountains represented adventure. Like the war zone the mountains tested people. And in the mountains, as at the Front, Mary could demonstrate that she could take it like a man, better than most men. Moreover, as we shall see, Mary had an uncertain, vacillating attitude toward the life she and her family had begun to live with the considerable money she was earning. She had no romantic notions about poverty, but there were aspects about the life of women of the leisure class that she disliked, and in her novels the only unredeemably weak and vicious people are such women. As she said a number of times in *Through Glacier Park,* to ride through the mountains, sleep out of doors, sit around a campfire forgetting dressmakers and hair curlers and social calls was *to live.* Finally, Mary was uncomfortably aware of reaching the age of forty. Even in 1915, as her thirty-ninth birthday approached, she had begun to think of herself as "almost forty years of age."[21] No one able to make those mountain trips could possibly be old.

In the fall of 1915, the house in Sewickley began to feel very large and very empty. Stan, Jr., entered Harvard in September and Alan went off to Morristown School. It distressed Mary to watch her two older sons leave for school and college, and she knew that it would not be long until Ted, too, would be at Morristown, leaving her and Stan and Cornelia alone in the twenty-room house, "the big house gay with light, and very quiet—and empty." Thinking later about those years and the separations they entailed, Rinehart concluded that much of it was unnecessary. Fancy colleges and universities were simply a "fetish"; education—if that were really the goal, which she doubted—could be had much closer to home. All in all, she decided that the fetish was made up of two parts, "of a certain snobbishness on the part of the parents, and of escape from home on the part of youth.[22] Still, all three sons attended Morristown and all three went on to Harvard.

At Harvard, Stan, Jr., nurtured ambitions to become a writer and by November he sent home the exciting news that he had been invited to

"Copey's" Thanksgiving party. Professor Charles Townsend Copeland was Harvard's celebrated writing teacher, in young Stan's words, "a big bug in contemporary writing,"[23] and places in his class were hard to come by, but Stan wrote soon after that he had gained admittance to the course. At Morristown, Alan hoped to concentrate in science, preparing for Carnegie Tech. It was not long, though, before he too began to think seriously about writing, and by 1916, when Stan had joined the staff of the Harvard *Lampoon,* Alan was writing stories and poetry for the *Morristonian.*

Reports from Stan, Jr., about social life in Cambridge and Boston included complaints about the green youth of the girls attending the Friday night dances. They were, to his eighteen-year-old eyes, offensive "sub-sub-debs."[24] Mary's comic imagination began to play with this idea and early in 1916 she sent Lorimer "The Sub Deb." The Boss was very pleased: "When they're as good as The Sub-Deb, I send the check gladly"—quite a tribute considering that Lorimer was now paying Rinehart $1,750 for a short story. In a postscript he added that the Sub Deb was worth a series and that Mary might well think of writing enough Sub Deb stories for a book.[25] Rinehart had discovered her third memorable character.

Bab, the Sub Deb, is an underage precursor of the flapper. Confined to boarding school and bitterly jealous of her older sister who has already "come out," Bab plots and schemes for her freedom, consequently landing in jams worthy of Tish. As Barbara Putnam Archibald, she customarily reaches the public through the themes required for her English class. These themes are studded with misspellings and ornamented with Bab's extraordinarily inappropriate misquotations. For example, fearing quite needlessly that her infuriated father will find and thrash a man she has developed a crush on, Bab wonders if she has led her "poor paternal parent into crime," and adds, "Hell is paved with good intentions. Samuel Johnson." Bab's essays are modes of defense against the injustices she has suffered and the punishments she is undergoing. Beyond the surface comedy of the Sub Deb stories, Rinehart gives us a realistic adolescent girl. Bab is always in love and always forswearing marriage. She vacillates between desire for jewels and desire for ice cream. Her hero is her father; her enemies, her mother and older sister. "My father has always been my favorite member of the family. . . . He has a great deal of tact, also, and later on he slipped ten dollars in my purse."[26]

Probably in no other writing did Reinhart ever find so successful a voice for comic absurdity. Bab's narrative carries the stories. On a well-developed jam: "I had made my own Fate, and must lie in it." On a novel she particularly liked: "The villain's only hold on her had been the letters, so he went to South Africa and was gored by an elephant, thus passing out of her life." On her mother: "My mother who had cared for me as a child, and obeyed my slightest wish, no longer understood me." And, preparing for a school vacation, on the Great War: "It is strange to be going home in this manner, thinking of Duty and not of boys and young men. Usualy when about to return to my Familey I think of Clothes and *affairs de couer*, because at school there is nothing much of either except on Friday evenings."[27]

Between April 1916 and June 1917 Rinehart published five Sub Deb stories in the *Post*, eventually receiving $2,000 for each one. Later in 1917 Doran brought them out in book form, as *Bab*. At the time when Mary was sending the Sub Deb stories to Lorimer, she was a little put out with him. She wrote, late in 1916, that she hoped the new story would be suitable for the *Post*, adding caustically, "Every now and then I appear to get out of my 'Post' stride." Behind this letter lay Mary's annoyance at Lorimer's refusal of a new novella, *The Confession*. It was not simply that Lorimer had turned it down—Rinehart was too much of a professional to take offense at that—but he had done so in terms she found particularly wounding. The novella was, said Lorimer, "much more calculated to appeal to your woman's magazine audience." Mary had the pleasure a few weeks later of informing the Boss that Edgar Sisson of *Cosmopolitan* had been happy to have the story for $5,000 and that she had accepted his offer "just in time to be obliged to refuse an offer from *McClure's* of seventy-five hundred, which is going some!" The reply was vintage Lorimer: "So glad you have taken the money away from the Philistines and have added it to your own bankroll."[28]

The Confession was another gift of celebrityhood. On October 11, 1912, J. A. Szydowski, a telephone installer, was replacing an old telephone box in the Savoy Hotel in Glassport, a town about fifteen miles up the Monongahela River from Pittsburgh. In the old phone box he found a piece of paper, folded up and tucked between the telephone bells. The paper was a small jagged piece torn from a cheap tablet, and on it in the spidery handwriting of the last century was written:

> To whom this may
> concern: on the 31st
> of May 1906 I killed a
> woman in my house of
> sin in Pittsburg 2nd Ave.
> I hope that you will
> not find this till i'm dead.
> M. M. Bennett.

Szydowski turned the confession over to the district attorney, W. A. Blakely, but with no evidence of a crime the D.A. could make no arrest.

Blakely assigned Detective B. Koehler to the case, and on October 25 Koehler reported that a Millie M. Bennett had run the Savoy Hotel for five or six years, selling out several months earlier in 1912 and moving to nearby Mc-Keesport. The coroner's office had no reports of the "sudden or mysterious death of a woman" in Pittsburgh any time from May 1 to June 16, 1906. A second report, on October 31, had more detailed information on Mrs. Bennett. She was widowed, had once kept a house ("sporting" or boarding?) on Second Avenue in Pittsburgh, and had subsequently bought a new house in Glassport, taking in forty-five boarders. Ten of the boarders were female and neighbors complained that they were "sporting girls." Bennett now lived with a young girl she claimed she had adopted and she appeared to have a lover. Otherwise, she was a quiet and respectable neighbor.[29]

Blakely had no case but apparently he remained curious about the confession, for sometime later he showed it to Rinehart and asked if it seemed genuine to her. Rinehart thought it was a real confession and the idea of the damning note hidden in a telephone box intrigued her. When she came to use that idea for *The Confession,* she altered the story, of course, since mur-

This torn and folded paper, found in a phone box, provided the idea for *The Confession.*

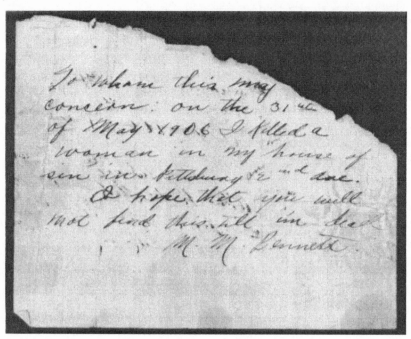

ders in brothels were not topics salable to magazine editors, but she kept the idea of the confession written on a scrap of paper and secreted in the telephone box of the house where the murderess lived.

In February 1916 Mary and Stan, along with Ted, took a cruise to Cuba, Panama, and Costa Rica. Mary was recuperating from another operation and from what had by this time become recurrent episodes of exhaustion and sickness. A seesaw pattern of alternating periods of energy and sick depression was becoming fixed in her life. The best tonic was travel. Although Lorimer was chary of travel pieces, he agreed to buy an article on Cuba, a newly fashionable resort. By the time the family had settled into their Havana hotel, Rinehart had found the title for her article—"The Pirates of the Caribbean," for, she wrote to her sons, "pirates they are." Among the least charming aspects of Havana was the "Cuban roach, which is a cross between a flea and a Rocky Mountain goat, and has a cold and malevolent eye." The native food was worse, "fish stewed in rancid oil, and smelling like a burnt case in a hospital." Piracy was best represented in the hotel trade. The three Rineharts were sharing one room, at the then considerable rate of fifteen dollars a day, without meals, and Mary felt a particularly strong animosity toward the hotel clerks. Rooms confirmed by wire were suddenly "not available," and tourists were paying a good deal for the privilege of a cot set up in the bar. Still, the cold room with its shabby blankets was not the hotel's greatest offense; that was the worm discovered in Dr. Rinehart's corn muffin.[30]

The *Post* published "The Pirates of the Caribbean" in November 1916. With such observations as "Dying in Cuba is very interesting. For the poor it must be much more so than living," the article enraged the Cuban government. Nor was it amused to read that "a week in Havana is longer than a cycle in Cathay." However, the outstanding outrage in Havana's eyes came in Rinehart's comments on the penitentiary, which, she observed leniently, was "full of political prisoners clothed in white" and seemed "to be most humanely conducted." There were no political prisoners in Cuba, Havana protested to the State Department of the United States. Rinehart and the *Post* were attacked in a number of editorials and both received a good deal of unpleasant mail. Mary remained serene, remarking to Lorimer, "I daresay there will be a marked improvement in tourist conditions this coming fall." As for the political prisoners, she continued, the Cuban consul was absurd, neglecting "to mention that the prison was built [for] and is now filled only by political prisoners as a result of the last Cuban revolution, and that most of them have life sentences." She assured Lorimer that she was entirely sure of her facts; moreover, she wondered if he would like an article on the Panama Canal—although "I daresay you will have lost your courage since the Havana article."[31] In fact, Lorimer had insisted on cutting some of the stronger parts of the Cuban piece before it went to press, and he did not care to take another.

When Mary returned from the cruise, she found yet another evidence of her role as a public person. The *Philadelphia Public Ledger* Syndicate wanted her to report on the 1916 national conventions. That year there were three nominating conventions, including that of the Progressive party. The Progressives and the Republicans were to meet simultaneously in Chicago; the Democrats, immediately after in St. Louis. Although, as Rinehart admitted, her "interest in politics was still purely academic," she accepted the assignment.[32]

The job presented new challenges, for Mary had no experience as a reporter. Her war articles had, with the exception of the interview with the king of the Belgians, been written after the events had occurred. Now she had to file daily reports, keeping up with the activity on the convention floor. Moreover, Mary was not comfortable competing with the male-dominated press corps. As she discovered at these conventions and later at the Disarmament Conference in 1921, the newspaper boys had their own sources, their own deals, and they were not at all eager to share them with a celebrity-novelist—and female at that.

Rinehart's way of counteracting the disadvantages inherent in not being one of the boys was effective, but it was not calculated to bring her into the fold. She found her own stories and sources through the famous people she either knew or could get introductions to. The reporters in Chicago might have had all kinds of inside dope, but Mary Roberts Rinehart had already been to Oyster Bay, where it had been arranged for her to meet and talk with Teddy Roosevelt, a possible candidate of either the Republicans or the Progressives.

Mary liked and admired men of action. The famous friends she would make and cherish were not artists or writers but generals and statesmen. Teddy Roosevelt was the kind of man she liked. He might have been, as she remarked, hard to interview, but Mary found his energy and forcefulness attractive. TR was difficult to interview because he did not particularly want to talk about the conventions; he was much more interested in the war, the West, the Indians, and "he wanted to talk, to tell stories." Mary was, nevertheless, pleased with the article she wrote, an article that seemed to admit her into the journalist fraternity, even if the fraternity was in this case a sorority of one: "It was the ideal interview handed out to the press to keep it quiet, while real affairs went on in secret."[33] But as the interviewer who had carefully masked what could not be revealed, Rinehart was in on the secret.

She did not, on the other hand, enjoy the actual reporting of the conventions. Chicago was hot and dirty, and the need to rush her work was disconcerting even though she had brought Helen Mayall with her to prepare the typed copy. There were diversions of a sort. Mary marched with the suffragettes in Chicago although she did not particularly believe in the effectiveness of votes for women. Her own career had taught her that economic independence, the right (and the willingness) to work and earn money, represented the route to freedom for women. As far as Rinehart could determine, the American voter had to fight a system that was for all real purposes unbeatable. The people were "jockeyed into position by a handful of men whose very names [they] hardly knew."[34] She did not see that it would make much difference for women to cast a vote within this system.

Although Rinehart only infrequently accepted such journalistic assignments, the work she did at the national conventions in 1916 was important for her, providing her first real taste of American politics and her first meeting with some of the men with whom she would be working closely only a few months in the future. Less than a year of peace remained for America, and Mary Roberts Rinehart was going to become an important propaganda weapon for the U.S. government. Not only had she seen and reported on the war in 1915, but she was a woman whose writing had created a deep affection for her in the American public. As a woman, a mother, a patriot, a celebrity, and a skilled writer, Rinehart would prove very useful for the government.

At about this time Mary went in for self-improvement, deciding to give up cigarettes—and never succeeding. The daughter of the Victorian household on Arch Street had taken up smoking when she first began to spend time in New York with theater people. Now she smoked regularly and decided to pit her willpower against the seduction of tobacco. The result, she announced to the more and more frantic staff at the *Post,* was that she could not write. On September 18, 1916, Mary wrote to Churchy Williams boasting, "I have not had a cigarette for ten days!" She promised that when she recovered from the effects of "abstinence," she would finish a Sub Deb story and admitted that, unfortunately, she was at present writing only about half a page a day and that half a page was "punk." Three days later Churchy suggested that maybe one cigarette would be all right, just something to get her back to the story. On the twenty-fifth, when no story had appeared at the *Post* offices, he urged Mary, "Please buy a box [of cigarettes] and charge them to the Saturday Evening Post." But Mary kept it up, sending periodic reports on her abstinence—but no fiction. The last such report was dispatched on October 2, and on the eleventh Churchy wrote with relief, "You must have cheated . . . for you never could have written so good a story as that in the first throes of a swear-off." No more was heard of the "cigarette-wagon."[35]

Perhaps the concern about smoking was one of Mary's responses to turning forty. Certainly she thought seriously about reaching that age, sometimes thinking how young, after all, her father had been when he shot himself and sometimes reviewing what she herself had accomplished. It was at about this time that Mary wrote her first autobiographical essay. Bit by bit, in the interviews she had given over the years, Mary was constructing the Rinehart myth, shaping and fitting the events of her life into a pattern that accommodated her ambivalence toward her career. Late in 1916 or early in 1917 she took that process a little further than before in a piece called "My Creed."

American Magazine published "My Creed" in October 1917 and in so doing at once exploited and extended Rinehart's celebrity. The article was subtitled "The Way to Happiness—As I Have Found It." It is a combination of autobiography and philosophy, though the latter predominates. Rinehart describes the beginnings of her career, emphasizing those times when she hazarded her talent and perseverance and luck against the world. In the story of her first trip to New York with the manuscript of her poems for children, Mary Roberts Rinehart becomes very much the female Horatio Alger, newly arrived in the city to pit her energy and wits against the power and wiles of urban America. "I remember looking at the silhouette of the city, rising above the morning mist, and wondering what it had in store for me."

Philosophically, Rinehart says in "My Creed" what she would say in all her autobiographical writing: The family comes first; she is "fiercely a mother." At the same time, "My Creed" is a statement for women's freedom —up to a point. Rinehart has been "among the pathfinders of the new world of independence," and she is proud of that; on the other hand, she believes "this *new* woman" may sometimes go too far. "Perhaps in a few years, it will be the accepted thing to consider that, having brought her children into the world, a mother may then pursue a gainful occupation without further serious responsibility for them. I hope not, but I fear it is coming."

Mary Roberts Rinehart had become a symbol of the woman who had made it. She was successful, wealthy, famous, and a celebrity in the special American sense of the term. Somehow she had achieved this while remaining identified with the home and the family. It was, no doubt, a tricky bit of tightrope-walking, but Rinehart insisted that women had to walk that tightrope. Unlike men, she said, women with careers will always encounter those moments when they must choose between the opposed demands of the career and the family. That dilemma is uniquely a woman's and eternally a woman's. And Rinehart's belief was that, in the end, the "new woman" would always choose correctly: "We need not fear for this *new* woman, where her home is concerned. Between her work and her family, the family will always win."

In an interview granted Montrose J. Moses for *Good Housekeeping* at about the same time that Rinehart was working on "My Creed," she elaborated on her ideas about the nature of women. "I have a conviction that the economic independence of women does not mean sexual independence of women." A woman may have a career, but marriage and children *"are* life" for a woman. "Nature is very strong," she continued, "stronger than art, or ambition, or avarice. . . . And because love-making and marriage are so fundamental, I can not imagine a normal young woman deciding against them in favor of the gratifying of her personal ambition." In writing his interview, Moses found that "even though she may be a woman with advanced ideas, tempered with a certain inherited love for family life, she is what she is, largely because of her family.[36] Moses' judgment is doubtful, but it was certainly what the audience of *Good Housekeeping* wanted to read and just as certainly what Mary wanted them to read.

With time Rinehart's position on women and the family has grown antiquated, conservative. Still, it is only fair to recall how great a freedom she had attained for her day and how far she had moved from the constraints of her upbringing. While there were times when she resented what she sometimes called her "chains," the fact was that she needed her sons and she needed Stan. As she grew older, she came to rely more and more on her husband's "steadiness and his sanity and his humor." Envying at times the freedom of unmarried women—the actresses she had met in New York, widowed Corra Harris who traveled as she wished on *Post* assignments, spinster Tish, absolutely her own woman—Mary Roberts Rinehart knew that she had the best of both worlds, and she wanted to preserve both.

> So—I work hard, and alone. And tonight I shall go home where the house lights shine out over the wintry garden and the dogs run out to meet me, and the glow of a wood fire flickers on the long windows that open to the terrace.[37]

But by the time that "My Creed" was published in October 1917, there were no lights shining out from the Sewickley house. It had been closed for the duration of the war.

7

The Rineharts at War

1917–1918

Lt. Stanley M. Rinehart, Jr., France,
To Maj. Stanley M. Rinehart,
Washington, D.C.,
November 24, 1918

"What is mother doing over here?"

BY THE BEGINNING of 1917 it was becoming increasingly apparent that only a matter of months, even of weeks, lay between peace and war for the United States. The formal break with Germany came on February 3, 1917, and the declaration of a state of war on April 6.

The Saturday Evening Post declared war on Germany on April 21, 1917, in an extraordinary issue. On the cover an American eagle, its claws extended, swooped down, screaming defiance on an unseen enemy. For this issue the pale peach-colored wash that characterized the covers of the *Post* was deepened to red orange, intensifying the power and belligerence of the American eagle. For the magazine's contents Lorimer was equally prepared to abandon pacifism for patriotism. He had wired his two most influential and popular writers, asking them for pieces on the war. One was Irvin S. Cobb; the other was Mary Roberts Rinehart.

For the April 21 issue of the *Post,* Rinehart wrote "The Altar of Freedom," supporting the new war effort in the most effective way she could. She spoke with the authority of celebrity, but at the same time she spoke as a woman and a mother to the mothers of America, urging them to courage and sacrifice. "Because I am a woman, I cannot die for my country, but I am doing a far harder thing. I am giving a son to the service of his country, the land he loves." Rinehart gave special force to her plea by referring, as she almost never did in her published work, to a family incident. Stan, Jr., had asked permission to enlist, and Mary had "weakened." "I wrote my oldest son a letter. . . . I asked him to wait. Womanlike, I wanted time. . . . Then—and may he forgive me for telling this . . . after a day or two, he wired, asking his father and myself if we wanted him to be a quitter."[1]

Although Mary had long known America would be at war and had long believed it was America's moral duty to join the Allies, it was not easy for her to write an article urging women to sacrifice their sons. She had seen the war and she had no illusions about its horror and brutality. In fact, Mary

108

who was to survive this world war and the next, lived to regret "The Altar of Freedom" and its profound effect on the women of America.

> Perhaps only God knows what a terrible thing that was to do, or how it haunts me now. Those women, with their letters that came in by hundreds, literally I believe by thousands: "I have just said good-bye to my son." "My boy left today." "I have read your article and my boy has gone. I sent him smiling, but I shall never see him again, for I am dying of a cancer."
>
> That was not all. When the war was over they wrote me again, those gold-star women; never bitter, accepting the empty chairs, the empty beds, the terrible emptiness of their hearts. "My boy did not come back."[2]

But that day in April 1917, Rinehart went to her office downtown, locked herself in, and wrote for twelve hours. She told the women of America that war is "a great adventure, the greatest adventure in the world," and promised them that it would make men of their sons. War is, as well, terrible, but America, the "last stand of the humanities on earth, realization of a dream and fulfillment of an ideal," will not fail. Nor will America's women fail; "we mothers stand ready."[3]

With the United States at war, Mary's determination to return to Europe grew although Stan's opposition had not diminished. Writing to Curtis Brown, agent for the foreign rights to her books, she said: "I have been hoping to get over to your side this spring. The vigilantes have been wanting me to go for them. But Doctor Rinehart is so unalterably opposed to my crossing just now that I have been obliged to give it up." But Mary was giving it up only for the moment. In a combination of professional, patriotic, and parental zeal, she added the assurance: "If we send an Army over I shall be there, if the thing can be done. My son is in training at Harvard, and of course I shall cross if he does."[4]

Mary set about assuring her return to the Front the very day that war was declared. She expected that she would be sent across with the first wave of troops in the American Expeditionary Force (AEF), and she wrote to Lorimer reminding him of that fact. In the hope that the *Post* would send her as a correspondent immediately, she added, "I find I have quite a pull with Washington." Lorimer was not enthusiastic: "I don't myself see any reason for all this haste about exporting our best writers to different parts of the world." Of course, he went on to say, if she should be sent with the AEF, he would not waste the opportunity—"we can use you in our business." In other words, Rinehart was not going to be sent Over There at the *Post*'s ex-

Rinehart at about the time of "The Altar of Freedom."

pense. Leaving nothing to chance, Mary also exploited her nurse's training and, that same day, enrolled in a "post-graduate operating room course at the hospital,"⁵ preparing herself for front-line duty in France.

Even before war was declared, Stan, Jr., had joined 1,400 Harvard undergraduates in military training. The training was unofficial, that is, it was not under the auspices of the government, but it was nonetheless serious. French officers had come to America to guide this program, and their realistic preparation for conditions of contemporary warfare was far more practical than the conventional training still followed in army camps. Writing to his mother in the middle of January, Stan asked her what Secretary of War Newton D. Baker had said about the Harvard training program and wondered why the government did not send his group over. "We are getting the best training in America, doing everything the French way—trench digging, bayonet drill, combat order."⁶

Mary had mixed feelings about the Harvard ROTC program. She was prepared to have Stan, Jr., in the army although she underwent the terrors of other mothers. On the other hand, she wanted him to be an officer and, regardless of his place in an ROTC group, he was not old enough to receive a commission. But Mary stopped worrying about Stan's rank when he mentioned, early in March, that the cadets had rifles "but not 'Springfields,' as yet."⁷ Although American factories were not yet producing anything like an adequate supply of ordnance and many recruits would soon be going through the manual of arms with wooden guns, Mary was appalled to discover that her son's group was training with outmoded rifles.

At the beginning of April, Rinehart decided to find out just what kind of leverage she had in the matter of small arms. On the third she sent a wire to the White House and another to Baker requesting Springfields for Harvard. By the fifth she sent Stan, Jr., a letter announcing her receipt of a wire from the White House, promising that it was "taking the matter up at once." Stan passed the news on to his captain, who "was overjoyed." That apparent success prompted Mary's remark to Lorimer on the extent of her pull at the White House. But Mary—and the cadets—were to be disappointed. On the seventh Baker wrote to President Wilson's secretary, Joseph P. Tumulty, acidly remarking that "the latest models [of Springfields] were not available for issue to educational institutions."⁸ Courteous letters from various government officials followed, but the matter was closed and new ordnance ended up at the Front rather than at Fresh Pond in Cambridge.

Springfields or not, Stan's enthusiasm was undimmed. Like other Harvard students he found that the outbreak of war made college inconsequential. It was hard to concentrate on his studies, and he expressed his frustration at college life and his eagerness to enter the war in a theme for Copey's class.

Early in March, Stan wrote home with mixed news. He had been placed on academic probation, but Copey thought his essay so good that he suggested sending it to a Boston paper. On March 7 the *Boston Evening Transcript* printed "A Fair Chance," by Stanley M. Rinehart, Jr., Harvard, '19. The essay carried the subtitle, "An appeal from a soldier of tomorrow," and argued for the right of his generation to fight in America's war. The essay made quite a stir and was, Stan reported, being read from the pulpits.[9]

Throughout America war enthusiasm was running high. Simple distinctions were made: one was either a patriot or a slacker. Lorimer, despite the cautious course he had been steering since 1914, now lent his magazine to the American war effort, encouraging men to enlist, women to economize, workers to save their higher wages for Liberty Bonds, farmers to win the war on the food front, and all aliens or first-generation Americans to raise their voices in support of the Allies or to shut up. Above all, the *Post* reminded America of its special meaning as a nation and exhorted the American people to supreme efforts.

Despite her wealth and fame, Mary Roberts Rinehart was a fair reflection of the mind of the American people in 1917. Her patriotic feeling and her ideas about the war and what it meant for her nation were those of most of her countrymen. A serious letter to seventeen-year-old Alan at Morristown tried to impress on him the significance of the war:

> These are very serious times. I want you to think about them. You may yet be called to serve your country. . . . We bought each of you $500 worth of bonds, but that cannot count as your contribution. Good hard work, a high and lofty perception of what it all means, a little additional seriousness and a new and *active* humanity, these must be the attributes that war demands and produces. It will be a long war. It is not across the sea. It is here. And we are going to need all our strength and all our religious faith to come through.[10]

Mary was prepared to contribute to the war effort in any way she could. The military and the government thought she could be most useful as a propagandist, and soon after the United States entered the war, Josephus Daniels, secretary of the navy, offered her an assignment. The United States Navy had been allowed to grow obsolete. In order for the fleet to be enlarged and modernized, it was urgent to raise public interest, thereby encouraging both congressional appropriations and enlistments. The navy mounted a fair-sized publicity campaign in the press and Daniels wanted Mary Roberts Rinehart among its campaigners. As Daniels put it in a memo to Adm. Henry Mayo, commander in chief of the Atlantic Fleet, Rinehart's 1915

pieces had been "of untold value in the stimulation of public opinion."
Now, it was "highly important to have the Fleet painted by a master hand"
by "one of the foremost writers of the day."[11] The Department of Navy asked
Rinehart, therefore, to spend a number of days with the Atlantic Fleet and
then write a story for the *Post.*

Lorimer was, under the circumstances, willing to print such an article,
but he wasn't promising a lot of money: "When I see how long it is, and how
good it is, and how different it is from the million other articles which the
thoughtful Navy Department is putting out through every correspondent in
the country that they can coax to take a stateroom for a trip with the fleet, I
will talk prices with you." In closing he took the time to repeat himself; this
article better be "pretty individual and different." In fact, Lorimer liked it to
the tune of $1,750, a good deal of money for nonfiction, and admitted "it is
individual enough."[12]

Rinehart's navy article, "The Gray Mailed Fist," did take an individual
slant, precisely the slant most useful to the navy and most effective for her.
She wrote as a woman, ignorant of ships: "This article is a landman's impression, in a landman's tongue, of one of the most impressive experiences of my
life." She mixed a description of the ships themselves with a narrative of the
day's activities for a typical bluejacket. Her eye again on the mothers of
America, she stated the major purpose of her article: "To give to those whose
lads have gone to the fleet some idea of what the fleet is; to tell the average
citizen how the fleet appears to another citizen—for I take it a woman is a
citizen."[13]

Mary had gone to Washington early in May for a briefing on the navy
and left for Yorktown and the new battleship *Pennsylvania* on May 8. For
four days she was given a crash course on the ship and its men, and she was
accorded red-carpet treatment—as far as that was possible. Admiral Mayo
turned his suite over to her and she ate her meals with the admiral and his
chief of staff, but to Mary's dismay she was sent ashore each night. Women
were not permitted to sleep aboard a naval vessel; in Mayo's words: "It would
require an act of Congress to keep you on a battleship overnight!" So each
evening the admiral's barge took Mary to "a dreadful little country inn, outside toilet, oil lamps and so on."[14]

On Mary's last day with the fleet, Daniels and Baker arrived in Yorktown on the presidential yacht, the *Mayflower.* A high-level, all-male luncheon was arranged on the *Pennsylvania* and Mary was again put on the
barge and sent ashore. When Daniels arrived at lunch and asked for Mrs.
Rinehart, the barge was sent to retrieve her. Unprepared and rushed, Mary
returned, shod in borrowed tennis shoes. But when the press was called in
"to view this historic occasion," Mary glowed; her presence "alone in a world

of men" was another triumph over the newspaper boys. She sailed back to Washington with Baker and Daniels on the *Mayflower,* standing on deck as they "steamed between that double line of great gray ships."[15] Dinner on board and—naval rules not pertaining to the presidential yacht—she was assigned Mrs. Woodrow Wilson's cabin.

However, lying in the first lady's quarters, Mary become horribly sick. She summoned a doctor who gave her some morphia, but in the morning she was still weak as well as nauseated by the medication. After her triumph, ignominy. As the yacht sailed into the dock, Mary vomited into the Potomac. She wobbled ashore and Baker drove her to the Shoreham, trying not to jolt his miserable passenger. One day in bed and then Mary was off to New York, overnight, and to New London to visit the submarine base there. Once back in Sewickley, she wrote and revised "The Gray Mailed Fist" in ten or twelve days.

The Navy Department was not alone in perceiving Rinehart's special usefulness. Late in May *The Ladies' Home Journal,* still under Bok's editorship, asked for a monthly war column, "Mrs. Rinehart Sees It Through." Although the *Journal* was more or less the *Post's* sister publication, Mary was not at all eager to comply, so she told Bok that she was pretty much pledged to the *Post.* But Bok replied that he had checked with Lorimer, who thought the idea a fine one. Mary wrote angrily to the Boss, complaining that he "took away the only ground I had to stand on"; once again he was willing to push her into the women's market. "I have very little interest in Woman's Magazines," Mary continued, pointing out that she was not a women's writer and that of the hundreds of letters received from "The Altar of Freedom" many were from men. "I do not," she emphasized, "appeal to a purely feminine audience." Finally, she conceded that if Lorimer did not want her war material she would have to accept Bok's offer, but she was indignant: "I cannot believe that you are going to turn me over to the Home Journal in this summary fashion."[16] Lorimer could not afford to overlook Rinehart's irritation; he wanted her fiction too much. The *Journal* gave up on the war column, but publisher Cyrus Curtis kept his eye on Mary for a future proposition.

A much more attractive opportunity came shortly later, the chance to visit a number of army camps and cantonments and to write about army training for the *Post.* It is hard to know whether the plan was initiated by Rinehart or Newton Baker. Perhaps they had talked of it together in general terms, leaving the matter open until Rinehart could assure Baker that she had a market for her articles. At the beginning of June, Mary tried the idea out on Lorimer. As with the navy piece, he was willing, but found it irresistible to rub salt into *The Ladies' Home Journal* wound. Write a story, he advised her, "that will appeal to the women—heart stuff, mother stuff, son stuff, your-boy-doing-his-bit stuff."[17] With the *Post*'s approval in hand, Mary probably got in touch with Baker, for a week later Adjutant General John R. White wrote telling her that Baker would be pleased to have her visit the camps for a *Post* article, although he could not guarantee exclusive rights.

Rinehart described army training camps in two pieces for the *Post*, "The Boys Are Marching" and "For the Great Adventure" (August 18 and 25, 1917). She spent about two weeks collecting materials, visiting Forts McPherson, Myer, and Niagara, as well as the training camp at Plattsburg, New York. Besides the *Post* pieces, Rinehart prepared a fourteen-page document for Baker, marked in her hand "Confidential to Secretary of War." In that report she mixed observations and judgments about each camp with a very positive review of the training system at Harvard.

The *Post* articles were upbeat and encouraging; the report to Baker pulled no punches. At Fort McPherson, outside Atlanta, she found a colonel who lacked "executive power" and who was in fact "rarely in evidence" at the camp. McPherson was, overall, the least satisfactory of the camps Mary visited; for one thing, the "vice conditions are not good in Atlanta," and for another, there was a "spirit of pessimism." Mary had been told there that the German machine was unbeatable. About the young men themselves she had no reservations; they were "all members of good family and of fighting tradition." Her investigations were everywhere thorough. At Fort Niagara she found the "kitchens very dirty, sinks full of greasy dish-water, menus ill-balanced, and unappetizing." In general, Rinehart lectured Baker on the outdated training the men were receiving. At Harvard the cadets learned trench warfare; in the army camps they were "in effect still using the combat methods of the Spanish War." One commanding officer had even, she marveled, "consulted my ignorant self as to the building of the trenches." And she repeated that "this is trench warfare."[18]

Mary had returned to Sewickley to write the material for the *Post*, making frequent trips to Washington during the summer. A major preoccupation now was the military future of her husband and son. The matter of young Stan's commission continued to rankle. Mary wrote to tell him that she had taken "the matter of the Harvard commissions up to the President himself last week." Wilson was tactful enough to take "careful notes," but no commission was forthcoming. A combination of admiration for the Harvard system of training and frustration over Stan's failure to receive a commission drove Mary beyond good sense, and she suggested in a letter to her son that she might have a senatorial investigation made "if there are no commissions to be issued in any other way." Leaving no stone unturned at this point, she also looked into a West Point appointment for Stan, taking that request to the secretary of war. Baker turned Mary down with the report that "the certificate board had closed its proceedings in June" and added that it would take an act of Congress to change the present system.[19]

At the same time that Mary was in something of a state over her son, she tried to take a hand in her husband's army career as well. Right after war was declared, she wrote to the assistant secretary of war asking what the plans were for medical men. She explained that her husband was a specialist in heart and lung diseases as well as "a sanitarian of twenty years standing, having had charge of the health of Allegheny County . . . for that length of time." It was not a question of rank or pay, but rather of "doing his bit" where he would be "most valuable."[20]

Stan found his first war work as one of three men in charge of draft registration for Allegheny County. It was an important job, mostly administrative, rounding up and training volunteers to help find and list all the men in the county in preparation for conscription. Registration completed, Stan went on to work on the Exemption Board, meanwhile taking and passing his physical examination and awaiting his army commission. And then, after two and a half months, he learned that his commission was being held up on account of his work on the Exemption Board.

Mary tried again. On the first of August she wrote a long letter to Enoch Crowder, judge advocate general of the army. She reviewed the situation for him, including the fact that during her recent trip to Washington, the last week in July, it had finally been arranged for the doctor to take "executive charge of the tuberculosis situation in one of the large army cantonments," and that on the last day of July word had come that he would have to remain on the Exemption Board. Mary went on to argue, "Many other men who cannot leave their practices to do special work in the field are not only willing but anxious to serve their country at home." Dr. Rinehart was willing to do more and to find a substitute for his present position. There was also, Mary continued, a "personal" side; the doctor was having "the hardest part of all since war was declared" for he could only watch "his wife going about doing her bit for the country while he sat at home and waited." Finally, Mary made it clear that she had troubled the general with "a family matter" only because she hoped he would make an exception for them. "I am perfectly willing," she added, "to have you do it against your better judgment so long as you do it!"[21]

He did it. On August 13, 1917, Stan received his commission as a captain in the medical section of the Officer Reserve Corps. In September he was to report to Camp Sherman in Chillicothe, Ohio.

Obviously the spring and summer had been difficult for Mary. The boldness and sometimes the stridency with which she made her demands on Washington were not characteristic, but the military careers of her son and husband had become obsessions with her. She had, as well, the younger boys to think about and plan for, and at the same time she was traveling a good deal, to the fleet, the army camps, to Washington and New York. Constantly, she brooded about getting to the war again. Through these months she was "highly emotional." She broke into tears before the Women's Club of Sewickley Valley when she tried to read them "The Altar of Freedom."[22]

It was in this highly charged state of hypertension and anxiety that Mary discovered spies in Sewickley, or so she suspected. It is not possible to exaggerate the fear of spies in America in 1917 and 1918. Not only did newspapers and magazines tell of the fearsome work of German agents, but Americans themselves were suspected, in particular those who were then called "hyphenated Americans," first-generation Italian Americans, Polish Americans, German Americans. The *Post,* for example, ran a series of articles on captured spy documents, most of them hardly credible; in one a letter from a German spy in America was quoted, "Ha! Ha! Evil seeds flourish. . . . The people are stupid."[23] Magazine fiction dwelt on the bomb-carrying saboteur, usually a hyphenated American bent on the destruction of U.S. factories.

The Rinehart men during World War I. From left to right, Stan, Ted, Alan, and Stan, Jr.

Rinehart suffered no less anxiety over spies than did her fellow Americans. Some of her suspiciousness was apparently justified for her office was broken into. She thought someone must have been looking for material on the fleet or the training camps. The general air of pessimism she had noted at Fort McPherson she laid to enemy agents too. There she had grown suspicious at the unusual dispiritedness of the men and decided to spend more time just listening: "Gradually one officer's name began to stand out." She met him at a dinner party where he sought her out and asked her "very indiscreet" questions and then went on "to exalt the Germans and minimize our services."[24] Rinehart included this information in the report she prepared for Baker.

In an episode that sounds like the plot of *The Man in Lower 10,* Rinehart lost that report. She took it with her on the train for Washington and was "bothered by a middle-aged man." She snubbed him, went to bed, and took "the precaution of placing my dressing case between myself and the window." In the morning the dressing case was in the aisle and the report was missing. Sometime later the officer Mary suspected was discovered to be one of a dozen men "planted by Germany in the ranks of our army a number of years before."[25]

By the time that she was back in Sewickley for the summer, Mary was intensely spy conscious. A small hotel near the railroad station at Glen Osborne had, some months earlier, been bought by a German, and "since that time people residing in the hotel have reported at various times strange and mysterious events." Reporting in a letter to a Col. R. H. Van Deman in Military Intelligence, she conceded that anti-German sympathies and the natural suspicions of a small town might be playing their part in these rumors; nevertheless, she was worried: "I am reliably informed that foreign gentlemen carrying valises are constantly appearing at this hotel . . . at all hours of the day and night, remain for a few hours closeted with the proprietor and then depart." Although this could mean nothing, Rinehart suggested an investigation. Since an agent at the hotel would arouse suspicions, she offered her own house as a base. "It is," she concluded, "a matter for quick work."[26]

Van Deman sent Rinehart's letter on to the Department of Justice. It is impossible to tell whether he was simply discounting her story or whether he was handicapped by real problems of staffing and jurisdiction. The War Department had no authority except within the armed forces; nor did it have any agency in Pittsburgh at that time. Without question, Van Deman took spies in general very seriously. He told Rinehart, "If the industrial agitation [in Pittsburgh] increases proportionally in the next few weeks, as it has in the past three or four, and if the evidence of German activity in labor circles becomes more apparent, the War Department will have to establish a section in

Pittsburgh." Meanwhile there was not much he could do. Mary was ready to take the matter directly to Baker at this point, an idea that made Van Deman considerably uneasy: "He is such an extremely busy man and so full of responsibilities . . . that I hesitate to bother him with matters of detail which can be kept from him."[27]

By fall Mary had new problems to contend with. With the doctor and Stan, Jr., both ordered to Camp Sherman in September, Alan entering Harvard, and Ted off now for Morristown, she faced the prospect of being alone, except for Cornelia: "I found myself entirely on my own resources, and with a large and expensive property to support." She had thought of closing the house before; now it seemed certain she would have to. It was, after all, very expensive to maintain. The doctor would be making only his captain's salary and Mary's own income had been somewhat reduced as a result of the time taken away from her fiction-writing by the work done for the army and navy. Moreover, the twenty-room Sewickley house depressed Mary; in what had been the center of active family life, there were now too many empty rooms. But the decision was hard to come to. Stan, Jr., left for Camp Sherman; the doctor was to follow in two weeks. Still Mary had not made up her mind. While Stan saw to the closing of his office, inventorying and storing the furniture, medical equipment, and records of twenty years of practice, Mary went to Atlantic City for a brief vacation. Helen Mayall sent her daily reports and they were not encouraging. The servants wanted to know what Mrs. Rinehart planned. William had two offers for gardening positions. Maggie the cook was "on the verge of nervous prostration" and was threatening to leave the next day. "I am afraid this is final," Mayall judged.[28]

Not until Mary had returned and seen Stan off did she finally decide that she must close the house. She would take Cornelia to stay with Olive and find herself accommodations in New York, near both Alan and Ted, within a short train ride of Washington, and right at hand for the hoped-for rehearsals of *Otto*.

In New York, Mary moved into the Langdon Hotel at Fifth and Fifty-Sixth. Shortly after she was settled, Winthrop Ames postponed *Otto* again; the whole play had to be done over. Mary continued work on a new novel despite her frustration and loneliness. Then there was a new calamity. Visiting Ted at Morristown, Mary found him "jerking with nerves and looking very ill." She took him back to New York where his condition was diagnosed as "a dilated heart with incipient chorea."[29] Ted went into the Roosevelt Hospital and Mary divided her days between visiting him and working on her novel at the Langdon.

The new novel was *The Amazing Interlude*. By November the typescript was at the *Post* and Lorimer planned a five-part serialization to start in February 1918. Rinehart wanted a good price for *The Amazing Interlude,* but Lorimer would not pay any more than $2,000 an installment, the same price he was paying for her short stories. Ten thousand dollars was more, he said, than he had ever paid for a serial, "and the absolute maximum of value that I can see in anything short of the New Testament."[30]

Lorimer bought *The Amazing Interlude* for ten thousand and he bought himself a bargain. The most popular of Rinehart's romances, the story of Sara Lee and Henri appeared at a very propitious time. At the end of America's first year of war, the story of a brave American girl who goes off to the Front to aid the war effort and falls in love with a romantic Belgian aristocrat was precisely the kind of story ten million Americans wanted to read. Doran brought the book out later that spring and by early summer reported to Rinehart that it was "the success of the year" and would certainly "sell 100,000 copies."[31]

After the New Year, Mary continued to press for a way to return to the war but to no avail. With work completed on *The Amazing Interlude* and no good news about *Otto,* she was restless and when Howard Eaton suggested a trip to the Southwest, she was delighted to accept. There was even a chance that Teddy Roosevelt, Mary's neighbor at the Langdon, would accompany them. As it turned out, Mary took the trip, but neither Roosevelt nor Eaton went along.

Moreover, what had started out as a trip to the Southwest turned into a trip to Mexico. The change in itinerary occurred as a result of government interest in Mexico, friendly to Germany and suspected as a retreat of German agents. Mary was joined by an intelligence agent from the War Department and a border official from the Treasury Department. The border official was tracking down smugglers; the intelligence agent was crossing the border into Mexico for counterespionage purposes. The situation grew yet more involved. Mexico had its own suspicions, whether of Rinehart or of the intelligence agent disguised as an interpreter is hard to say. The Mexican government decided to protect its interests by providing an escort for the party: two army officers and five enlisted men, "all mounted and in uniform."[32]

They set off from San Diego on March 7, 1918, and by that time had taken on "all the aspects of a small army." Mary herself was well equipped.

> With each alarm I had added to my personal armament. When we finally started I carried in a scabbard slung under my right stirrup the Winchester thirty-thirty; hanging to the horn of the saddle was a small combination rifle and shot gun, and in my leather belt was a Smith and Wesson thirty-eight caliber revolver! And I was so loaded with ammunition that a substantial blow would have exploded me.[33]

If they had become by then "an expeditionary force," Rinehart later said they were more distinguished for what they did not accomplish than for what they did. They found no radio sets and no smugglers, and had to be satisfied with the presence of a number of slackers in Enseñada. There were not even any bandits.

Still, the trip was difficult and not particularly pleasant. They traveled through the desert and mountains on the coast of the Baja Peninsula to Enseñada. Typically, Rinehart commented "I do not know of any other women who have taken that trip to the head of the Gulf of California and then across the mountains to the Pacific." "After all," she added, "why should they?" They had taken no tents, believing the desert nights would be warm. As a result they broiled all day and froze all night and toward the end of the trip found their supplies running low. Enseñada seemed a paradise by comparison, but unknown to Mary, the American Consul there, suspicious of her German name, had wired the government. Later she learned that "a navy gunboat [had been] on its way to Ensenada to arrest us!" When Secretary Daniels heard about the incident a few weeks later, he wrote to Mary that he hoped there had been no inconvenience. And then, knowing his woman, added, "But would it not have given you a chance to write a fine story if they had arrested you?"[34]

The party returned to San Diego on March 20 and after two weeks in California, Mary made one of her fairly regular visits to Chillicothe to see the doctor, now a major, and Stan, Jr., just back from a short inspection tour in France with Gen. Edwin F. Glenn. More changes were at hand: Stan, Jr., was engaged to marry Mary Doran, the daughter of Rinehart's new publisher, George H. Doran. Writing from Morristown, young Ted was not at all sure how he felt about the "fatal news" that his older brother was planning to become a married man.[35]

By early in May both the doctor and Stan, Jr., expected to be shipped overseas shortly. Mary was in New York working on a new mystery play and a comic army-camp story, "Twenty Three and a Half Hours Leave"—destined for instant popularity as a story and a movie. She wrote some serious war pieces as well, one of them an inspirational essay for men returning with permanent disabilities ("Going to the Sun," *Post,* July 20, 1918) and another a discussion of the changes war had brought to America and, by way of example, to Sewickley ("The Gains of War," *McClure's,* September 1918).

The doctor's plans to be shipped overseas were frustrated in the end. He was transferred to the surgeon general's staff in Washington to implement new health policies for the training camps. But Stan, Jr., was about to go, not this time on a special tour with Glenn but as a part of the AEF. He came to New York where the troopship waited and he and his mother had dinner together the night he was to sail. Mary maintained her composure as she saw him into his taxi and the next day forced herself to continue work on "Twenty Three and a Half Hours Leave." But the sailing was delayed. Stan made a surprise return to the Langdon to say good-bye again. The shock and the sight of her son, "a soldier in full fighting equipment," swept away her control. "I gave one long terrible look, and then I screamed."[36]

With her oldest son overseas, Mary intensified her own efforts to get to France. In June she was officially made a Red Cross nurse with the promise of a September crossing. She told her husband: "A man came from Washington yesterday to see me. He brought credentials and my [Red Cross] nurse's pin, and I am to have every privilege in France when I go late in September, to choose my own places of service, to move about at will, and so on." But a month later she wrote him that there was a delay: "Baker is afraid to let me go while the present ruling exists."[37] The "present ruling" disallowed the wives and mothers of soldiers at the Front from serving as nurses in France.

Mary had sent Baker a letter as soon as her Red Cross credentials came through and he replied on July 8. He was tactful, congratulating her on her earnest desire to help, her willingness to "go back from the distinguished position" as a writer in order to return to her "old profession of trained nursing." However, it was at Pershing's own request that the ruling had been made keeping mothers and wives from the Front. Mary wrote again, apparently bringing to Baker's attention the services she had performed for the army, but he was adamant: "I wish I were in a position to act in accordance with my personal desire to show our appreciation of all that you have done, but after all, I don't think you would think much of the army if it did not treat all alike."

Mary was not going to take no for an answer, and on August 2 she wrote directly to General Pershing at his headquarters in France. Pershing did take time out from the war to reply: he would not make an exception; Mrs. Rinehart should continue her fine work at home.[38]

The summer was a low point. The major was in Washington or traveling for the surgeon general, able to spend little time with Mary. But the two younger boys were out of school for the summer and, with the Sewickley house closed, Mary decided to rent a place at Bellport on Long Island, where she could spend the summer with them and Cornelia. It was the best plan, but Mary was lonely and restless. "It is unspeakably lonely, dear, without you," she wrote to Stan. "The evenings are dreadful. Grandma plays solitaire, and at last in desperation I come up to my little study and write."[39]

Both Mary and Stan talked now of her writing less, even of her not writing at all for a time, for she was tired and often ill. But during the summer she started work on a new novel. It was an ambitious project, concentrating on the war from the point of view of the home front and dealing with problems of profiteering and industrial agitation. The intricate plot combined German espionage and subversion with romance—remarkably a love story about a mature man and woman both trapped in unsatisfactory marriages. As had become customary—especially with serious fiction—Mary complained to Stan that the work she was doing was not satisfactory. "I am very nervous. The new novel worries me, too. It is moving slowly and very uncertainly." On the other hand, she reported that *Pictorial Review* had offered her $25,000 for serial rights, an enormous advance over *The Amazing Interlude*.[40] She accepted that offer and *Pictorial Review* began serialization of *Dangerous Days* in March 1919.

The summer at Bellport was not altogether uneventful. In fact, the house they rented shared some of the characteristics of the rented summer houses Mary Roberts Rinehart created for her mystery novels—it appeared to be haunted. "There is," she wrote to Stan, "a ghost! I knew, right after I came here that the place was queer. Now laugh!" Waking one hot night, she felt "a cold wind blowing over me" and was "paralyzed with terror. Then something banged the bed with a perfectly shattering noise." Other strange incidents followed. The maids, kept in the dark for fear they would leave, reported things they had seen and heard. Nor were Alan and Ted told, and yet Alan "heard something climb up to his room and stand in the doorway—at 3 A.M. He got his gun and went all over the house" but found nothing. Subsequently, Mary learned that they had rented "the haunted house of Bellport, written up in the [New York] Herald of 1902."[41] The incidents at Bellport were stored up, to be used a few years later in *The Red Lamp*.

In September the boys returned to school and Mary went back to the Langdon, writing and waiting for Baker to change his mind. In a state of tension and anxiety she completed *Dangerous Days*. The effort of writing long serious fiction had begun to tell on Mary since at least the time of *"K,"* and she was now severely depressed. It was at this low point that Rinehart at last received word from the War Department that she was to go to France. She reported her triumph to Stan in a strangely unenthusiastic letter, as though she might have wanted to spare his feelings about his own stateside assignment: "I am to be sent abroad soon as official representative of the War Department." Moreover she was, as she told him, not well, generally depressed, "almost suicidal." "I finished the novel, 150,000 words, written twice, all of it, on Monday morning, and went into a sort of nervous collapse."[42]

Baker did not give Mary much notice; she had only three days to prepare to sail. The family was, in its way, settled. Alan had joined the Marine Corps and was about to go into training at Harvard. Ted, at Morristown, had joined the Home Guard. Rinehart's writing commitments were something of a problem though. *Dangerous Days* was completed but a mystery play was not. Mary got in touch with Avery Hopwood, with whom she had collaborated so successfully on *Seven Days,* and asked him to finish it. Then she went to Washington to say good-bye to Stan and to receive her official State Department passport.

On November 1, 1918, Rinehart made her second crossing to the war. It was a cold, rough trip and most of the time the passengers stayed below. Nor was a sea crossing in wartime at all like the luxurious days now gone. No lengthy menu, not even at the captain's table where Mary sat. The fare was spartan: butter only at breakfast, no desserts at all "save apple sauce or prunes," and no second helpings. Other economies were made on linen. A napkin, issued in the morning, was to be used all day. Bed sheets were unchanged during the voyage. The only touch of glamour was the presence on board of Sarah Bernhardt, whom Mary saw only as she was carried on board, for the aging actress, now with only one leg, remained in her berth all day.[43]

Unlike most of the official or semiofficial passengers, Mary was alone with time to worry over her assignment in France. Writing to Stan from the ship, she said that she intended to go first to Paris and locate "the various men I am to see, and map out a plan of some sort." Although she carried "a mass of cabalistic papers," she could make nothing much out of them except the fact that they were "vastly important." Finally, she reported: "The wireless last night tells of a mutiny in the German navy, and of a revolution in some of their cities. It looks as though it is all true. I surely hope so."[44]

They reached France on November 9; a pilot came on board to bring the liner up the Gironde River. Ashore, representatives of the French government waited to greet Rinehart and offer their services. Mary wanted help only in hotel reservations and they assured her of a room at the Ritz. She took the train to Paris and arrived at the Ritz to find that they had heard nothing of her and could do nothing for her. She found accommodations for one night only, November 10, in the nearby Hôtel Castiglione.

The next morning, November 11, Mary went to look for another hotel. With her incredible luck she was out on the Paris streets at eleven o'clock in the morning, suddenly seeing a captured German plane "rolling and looping" in the sky and hearing the signal guns. The armistice had come.[45]

That night she wrote home, dating the letter, "Monday, the day of the peace." "This is a great time to be here," she remarked with extraordinary understatement. "Paris is suddenly going crazy."

The city is on the streets, singing and waving flags. Every now and then, out of the riot below, an American voice rises, in song usually. But the gaiety seems tempered. There are no bands, as all of them are at the front, and there are too many women shrouded in black, for whom the victory has come too late. I have a great thankfulness in my heart, of course. At last it will be possible to think and plan ahead. Unless he becomes ill, our boy is saved to us. Two boys are saved to us. God has been very good to us.

An unfortunate encounter with French oysters made Mary a little queasy, and the letter was not continued until the next evening. A Red Cross official had procured a place for her on a balcony overlooking the Place de la Concorde, and from there Mary watched more of the Armistice Day celebration.

American boys dragging about captured German guns, captured Hun planes overhead, mad processions of poilus and girls dancing, and kissing every one they met. But the procession of the mutilés was too tragic, men with one leg stumping along and singing. It broke my heart. The Place and the Champs Elysée [sic] are filled with captured tanks, guns, observation balloons and aeroplanes. Even the fragments of a Zeppelin.[46]

It was thrilling but it was also lonely; Paris at armistice was no place to be alone. "Every one has his or her own group of friends, and I am terribly alone."[47] As the excitement abated, Mary had to think of what she would be doing; certainly her assignment would change now that the war was over. It looked as if she would go on tours for the Red Cross, accompanied by Elizabeth Hoyt—the daughter of the American banker, Colgate Hoyt, and later, as Lady Lindsay, the wife of the British ambassador to the United States.

Paris was, after the emotional outburst of the armistice, a sobering experience. Prices were high but there was little to be had. At her hotel, the Westminster on the Rue de la Paix, there was no sugar, only saccharine, and butter only at breakfast. No fresh milk was available, "only canned milk, diluted to an incredible degree," and bread was "served only with bread cards or tickets."[48] The women on the streets were dressed shabbily and there were practically no private cars.

Far worse sights lay ahead. On the thirteenth Mary started for Chaumont by train, to meet briefly with Pershing at his headquarters in an American Pullman car and to continue on for a tour of the battlefields. With an army chauffeur and a lieutenant she drove seven hundred miles, covering the Vosges, the Saint-Mihiel salient, and the Argonne Forest. It was only days since the last drive of the war had ended and Mary discovered the appalling litter of battle—shells, mines, rusted wire, and the more startling personal debris, cigarette butts, letters, a notebook discarded at an observation post with its last entry: "11 A.M.: Guns cease firing."[49]

"It is a dead country, the battlefield, no troops, no anything, the ground covered with pathetic and tragic signs of what has been going on." The dead had been buried, but otherwise no cleaning up had started, for Mary was the first to visit the Front since the armistice. Caution was needed everywhere because of unexploded shells and grenades. "The Argonne forest is particularly terrible, a mass of underbrush through which our men fought and died under dreadful conditions. Our losses are much greater than has been told. Ghastly indeed."[50]

From the Argonne they continued on to Verdun, having spent the night at Bar-le Duc, "in a dreadful place, dirty and jammed." For dinner they ate horsemeat. Much more comfortable were some of the abandoned German trenches, "with electric lights, outdoor arbors with flowers, hammocks."[51] These were dangerous to examine, however, for some had been left mined. During the entire trip there was little to eat, for some meals only a slice of bread.

Foremost in Mary's mind was to get in touch with Stan, Jr., stationed at La Valbonne, near Lyons. On arriving in France he had been sent briefly to Chaumont and afterward ordered to Montigny and officers' school. Since then he had been at La Valbonne, hoping to get closer to the fighting. Mary wired him on her arrival and he wrote back expressing his surprise and also his disappointment at having missed the real fighting. "What hurts me is the knowledge that if I were up with a real fighting unit instead of being away back here in S.O.S. [Service of Supply], I'd stand a better chance of seeing you. I should wear the service flag pin, not you."[52]

By the time Mary returned from the battlefield tour, it appeared that she could spend Christmas with her son. For the moment there were other assignments for her, principally a tour of Red Cross facilities near the Front. Mary received a special pass, good from November 30 to December 10, permitting her to enter Luxemburg. With that, her Red Cross card, and her passport marked "on official business for the War Department," Rinehart set off again for Chaumont and Pershing.

She and Elizabeth Hoyt planned to be gone for three days, but in fact they spent a week. Some time was taken with interminable automobile breakdowns. After the first occurred near Meaux, they turned back, had the car repaired, and started off again. Another breakdown and "after limping for two hours our fine limousine burned up entirely, leaving us on a desolate road, with our baggage beside us."[53] It was raining and very cold, and they waited a long time before a French convoy stopped for them and took them as far as Provins. There the two women were fortunate to share a single bed.

Early the next day another car arrived for them from Paris and they continued toward Chaumont—and dinner with Pershing—and from Chaumont to Alsace-Lorraine, Luxemburg, and eventually into Germany. The car held up for a day or two but then they began to have tire trouble. Driving through rain and fog, foraging for tires to replace those they lost, they eventually reached Trèves—and Germany. Accompanied by Gen. Joseph T. Dickman, they crossed the Rhine and, as she reported home, Mary spat into the river. "It seemed very odd to be there. Children gathered around the car in crowds and the eyes of the Germans were not very friendly. We were the first civilians in Treves."[54] There the women visited hospitalized allied soldiers who told them they had been well cared for. A few German nurses had, in fact, stayed behind to see to them. Mary was uneasy, not only in Germany but back in Alsatian Strasbourg and Metz, where small boys threw stones at them. Moreover, the hospitals there were untended, for the Germans had left and the French had not yet taken them over. Mary found them filthy, out of supplies, with convalescents struggling to prepare their own food.

It was in Strasbourg that Mary saw the first return of prisoners. Released by the Germans, they were walking home, in rags, without money or food. She heard first a shuffle of feet, and then she saw them, "often mere skeletons of men, unshaven, emaciated, listless." In the morning, with the help of Schuyler Parsons of the Red Cross, the women had some cocoa prepared and found some cigarettes. "Each man who came received a tin cup of cocoa and a few loose cigarettes that morning, and then they started off again, bound for God knows where."[55]

Back in Paris there were letters, cables, and official assignments to deal with, principally tours of French hospitals, including the twenty-two facilities in Paris. Among these was the American Red Cross Studio for Portrait Masks, where two artists made masks for the "unfortunate soldiers whose faces have been so shot away as to appear barely human."[56] Mary visited the ward for these soldiers whose faces had been destroyed and remembered that it took all her courage and that she was sick after she left.

Meanwhile, in Brest, there was an outbreak of influenza, and charges of "congestion, mud and terrible living conditions" at the American camp were threatening to lead to a senatorial investigation. Rinehart was sent to investigate and report. There, "in boots and slicker I hunted trouble, maladministration," checked the kitchens, and ate the food, which she found "good . . . hot, abundant, well seasoned." She met Marine General Smedley Butler, as well, and asked him what he needed to improve conditions. She radioed a coded report and Butler's list of necessary equipment to Baker, who later told her she had "helped to save a delicate situation." When she returned to Brest in January, she found conditions "incredibly" improved.[57]

Mary was kept busy and she was useful, but the longed-for trip to the war was not satisfying. It was a long way from 1915; there was greater devastation, greater deprivation, and finally the slow postwar letdown. Before she had been the extraordinary woman alone, the first correspondent at the Front—half official, half living by her wits. Now, the full officialdom of Washington behind her, Mary was trapped in her own established importance. Instead of the camaraderie of 1915, there was formal cooperation and personal isolation. Even so, had Mary been clear about what her responsibilities were after the war ended, had she had a sense of participating in an important way, she would not have been so eager to leave France. As it was, her assignments lost their urgency. She wanted only to see Stan, Jr., and to leave Europe with him on the earliest transport.

Waiting for her son, scheduled to take some men to Le Mans and then to stop in Paris, Mary tried to arrange for passage on January 15. "If it were not for Christmas with Stanley I'd try for a chance sooner." American civilians were leaving France and Mary did not blame them. "It is cold and gray and rainy here. Dark at four." And it was lonely; Mary had "made a few acquaintances but no friends" and found the time in Paris "unutterably long and dreary." Mary knew, however, that "feeling a little low," as she put it, was unjustified. In her memory were burned pictures of "the lines of white crosses, with the identification tags nailed to them, in rows on the battle fields, in the rain and mud." Worse yet were those forever unidentified, with only a helmet on a stick to mark the grave. "And I think of what Alan calls the luck of the Rineharts, and what I think is God's mercy."[58]

Mary and Stan, Jr., did spend Christmas together and, in the middle of January, sailed on the same transport from Brest, Stan with the troops and Mary in the assistant engineer's cabin. At home the doctor awaited their arrival in a small apartment in Washington and, in his letters to Alan, tried to cheer up both his son and himself. They had missed the war, he conceded, but added, "Both of us, like good soldiers, must accept things philosophically." Although the disruptions and dislocations of family life seemed more difficult to endure now that the war had ended, he was looking ahead. "It won't be very long now until both mother and Stan will be back, and then some time later, we shall have a permanent place of abode where we may hang our hats and consider ourselves at home."[59]

Home had been on Mary's mind as well. Should they reopen the Sewickley house? "In a way I'd like to," she wrote to Stan. "Some of my feeling has changed with the coming of peace. I want all of us together again—I always did, but I was afraid to count on it—and I want to get back to normal ways as soon as possible." Perhaps they might have "a few months together in the old place before Stanley's marriage. I don't know. I only know that I want my own all around me once more." But Mary was to find that the old days were over for the Rinehart family. The boys were grown; Stan was about to be married and the others were away at school. The doctor would not find it comfortable to return to his old medical practice in Pittsburgh. And Mary herself discovered that the war years had created an unbridgeable chasm in her life. "For almost five years I had been obsessed by the war; I knew nothing else. It was impossible to think back to the life before it, across that gulf."[60] The Sewickley house would be reopened, but "normal ways" would never quite be established again.

8

The Bat

1919–1921

WHILE MARY HAD BEEN WAITING in Paris to arrange transport home, she received a cable from George Doran, authorized to make her an extraordinary offer. After thirty years Edward Bok was resigning as editor of *The Ladies' Home Journal* and Cyrus Curtis wanted Mary Roberts Rinehart for the job. He was willing to meet almost any terms, as Doran's cable promised: "YOUR DUTIES WOULD BE EXECUTIVE ENTIRELY AND NOT DISTURB YOUR REGULAR WRITING PLANS OR INCOME." So eager was Curtis to have Rinehart accept the position that, in deference to her feelings, he offered to change the name of the magazine to the *Home Journal.* Moreover, he offered her the astounding salary of $50,000 a year. Doran had talked it over with the doctor, who sent his own cable advising Mary to consider the offer favorably but not to accept it finally until her return. "MY PLANS UNCERTAIN BUT NEED NOT INFLUENCE DECISION . . . COME HOME DIRECT SOON AS WORK FINISHED XMAS LOVE." A second cable from Doran assured Mary that the Curtis Publishing Company would give her sixty days to make up her mind.[1]

Almost immediately after Mary landed in New York, she went to see Lorimer in Atlantic City. Apparently he advised her to accept the offer, for on February 6, 1919, the doctor wrote to Alan telling him that they had plans to rent or sell the Sewickley house. But then Mary had second thoughts. She did not want to give up the family home and she talked to Lorimer about the possibility of commuting. That seemed reasonable to him, and Mary began to lean even more strongly toward accepting the job. She went to Philadelphia, where she was assured again that the editorial post would leave adequate time for her own writing and where she was given a seductive glimpse into the editor's office. "I looked about Mr. Bok's imposing suite, and womanlike I could see myself there, dictating policies, influencing public opinion."[2]

But in the end Mary did not succumb. On February 12 the doctor wrote again to Alan—Mary was back in Washington with him, "already beginning to think about going home and opening up the house," for the *Journal* proposition was off.

In fact, I think she is rather relieved, but, of course, it was a source of a great deal of worry to her while she was deciding, and a total reversal of all her plans has left her sort of empty. I think it is all for the best though. I gave her every encouragement to do the work and she decided the matter entirely herself after looking over the situation.[3]

Stan's observation that the reversal of all her plans had left Mary "sort of empty" was accurate. The emotional letdown from wartime activity to peacetime routine was acute and distressing, as was the realization that the customary rhythms of their family life were as much a thing of the past as the innocent world of prewar America. Mary had a great deal to come to terms with emotionally. It was the right time for taking stock, but she did not do so. Instead, she plunged into a maelstrom of activity. Back in Sewickley, awaiting the doctor's demobilization, she began another long novel.

Like *Dangerous Days*, the new novel, called *A Poor Wise Man*, was an ambitious project, attempting to mix romantic fiction with political analysis and social criticism. Both depend for plot on the dangers of subversives, in *Dangerous Days* immigrant German socialists, in *A Poor Wise Man* native-born anarchists. In neither case was it Rinehart's purpose to create spurious adventure. Like many Americans during that period, she feared subversion, anarchism, and Bolshevism, and she addressed these fears in both works.

Rinehart based the anarchist plot in *A Poor Wise Man* on information she received from a curious encounter in the spring of 1918. After her return from Mexico, she met a man, by appointment, in a "small shabby restaurant" in Los Angeles. He had information for her about "the Seattle strike, and out of it the abortive attempts of I.W.W. wobblies to take over the city."[4] That story seemed to Mary to confirm America's worst fears, for the Wobblies had become the nation's bête noire. Almost alone among labor organizations, the Industrial Workers of the World (the IWW) adhered to the socialist disavowal of international warfare, understood as benefiting only the masters of capital and as exposing to hardship and death the brotherhood of workers. Socialist expectations of avoiding war had collapsed all over Europe in the summer of 1914, and in 1917 American labor unions also had pledged the support of the working man to the war effort. Not so the Wobblies. As a result generalized fears of German sabotage, followed shortly after the 1917 Russian Revolution by equally dire expectations of Bolshevik subversion, found a particular object of terror in the IWW.

By August and September 1917 the Northwest had been riddled with anxiety. Some believed the Wobblies would, in the interest of the German military, attempt to take over Seattle. To Rinehart the situation in the state of Washington seemed only one more piece of evidence for the widespread network of sabotage she had discovered signs of elsewhere. She saw the Seattle strike as the first link in an operational chain that would lead to the takeover of a series of American cities by cutting off communications, light, water, and the food supply. "The Boston police strike was," it had been claimed, "a second and similar experiment."⁵

The man in the Los Angeles restaurant told Rinehart that he was a member of the IWW and privy to its plans "to enter the city [of Seattle], take over the City Hall, substitute their own constabulary for any police who became recalcitrant, and cut off the power plants. . . . They would also control the water and light plants, and they would cut the railroads."⁶ A few hours before the signal for the strike to begin, however, the man got cold feet, thinking of his own wife and children safe in Tacoma and then of other wives and children not so fortunate. With little time to spare, he telephoned city hall and warned officials of the plan. Thus, when the insurrection began, the armed citizens were ready for it and the city of Seattle was saved.

Taking this story at face value, Rinehart based *A Poor Wise Man* on it, but except for an occasional dyed-in-the-wool villain, her subversives are more victimized than vicious. Even in the bitter prejudice of the first postwar years, Mary had not altogether forgotten what she had learned of the lives of the poor in her hospital work in Pittsburgh and on the streets of Vienna. They had seemed to her then the victims of something "rotten," and she did not abandon that point of view. At the same time she believed, as most nineteenth-century Americans did, that the very strong could rise above ignorance and poverty. The others needed help, and Rinehart was willing to admit that help had not always been forthcoming, that there were culpable weaknesses in the American system. For instance, in writing of the deluded anarchist immigrant in *Dangerous Days,* she observes that he had "the making of a good American," but that after his arrival in the United States "nothing was done to stimulate in him a sentiment for his adopted land."⁷

Behind the plots of subversion and sabotage in *Dangerous Days* and *A Poor Wise Man,* Rinehart examines the social system, trying to discover what had gone wrong. In both she gives considerable attention to wealthy characters from powerful families, and among these men and women are those whose selfishness and vanity cause just as much havoc as do the subversives. It is difficult to locate a group of Americans with whom the problems of social inequity can be resolved. In *A Poor Wise Man,* Rinehart gives us the "plain people," neither rich nor poor, who maintain American values, and she makes her hero, Willy Cameron, their representative. But in fact, with the exception of Willy, the plain people are neither interesting nor particularly high-minded, and at the end of the novel Willy is rewarded by the chance to move out of the middle class, marrying the heiress to the great Cardew fortune.

In attempting to come to some thematic resolution, Rinehart could do no better than a softened Social Darwinism. Willy, the man whose foresight and planning saves the city (in her story Pittsburgh, not Seattle), has risen by dint of his own strength of character, and in his success lies the moral: All societies divide themselves into higher and lower classes, but as long as a society provides a chance for the talented and brave to climb, it is a healthy society. Conversely, "to destroy the chance of gain was to put a premium on inertia; to kill ambition."[8]

Besides working with large social questions, Rinehart used *Dangerous Days* and *A Poor Wise Man* to try out new ways of writing, and thinking, about love and sexuality. In *The Amazing Interlude* she had gone so far as to have Sara Lee break her engagement in order to return to Belgium and Henri. (Actually, Rinehart recalled that she did not plan to have Sara Lee return to Henri and she credited George Doran with the suggestion that she change the ending of the novel.) In *Dangerous Days* she went further, dealing for the first time with unsuccessful marriage and adulterous—though innocent—love.

Dangerous Days resounds with overtones of sexuality. The smart young set is flatly promiscuous. Nor is the older married group marked by connubial fidelity. The husband of Audrey Valentine has an affair with a chorus girl and, when his wife discovers this, flees into the French Ambulance Corps. Clayton Spencer, the hero of the novel, is trapped in a sexless marriage. His parasitic wife Natalie becomes involved in her own particularly nasty flirtation with the architect-decorator Rodney Page. At the center of all this sexual groping, Audrey and Clayton fall in love. Rinehart manages to elevate them above their moral environment by denying them any pleasure in that love beyond the knowledge of their mutual attachment and the sacrifice they are prepared to make of it. The sacrifice is not easy, though, for "the passions of the forties, when they come, are to those of the early years as the deep sea to a shallow lake, less easily roused, infinitely more terrible."[9] The adulterous, if unconsummated, passion of Clayton and Audrey is the emotional heart of the novel. Rinehart unites them, but only after Audrey's husband is killed in France and Clayton's wife (for entirely other reasons) divorces him. That ending, at once a happy and a moral one, was suitable for the magazine audience of the day. But the mechanics of the ending are much less important in themselves than Rinehart's willingness to explore the problem of dead marriages and mature passions.

Dangerous Days and *A Poor Wise Man* were Mary Roberts Rinehart's most ambitious novels to date. They commanded large prices for serialization, they sold well as books for Doran, and they met with what was becoming a typically mixed critical reception.[10] Like all Rinehart's fiction they are written well. And like almost all her serious fiction they are considerably bolder in the issues they raise than in the resolutions they reach.

Mary's own marriage had reached a difficult point by 1919. Until the disruptions of the war years, Stan had been a successful professional and an important medical man in Pittsburgh. After the war, in the months between the armistice and his demobilization in April 1919, he began to have serious doubts about returning to private practice. Just a few days before he was discharged from the Medical Reserve, Stan wrote to Mary telling her he was already looking for a government job, perhaps with the Public Health Service. Nothing came of that, however, and on the day of their twenty-third wedding anniversary the Rineharts returned to Sewickley and the doctor resumed practice. With whatever tensions accompanied readjustment and with whatever compromises were made on either side, Stan and Mary picked up at least a semblance of their old life.

For Stan, however, the situation was not satisfactory. Medical practice had soured, as he explained in a letter to an army friend, recalling the days they spent together at Camp Sherman and "all the high purposes that possessed us, the momentous things that were happening, and the part we hoped to play in them." The return to civilian life seemed to signal the end of those aspirations but not of the emotional energy behind them. Civilian life was flat and dull: "Like a great many other people, I have never gotten back in spirit to private practice since the war."[11] During this time, perhaps in search of a new interest or in an effort to unite his life and Mary's more closely, Stan took over his wife's business affairs. Certainly she needed the help, for the business side of her writing had grown vastly complicated and her record-keeping was spotty and untidy.

Recalling this decision in her autobiography, Rinehart took the time to comment on the problems of a man married to a successful woman. There can be no question, she wrote, that "the husband of any woman with a successful career finds himself in an anomalous position." Mary had always assumed that she could cope with this if she simply did the work of two women —the domestic and the professional. But no matter how smoothly the house ran and how much time she gave to her husband, "a psychic cruelty" could not be prevented. The years right after the war were more trying than any time before—an "emergency" in Rinehart's words.[12]

Ironically, the tempo of Mary's professional life increased in these years —though one wonders how. A significant new commitment came with an offer from Samuel Goldwyn in 1919. He was starting a project called Eminent Authors, contracting with a small number of well-known writers to come to Hollywood "to produce their own stories on the screen." Rinehart signed a contract with Goldwyn in June and a month later was on her way to the coast to work on the film version of *Dangerous Days.* Her high and innocent expectations about Hollywood were blasted even before she arrived there. On the train she received a wire: "Do you object if baby blimp meets you at station? Safer than taxicab."[13] From there it was all downhill. For one thing, it quickly became apparent that most motion picture people did not know, nor want to learn, how to use the Eminent Authors. Moreover, there were from the very start disquieting indications that the buying and selling of literary properties for the movies did not work along the more conventional lines Mary was used to.

By the time that Mary, along with Alan and Ted, was settled at the Beverly Hills Hotel, she found herself "somewhat disturbed by a growing conviction that Griffen my agent, who sold D.D. [*Dangerous Days*] to Lasky for twenty thousand, bought it back cheap himself."[14] It is difficult to reconstruct the situation, but apparently Griffen sold *Dangerous Days* to an agent for Lasky-Famous Players, who then, according to Griffen, "repudiated" the sale. Furthermore, Griffen asserted that he had to buy the property back for $20,000, and Mary hoped that Goldwyn would guarantee that money to Griffen. The difficulties seemed eventually to be ironed out, but then, in January 1920, with *Dangerous Days* scheduled for release, Goldwyn and Rinehart discovered that Lasky-Famous Players were about to release their own film called *Dangerous Hours.*

Mary spent her first week in Hollywood waiting for Goldwyn to return from Santa Barbara to make the final decision to film *Dangerous Days.* When Mary finally started work, she discovered that she had no function whatsoever. Outside of the studio executives, the movie people wanted nothing more from the Eminent Authors than to arrange a story sequence. As Rinehart summed it up, "All they asked of me was to go home and draw my guarantee of fifteen thousand dollars a year and a small percentage of profits which never developed."[15]

In general, the studio—where Mary's "office" consisted of a chair in the cafeteria—was "a worrying place." "The scenario people resent an author being on the job. But they are a poor lot, and if a thing is left to them it is going to go bad," Mary fretted, as time passed with little but the "big splurge" about her presence there. Callers and flowers "pestered" her and she found Hollywood "dreary beyond words." She had come to do a job, but there was no one preparing material for her to work with. In short, "when I look at D.D. and try to think of pictures I just go bugs again."[16]

While the production of *Dangerous Days* dragged, publicity moved apace. Mary had turned down the blimp ride, so the studio came up with a second idea—this time an airplane. Mary agreed to go up in a Curtis biplane and was enjoying the ride until the pilot began rolling and spinning in a series of stunts. She was frightened at first, but, as always, game. She told Stan the stunts were "horrible," but pointed out that, since a photographer had gone up in a second plane, she had "some good stunt pictures." That was on Saturday and, stunts notwithstanding, Mary was not at all ready to give up flying. She went up again the same day and again on Sunday. Then on Monday she flew 150 miles to Coronado Beach. "I thought it quite simple, but it seems no woman has even done it here. Indeed, I think no passenger not a flyer has done it." Alan and Ted were sent ahead by car, not without grumbling, while Mary took her two-hour flight over the San Luis Capistrano Mountains. She ate her lunch "at six thousand feet" and altogether enjoyed herself hugely except that the next day she was "still rather deaf."[17]

Stan could not have been delighted with the news that Mary was flying around California. She dutifully promised him not to fly again without his permission and, in a bizarre blend of the cautious mother and the daredevil ace, informed him that the recent deaths of two women "in a different type of plain [sic] from a different field" made her "reluctant" to allow the boys to fly. "I'll try to keep them so busy that they won't mind."[18]

When Mary left Hollywood, *Dangerous Days* was under way, and she and Stan returned in January for some final work including the writing of titles. To Mary's disgust the studio "decided that the underlying motive of sabotage in a munitions plant during the war might offend labor." On the final day of her second stay in Hollywood, Mary had to rewrite the titles eliminating this part of the story and, to all intents, eliminating as well any continuity that remained in the "enfeebled" film.[19]

Rinehart had a three-year contract with Eminent Authors and after her experience with *Dangerous Days* came up with a plan to beat the game. She asked that a scenario writer be sent to Pittsburgh to work with her. The studio agreed and sent Frank and Agnes Dazey to Sewickley for several months early in 1920. In the morning Mary met with them to discuss each day's work; then the two young movie writers developed the scenario. The plan seemed to be working well, but when the Dazeys returned to Hollywood, the scenario department discarded the script altogether and began a new one.

Rinehart made a small number of films with Goldwyn. Besides *Dangerous Days*, Goldwyn released *It's a Great Life*, adapted from "The Empire Builders," and a year later *The Glorious Fool*, from two of her hospital stories, "In the Pavilion" and "Twenty-Two." Rinehart's final comment on her early experiences in Hollywood was left to Tish in "The Baby Blimp." Tish wants to go to Hollywood to study the movies, believing "that the over-

Rinehart as "air ace": part of the promotion engineered in Hollywood for Samuel Goldwyn's Eminent Authors project.

emphasis on love in the pictures was weakening the moral fiber of the nation." Anyway, adds Lizzie, Tish has been bored since the war. Stein, a producer, visits the famous Miss Carberry and offers to buy her story and to star her in the picture—she can do her own stunts—at $1,000 a week. Tish agrees on the condition that "this is purely a picture of adventure and is to teach a real moral lesson." "Absolutely," asserts Stein. "Virtue is always triumphant on the screen. It is our greatest commercial asset."[20]

Mary had returned from Hollywood late in the summer of 1919 tired and ill—and with the prospect of a hectic autumn. A mystery play, scheduled to go into rehearsal in the spring of 1920, demanded considerable time and energy. Rinehart had been working on *The Bat,* as the play was finally called, since the spring of 1917. She had asked Edgar Selwyn, the producer, what he thought of the idea of a mystery play in which "the audience was kept completely mystified . . . until practically the drop of the curtain." Selwyn's response turned out to be conservative: "It would be worth a million dollars."[21] Rinehart's first intention had been to dramatize *The Circular Staircase,* but she soon discovered that her popular novel needed some significant changes in order to succeed in the theater. Most important was the introduction of the criminal, called "The Bat," whose identity would not be revealed until the final moments of the play. Despite the changes Rinehart made, *The Bat,* still bore strong resemblances to *The Circular Staircase* and the similarities between the two led eventually to some unpleasant litigation.

America's entry into the war interrupted serious concentration on the play, but Mary worked on it off and on and early in 1918, while she was living at the Langdon, "in a white heat I rewrote the first and second acts."[22] When Mary received word from Baker sending her overseas, she asked Avery Hopwood to write the third act. But Hop did not complete the play, and in the spring of 1919 he had come to Sewickley to work on the last act with Mary. Over the next few months the two continued their collaboration, sometimes in Sewickley and sometimes in New York. Now, in February 1920, they were again in Sewickley, still working out problems in the last act. Timing was crucial to the effect of the final discovery of the criminal and Mary and Hop continued to tinker with the conclusion.

It was impossible to give undivided attention to the play, however. Rinehart recalled that "the distractions were almost overwhelming."[23] There was a vast mail, other writing obligations, and the problems with Goldwyn and *Dangerous Days.* At the same time Mary had a play running on Broadway, for in 1919 the early Rinehart-Hopwood collaboration, *Seven Days,* opened in a musical version called *Tumble In.* It had a respectable run of 128 performances (although nothing like the 397 enjoyed by *Seven Days*), despite

A softly glamorous Rinehart in a Hollywood photograph.

a musical score that boasted such titles as "I'm Just a Little Chicken Made for Old Broadway" by Harbach and Friml.

There was also some family excitement. Stan, Jr., had been in New York since March 1919, working for George Doran, first in the advertising department and soon after as the business manager of *The Bookman Magazine*, published by Doran. He had been married that spring and, as he reported to his father late in August, he and Dorrie (Mary Doran Rinehart) were expecting a baby in April. And, in Rinehart's words, "there were other complications"; Alan flunked out of Harvard and went west for a while to be a cowboy.[24]

Work, sporadic and often unsatisfactory, continued on *The Bat*. Rehearsals were now scheduled for the middle of May, and in March, with the final act still not quite right, Mary went to New York to work with Hop. Frustrations increased as effective changes in the last act necessitated adjustments in the earlier parts of the play. By the end of the month they were almost done with Act 3 but found that Act 2 was giving them real trouble: "We were five days on it, but it is in satisfactory shape now." The draft seemed almost completed except that some dialogue had to be added and adjusted for humor, as Mary wrote to Stan on April 2: "The revision of the play for humor goes slowly. It began this morning, and I only hope I can hold out to the end."[25]

Mary and Hop spent some ten days revising for humor. Just when they had accomplished that task to their satisfaction, Mary received a phone call from Stan, Jr., telling her that Dorrie was in labor. Mary Roberts Rinehart II (called "Bab") was born on April 12, 1920. On the fourteenth, producers Wagenhals and Kemper were to hear the play read, but the new grandmother had more compelling duties and would not be present. Nor did Mary attend rehearsals of *The Bat*. Hop agreed that it was not necessary but did ask that she plan to be in Washington for the pre–New York opening on June 14. Hop kept Mary informed about rehearsals of *The Bat*—and about rehearsals of another Rinehart-Hopwood collaboration. W&K had asked them to adapt the classic Spanish play *María del Carmen*, and *Spanish Love*, as their adaptation was called, was scheduled to open in New York just six days before *The Bat*.

Mary had a great deal invested in *The Bat*. She had spent considerable time and energy on the play, hoping to produce another success like *Seven Days*. She had also put money into the new play, having learned from *Seven Days* that even the most generous royalties did not earn the really big money from hit plays. Together Mary and Stan invested $5,000 toward the $20,000 cost of the original production, so that each of them owned 12½ percent of *The Bat*; Wagenhals, Kemper, and Hopwood each owned 25 percent. The contract for *The Bat* split the net profits among the shareholders and divided movie, stock, and other rights the same way. W&K each received $200 a week for the first company. Should subsequent companies be formed to take the play on the road, they would receive another $200 a week if the weekly gross ran over $5,000; otherwise, their salary on each road company would be $100 a week. Royalties, figured on the gross profit, were fixed for the first company and for any subsequent companies. Based on weekly income, the authors received 5 percent of the first $4,000, 7.5 percent of the next $2,000, and 10 percent of anything over $6,000.[26] Since there were eventually six road companies simultaneously playing *The Bat*, it is clear that everyone involved earned a lot of money.

Mary and Stan went to Washington for the pre-Broadway production of *The Bat* and on for the next week's run in Atlantic City. After that the family went west, and for whatever combination of reasons, Mary did not attend the New York opening of either play. Perhaps it was her desire to stay out of the public eye. Perhaps it was nerves, or even some kind of private way of ensuring luck.

When the two Rinehart-Hopwood plays opened, Mary, Stan, and their two younger sons were driving through the Arizona desert, on a motor trip with Howard Eaton. Wires from W&K first reached her in New Mexico with mixed reports about *Spanish Love*. Wagenhals wired that he was "amazed at critics," who were apparently less enthusiastic than the audience: "EVERYONE SAVE CRITICS SAY BIGGEST THING COUNTRY HAS SEEN IN YEARS." The play created some excitement by introducing what was then a novelty in the American theater: certain characters entered from the audience. The critics did not approve, but Lee Schubert, according to Wagenhals, said "it was the biggest attraction he has ever seen in New York—that it was something like a three ring circus."[27] Although greatly overshadowed by the success of *The Bat*, *Spanish Love* did very well, running for 307 performances.

The Bat opened August 23 at the Morosco, and Hop wired on the twenty-fourth: "CONGRATULATIONS PLAY BIG HIT   NEW YORK EVENING TELEGRAM SAYS THE BAT IS BEST MYSTERY PLAY EVER SEEN IN NEW YORK." W&K sent word that about 1,100 attended the opening: "AUDIENCE WILDLY ENTHUSIASTIC." Also, "PAPERS IMMENSE GIVING AUTHORS GREAT PRAISE"; for example: "THE BAT BIG HIT   A BABE RUTH HOME RUN."[28]

More wires followed Mary across the desert; the initial success of *The Bat* continued, increased. Mary returned home in the middle of September and planned a New York trip immediately. She wrote to her producers, "I have been simply wildly thrilled by the news from the plays [and hope] you can find seats somewhere for us!"[29] The popularity of *The Bat* grew and grew, and, to add to Mary's sweep of the theatrical field, two other plays based on her stories, but dramatized by others, also played in New York that fall. One was *Tish* with May Robson; the other *Bab*, starring the young actress Helen Hayes.

Eventually *The Bat* ran for an extraordinary 878 performances in New York. In December 1920 a second company was formed to take the play to Chicago. By September of 1921, in addition to the New York production, six companies were playing *The Bat* in large cities and small towns all over the country. When the play reached Americus, Georgia, Wagenhals penciled a note to Mary: "Did you ever hear of this town? One performance." The receipts were $1,343.[30]

The receipts everywhere were astonishing. At the end of 1921, Rinehart received an accounting of royalties on each of the seven *Bat* companies. Her royalties were, of course, only half; Hop received a like amount.

New York Company	$25,632.59
Chicago Company	26,323.87
City Company	10,729.44
Coast Company	8,123.39
Eastern Company	3,552.33
Western Company	4,012.16
Philadelphia Company	7,123.00

Rinehart's royalties for 1921, *The Bat's* most profitable year, came to $85,496.78. The single season of 1920 brought over $16,000; 1922, just under $75,000; 1923, the final year, almost $25,000. Rinehart's total royalties —excluding the London production, stock performances, revivals, and movie rights—came to $200,902.35.[31]

On top of royalties, of course, was the Rineharts' share in the profits of the play. By 1923 Mary and Stan had each received $137,663.09. With royalties, that brought the Rineharts' income from *The Bat* to nearly half a million dollars. The total income, however, with other rights and residuals, can only be estimated. In a *Life* magazine "Close-up" of Rinehart in 1946, Geoffrey T. Hellman wrote that the play was seen by over ten million people and grossed more than nine million dollars.[32]

The enormous success of *The Bat* brought legal entanglements. Selig had purchased movie rights to *The Circular Staircase*, probably in 1915, for a very small amount of money. In the spring of 1920, Rinehart bought the rights back for $7,000, and "that seemed to clear everything entirely." (She had also paid Bobbs-Merrill $15,000 for its residual rights.) But now Selig released his 1915 *Circular Staircase* under the name of *The Bat*. Rinehart insisted that the two works were distinct and wanted to enjoin Selig from using the new title. Meanwhile, reviews and advertising of Rinehart's novels compounded the difficulties by advertising the old mystery novel as the source of the new play. Mary appealed to Doran for "an expert motion picture lawyer, one familiar with all the tricks Selig will try to pull."[33] Eventually, *The Bat* itself was fictionalized (anonymously, by young Stephen Vincent Benét) and published by Doran in 1926, no doubt partly to support Rinehart's claim that the play was unrelated to *The Circular Staircase*. The same year Feature Productions bought the rights for a silent-movie version of *The Bat*, and in 1930 a talking picture called *The Bat Whispers* was produced by the Art Cinema Corporation, which paid about $50,000 for the rights.

A smash hit on Broadway added lustre to Rinehart's reputation as novelist and war correspondent, and she received ever more flattering accolades and invitations. Public appearances certainly had to exacerbate the pressures at home, but some were too tempting to decline. An attractive opportunity came in October 1920 for Mary to join a delegation of women visiting Warren G. Harding in Marion, Ohio. Harding, the Republican candidate for president, had neglected to make "concessions to the woman vote."[34] Now, with a small group of other notable women, including Alice Roosevelt Longworth, Rinehart went to hear Harding's suggestion for a new Department of Public Welfare.

At about the same time Mary accepted an invitation to speak at a Bryn Mawr College fund-raising function about women and the new opportunities open to them. *Post*-editor Adelaide Neall, from that time on one of Mary's closest professional friends, was a Bryn Mawr alumna, and she had asked Mary to come to Philadelphia to give this talk. Some kind of mix-up over dates occurred and Mary was unable to appear in person; instead, she sent the women her speech called "The College Woman and Life." The essay tempers excitement over women's new responsibilities as citizens and wage earners with conservative respect for traditional roles, assuring the women that "marriage and home-making are professions." But overall Rinehart preached careers and professions and delivered the heady promise that out of "our women's colleges," described as "national assets," would come future leaders of America, including someday even cabinet members.[35]

Perhaps the most flattering invitation came from Cyrus Curtis, who wrote asking Mary to be toastmistress at the New England Day Dinner in Philadelphia in December 1920. The day the letter came, Stan—who had already taken over a good deal of Mary's business correspondence—wrote to Adelaide Neall to tell her that Mary was tired and not at all able to take on new responsibilities. He planned to write to Curtis that day "in as diplomatic a style as possible . . . declining politely but nevertheless firmly and finally."[36] Be that as it may, two weeks later Curtis wrote again, expressing his delight in Mary's acceptance.

The New England Day Dinner was more than Mary could pass up. Only three years before had women first been allowed to dine with the men at the New England Day festivities and Mary would be the first woman speaker they had ever had. The other speakers would be Gen. Leonard Wood and Congressman J. Hampton Moore. Moreover, the dinner was a major social event in Philadelphia. Mary developed some stage fright in advance, but Curtis was encouraging: "But, my dear woman, don't be afraid of this little bunch of Yankees, sitting down once a year in a sociable way to brag of the Mayflower, and perhaps fib a bit about their descent." Mary went, but Stan did not accompany her. She gave a charming speech and Curtis wrote immediately afterwards, "You made the hit of the evening."[37]

With so much time devoted to *The Bat* and *Spanish Love* and to the two long novels she had recently published, Rinehart had done virtually no writing for the *Post*. Lorimer wrote occasionally with requests for stories and promises of bigger fees: "I see that the Standard Oil has just granted a ten percent increase to the help. We could do the same, if we had a Bab story in the shop to operate on." His pleas were seconded by those of Adelaide Neall, looking for a Tish story; she wrote, "Our good old pal, Tish [might] take a little plunge into politics."[38]

The *Post* would not, in fact, receive any more Rinehart fiction until the fall of 1921. Lorimer had written again: "I suppose it's very hard to get down to anything so trivial as fiction with three or four plays running and pulling down big money for you." Ten days later he had a story and he sent a letter expressing his pleasure, as well as some uneasiness. "We have had no dealings with you for so long and you have become such a high priced soubrette, that I do not know what you think you ought to get for a story of this kind. Tell me the worst." Mary answered: "I hope you will not drop dead when I tell you that I am getting four thousand dollars for a story of this length. However, I much prefer not to set any price where you are concerned, and to do, as I have always done, give you the best and trust you to give me the best price you feel I deserve."[39] Lorimer paid Mary $4,000 for "A Midsummer's Knight's Dream," published in the *Post* in December.

More and more frequently Mary complained of feeling exhausted and ill, but by early 1921 she was again committed to a full schedule of writing. She told W&K in February that she had just finished a new movie and was revising a new novel. Moreover, she had, surprisingly enough, committed herself to *The Ladies' Home Journal* for a monthly editorial. Sometime in 1920 Mary had sent the *Post* an article called "A New Citizen in the White

House." Lorimer wrote back: "Your article is fine—so fine that we are going to use it to lead the next number of the Ladies' Home Journal. Now back up," he urged, anticipating Mary's annoyance, "and be a good fellow." The Curtis Company was hard at work to change the image of the *Journal*; he explained: "We are asking all the good fellows and fellorines to come along with us in the good work. This, however, is the last one that I will put over on you." Adelaide wrote two days later to say that they were all "trying to make a new woman" out of the old *Journal* and needed Mary's help.[40] In the end Mary agreed to have her article appear in the *Journal* and promised as well to provide the monthly editorial.

The new novel Rinehart was revising early in 1921 was called *The Breaking Point*. It earned her the high prices she had warned Lorimer of: *McClure's* paid $30,000 for serialization; Lasky-Famous Players, $20,000 for film rights. The novel is a compendium of favorite Rinehart subjects: a murder mystery, theatrical people and settings, some western scenes, and a doctor-hero; moreover, *The Breaking Point* returns to the theme of amnesia. The hero, who has lost his memory and is living under a contrived identity, undertakes a kind of psychoanalytic journey into the West and his past to recover the story of his life. It is significant that Rinehart turned again at this time to the subject of her first story, "His Other Self." Without question the pace of her professional life had become frantic and the unresolved tensions in her personal life were building up enormous pressures. Her renewed fascination with amnesia and false identity seems a means of escape—into forgetfulness, into a kind of suicide without death.

Certainly Mary was ill, confused, often exhausted—in her words, "in a condition close to a breakdown." But she could not slow down: "Years of necessary activity had trained me to work, and without work of some sort I was lost." The physical symptoms she had long suffered as a result of emotional distress were intensified by a more serious illness. During the winter of 1920–1921 she was often in great pain. "Sometimes I found myself on the floor, holding to a piece of furniture until the agony passed; then there would be a hypodermic of morphia." With the drug, however, sleep did not come. "My mind would race at lightning speed. I would project books of huge conception, brilliant plays. I became a sort of super-woman, lying in that big four-poster bed with its tester and valances, planning heroic adventures, explorations."[41]

Emotional and physical breakdown came together, in June 1921, significantly enough on the day she and Goldwyn saw the screening of *Dangerous Days*, a picture Mary found bitterly disappointing. Leaving the theater she collapsed on the street and was taken by ambulance to the hospital. There she learned that she must undergo surgery to repair her gall bladder, much more dangerous than any of her previous surgery, most of which had been gynecological. For the first time Mary was afraid that she would die, but "I did not greatly care, save that I was leaving my family."[42]

Recovery was slow and, a month after the operation, Mary went to Eaton's Ranch to recuperate and to think about her life. "I had been too busy, too engrossed. I had missed much of the happiness I might have found, and in its place I had put work, hard grinding work." Awaiting her forty-fifth birthday, Mary vowed to change the pace of her life. No more monthly pieces for the *Journal*. No more work in Hollywood. No more "semi-hysterical rushing about the country, with its equally hysterical dashes back to the family." She recognized that she "was still the head-strong and self-willed woman who out of some intense curiosity of mind must do, see, adventure."[43] Now she felt sorry for her family—certainly for Stan—who lived with her ambition, her curiosity, and her furious energy.

Mary made a decision to cut down on her work in order to achieve a more rational balance between her professional and her personal lives, and she always believed that she stuck to that decision. In a way she did; at least she found a better rhythm between work and rest in the years to follow. But ambition, curiosity, and energy continued to dominate. No sooner had Mary recovered her strength than she agreed to go to Washington in November 1921 to cover the Disarmament Conference for a newspaper syndicate.

The conference was a repetition of Mary's experiences at the nominating conventions in 1916. Again she was excluded from the camaraderie of the press corps, and again she moved in her own world of famous and influential men. She complained to Stan of the difficulties of her position: "The men are jealous of a woman and become very close-mouthed all at once," even old *Post* colleague, Sam Blythe. The conference delegations had "had meetings for the men and . . . explained their position," but Mary was excluded from those meetings. "The men have a club, and know what is going on, I have no contacts whatever. They have all the dope in advance and I can only guess." "No contacts whatever" was something of an exaggeration, for she had occasion to meet with General Glenn and Colonel Forbes, to attend a dinner party with the Alex Mellons, and to spend an evening with General Foch. Still, Mary hated being treated as a "trained seal," the journalists' name for a celebrity poaching on their preserve, and claimed, "I have written out of observation and my own head entirely."[44]

Mary remained in Washington for three weeks, sending in some fine dispatches, particularly one on the burial of the Unknown Soldier on the anniversary of the armistice. But during the conference Mary found time for some personal business as well. Through Colonel Forbes of the new Veterans' Bureau, Mary was arranging for the possibility of a Washington job for Stan, who was interested but cautious about getting his hopes up: "There's no use discussing the general proposition yet. Let's hear it first. It listens pretty good, though, if there is any prospect of its lasting more than a year or two. But it means breaking up the home here, which must be seriously considered."[45] Stan badly needed some new professional interest, and an offer to join the Veterans' Bureau as a tuberculosis consultant looked very good to him at the end of 1921.

The Rineharts gathered for their last Christmas in Sewickley, just days after Stan accepted the Washington offer. Then they closed the house, planning to be away for a year. In fact, they were never to return. "So we said goodbye to the white house, there on its hill over the river; to the steps and the cinder path along the railroad which we had traveled to our work, to our vacations, to see the boys to school, to see our young soldier off to camp."[46]

Necessary items were packed, a good deal was put into storage, and the family set off in two cars for the capital. Stan and Mary went ahead in the larger car, Alan following with a friend and the family liquor supply. Some of that they sampled on the way, chilling their glasses with snow from the side of the road. When Alan arrived at the Wardman Park Hotel, where the family had taken an apartment, he was shown—unshaven and "boozy"—into his mother's suite and there introduced to President Warren G. Harding.[47]

9

The Public and the Critics

1922–1927

MARY ROBERTS RINEHART'S WORK with the federal government from 1914 to 1918, with men like Newton Baker, Josephus Daniels, and Woodrow Wilson, in no way prepared her to understand the sordid cronyism of the Harding administration. Through a combination of wifely concern, egotism, and political naïveté, Mary brought Stan—a man of almost unbending rectitude—into the Veterans' Bureau and the sphere of Charles R. Forbes, who, in the words of Frederick Lewis Allen, was "a buccaneer of fortune (and one-time deserter from the army)." The cynical mishandling of the Veterans' Bureau, although greatly overshadowed by other malfeasances connected with the Teapot Dome and associated oil scandals of Harding's administration, was an example of gross corruption. Frederick Lewis Allen sees Forbes in his two years as head of the bureau as responsible for an estimated 200 million dollars of "graft and flagrant waste." He traveled around the country, purportedly to investigate future hospital sites; in fact, the sites were already selected. He let contracts with so little regard to cost that he was charged with taking kickbacks of over 30 percent. Equally suspicious were purchases of supplies; he secured $70,000 worth of floor wax and cleaner, "enough, it was said, to last a hundred years."[1] Eventually Forbes was convicted of fraud and sentenced to Leavenworth.

Stan began his work with the Veterans' Administration with considerable enthusiasm. His particular interest lay in tuberculosis, and by March 1922 he was investigating facilities for tubercular patients at Saranac Lake. By summer he had begun to develop plans for establishing a major tuberculosis hospital but was already somewhat uneasy about Forbes and his staff. Still, he expected to stay on at least long enough to formulate policy about tuberculosis treatment: "The situation at the Veterans' Bureau is not altogether satisfactory, but it is much better than it was several months ago. I am still determined to straighten things out or get out." That determination carried Stan through most of another year, but in June 1923, his project for training personnel to care for tubercular patients having been shelved, he resigned.

"Father sent in his resignation Saturday," Mary wrote to Alan. "He had borne it as long as he could, and I am heartily with him in his desire to escape."[2]

Two months later Harding died; murky questions of suicide or poisoning were raised and, shortly after, information about the scandals began to surface. Even five or six years later, writing about these years in *My Story*, Rinehart was guarded about the Harding administration, Forbes, and the Veterans' Bureau, although she did mention the pressures brought by special, and greedy, interests and the fact that "scandals had begun to be whispered."[3]

At the time of Harding's death, Mary was engrossed in her own immediate problem—her newly opened play, *The Breaking Point*. When the novel had appeared a year earlier, it received a number of very unfavorable notices. The *Literary Review* observed that the book should find "popular favor," and that was not a compliment. Rinehart, the reviewer said, "has skated over the surface of her mental problem" and overwhelmed the "psychopathic" interest of the novel with excessive plotting. The *Times* thought the plot unconvincing but preferred it to the characters. And *The New Republic* warned its readers off: Rinehart had written an "old-fashioned novel for old-fashioned readers."[4]

As it turned out, there were still a great number of old-fashioned readers around, and *The Breaking Point* held the best-seller list for two years—in sixth place in 1922 and in tenth the following year. Still, such reviews were deeply distressing. Stan tried to cheer Mary, sending her the more favorable notices. "These clippings about The Breaking Point should hearten you up a bit. They're bully. I've kept nothing bad out. So cheer up. You're getting stronger every year—perhaps because you are taking your work more seriously. You are not Mrs. Goin's but Mrs. Cummins."[5] But the critical reception of her novel dismayed Mary, and after *The Breaking Point* she did not attempt another major novel for four years.

The Breaking Point, however, looked like good material to Wagenhals and Kemper, eager to follow up the great success of *The Bat* with a new play. In the fall of 1922 Mary began to dramatize her novel, but she was not writing with her usual energy and speed. For one thing, the Rineharts were not really settled. Still living in an apartment at the Wardman Park Hotel, they did not know whether they would remain in Washington or return to the Sewickley house, now rented. Also, as Mary was beginning to discover, social life in the capital was very demanding. She loved being part of the elite world of Washington, but maintaining a position in that society was almost a career in itself. Moreover, Mary was often tired and complained of illness more frequently than in the past. Her output declined dramatically over the next years. In 1922 she published only two Tish stories and one travel article; the next year, one Tish story and one travel piece. In 1924 she did somewhat more

—five stories and two articles—but by Rinehart's standards, this was meager.

Nineteen twenty-two was, as well, the year of her mother's death. Cornelia Roberts had not been happy in Washington; she missed the Sewickley house and the life she had grown accustomed to there. Occasionally, Mary found her in her room, crying. Then she died in a manner so bizarre that Mary wondered if Cornelia had not planned it years before. After a bath had been run for her, her companion was called away for a few minutes. Somehow, Cornelia, still paralyzed—"one arm was useless, and one foot still dragged"—managed to climb into the bathtub.[6] The water was scalding; badly burned, she could neither call for help nor lift herself from the tub.

Mary had started for Wyoming that day and was called back by wire. She arrived in time to watch her mother die, a death Mary found herself wishing for, so painful were Cornelia's attempts to breathe. Mary took Cornelia Roberts back to Pittsburgh to be buried in the old cemetery in Allegheny with the family.

Despite her absorption with the griefs and tensions and uncertainties of her private life in 1922, Rinehart developed ever more the image of success in the public mind. That summer the *New York Times* sent out questionnaires in an attempt to discover the twelve greatest women in America, and Rinehart was among the twelve. Grant Overton's *When Winter Comes to Main Street,* published that same year, included an essay on Rinehart, praising her vitality and freshness and commenting on the great variety of her work. And with continued royalties from *The Bat* and with *The Breaking Point* a best-seller, Rinehart made so much money that her federal taxes came to $46,612.

In 1923 George Washington University awarded Rinehart the honorary degree of Doctor of Letters. On June 3 Mary attended the baccalaureate ceremony wearing her cap and gown. As she wrote to Alan, she now owned "a beautiful diploma and a silk and velvet doctor's hood." A photographer was engaged to take her picture in the academic regalia. A further delight was afforded when Mary received a letter from the president of George Washington, addressed to "Dr. Mary Roberts Rinehart."[7]

The day after the presentation at George Washington, rehearsals began on *The Breaking Point*. The play was to open its pre-Broadway run in Washington at the end of June and then move on to Atlantic City by July 1. W&K had high hopes for the play, as did Mary, whose investment of $10,000 bought her a third of the property.

Mary had written most of the play in the first months of 1923 but was still sending in revisions a week before rehearsals were to begin. Even after rehearsals were under way, she continued to make changes, working with

W&K in New York. As late as June 20, she wrote to Alan that she was working day and night on the play. She was no longer particularly sanguine about its chances, though. The cast was all right, no more than that, and the production left "much to be desired, as W. and K. have been rather too economical!"[8]

Mary returned to Washington from New York on June 24, the night before the opening. Stan sent Alan word that Mary was exhausted and added, "Of course we are all rather on the tenterhooks of expectancy about the play which opens here tomorrow night." The producers were very cheerful, "apparently without the slightest apprehensions," but Mary was "rather low in her mind."[9] As things turned out, Mary was right. The Washington papers, all but one, roasted the play.

The flop in Washington sent Mary back to work even more feverishly on the script. She worked harder, Stan said, than he had ever seen her work, and she became increasingly ill, wakening with violent headaches. As early in July as was possible, she left for Eaton's Ranch and there continued to revise the script. W&K kept the play on the road, attempting to improve it before the August 16 opening in New York. By late July the producers were wiring Mary for more third-act revisions and urging her to join them. The situation was pressing enough for Mary to leave Wyoming for a week with W&K in New York.

Mary was back at the Ranch when *The Breaking Point* opened. Wagenhals sent his typically hyperbolic wire: "BIGGEST DRAMATIC OPENING IN HISTORY OF NEW YORK AUDIENCE ENTHUSIASTIC CAST GREAT." But he closed on a more cautious note: "TIMES [GOOD] BUT NOTICES OTHERS VERY BAD NOBODY DISCOURAGED HAVE COATS OFF WILL PUT IT OVER." Over the next few days it became clear that the play was in trouble despite Wagenhals's doubts about the critics' ability to "kill as big a play" as this one.[10] There might be weaknesses in the third act, but the audiences, W&K asserted, remained enthusiastic.

Unfortunately, the audiences grew smaller. Wagenhals was filling the house with passes late in August to create the impression of a sellout. His wires west were, as a result, baffling in their contradictions, for example, "RECEIPTS [$]800 HOUSE PACKED."[11] By early September the Klaw Theater threatened to close the play if the receipts were not kept up and demanded a guarantee of $8,500 a week, meaning that W&K and the Rineharts had to buy up the empty seats. On September 11 Mary and Stan contributed another $5,000 to *The Breaking Point.*

By mid-September, though, Mary seemed to feel the worst was over: "We had to get by the sensational attacks of three or four critics." Moreover, she thought the slow first weeks might have been due to the season: "It was not a hot-weather play." Now, fairly buoyant, she reported to Alan that business was growing and that she "never saw audiences more enthusiastic."[12] Her optimism was ill-founded.

As each week's subsidized gross fell slightly under the $8,500 guarantee, W&K took to the streets with a wild advertising campaign. New York was in the midst of a newspaper strike, and W&K decided to print a "Special New York Newspaper." The lead story carried the heading "Jud Clark Is Declared Legally Dead," and boxed on the front page was a "Summary of the Clark Mystery," including such items as:

August 16, 1923	Opened to capacity
August 17, 1923	Most widely discussed play in New York
August 18, 1923	Sold out, matinee and evening
August 26, 1923	Mary Roberts Rinehart sees play for first time
September 11, 1923	Klaw Theater arranges to keep play for one year
September 13, 1923	One thousandth letter of praise received by Wagenhals and Kemper[13]

But on October 1 Wagenhals wrote to tell Mary that they would close the play in three weeks. Don't be depressed, he counseled her. And on the theory that misery loves company, he added that Tarkington had had a play close and that Anita Loos was sinking thousands into a play of hers in an attempt to keep it open.[14]

A few years later Rinehart attempted to explain why *The Breaking Point* had failed. She knew that it was technically sound, "but the story simply did not hold the audience. . . . they had expected another *Bat,* and here was a quiet little drama of human emotions." She had spoken more frankly of the audience in a letter to Alan: "Those who like it love it, but it is not I am afraid for the mass."[15] In fact, the play, like the novel, suffered from Rinehart's inability to make it either one thing or another. In some ways it is a serious story, dealing with amnesia and the psychological shock of discovering that one's identity is not real. At the same time Rinehart continued to give to her audiences the things they had come to expect of her: very involved plot complications and a conventionally happy ending. *The Breaking Point* moved in the direction of serious fiction, but it did not move far enough. As a result, it remained an uncomfortable marriage of two diverse intentions.

The question of serious fiction was an important one for Rinehart by this time. *Dangerous Days* and *A Poor Wise Man* both had been bids for attention as a serious, rather than a popular, fiction writer. No doubt, it had once seemed a simple thing to Rinehart to distinguish one kind of fiction from another. She had made her name in mystery and farce and, then, with *The Street of Seven Stars* attempted a new kind of writing. Despite her reputation as a mystery writer, she had in fact written no long mystery novels since *The Case of Jennie Brice* in 1912, although she had done two mystery novellas —*Sight Unseen* and *The Confession*. From 1914, when *The Street of Seven Stars* was published, to 1922, when *The Breaking Point* appeared, she had written six serious novels, and with each one the critical reception had grown colder, although five of the six were best-sellers.

Through the 1920s, the critical reception of her serious novels continued to dismay Rinehart, at times to contribute to her growing depression. One explanation that Rinehart came up with had to do with what she continued to call "realism." In 1922 *The Bookman* (published by Doran) printed a Rinehart article called "The Unreality of Modern Realism." In fact, the essay is a defense of Rinehart's own work, particularly in relation to the new school of fiction writers so different from anything she had known in the past, writers like Sherwood Anderson, F. Scott Fitzgerald, and the best-selling new novelist Sinclair Lewis.

Realism, says Rinehart in this piece, is the opposite of idealism, the quality that separates man from the "creature." In literature realism is simply reportage and thus a kind of journalism. It is the literary counterpart of the office building, rather than the cathedral. The question turns on the responsibility of the writer. If he "sees life only as cheap, drab, . . . is it his province to spread broadcast this conviction?" Certainly not, for literature must be more than "merely the egotistic attempt to interpret the world" in the writer's own terms. And then Rinehart extravagantly labels the realist a "ruthless iconoclast . . . the Hun of Literature."[16]

The new young writers Rinehart labels simply cynical. She particularly objects to the sexuality in their books ("They stress the life of the body") and to the emphasis on psychological probing ("with a sort of indecent honesty they violate the sanctuary of the human mind"). It was, of course, possible that these young men would outgrow such writing—"when they have discovered that every man has moments when he ceases to be the thing he has made himself and becomes the man God made him." If not, contemporary American literature would not live. "Certainly we have no survival of non-idealistic literature from the past. . . . The job of the writer is to preserve our dreams, not our failures."[17]

Coming as it did at the beginning of one of America's most brilliant literary periods, Rinehart's article was desperately out of step. At the same time it shows us a good deal about what made her writing so popular for so long, for most of the American public preferred those novels which provided them escape from the reality of their lives, and for a considerable period a good part of that public remained intensely prudish about literary sexuality as well. But the essay is most important for the insight it gives us into Rinehart's defensiveness about the quality of her own writing.

Popularity and success carried, as it turned out, something of a curse. Sometimes it seemed as though the critics would not take seriously a writer who had made a name first in the mystery field. Sometimes, however, Rinehart saw her failure to capture critical attention as a deliberate choice on her own part—the choice not to exploit sexual themes and not to emphasize the sordid. In 1920 she had written, also for *The Bookman*, that she had an obligation "to keep the faith of my readers, to give them my best, to spread such happiness as I could, never to preach an evil thing nor to exalt a wicked one." In that article, called "My Public," she asserted that she "would rather have the liking and confidence of the many than the praise of the few," that she would rather be "in the hearts of the multitude [than in] high places where the mighty sit alone."[18]

Just about the time when W&K decided to close *The Breaking Point*, Mary and Stan made up their minds to stay in Washington. On September 30, 1923, Mary sent Alan the news. "We have bought a house!" The house at 2419 Massachusetts Avenue, formerly the home of the Dutch minister, was a good-sized red brick, "with quite a little ground for a city street."[19] They went back to Sewickley to arrange for the furniture and some of the bushes and trees (favorite Rinehart gifts to one another) to be moved. By Christmas they were in the new house and for that holiday Mary and Stan gave one another saddle horses.

Not long after Christmas, the Rineharts were out riding together when Stan was seriously injured. He had taken his foot out of the stirrup momentarily when Mary, who had not noticed, took her horse into a canter. Stan's horse bolted, half throwing him, so that the free stirrup struck him a number of times on the head. Finally he fell and Mary reached him a good distance up the road. He was unconscious, with a severe concussion and a broken leg. The leg was long in healing, he had recurring attacks of dizziness, and the concussion impaired his memory.

By late spring it was apparent that Stan was not well enough to spend the summer in Wyoming, so the Rineharts rented a house on the coast of Maine, where they went immediately after Ted's graduation from Harvard. Alan was back from several months in Haiti and he and Ted spent the summer with their parents. Then in the fall, the two boys traveled together in Europe. When they returned, they joined Stan, Jr., at Doran. Now all three Rinehart sons were working in publishing.

In Maine, Mary began work on a new mystery novel, *The Red Lamp*. It is a well-plotted and well-crafted novel that mixes crime and mystery with elements of spiritualism. Mary's interest in spiritualism was not new; she had used mediums and séances in her 1916 novella *Sight Unseen*. She had also had experiences with what seemed to be haunted houses, both at Bellport in the summer of 1918 and at the Wardman Park Hotel in Washington, where the spirit of Boise Penrose was supposed to manifest itself. Throughout the 1920s there was considerable public interest in what was then called "spirit return," and even so hard-headed a journal as *Scientific American* took the matter under consideration—with negative results.

Mary and Stan probably had their first experience with spiritualism in 1909, at Lily Dale near Chautauqua, where there was a spiritualist camp. Both had sittings there with a medium named Keeler. First they wrote notes on a slate and awaited replies that were to come through Keeler. Stan wrote notes to his father, his brother Charlie, and a young doctor friend, but the replies he received were unsatisfactory. A trumpet séance followed and Stan's brother Charlie spoke, but again it was unconvincing. As Stan explained in a

The house in Washington, now the Embassy of the Republic of Zambia.

letter a decade and a half later, "Both of us would really like to be convinced, but as yet nothing has brought about conviction."[20]

Continued experimentation with spiritualism eventually led the Rineharts to initiate correspondence with Sir Arthur Conan Doyle, who had himself developed a profound interest in spirit return after World War I. Mary and Stan first wrote after a particularly unsatisfactory episode in a séance held in 1926 by the well-known medium Valiantine, who worked in America with Conan Doyle's endorsement. By that time Mary had attended a number of séances, sometimes alone and sometimes with Stan. Mary, like her husband, seemed willing to believe in spirit return, but she also maintained some skepticism. She had transcripts made of several séances, among them one in Sewickley in 1921 and two in Washington in 1926. At the sitting in Sewickley, Mary was asked by Black Hawk, the medium's control, if she knew a John Roberts and an Abraham Roberts. John was her great-great-grandfather's name; Abram Roberts was the name of her great-grandfather. When it came time to ask questions of Black Hawk, however, Mary asked only general questions about the state of the world situation.[21]

In Washington, Mary spoke with a voice who seemed to be Tex Hale, a Marine Corps friend of Alan's who had died in a plane crash, but neither Mary nor the voice would actually state the name. "Do you know who I am?" asked the voice. "Certainly," replied Mary. Another voice identified itself as Ella, probably Cornelia's sister, and talked of family matters with Mary. Mary asked for confirmation: if it was really Ella, she wanted a sign that night, a light or a rap in her bedroom.[22]

The séance with Valiantine took place at the home of Thomas Bell Sweeney, and it progressed satisfactorily until at the conclusion—or what he thought was the conclusion—Sweeney turned on the lights. There was Valiantine in the middle of the floor replacing the trumpet that was, theoretically, moving about in the air of its own volition. At that point, as Mary and Stan reported, Valiantine swiftly decamped. Valiantine, on the other hand, told his supporters that he had merely replaced the trumpet at the end of the sitting because it had ended up close to his feet and had not raced from the house.

It was then that Mary and Stan wrote to Conan Doyle. He answered readily enough, in part to interest them in buying books from his spiritualist bookstore ("I am a persevering drummer"). In the correspondence that followed, Conan Doyle assured them that Valiantine had come with the highest recommendations, including that of the well-known spiritualist-expert H. Dennis Bradley, who had found Valiantine's conversations with such figures as Confucius "remarkable." In explaining the episode at the Sweeneys', Conan Doyle offered the possibility that Valiantine was an "intermittent" and that his power was sometimes "taken away as a punishment by the intelligent forces which lie at the back of this business." When his powers were gone, perhaps Valiantine allowed his weak "morale" to push him to "mumming."[23]

Conan Doyle provided the Rineharts with very specific instructions about the proper atmosphere for sittings. Not only did such an atmosphere bring better results, but it made it possible to hold séances without mediums. Darkness was crucial, and "a musical box playing a succession of quiet tunes" very useful. Above all, there must be "no straining or anxiety." Under these conditions, he assured the Rineharts, they would have better success, but they had to think positively. In a final and practical note the creator of Sherlock Holmes suggested that they adopt the measures he used with his favorite medium, Powall: "I tie him tight to a chair."[24]

Although the spiritualist element in *The Red Lamp* may have been the most interesting to Rinehart, the most appealing to the reader is the narrator. Rinehart typically used a first-person narrator for her mysteries and a third-person narration for her serious fiction, and usually her narrators were young women who also served as the center of the romantic interest. But in *The Red Lamp* Rinehart created a middle-aged man, a college professor whose diary provides a record of the summer's experiences. The professor has his own voice—dry, precise, "academic":

> Show me any man who teaches literature, and I will show you a man thwarted. For it is our universal, hidden conviction that we, too, could write, were it not for the necessity of earning our daily bread. We start in as writers, only temporarily sidetracked. "Some day—" we say to ourselves, and go to our daily tasks of Milton or Dryden or Pope as those who, seeking the beauties of the country, must travel through a business thoroughfare to get there.[25]

Professor "William A. Porter, A.B., M.A., Ph.D., Litt.D., etc.,"[26] is a delightful character, but he is at the same time an exercise in revenge. Not only had critics but professors participated in the cabal that labeled Rinehart "popular," meaning insignificant. Speaking about college education in her autobiography, Rinehart wondered whether it had been worth it to send her three sons to Harvard. "When it gradually dawned on them, in literature classes, that 'mother' was no light of the world, but only a good professional writer, they bore up under it." Later they learned a more important lesson: "As they became publishers themselves it was to discover that lights of the literary world were mostly poor business."[27]

The Red Lamp, Rinehart's first full-length mystery novel in over a decade, received splendid critical notices—an irony that could not have been lost on her. The reviewers praised the plot, the structure, the characters, the writing. The *New York Tribune* called her mystery technique "practically perfect," and *The Literary Review* went even further, saying that the novel "comes about as near to fulfilling all the requirements for a bang-up mystery yarn as anyone could ask." The staid old *Boston Evening Transcript* asserted that "with her versatility there is nothing she cannot do next."[28] But *The Red Lamp* was not a best-seller.

Mary was not at all well during that summer in Maine. A nervous condition persistently worsened. More alarming was the evidence she discovered on the yellow pages filled with her handwriting: "I would leave out letters, or only partially form them."[29] The hand cramps that she had experienced for a number of years intensified as well; it was diagnosed at some time as a real enough condition called Dupuytren's contracture or shoemaker's disease. By the late fall the cramps had become a kind of hysterical paralysis, and Mary could not hold a pen in her hand.

By the winter of 1924–1925, Mary's psychological condition was yet worse. Even the fairly cautious language of her autobiography describes a state of deep depression and suggests that she struggled with strong suicidal tendencies. "At night I lay awake and fought a new and terrible impulse, unreasoning and without cause." Despite efforts to remind herself of the blessings of her life, particularly her husband and sons, she "seemed remote from all of them and dreadfully alone." Dr. Rinehart was sympathetic and watchful. "Probably he knew that I would do nothing, that it was hysteria, but I might make the gesture."[30]

Mary's neurotic depression had a number of sources. One was her knowledge that the family no longer existed as it once had; her sons were adults and they all lived away, in another city. Her husband, too, caused her concern, for having left the Veterans' Bureau, he was without work of his own. Growing older troubled her. She had worried about her age at forty and forty-five; soon she would be fifty. Menopausal stresses probably added to the concern over aging. In a letter written in the summer of 1925, Mary commented, in reference to another woman, that "passing through the climacteric [is] a wretched time with strange inhibitions and great mental distress."[31] And then there were the problems attendant on Mary's writing, especially on her attempts to write serious fiction and the critical reaction to that fiction.

It became more and more difficult for Mary to write at all. In 1925 *The Red Lamp* appeared, but otherwise only three stories and two articles. The following year was slightly more productive, with four stories, six articles, and a short novel called *Two Flights Up*—but that was a slight effort, nothing more than a five-finger exercise for Mary Roberts Rinehart.

One of the short stories published in 1926 was called "The Rock River Fugitive." It appeared in *Youth's Companion* as the result of a strange course of events, described in Eric Hodgins's autobiography, *Trolley to the Moon.* The company owning *Youth's Companion* had gone bankrupt in 1926 and the magazine ended up under the ownership of Ellery Sedgwick, editor of the *Atlantic Monthly*. Among the assets "was a massive manuscript inventory carried at a value of $1 million." There were thousands of purchased but unpublished manuscripts and among them was discovered "an early indiscretion of Mary Roberts Rinehart's." That story, probably written in 1904, had been purchased for forty dollars.[32] When it was published Rinehart's stories were receiving exactly one hundred times that amount.

It is in some ways astonishing that Rinehart wrote even what little she did in 1925, for she was away from home almost continually from early in January until the end of September. Once again travel was to provide the psychological boost Mary desperately needed. In January she and Stan sailed for the Near East, a long cruise to be followed by about four weeks in Egypt. From the ship Mary wrote to her sons, reporting optimistically on her condition. "I seem at last to have reached rock bottom and started up again. Now that it is over I can say that I was pretty bad for a while, no sleep, black melancholia and all the rest of it. But today I know the worst is over, and the rest shall be all velvet." A few days later she told them, "I am slowly getting better, but am still nothing to write home about." The ship made stops in Athens and Constantinople and Mary commented, "I hate sight-seeing, but if it is going to send me back normal and ready for work, I'll sight-see or die."[33]

At first, in Cairo, there was little change, and Mary talked dismally about the end of her career. But after a few days a camel trip into the desert was suggested, and with that incentive she "slipped out and bought a notebook! . . . what was a camel camping trip but material to write about?"[34] Even the outfitting was fun, if fruitless. Advised of the benefits of native costume, Mary purchased a gold underdress, a turquoise aba, a yellow scarf, and white veil. Modeling this costume while Stan tried on his green and white cloak and white turban, Mary had to conclude that it could be used only for fancy dress back home.

They set out on camels with an extraordinary retinue: four "luggage camels" with tents, beds, washstands, stove, oriental rugs, and even a collapsible dinner table. The tents were embroidered with "scenes and carvings from famous tombs." Inside, rugs were laid and beds set up with mattresses and pillows. Outside, they reclined in deck chairs while elegant dinners were prepared: "soup, entrée, roast with vegetables, salad with quail and dessert. Then fruit, coffee and candy." Despite an attack of the flu, Mary realized she was "coming back."

> In those quiet nights under the stars I found a new peace, and something more; I learned to be thankful for what I had, and the folly of aspirations beyond my reach. I saw the Arabs in their thin cotton clothing, grateful for a little food, a bit of fire, singing because for once they were warm and fed. And I was ashamed.[35]

By the time they returned to Cairo, Mary's notebook was filled and her handwriting was firm and steady.

Although they planned to leave at this point, Mary explained, "With our usual capacity for getting into trouble, we found ourselves one day, not bound for home at all, but for Bagdad."[36] The first idea was to fly over the desert but fear of a forced landing among unfriendly Bedouins defeated that plan. There was a new automobile route, taking three days from Beirut to Bagdad, and the Rineharts decided to go by car. Even that was dangerous. A week earlier Bedouins had held up a similar convoy and killed the wife of the French vice-consul. All in all, an irresistible trip.

A train to Haifa, and the Rineharts rented a car and driver to cross the desert, stopping in Damascus to be joined by the French mail truck and an armed pilot car. On the way to Bagdad they met the desert camel patrol, still seeking the murderers. They reached Bagdad and Maude's Hotel—and they were appalled. Garbage lay rotting in the sun; it would be washed away when the river rose. Sparrows flew into the dining room and picked food off the plates. In the city itself Mary saw poverty and conditions of labor unlike any she had ever imagined: "In the bazaar at Bagdad I saw coolies, carrying on their backs steel I-beams, fifteen feet long or more. Their feet wide apart, their faces pallid and dripping with sweat, their breathing a series of gasps."[37]

The return through the desert was unpleasant. A sandstorm shaved off Mary's hair where her hat left it unprotected; a subsequent rainstorm turned the road to mud, and the jolting of the car was sufficient to eradicate altogether the seat of Stan's trousers. They met the camel patrol again, this time with the murderers apprehended. The train from Beirut took them back to Cairo where Mary was presented to the King, and then they sailed for home. It had been a successful trip: "The morbidness was gone, never to return; and my notebook was full, bursting."[38]

Back in New York, there was wonderful news: Alan had become engaged to Gratia Houghton, the daughter of Arthur Houghton, co-owner of the Corning Glass Company, and niece of Alanson Houghton, American ambassador to the Court of St. James. Mary was thrilled. Alan, her restless son, had made a brilliant match.

Mary went almost immediately to Eaton's Ranch, where Stan planned to meet her sometime later in the summer. She worked on a series of Near East articles, to be published in *Cosmopolitan* the following spring, and on *Two Flights Up*. But mostly she thought about the wedding, set for September. Part of July was devoted to preparing the list of wedding guests, part to planning her clothes. Practical letters to Alan dealt with the interest in Doran she would buy him (as she had for Stan, Jr.). Other letters, both to Alan and to Gratia, expressed Mary's profound pleasure in this marriage; she wrote to Alan, "You have chosen beyond my greatest expectations and I know she will not let me down, as to my faith in her."[39]

Alan and Gratia were married on September 19, 1925, in what the *New York Times* labeled "the most brilliant marriage of the season in Southeastern Massachusetts."[40] The ceremony took place in the private chapel at The Meadows, the Houghton estate in South Dartmouth, just below New Bedford. A wedding breakfast and reception followed in the garden overlooking the bay. Back in Washington, Mary wrote to Gratia and Alan, honeymooning in London.

> Just a week ago today I was standing in the chapel ready to howl like a dog at something that was going on. And yet with such happiness too that I simply would not cry. . . . Here I would like to sit down and think up a new story, and all I can do is wonder if you are as happy as I want you to be! I'd be a better writer if I were not such a darned good mother![41]

During the fall, in an effort to write more productively, Mary rented a downtown office. At the same time Stan was trying his hand at writing. In November, Lorimer sent him $500 for an article called "The High Cost of Keeping Alive." Lorimer was glad to keep the article and to "consider a list of subjects dealing with popular medicine." This was not Stan's first work in this area. In 1919 and 1920, while still in Pittsburgh, he had written eleven articles on medicine for popular magazines, and most of them were published in the *Post* and subsequently collected by Doran as *The Common Sense of Health*.[42]

Then, in January 1926 Alan sent a special delivery letter announcing his desire to leave his job at Doran and devote himself to writing. The idea was not news to his parents; he had talked of it for some time. As Rinehart put it in her autobiography, Alan turned to the idea of writing shortly after "having abandoned the idea of going around the world in an eighteen-foot boat." Mary thoroughly disliked the notion of his becoming a writer, looking back "on my own struggles, on the virtual solitary imprisonment of that more than twenty years of grinding labor." But when Alan sold some of his stories, "I was compelled to admit his ability." Nor did Mary approve of Alan's giving up his job. She suggested that he wait: "Some day, when you can't hold off any longer, you will take a Sabbatical year and see what you can do in it." Sabbatical years, she pointed out, come only one in seven. Meanwhile, she advised that he try short stories, "fine training and preparation." That kind of work could be done after hours, for "if you are a writer in your heart you will do it, time or no time."[43]

But Mary had more to communicate in this letter than her belief in hard work; she also had a warning for Alan: "Don't get the magazine idea," Mary told her son. "I think it is fatal to real work." She herself had caught the "magazine idea," for she had had to earn money. The result was a set of "such habits of writing down that I am afraid to do anything else. I am literally afraid I cannot."[44] Success had sprung another trap.

Only a few weeks after this letter to Alan, Mary began work on another serious novel. The idea came from Adelaide Neall. On February 3 she wrote to tell Mary of her conversation with W. H. Koerner, the book and magazine illustrator, who told her of an experience his young niece was going through. Adelaide thought there was "a wonderful idea for a story in it." The girl of eighteen, brought up in a wealthy and very conventional home, had been taken west by her uncle to help her get over the death of her father. She loved the ranch, and the cowboys loved her; "on the day she left camp she had six proposals from the cow-boys and others around the place!"

> There was one cow-boy rather more picturesque than the others because he was somewhat more of a daredevil—you know, the kind who goes off on terrible sprees and then comes back and repents picturesquely all around the place—that she met only two times. It appears that they kept up a correspondence after she got back to Chicago and just before Christmas the Koerners got a wire from the niece to say that she had gone West and married "Bill."[45]

Bill was a railroad brakeman and the two set up housekeeping in a one-room log cabin. Adelaide was fascinated to contemplate "what she and Bill will make out of married life," for "she is the daintiest, most immaculate little person [and] writes charming poetry." She went on: "I imagine there are lots of Eastern girls who fall for a pair of chaps and a red silk handkerchief and marry western boys similar to Bill, but I cannot remember reading any story about how such a match works out. Have you?"[46] If a brilliant editor is one who brings the right story to the right author, then Adelaide Neall was a brilliant editor, for in her letter she provided Mary with the basic story of *Lost Ecstasy*.

Within the week Mary sent back her idea for a serialized novel along the lines Adelaide had suggested. By the end of March, they were discussing the price. The Boss "seemed to think that forty thousand would be about the limit" and, Adelaide reminded Mary, that was "big money" for the *Post*. By early spring Mary had gone west, this time to the 101 Ranch in Oklahoma, in search of local color.[47]

Back in Washington, Mary worked rapidly on the new novel although there were distractions. She tried to fit a full work schedule around family responsibilities. In April, Dorrie had an operation and Bab was sent to Washington to stay with her grandparents. Mary told Adelaide, "This business of being a sort of mixed grill of mother, grandmother and writer is not as easy as it sounds."[48] But by early summer Mary traveled to Wyoming where she could write fairly uninterruptedly. Stan came later for a few weeks and returned to Washington ahead of Mary. For whatever reasons of anxiety and tension, and with whatever immediate cause, they quarreled badly when he left.

For the next two weeks they wrote each other the careful, tentative letters of badly wounded adults, but they wrote lovingly. Stan's first letter referred to the "emotional storm" in which they had parted. "I haven't had time to clear the wreckage. I only know that I love you and I'm holding fast to that." He felt certain Mary needed time alone: "For your peace of mind we should be separated for a while." She could stay at the Ranch or, if she wished, return to Washington, in which case he could "arrange to go elsewhere." Mary replied that she would return immediately to Washington if the weather were cool, and then she went on to analyze her feelings—her letter was less ardent than Stan's, but marked with insight.

> And if you have any idea that I am staying so as to be away from you, get rid of it at once. I feel as if I had had an amputation and lost a leg. Maybe the leg bothered me a little now and then, but I am certainly lost without it! And if it bothered me, what about the way I treated it? Don't I know I cramped it and generally gave it pretty hard going?[49]

Mary returned in October, to work on *Lost Ecstasy* and take up their busy social life. Lunch at the Edward McLeans' (of the *Washington Post*) for 250 people. A diplomatic dinner at the White House. Over Christmas a month of family visits. Although Washington was not the place for hard work —as she wrote to Adelaide, "quite and completely rotten as far as work is concerned"—Mary made considerable progress on *Lost Ecstasy*. Adelaide was now receiving sections of the novel, and Lorimer wrote early in 1927, "If the story pans out as strong as Miss Neall seems to feel that it will, I am perfectly willing to increase the ante to $50,000."[50]

Mary continued to write out her drafts and revisions in long hand, but now she had a new secretary to prepare the typed copy. In 1926 Stan inquired at a local business college for someone interested in a secretarial position. Enrolled at the business school for a course in shorthand was a young man named William Sladen, a graduate student in history at George Washington University. The shorthand instructor told Sladen of the job possibility and he went for an interview and typing test with Dr. Rinehart. It was only a temporary job, of course, for Sladen intended to go on with his work in history (indeed, he received his M.A. in 1929). In fact, Bill Sladen was to remain with Rinehart for the rest of her life, handling her correspondence, typing her manuscripts, a dependable, intelligent confidant who would become part of the Rinehart publishing firm. He started his job typing the manuscript of *Lost Ecstasy*.[51]

Precisely one year after Adelaide Neall had written Mary about Koerner's niece, Mary mailed in the final chapters of *Lost Ecstasy*. Stan wrote to Lorimer: "It has been a terrible grind. . . . I have never seen her so tired. . . . You have no idea how much the novel has taken out of her. . . . But believe me or not, I think the story is worth it." Now Mary "was taking up the idea of resting with the same intensity of purpose that helped her to put over the novel." Resting, as Stan wryly informed Lorimer, meant a routine of hair dressers, masseurs, and special baths.[52]

In March 1927 the Rineharts sailed for Hawaii on a vacation planned as a real opportunity for Mary to relax. As it turned out, she would have been better off on horseback or in the desert. No sooner had they arrived, than Mary slipped and fell in the bathroom and broke a rib. Although she was in some pain and miserably confined to her room, she still saw the absurd side of the accident. Actually she had slipped and fallen against the toilet seat, but, as she wrote from Hawaii, describing the situation to the family, "I am politely supposed to have slipped in the bathtub." But more was to happen.

> The night of my accident I had had my second hypodermic of morphia and was gloriously calm . . . when the chandelier began to sway like a ship at sea. So did the bed, and so did the island. It lasted nine minutes. I had not lifted a finger up to then, but I leaped like a young gazelle out of bed and shook father. "Earthquake!" I yelled. "Earthquake!" But he only turned over and slept again! . . . I just crawled

back—and I've never got back [up] since without help—and let it shake itself out.⁵³

They returned home to the enthusiastic mail about *Lost Ecstasy*. Letters were pouring in, and more than half "from men, busy lawyers, newspaper men, doctors, bankers." It was the greatest reaction Mary had ever had to a serial. The *Post* wrote to tell her of a man who wired the magazine, "begging for an advance copy of the last installment."⁵⁴ The story of the cowboy and the rich girl was a smash, not only for its love interest but for its detailed handling of the hard life of the cattle herder in dry summers and snowbound winters.

Of all the letters Mary's favorite came from the foreman of the Double Cross Ranch in Grand Junction, Colorado.

No story since "The Virginian" has created such furor around the Double Cross. The atmosphere is becoming so saturated with romance from the absorption of this story that it bids fair to become a hindrance to everyday activities, for, as you know, a cowpuncher full of romance is about as useful as an Eskimo full of blubber. . . . [This problem] is nothing compared to what we will have to face when the remaining installments have been absorbed. By that time we will have a bunch of soft-hearted, bow-legged cowpunchers on our hands teeming with romance and no immediate outlet for their pent-up emotions.

The foreman added the note that the novel was "proving educational as well as entertaining: two of the boys have already given up their sweethearts—for they were merely small town girls," and he added, "We have only reached the fifth installment."⁵⁵

The reaction was so powerful that Stan felt sure it would cushion whatever attack the reviewers leveled when Doran brought the book out. "Now let the TIMES and other cocky news reviewers say whatever they please. Books are sold, in my humble opinion, by individual recommendations." He was right about the sales; *Lost Ecstasy* was sixth on the best-seller list. He was not right about the effect of the reviews on Mary. Arriving at the Ranch in early July she wrote to Stan: "I have never seen such bad reviews as the book is receiving. They fairly daze me. One I picked up on the train (a Denver paper) said it was the worst thing I had ever done. It helped to sweeten the trip considerably."⁵⁶

The *New York Times* made some brutal observations about the novel, but in some ways the review was not altogether unflattering. *Lost Ecstasy*, as the *Times* saw it, started out dreadfully and got better, becoming "increasingly engrossing" as a tale—not of ecstasy, but of discovery. Trying to understand how a novel that starts out so poorly as to be "dreadful to contemplate" is then able to move on to some passages of considerable power, the critic tried to take a psychoanalyst's view:

> If one got down to the root of the matter Mrs. Rinehart would probably be found to be an artist governed by a subconscious feeling of fear. She was afraid of her novel, she was afraid of the people in her novel, lest they climb up on their hind legs and insist on acting for themselves. And it is only when they do get out of control and act for themselves . . . that the characters . . . become genuine human beings.[57]

A fairly canny observation, after all, particularly in conjunction with Rinehart's own comments on the "magazine idea" and its effect on her writing.

Lost Ecstasy, then, fared very much as *The Breaking Point* had, with a great popular sale and negative critical reaction. Mary tried to put all that behind her when she went to the Ranch for the summer of 1927. She had other things on her mind. She was not at all well and suffered a good deal of pain, sometimes attributed to the broken rib and sometimes to continued gallbladder trouble. A merger was pending between Doran and Doubleday, Page, with obvious implications for her sons' careers. Gratia was expecting a baby during the summer. And, reviewers be damned, she was beginning to work out the idea for the most ambitious of all her novels—*This Strange Adventure.*

10

"Gesture Toward Truth"

1927–1928 and Beyond

In 1927, when Mary went to Eaton's in early July, she had begun work on a major novel. She traveled to Wyoming alone that summer, for Stan remained in the East to await the birth of Alan and Gratia's baby. Early in August a baby girl was born—named Gratia, but called Topsy. Mary received the news by wire during an afternoon bridge game. She left the table to "shed a tear or two of pure relief" and then returned to "say 'two hearts.'" Letters to Gratia philosophized about family and reminisced about her own early experiences of motherhood. "I shall never forget, after Ted came, the maid of all work leaving, and throwing ink on her walls . . . before she did so!" Other family letters dealt with Mary's plans for the coming Doubleday Doran merger. She prepared to buy Ted some shares in Doran before the merger, "so he can go over on a very nice basis." Like the other boys, Ted was to have had shares bought for him when he married, but the merger changed the timetable. And throughout that summer Mary was trying to deal philosophically with the reviews of *Lost Ecstasy*.

> My depression over the failure of Lost Ecstasy stayed with me steadily. Now however I begin to realize how unimportant it all is. That the real thing is still, as it always has been, my family and its happiness. And after all I have given a good many people pleasure with the thing. That ought to count a point or two. I found a raft of letters about it out here, and all wonderful. Well—[1]

When Mary returned to Washington in the fall, she continued to work on her new novel, one that would at least partially reflect the new literary mood of America, for despite her derogatory comments about realism, Mary Roberts Rinehart had not been immune to changes in American fiction brought about by the new young writers. She continued to express her reservations about the work of such writers as Sherwood Anderson, F. Scott Fitzgerald, and Sinclair Lewis. In 1926 she told Jean West Maury, in a long interview for the *Boston*

167

Evening Transcript, that "Mr. Lewis can take a half-dozen pages to get Babbit out of bed and into the bathroom. It is all very well," but she felt she would be cheating her public with that kind of writing. Still, she told Maury, she was only a storyteller who hoped "before I die, to have sufficient time to write a novel in which I am able to tell the truth as I see it, avoiding both the ultra-idealism of the one school and the too sordid realism of the other school of fiction writers." Such a novel, Rinehart said, would be "a gesture toward truth,"[2]

During the fall she prepared three articles for different magazines, on subjects both trivial and serious, revealing some effort once again to analyze her life, to understand the interplay of roles. The first to appear was "Just a Touch of Celebrity" in the *Post* in January 1928. In it Rinehart writes of the hard work required of her and of the inordinate numbers of "reporters, delegations, letters, manuscripts, speaking requests, endorsement requests" she has to deal with. "It has taken an iron determination, an unlisted telephone, and a secret office downtown to enable me to do any work at all." Female celebrities, she feels it important to add, have more problems than their male counterparts; they have to pay careful attention to their makeup, hair, and clothing, and to deal with "the essential feminine instinct to be all things to all men." As for fame itself, "it is not all beer and skittles." And, searching for the reason for her own celebrity, Rinehart concludes simply that "it is rather . . . a matter of appealing to the general imagination."[3]

For the *Journal* Mary wrote a piece called "I Buy Clothes Twice a Year," an article sufficiently dated to outrage most career women of our time. Writers, says Rinehart, are "a notoriously dowdy profession," and she determined from the start of her career that her work was not to change her "interest in dress." The tendency for writers to dress poorly is nothing more than "a tradition and a pose."[4] All that it takes to dress nicely, Rinehart opines, is organization and systemization; twice a year she tackles the problem of dress. First there is the preliminary survey of her clothing; second, a careful consideration of her schedule for the next six months and what that schedule would require in the way of dress. Only then is the third step, the actual purchase of clothes, undertaken.

The next section of the article is surprising, for the *Journal* audience was not the audience for *Vogue,* and the extent of the Rinehart wardrobe must have stirred the demons of jealousy in a good many middle-class bosoms that March. "If I outline a rather extensive wardrobe," she explains, "please remember that I live rather an extensive life." Some lists follow—for example, her furs:

full sealskin cape
ermine evening wrap (floor length and full)

caracul coat—collar and cuffs of Kolinsky
old ermine wrap (from Vienna)

The final body blow is delivered in the statement, "I still have the rather out-of-date idea that a gentlewoman's clothes should be made for her." Still, Rinehart explains, she is not extravagant, for she is neither promiscuous nor impulsive in her shopping. "And I know my own weaknesses. If I stay out of shops I do not purchase."[5]

That same month, March 1928, *McCall's* published "Companionate Marriage," Rinehart's views on a new question. Judge Ben Lindsey had formulated the idea that marriage should be led up to in stages, culminating in a legal marriage with the expectation of children. Rinehart dissented. Behind that idea she spied the theories of Freud and Marx. Freud, asserts Rinehart, was wrong in his theory of sexuality, especially for girls. "Practically always, the girl gives herself in marriage because she loves, and not because of any overwhelming sex urge." Men may be different, but a girl "normally gives herself where she loves, and for life." She dismisses Marx even more summarily. All in all, marriage should not be tampered with, for it has "spiritual values and compensations which cannot be ignored." Marriages fail not because there is any basic flaw in the institution but because parents do not educate their children to understand that "happiness in marriage must be earned."[6] The question of failing marriages was not an academic one for Mary. Stan, Jr.'s marriage was in serious difficulty, and he would be divorced by 1930. Alan's marriage would also end in divorce within the next few years.

The question of marriage and divorce was crucial to the new novel Mary was working on, the novel that was to be her "gesture toward truth." *This Strange Adventure* (its working title had been *The Dark Midwife*) was written during 1927 and 1928. Then, after an interruption to write a mystery novel for the boys' new publishing house, Mary began work on *My Story*. The two books are counterparts of one another—fictional and nonfictional views of Mary Roberts Rinehart. The troubled decade after the war had finally brought Mary the ability to see deeply into herself and the courage to write at least some of what she saw and some of what she had come to believe about women and their lives.

In *My Story* Rinehart talks of *This Strange Adventure*:

It was not my own story, but at certain tangential points Missie's life and mine met. We had lived through the same cycle, known the same people. . . .

And Missie thought much as I did. She was cursed with the ability to see both sides of everything, so that she seemed often to be a poor shilly-shallying sort of creature. Also she believed with me that cruelty is the great sin and love the great virtue.

One of the boys told me I would have hated Missie, had I lived with her. I wondered if I had not lived with her, for as many years as I had been alive! But I did not say so.[7]

In many ways Missie Colfax is not Mary Roberts Rinehart. She has no career and no ambitions for one. There is no adventure in her life, a life which Rinehart calls "a triumph of the ordinary."[8] She marries, falls in love with another man, gives up even the hope of having him for the need to devote herself to her child, and endures a life without glamour, love, or self-expression. But in many ways Missie is Mary. Or to put it more accurately, in creating Missie, Rinehart explores certain parts of her own experience, feelings, and frustrations, partly by recapitulating events in her own life and partly by altering events, as if to test the effect had certain circumstances been different.

We meet Missie as a child in the Arch Street house. In fact, Mary has split her own personality—the romantic and the practical sides—into two characters, each with a name that echoes Mary's own. Missie echoes Mamie; her real name, Marcella, differs in only one letter from Mary Ella. She is the sensitive, romantic child. Her older sister is Ellen (Ella again), practical, fairly cold, determined to get ahead. They are, actually, half sisters, with the same mother, Stella Colfax, a former burlesque actress. Stella bears no resemblance whatever to Cornelia Roberts. Lambert Colfax, on the other hand, has a good number of Tom Roberts's characteristics. He is elegant, convivial, spoiled, and he has Tom Roberts's white hands, unmarked by work.

Missie's family has little money. When Lambert had run off with Stella, he ran afoul of the old Colfax family—aristocrats who would have nothing to do with the world of the theater. The household grows progressively more disorganized and demoralized as Lambert begins to take up with other women, sometimes staying away from home for days at a time. Missie is the small receptacle of all Stella's laments and suspicions, hearing about "other women" long before she knows what the phrase means. It is not long, though, until she develops a powerful suspicion of and dislike for men and their sexuality.

Missie's life is a series of failures and losses; the first comes when Stella commits suicide. Here Rinehart has reversed the facts of her own life, permitting father Lambert to survive. He has run off again, this time perhaps permanently; and Stella, adoring him, goes upstairs to the small back room —the "back room" of Mary's childhood on Arch Street—and turns on the gas. Her daughters find her the next morning. Missie has nothing but pity for Stella; her father she loathes. Like Mary, sister Ellen is married shortly after her parent's death, but Missie is taken to live with her grandmother Colfax and her maiden aunt Adelaide.

By the time that Missie moves to her grandmother's house, she has shared many of the experiences of Mamie Roberts, most of them recalled as well in *My Story*: stringing morning glories along the back fence (Mary did that with her father, Missie with a neighbor), the fear of ghosts in the back room up the stairs, the simulated funeral in imitation of one in a nearby household, the make-believe bustle made of paper in a childish attempt to mimic a womanly figure, a long day in the park as the result of an errant father's behavior, a profound love for the escape offered by books, an innocent and hopeless love affair, and a deep horror of labor and childbirth. Like Mamie, Missie had learned all this in the little house on the Street.

As in a number of Rinehart stories, Missie is rescued from a life of poverty by her "real"—and aristocratic—family. But Missie regrets leaving the old house and is lonely and repressed in her grandmother's mansion. Both her grandmother and her aunt are deeply neurotic and, as bad as her preparation for life had been at the hands of her father and mother, the education she now undergoes is worse. Old Mrs. Colfax has three children. Lambert, her favorite, is irresponsible, selfish, lazy, and even now continues to take money from his increasingly impoverished mother. Adelaide is fat and ugly, a spinster with a passion for food, a loathing of her brother, and a fear of crossing streets. Another daughter, Cecily, had—like Mary's patient of years before—borne an illegitimate daughter and been sent to live some miles away in a small, dingy, remote house.

In the lonely years with her grandmother, Missie occasionally meets her childhood idol, Harry Sloane, but they are now separated by social class. After her debut Missie spends more time in society, without any marked success, until after a few months she is pursued by Wesley Dexter, a man of "no background, no family," who has insinuated his way into the local elite and is now looking for a way to consolidate his position through marriage. With something of a reputation for a wild youth, Wes, in his thirties and rather stout, has settled down—at least apparently. Although she is considerably put off, even repulsed, by his physical advances, Missie does accept Wes. She remains unmoved by Wesley's passion during and after their honeymoon, and at this point Rinehart begins to falter. All the book has worked toward a psychosocial explanation for Missie's coldness. Now, however, Rinehart turns the responsibility onto Wes, certainly an unlovely character, without understanding, warmth, or sympathy. While the problems of Missie's emotional education and Wes's character are essentially complementary, Rinehart does not use the one to intensify the other; instead she blurs her analysis of Missie.

As a matron Missie suffers the constraints of married life. She has no money of her own. "Wes was a true son of the nineties. His money was his. He earned it. His house, his servants, his wife, his money." He even buys and decorates their house himself. Her life holds no interest. Although they entertain at long and elaborate dinners, Missie is not a charming person socially and these dinners provide her no outlet. Otherwise, Wes is occupied with his business and his private pleasures, and Missie grows increasingly despondent. "Did every newly married woman feel like this? Feel that life was over before it had begun, that no longer romance or adventure awaited, that she had reached the end of the road before she had even turned the corner?"9

It is not long before Wes begins to have affairs with other women. The first involves a woman friend of theirs, and one night her husband comes to the house and knocks Wesley down. In that way Missie learns of his romances, and, in penance, Wes brings home a diamond sunburst pin for her. With that a pattern is established; each of Wesley's cruelties is paid for with jewels or furs.

In 1899 Missie meets and falls in love with Kirby Phelps, a brilliant young engineer who works with Ellen's husband. Missie moves into her own bedroom and locks the door. She lives for an occasional hour of talk with Kirby and for the hours in bed when she can lie awake "and hug a warm secret to her breast." Missie's love for Kirby is sexual, but they share only an occasional embrace. Kirby wants Missie, and he tries to tell her that he cannot "live on the bare bones of love." He urges her to divorce Wes and marry him. She wrestles with her conscience, her unhappiness, and her longing, and finally decides to have it out with Wes. She waits up for him, the connecting door open between their rooms. But he is very late and Missie falls asleep. When she awakes he is in her room, "smiling down at her."10 Missie becomes pregnant and the trap is closed.

All the thwarted love in Missie is directed to the child she bears, Colfax Dexter, called Eddie. And for a year she does not see Kirby. When they meet, he asks if the child is worth their separation and loneliness, and she answers that he is.

Three more years pass and then the latent violence in Missie explodes in Rinehart's most extraordinary scene. Eddie has been sick, a result of an intolerable heat wave: "People dropped on the pavement as if they had been pole-axed." In caring for the child, Missie becomes ill herself—and vengeful. They have remained in the stifling city only because Wes has been too busy to leave. Now she watches him pack for a weekend in the country, a party somewhere that he is attending alone. Through the hot weekend "a slow smouldering anger and resentment" begin in Missie. She wants to take Eddie away with her to the country. "The house was crushing her, the heat was driving her mad." But Missie has no money, only a little change left from household expenses. Not enough money. "She was his chattel, his creature. It was his house, his child, his wife, his carriage, his horses. A furious hatred began to shake her, and all that Sunday while Eddie slept she sat and rocked, backward and forward, her eyes sunken and her mouth set."[11]

Wesley returns and, a little drunk, begins to make advances. "She backed off. He was suddenly horrible to her, his mouth loose, his legs apart to steady himself."[12] Missie pushes him off, but he comes after her. Suddenly, with a gesture like a cat, Missie seizes a poker from the fireplace and strikes Wes with it. Sure that he is dead, Missie runs from the house. Out in the street, she sinks to the steps, trying to think. And then she hears him. He comes down the stairs slowly, slowly to the door. He bolts the door, disconnects the bell, and goes back to his room.

The next major section of the book deals with Missie's punishment. After a few days, finding Eddie spirited away and her house closed to her, she goes to Kirby. They spend one night together in a hotel, but Missie remains pathologically frightened of sexuality. Kirby realizes that this fear lies very deep in her, "that a thousand early inhibitions, temporarily repressed by her desperation, were fighting him. She 'wanted to be good.' She didn't want Eddie to be 'ashamed of her.'"[13] The next months are spent at Cecily's. Eventually a reconciliation is arranged, on Wesley's terms, and Missie returns to a loveless marriage and a child who is, at best, a good deal less wonderful than Missie believes.

Rinehart had, to this point, gone further in exploring the essential frustration and emptiness of many women's lives than ever before in her writing. But as the book moves toward its close, she wavers. Missie is not a wonderful character, but she is a character whom the reader can watch with interest and pity. Her life is a shambles. But Rinehart cannot leave things that way. She begins to give Missie a new philosophy, has her find meaning in life through sacrifice. Her reward comes when Wes is hurt in an automobile accident. Witnesses report that a woman, seen in the car with him, has disappeared. Missie hurries to the hospital and pretends that she was the woman in the car—all to protect Eddie's belief in his father. As a result of the accident Wes is paralyzed and Missie devotes herself to caring for him. Just before he dies, he and Missie come to understand that they do have feeling for one another, and that feeling Rinehart calls "love." Rinehart is on Missie's side at this point, but it is noteworthy that the other important characters in the novel have little patience with Missie's mourning.

By the end of the book, Missie is in her forties and World War I is just over. Eddie has married, Kirby has married, and Missie has nothing whatever. Even Harry Sloane is long dead, a victim of disease during the Spanish-American War. But Rinehart has one more blow. The thing Missie has most feared happens: Eddie finds out about Kirby. The impatient modern reader wishes nothing more than for Missie to slap her son's face and send him about his business. Instead she goes back to the little house where she grew up, climbs to the back room, and like her mother turns on the gas. But even suicide is not possible for the popular market. There is no gas, and Missie is left at the close of the novel with that discovery still ahead of her, the discovery of "the crowning irony of that gasless bracket." [14]

Rinehart believed *This Strange Adventure* to be her finest book, and in many ways it is. She had discovered new courage, though, in the end, inadequate to her task. As she wrote, she was alternately elated and depressed. Stan was excited about the first draft, writing to the boys that she had "a bully story, not black but rather gray in coloring, and different from anything she has previously written." Mary was less pleased: "The new book is not as good as [Alan] hopes. It is plotless; it might be made into a good book if I had the health and energy. . . . It is not a popular type. Indeed, it falls between two stools, it is not a critics book or the other thing." [15]

She sent the draft to Alan whose response Mary found "searching, candid, brilliant." They agreed that the story had to be carried up to a few years after the war, whatever cutting was necessary in other places. That was important because "naturally the post-war world is one [Missie] can never understand." Mary's letters to Alan sometimes make the characters clearer than does the novel itself—particularly Eddie, for the reader constantly sees him through Missie's adoring eyes. To Alan, Mary said: "One knows by [the end of the war] that the world is full of Eddies, not too good, not even too bad. It is only to her that he matters." She wrote as well that the further along she got, the closer to the modern world, the harder the story was for her, as it became "only a study of human relationships and of *tout passe*." [16]

The conclusion bothered Mary a great deal. "I wish I dared to kill her at the end," she wrote. "All that living and then futility. Well—" But the idea of the gasless jet seemed like a good solution, given the restrictions of her market. She told Alan, "It is ironic beyond words"; [17] still Mary knew that it was not, finally, enough.

Mary's own estimate had been correct; *This Strange Adventure* fell between two stools. It was her first important novel not to make the best-seller list, and the reviews were mixed. The *New York Tribune* and *The Nation* dismissed it as an antiquated period piece. Other critics objected to the "gray" cast to the novel. Having been castigated for excessive plot and for sentimentality in the past, Rinehart was now taken to task for the absence of plot and for the seriousness of her treatment. Mary's response to the reviews can only be conjectured, but in August she wrote from the Ranch to Alan and Gratia: "I am seriously considering the end of a career which has served its purpose and which I am now ready to abandon. If the financial part can be arranged I shall do it. Not a whine, but a resolve, this."[18]

Rinehart could not seriously consider giving up her writing for long. *This Strange Adventure* was only half her task. She had completed an exploration of her life as a woman, as a wife and mother, through the fiction of Missie. Now she had ahead of her the exploration of her life as a writer, and that, the less personal narrative, she would treat as autobiography.

She began to think about writing her life story for her sons—not for publication—as early as 1927, while she recuperated from her accident in Hawaii. It was on her mind while she worked on *This Strange Adventure*, recalling her childhood and sharing her memories with Missie Colfax. During 1927 and 1928 Mary found it possible to go more deeply into her own mind than ever before. In part she attributed that new ability to a Christian Science practitioner with whom she had worked for a while; those sessions, she wrote Alan, had "something to do with liberating the unconscious."[19]

Rinehart had known something about Freud's theories of the mind and the unconscious at least as early as 1906, for in *The Man in Lower 10* she jokes about sublimation and subliminal impulses.[20] Throughout her novels in the 1920s, especially in *The Breaking Point*, there are references to the unconscious mind or, as Rinehart usually referred to it, the subconscious mind. Letters to Alan, advising and encouraging him in his own writing, show that she had come to believe that it was important for a writer to unlock those parts of the mind that were more typically inaccessible. In one letter she suggested that he try writing in the first person: "It is fun to play with anyhow and sometimes it brings astonishing outpourings of latent things within the writer."[21]

That kind of process took place while Rinehart planned and wrote *My Story,* and during the time when she still intended the book for her sons alone, she experienced an especially creative freedom from the constraints of censorship. "So I began to remember," she writes.

> Around me was the house. All day it was very quiet. I would lie there and think about houses. The first little brick house, and Dicky dead in the bottom of his cage. Olive sick. . . . Other pictures of that little house; my mother is dressing for a euchre party. . . .
> And she is powdering her face. I am looking up at her, shocked and fascinated. I cannot see myself, but I must have been very small. She towers above me. Powder! Face powder![22]

So *My Story* began for Mary, almost like a series of analytic sessions, images of childhood, the reexperiencing of herself as little Mamie Roberts.

Rinehart does not make clear just when the story for her sons became a story for the public. In the second edition of *My Story* (1948), she says that in the summer of 1930 William Bigelow of *Good Housekeeping* sent Arthur McKeogh to Massachusetts to find Mary, who was vacationing there, and to read the manuscript that he had somehow heard about. He loved what he read and asked that his magazine have the first chance at publishing it. By July 16, 1930, Bigelow had sent Rinehart a check for $25,000, the first payment for *My Story*.

Serialization began in October, while Rinehart was still hard at work on the manuscript. She told McKeogh on the first of November that she had written 105,000 words and thought there would be 125,000 more. He could, of course, cut what he wanted to, particularly since the excised portions could be included in the book. As it turned out, *Good Housekeeping,* planning on seven installments, extended the serial into an eighth month and generously

This portrait, still stressing soft femininity, was chosen to promote *My Story* in 1931.

added $5,000 to the original payment of $45,000. Even with the extra installment, McKeogh had to cut about 200 pages of typescript.

McKeogh was careful to cut any passages that struck him as inappropriate for a mass audience. One such passage is referred to in a letter in late December; McKeogh wanted to excise "the incident of the atropine," because he could "see nothing but an injurious reaction." The editor and the public once again. Years later, in 1954, Mary wrote in an unpublished memoir the story of the atropine as it had occurred long before, in 1894 or 1895.

> I can tell here now, I think, of the mad and irrational thing I did in [the children's] ward on a quiet Sunday afternoon. I have no explanation for it, except for exhaustion and ragged nerves. Certainly I could not have meant to kill myself, although I almost did. But after putting a drop of atropine in one child's eyes I simply went to the medicine chest, got a small glass, poured the atropine in it and drank it.[23]

Mary collapsed in the hallway and for two or three days was unconscious but violent. No one on the staff knew what she had done and they classed the episode as a hysterical attack. Unable to understand her own motivation, Mary still considered the atropine incident sufficiently important to include in her autobiography, but even in the book version it did not appear.

Not all the omissions in *My Story* were McKeogh's. Rinehart explains in the book that she had written as honest an autobiography as she could. Some omissions and some evasions came as a conscious intention not to hurt the living; moreover, she had respected the dead. Rinehart also notes that if there are other places in which the truth is not accurately portrayed, it is because memory deceives: "Against the unpleasant and the horrid the mind has set up the defensive machinery of forgetfulness," and not all of "us can bear the truth, even about ourselves." In constructing the narrative of her life, even with the intention of concentrating on the public rather than the private life, Rinehart discovered that "there is no truly honest autobiography."[24]

Certainly she was right. Yet, she could come progressively closer to honesty, as she proved in two later autobiographical pieces, one in 1948 and the other in 1954. Only the first of these was published, as an extension of *My Story*; the other remained an unpublished draft among her papers. These later pieces were written with greater distance from people and events than the original *My Story* had been, and for that reason they provide, in some places, crucial comparisons with the earlier autobiography. Sometimes the comparisons reveal Rinehart's tact. Sometimes they reveal her sense of privacy about her personal life. And sometimes they show us that as Mary grew older she continued to gain insight and self-understanding.

The most difficult part of writing *My Story* was finding a way to handle her relationship with Stan and the question of his attitude toward her writing and her success. Almost nothing is said of the first years of their marriage, the years when Stan built his practice, Mary kept house, and the three boys were born. It was not possible for Mary to talk of her own feelings as a young woman that her life had ended at twenty, that she had chained herself permanently to the unromantic routines of housework and motherhood, without money or freedom or a career of her own. Some of that story—the bleakness of marriage as Mary had found it in the last part of the nineteenth century—is given to Missie.

But late in life, Rinehart did write about those years. She had married with the ignorance she came to recognize as typical of girls of her time. She felt, she recalled, "gratified ambition, yes, and delight in being cared for after the long hard years, and a great admiration for this strong young man whose wife I was."[25] But she did not feel love. Married life soon became a succession of chores; even with a maid the turn-of-the-century household was a considerable burden. And day after day, there was shopping to be done, meals to be prepared, ironing to attend to, the house to be maintained in perfect order. The Rineharts went nowhere; after dinner Stan had evening office·hours.

Money became an issue, of course, once Mary began to earn it. In *My Story* Rinehart refers a number of times to the question of money, pointing out that their standard of living changed with her success and that she did not intend to readjust that standard downward, although Stan had been brought up in an age when a man expected to support his family. Mary's insistence on using her money created considerable friction. She could not wait to buy the things she wanted for herself and her house. She had her eye on a $400 mahogany dining room set, and the *Man in Lower 10* paid for that. With further successes, she convinced Stan to move to Beech Street despite the extra fifteen dollars in monthly rent.[26]

She knew that she was willful and sometimes paid the price. In the later edition of *My Story* she tells the story of a diamond necklace. Mary had seen it at a jewelry shop "and was immediately carried away by it." Stan was not: "Why on earth would you want a thing like that?" Mary answered with a classic rhetorical question, "Why does any woman want a thing like that?" Stan preferred to see the money Mary earned invested in securities, and he did not intend to sell her stocks to purchase the diamond necklace. They discussed it a number of times, and "after several such talks the necklace itself ceased to matter." Mary made clear what did matter: "What I *did* want was to assert that the money my husband had so carefully invested for me was mine, after all." So she bought the necklace. Stan's comment was withering:

"I thought you had better sense." In 1937 Mary sold the diamonds, for a third of the original cost. "At last I had paid the price of that self-assertion of mine."[27]

My Story tells of a woman's escape from the restraints of a woman's life, an escape made through a career that had to be fought for not only in public but at home. The story of that struggle cannot be avoided, for it is the real story of Mary Roberts Rinehart's life. But the autobiography tells it cautiously and tactfully. Ironically, Mary and Stan grew closer as her work took her further and further from the sphere of domesticity. That closeness, in fact, was born out of Mary's freedom and even out of the battles she waged for that freedom. Missie's story, on the other hand, suggests what happens to women like Mary who never achieve freedom.

In 1948 Mary wrote again about her marriage and her career. Speaking of Stan's death and her widowhood, she remarked that "there is also some remorse" for those who survive.

> In my case it was more basic than that. He had disliked, not my work, but my career. He wanted a wife, not a more or less public figure. . . .
>
> I had done my best. Only in one room, wherever we lived, was there anything to indicate my profession. . . .
>
> In a way he was proud of my success, but he had resented its demands. And I have no doubt that I myself had given him only a divided allegiance. There were hours every working day when I was barely conscious of the world about me.[28]

Remorse notwithstanding, there was no other solution for women as far as Mary could see. The Missie's of the world threw their lives away. Other women squandered them in the vanity of social calls, parties, clothing. Nor was love, in itself, adequate substance for a woman's life. Toward the end of *My Story*, Rinehart wrote that she thought, as she grew older, that she had come to understand women "a little better": "They are quick to love and slow to forget, tragically, painfully slow. [I have] seen them holding on, hoping, praying, unable to believe that what was once so real, so passionate and so vehement is dead; unable to believe that men can forget what they cherish and remember."[29]

But in 1948 she was no longer so sure that, with whatever understanding she might have gained, she did not after all view women with considerable coldness and little sympathy. She had not, she felt, written well of women. "With one or two exceptions, such as Tish, my women were often dull and uninteresting. Only this past summer one of my daughters-in-law, having read my latest book, made a comment which has caused me to do some heart searching. 'You don't like women much, do you?' she said."[30] In fact, Rinehart's women are less often "dull and uninteresting" than they are, if "good women," pitiable, or, if "bad women," detestable. Mary parried her daughter-in-law's question, but in fact she had little interest in or sympathy for people whose lives were being lived without purpose, ambition, and some adventure.

Most of Rinehart's autobiography was, of course, devoted to the purpose, ambition, and adventure that had made up her own life. Narrative is much more prominent than self-examination. *My Story* is first of all the work of a powerful storyteller, not only because Rinehart had perfected her craft, but also because she had discovered a way to objectify her memories and experiences. She had started to plan the book by remembering the past and by becoming again little Mamie Roberts whose mother towered above her. By the time she came to write it, Mamie was a figure grown distant again, one in whom Mary felt "no great interest." "She seems to me now a rather namby-pamby little thing."[31]

But distance did not bring coldness, and the narrative is bright, sensitive, sometimes humorous and sometimes powerfully emotional. Certain episodes are particularly moving. From *Good Housekeeping,* McKeogh wrote of the effect on him of the passage about Stan, Jr.'s departure for the war. It made him recall the day his own mother packed his things and sent him off to the army—without a tear. "You mothers!" he wrote; "I'm crying! And the Doc and you won't *laugh*—will you, please?" McKeogh was not the only teary-eyed reader. At the Horseshoe Ranch in California, America's strong-jawed cowboy hero, William S. Hart, was having the same trouble. Reading *My Story,* he wrote Mary, had left him "a wobbly creature, dumb to the point of idiocy—fallin' over doormats 'n everything—too scared to even try to talk in Sioux." "Mike, the bullfinch," he admitted, "was my Waterloo—I busted right out—an' somehow—I was not ashamed of it."[32]

The episode of Mike the bullfinch had been an emotional one for Mary too. She loved birds, even hauling her parrot with her on the long train ride west each summer. Twice in *My Story* she refers to Dicky, the bird she had kept as a child that had died because her father neglected to feed it. Then, in June 1928, Mary "started into bed and stepped on the bullfinch who was hiding under the drapery of the couch, and he passed out with just one single tremor." As Stan wrote to Gratia, "Of course there was a storm of emotion. It was a great shock." She loved the bird, Stan thought, better than any living thing outside of the family, "and the thought of killing him herself was just about too much." Rinehart tells this story in her autobiography because she felt that writing it might relieve her of the painful memory, although

Mike's name had not been mentioned in the house for two years. "You see," she writes, "I killed him." Then Rinehart takes two pages to describe the tame bird and his ways—lighting on the heads of distinguished gentlemen and riding around the pool table on billiard balls. He had been, Mary confides, "my companion, my friend and my slave," and then, she repeats, "I killed him."[33]

The bullfinch was not, however, the only attraction of *My Story. Good Housekeeping* received hundreds of letters. People wrote "pouring out their very souls in personal confessions."[34] And many asked Rinehart for advice and for help with their own writing, for above all the other threads in *My Story* is the history of a woman—not a "new" woman, but a wife and a mother who had found through writing a way out of servitude.

The last pages of *My Story* turn to Rinehart's evaluation of herself as a woman and as a writer. The woman is seen, in the writer's posture, "sitting at the old Queen Anne desk on a not too comfortable Queen Anne chair, in a handsome study where some thirty-nine of her books are in a row in a corner, all bound alike in red leather." She has, says Rinehart, "an intense curiosity but rather a surface shrewdness of understanding than a deep comprehension." She is less "cocksure" than formerly, but just as "capable of a burning pity and compassion, and of indignation at injustice, but she is too much inclined to let other people do the reforming."[35]

The writer, optimistic and even buoyant, is found still trying to deal with that persistent problem of popular success and critical reputation. By 1929 and 1930 Mary was no longer the depressed woman she had been in 1925; no longer did the critical response to her work contribute to a "black melancholia." But the problem had not disappeared. With some bravado she announces in *My Story*, "Slowly the critical attitude toward my work had commenced to change." Her books were being used in schools and colleges; she had stormed the academic fortress and she had won.

> Only the other day . . . a Harvard man now teaching literature wrote me that he could teach structure and characterization from my stories better than from any others; that he believes I have done a grateful world a lot of good, and that I will have a place somewhere in the future histories of American literature!

Mary wanted that place badly. Did she believe she would earn it? "It is just possible. I still believe in miracles."[36]

Some five years before the publication of *My Story*, Mary had met Yale professor and critic William Lyon Phelps, and they began a correspondence.

Mary was immensely flattered by Phelps's admiration for her work, and Phelps's letters express something close to intoxication at Rinehart's celebrity as well as her personal charm. In 1926 he wrote, "Your letters are so really wonderful in their display of a mind and character so far above average I can only stand and admire." He confessed as well to suffering the same disquieting doubts about his criticism that she felt about her fiction. Then, in a sentence that Mary must have found perfectly simpatico, he added, "I have reached the conclusion that I must be content to stimulate the average mind and let the High Hats take care of themselves!" A year later, when Mary suggested that she send one of her manuscripts to him for his criticism, Phelps wrote back in astonishment: "To think that a writer of your fame and success should write such a letter to an old college professor is overwhelming. Indeed I should love to read anything of yours in MS—but what an idea!"[37]

But an "old college professor" was a wonderful kind of admirer as far as Mary was concerned, and Phelps's comment in the spring of 1929 that he had lectured on her new book in New Haven was certainly welcome news. "I was still no light of the world," she admitted in *My Story,* "but

Stan shortly before
his final illness.

university professors now and then wrote to me and encouraged me."[38]

All in all, as Rinehart wrote the final pages of her autobiography, she was filled with courage and optimism about her career. "I am singing no swan song. Sometimes I realize that I am just finishing my literary apprenticeship, and that soon I shall really start to write." As for those young men, those threatening realists, well, "perhaps I cannot compete with youth on the same terms. Not that it worries me, but there you are."[39]

Rinehart had earned that optimism in the months of writing her autobiography, for *My Story* is her finest work. In many ways it is her finest fiction —as well as the full realization of the Rinehart myth. The story of her life is shaped and structured in Mary's attempt to create a pattern and to find a meaning from the extraordinary welter of events and people that made up the first fifty-four years of her life. Unlike Missie's story, Mary's could bear the weight of that shaping. For Missie's life Rinehart could provide no meaning other than the late, and finally spurious, discovery of domestic affection. Mary's life, with its richness of purpose, discovered its own meaning.

As for the professors, they too admired *My Story*. In his own autobiography William Lyon Phelps commented that he found it "more thrilling than her mystery stories." Some years later, when the 1948 edition was published, word came from Harvard as well. The distinguished scholar of American literature, Howard Mumford Jones, wrote to Rinehart with a precious word of praise. He found in *My Story* "a simplicity and directness of writing that makes refreshing contrast to much of the pretentious aesthetic prose I have to read."[40]

My Story closes with a passage on Mary and Stan, who have grown together "like two branches of a tree." Their marriage, in which they "wrangle and argue and laugh," was built; "it did not happen. I do not believe that real marriage ever happens." Mary and Stan are alone, in the summer of 1930, on the coast of Massachusetts, the boys and their wives and children having returned to the city. They spend their time quietly, sometimes wading in a salt marsh.

> And one day we were marooned there. We had found the tide rushing out, and we had to wait for hours until it came creeping in. We did not mind, because we were together. But how slowly that tide came in! And with what incredible swiftness it flowed out again![41]

Only half a year after *My Story* was published, Stan would be dead.

11

Endings

1929–1932

IN THE SPRING OF 1929, at what seemed a very propitious time for business ventures of all kinds, the new publishing firm of Farrar and Rinehart was formed. Stan, Jr., and Ted went to Washington to announce the news that, with John Farrar, they were leaving Doubleday Doran to go into publishing on their own. It took Mary a little time to accustom herself to the changes in her sons' lives: "Everything had been fixed, apparently, everybody settled, so that at night after my custom I could picture them, permanent, established, safe. . . . And now it appeared that nothing had been settled at all."[1] Then, absorbing the news, she set about doing all she could—specifically, writing *The Door,* a mystery novel, for her sons' firm.

In letters to Stan, Jr., and Ted that spring, Mary spoke of progress on *The Door* and weighed the chances for F&R's success.

> I am never really worried over it. You three have ability, training, popularity and a reputation for fair dealing. You may have no big breaks this first year, but that does not matter. Actually, I think I am so anxious to make The Door a good seller that it has cut off my creative ability. But I will settle down soon and go abut my business as usual.[2]

Meanwhile, she reminded them that she wanted a first edition of every F&R book—charged to her account.

That spring F&R planned its first list, made up of eighteen books of considerable variety. Serious, substantial reading led the list: *The Peerless Leader,* Paxton Hibben's biography of William Jennings Bryan; *The Incredible Marquis,* Herbert Gorman's life of Alexandre Dumas; and the two-volume *Life and Letters of Stuart P. Sherman.* The classics were curiously represented by a Floyd Dell modernization of Robert Burton's *Anatomy of Melancholy,* the first in a promised series of new editions of classic texts. Also curious were books from important contemporary writers: Lizette Reese, the poet, provided a volume of prose reminiscences, while novelist Hervey Allen contributed a book of poems, in both a regular and a special edition (175 copies signed and numbered). Another deluxe item, also signed, was Du Bose Heyward's *The Half-Pint Flask*. The *Post*'s own *Alexander Botts: Earthworm Tractors*, by William Hazlett Upson, appeared in a collection. There were half a dozen works of fiction including a murder mystery and a collection of Mary Roberts Rinehart's short stories, called *The Romantics*.

Then, during the early summer, Farrar and Rinehart designed and distributed its first promotional piece, the first cannon in what they hoped would be a successful advertising campaign. As it turned out, that campaign was a masterpiece of ill-timing. A flyer, distributed in the summer of 1929, announced F&R to the world:

WE PROPHESY

That we have discovered the
Fall Book of 1929–1930
!

Simon and Schuster
made their bow with the Cross-Word Puzzle Books
The Viking Press
discovered a pastime with "Ask Me Another."
Farrar and Rinehart
believe that they have happened on a game that will
be played in every American house before Christmas.
SECRET
?

YES! We do not court imitations
This book will mean fun, sales and instruction.
With pencil—dealer's price 75¢, 80¢—or what have you?
Full Announcement August 15th

FREE copy to any dealer or clerk who hazards a guess (and a two cent stamp) on the idea of the new game, whether the guess is right or wrong![3]

The game, packaged as a book and complete with a gold pencil, was entitled *SPECULATION: The Wall Street Gamebook*. Published in October, the month of the stock-market crash, it was a spectacular failure.

Like many other affluent Americans, the Rineharts were slow to comprehend the seriousness of the economic situation. It was difficult to believe the financial spree of the 1920s had really ended, for their investments had soared and money was plentiful for all kinds of luxuries—for travel, early in 1929, to Useppa Island, off the west coast of Florida, where Mary took up tarpon fishing; for a motor launch in March ("We've just bought a 28-foot motor boat with cabins fore and aft, bunks for 4 to 6, galley, toilet, 6-60 engine, all the comforts of a tabloid home. . . . Cost $5150.00," wrote Stan. "Gosh, aren't we foolish?"[4]); and, in the summer, for a new wing on the Washington house—making twenty-two rooms. With construction underway Mary left for the Ranch.

The new wing included a study for Mary, an elegant room filled with books and mementoes. On a fine Queen Anne desk was arrayed the collection of items that had become part of her working inventory: a silver and crystal inkwell, a silver cigarette box, long scissors, and, in a crystal container, the straight pins with which her cut-and-pin revisions were done. A small silver figure of a piper stood near the inkwell. Only one item was still missing, the famous Parker Pen.[5]

Sportswoman with tarpon,
Useppa Island.

The Parker Pen arrived a year later. Kenneth Parker, company vice-president, had been reading *My Story* as it was serialized in *Good House-keeping.* In November 1930 he came across Rinehart's comments on writing by hand, dipping the pen and racing it across the yellow pages. As fast as her pen would go, Rinehart said, it could not keep up with her thoughts. Mr. Parker wrote a letter. His pen, he promised, would help to solve her difficulty. Just tell him what point she preferred, and "with my compliments and with the greatest of pleasure," he would send the pen. Stan wrote back that Mary was "a little skeptical," but that she preferred "a broad stub point, quite soft, one requiring no pressure of the hand, and about a medium size barrel." A week after Mary had received the pen, Stan wrote again. His wife was delighted. Furthermore, she discovered that she had customarily taken a breath each time she dipped her pen. Now, without the interruption of reaching for the inkwell, "every now and then she would find herself entirely breathless." In 1933 Rinehart wrote to Parker that she was "in daily fear" lest something happen to "the wonderful fountain pen." In 1939 Parker sent her two more pens, built specially to "duplicate the one you have and like so well."[6] Mary would write with those pens for the rest of her life.

Construction on the Washington house was nearly completed by the end of the summer of 1929, when Mary returned from the Ranch with a draft of *The Door,* to be published by Farrar and Rinehart after serialization in the *Post,* for which Lorimer paid $60,000. On October 31 Lorimer sent Mary an advance and the advice that she "make some money with it. I got in at the bottom of the break, low, wide, and handsome, and at the opening this morning the stuff I bought shows from ten to thirty points profit." The crash appeared to Mary, as to Lorimer, no more than "a temporary setback," perhaps even an opportunity. By the end of the year, though, the Rineharts began to feel the pinch in terms of cash on hand. Stan had been speculating on the wheat market, buying on margin, and those margins had to be covered. Depleted cash reserves, furthermore, made it hard to come up with the money to pay income taxes for the year.[7]

Mary responded to the financial emergency in exactly the way she had reacted in 1903, when the Rineharts found themselves $12,000 in debt, and in 1911, when she had overextended herself in the purchase and remodeling of the Sewickley house. She wrote. Around her she saw "people losing their homes and left bankrupt and ruined." And she saw and heard of suicides: "some, unable to face the situation, taking the easy way out, as so long ago my own father had done." In many ways Mary's whole adult life had been a preparation for such emergencies. She was not dependent; she could earn money. As often as she spoke of some future date when she would stop writing, or would write considerably less, it is clear that she would have been unable to stop working. And if, as she wrote, it appeared as if she would have to start writing again, there was never any greater incentive for her than the need to protect her family from financial catastrophe.[8]

It is not surprising, then, that during the long decade of the depression Rinehart wrote a substantial amount of fiction, nor that she turned back to the mystery novel, for which there was a large and ready market. She published five mystery novels during the 1930s, one long serious fiction *(The Doctor)*, enough short stories for two more Tish books and a collection called *Married People*, and over twenty nonfiction pieces on various subjects. The prices she earned for her serialized novels were remarkable, especially in the depressed market of the period. Magazines paid between $45,000 and $65,000 for her mysteries, depending on their length, and *Good Housekeeping* paid $75,000 to serialize *The Doctor*. She earned money as well from book royalties and movie sales. Her income during the 1930s averaged $100,000 a year. Thus, while the depression did not reduce Rinehart's earning power, it did have a profound effect on her work. The 1920s had been a decade of serious fiction for Rinehart. After 1930 she would write thirteen more novels, and eleven of these would be mysteries.

Early in 1930 Rinehart addressed the problems of depression America in two articles for *The Ladies' Home Journal*. She shared the rather general view that America had emerged from the war in 1919 to go on a ten-year binge. Now the party was over, but that was not altogether to be lamented. In May 1930 *The Ladies' Home Journal* published Rinehart's "The Chaotic Decade." The twenties, she wrote, had been a reaction to the war, an effort to "recapture the old thrill, the drama which is gone." Cocktails appeared, manners grew freer, a cult of sex developed. Moral reformers attempted to stem the tide, but they acted absurdly, trying to impose their reforms from without. Thus, prohibition made alcohol illegal but overlooked the drug trade. Proponents of censorship had been equally wrongheaded and ineffectual, said Rinehart, suddenly on the side of the realists: "Honest writers, writing for the adult mind, have been haled into court because their honesty might contribute to the forbidden knowledge of youth." Youth, she added, should not be forbidden knowledge.[9]

The article expresses views that, if not radical or "bohemian," were at least liberal and up-to-date. Then, as if recalling her editor and audience, Rinehart turned to the subject of women and manners. Charm had disappeared during the chaotic decade; now it was returning. And with charm came "the return of the feminine woman." Women will, Rinehart thought, "be relieved, be even happier," for the return of the feminine woman meant the return of "the strong man to protect her."[10]

It is difficult, perhaps impossible, to fit together the disjunct aspects of

"The Chaotic Decade," but they can probably be explained in terms of Rinehart's market and the audience of *The Ladies' Home Journal*. Rinehart's attitude toward the *Journal* at the time was ambivalent. Loring Schuler, the new editor, very much wanted her to write for him, and he was eager to print her nonfiction. Lorimer, by comparison, would print some of her articles but always preferred to have her fiction in his magazine. Rinehart enjoyed expressing her ideas for a large public (even a public made up predominantly of women); but, as Schuler's correspondence with Rinehart indicates, there were strong pressures to soften her ideas, "to give the customers some sugarcoated politics."[11]

Schuler's was a pedestrian mind. When he received the copy for "The Chaotic Decade," he wrote to Rinehart about the exciting "train of thought" her essay had set off for him. It could, he wrote, result "in a policy modification for the Journal and . . . very likely provide a new keynote for the whole of American living during the coming few years." It was not prohibition, censorship, or the education of America's youth that appealed to Schuler. It was charm. Charm had lost out in the twenties to "a highly militant, sophisticated minority" of women who turned their electricity on the innocent husbands of still-charming women and "won their men away from them." Charm was the keynote. Would Mary write an editorial on charm?[12]

Mary would and she wouldn't. There is, she wrote, "no editorial in the idea only of charm. There is, and I have almost finished, a very good editorial on the effect of fashion on manners." Schuler published that essay, "The Effect of Fashion on Manners," in October. Rinehart began with a historical overview, going back to the turn of the century and the rise of new fortunes leading to ostentation and vulgarity. The aftermath of the war had intensified these characteristics, but now the pendulum was beginning to swing in the other direction. Vulgar dress, she asserted, leads to vulgar manners, and "what seems probable is that bad dressing and bad manners led to bad art." America needs the return to idealism and romance, in dress and manners and art. "The average human being . . . must live only partly in reality, and partly in a world which he builds for himself." Rinehart predicted "a revival of romance in living, in literature, and in art."[13] For whatever combination of reasons—the confusion of the times or the pressure from Schuler—Mary had never written so senselessly.

A much more serious effort at understanding the depression, "A Woman Goes to Market," appeared in the *Post* in January 1931. In this piece Rinehart added her voice to the general plea for renewed confidence in the economic system: Americans must put their money back in circulation. "This depression will end very soon," she promised, particularly if people will "start buying and cease talking hard times." She had, moreover, seen

The rich and glamorous Rinehart in her furs.

harder times. Out of 146 million Americans only 2.5 million are unemployed, according to Rinehart's statistics. "To a woman who has seen men starving on the streets in preceding depressions, this is tragic but not fatal." Then Rinehart added to that brisk bit of comparative economics the information that she had "worked very hard in 1930" and earned some money, and that she had used that money—on stocks, some luxuries, mortgages—to get it back in circulation.[14]

The *Post* readers rebelled. Even Rinehart's candor in admitting how she too had lost her head in the excitement over the bull market of 1929 and in revealing that her father had committed suicide as a result of the 1893 panic did nothing to protect her from the fury of that audience. She received letters from men and women who had lost their jobs, their businesses, their homes. In fact, Rinehart was simply unequipped to comprehend either the economic situation or the measures devised to alleviate it. She had been brought up in a world of nineteenth-century self-reliance, and she had learned its lessons well. She had no patience with government interference, "a new angle to these recurrent depressions, and a dangerous one. When the American loses his self-reliance he has lost his birthright."[15]

Mary was not without compassion, but she was bewildered. In the 1948 edition of *My Story* she talks about a plan she worked out with the Washington police chief. Tickets were printed, each one "good for a substantial meal at one of a chain of restaurants, and each police officer to have one or more books in his pocket." Rinehart would pay for the meals. The recipients were to be the men who came through Washington on trains, on their way south looking for work. The plan failed and Rinehart could not understand why. In her world there was no reason to fear and avoid the police. Later, toward the end of 1931, when the hunger marchers arrived in the capital, Mary watched them from the side of the street. "A motley crew, of colored people and Jews," she wrote Alan. "They were daunted by the rigid police line, shoulder to shoulder, drawn around the building." And then an instinctual understanding of the meaning of the police for those men came to her: "I found myself pitying them against that terrible force of law and order."[16]

Pity did not, however, end her bafflement. The depression continually brought back memories of 1893 and of Tom Roberts's suicide in 1895. He had been a victim, too weak to survive the economic shock. Now Roosevelt's administration was aiding such men. But Mary did not come to the conclusion that her father might have been saved by government action; on the contrary, she continued to talk like a Social Darwinist, not precisely arguing that only the strong should survive, but certainly asserting that to struggle was to build character. In the mid-1930s she wrote to Adelaide Neall offering to do a satiric criticism of the New Deal; Adelaide sent back word that Lorimer was not interested and made the countersuggestion that Rinehart write her reminiscences of three depressions.

> [Write about] the experiences you had had under the American system, the improvement you had seen in the standard of living, the care and protection of the poor. . . . No one knows what would have happened during that first depression after your father's death if a paternalistic government had stepped in and not only made it easy for your mother to get help, but made it very difficult for her to do anything on her own to meet the problem.

Mary had, finally, a simple credo: "One worked and succeeded, one worked and got along, or perhaps one worked and failed. But always one worked."[17]

The depression was not a subject Rinehart explored very deeply in her fiction, although her mystery novels in the late 1930s frequently present characters who, once wealthy, are now saddled with the responsibilities of large houses and dependent servants. One exception is "The Tall Tree," which appeared in *Good Housekeeping* in 1935. Like *This Strange Adventure,* "The Tall Tree" is a very personal story, playing variations on themes from Mary's life.

Edith, the young heroine of the story, is a mother, a wife, and a successful writer. But it is the depression, and her husband Don is no longer able to support his family. Like Mary, Edith used to send the members of the family off on their various daily occupations and then settle down to work. Now Don has nowhere to go and Edith will not write with him at home. To the public Edith appears to be "a successful woman, a woman with a career, more than that a rich woman." In fact, with a sick child and a tormented husband, Edith is exhausted, frightened, unable to write. Money problems are exacerbated by Don's unwillingness to let Edith assume any of the financial burden.

The story reaches its climax when Don attempts suicide. Waiting to find out whether her husband will live, Edith despairs of "the thing they called success." She resolves never to write again. During the night, as Don falls into a safe sleep, she thinks of the bills to be paid; perhaps just one story would tide them over financially. By morning she is overcome by "an urge, an itch" to write. She goes to her desk and begins her story. Edith's story begins precisely as "The Tall Tree" had begun; she is writing her own story, for she has discovered its universal meaning:

> They were alone, the two of them, with their problem. All over the country these days were men and women facing the same thing, franti-

cally trying to adjust—the man to the loss of his pride, the woman to a double burden of home and work. The man suffered the most, perhaps; his pride of sex was greater, his tradition as the dominant factor more fixed.[18]

Although the long-term effect of the depression was to spur Rinehart to intense writing efforts and substantial production, the first months of the depression found her unable to write much fiction at all. *The Door* had been completed at the end of 1929 and *My Story* absorbed a good deal of Mary's time during 1930. Otherwise, she wrote articles, those for the *Journal* on fashion and charm, as well as others on topical subjects. Mary recalled 1930 as a year when fiction-writing seemed impossible: "Creation, so far as fiction was concerned, was definitely out that year. My world, the static world of the novelists, was going to pieces around me. I talked to other writers, to Joe Hergesheimer, to Kenneth Roberts, to Arthur Train and others. All of them felt as I did, empty and confused."[19]

But whatever frustrations Mary felt about fiction-writing in those months she kept from her son Alan who, deciding his sabbatical year had come, had given up publishing for full-time writing. Frequent letters to Alan sympathized with discouragement, discussed the need for personal isolation, and suggested technical exercises such as writing in the first person. Rinehart, who did not care to talk publicly about the task of writing—except to stress hard work and application—was a good deal more forthcoming in letters to Alan. In August she wrote about what she called "the creative well."

The creative well empties itself every so often. There is nothing in it. Chekov [*sic*] tears his hair and sits in the sun. Conrad writes his pitiful letters, re-reads his old stuff, calls in his friends to encourage him. And then, not as a result of any of this, but because the well has filled, each goes to work.[20]

Early in 1930 *Collier's* accepted a story of Alan's. Another, published a year later in *Liberty*, became the basis for a play, called *Volcano*. Then in the spring of 1931 Alan decided to try writing for the movies and, by April, he took a job with Paramount Studios.

At the same time, Rinehart's frustration over writing fiction and increasing alarm about the severity of the economic situation encouraged her to accept an offer from *The Ladies' Home Journal*. Schuler wanted a monthly page of editorial comment from her, at $2,500 a page. Stan wrote enthusiastically to Alan about the plan for "short and juicy comments on current events or any ideas that happen to occur to her," an assignment that allowed her to work productively when she did not have large blocks of time or large projects on hand. Stan was whimsical about his wife's work habits:

> This morning, for instance, she said that there was nothing for her to do because she was through with the autobiography; she is not ready to take up the article about the human side of the Presidency that she contracted for; and she wouldn't have to think about the dinner party we are giving tonight till late this afternoon, so she thought she would write a few editorials. Three exclamation points.

But by the second month the novelty had worn off and Mary was restive under Schuler's advice and constraints. As she wrote Alan, the editorials "sound like drivel to me"; the *Journal* "wants the first person singular smeared all over the page, which weakens it entirely."[21]

"Thoughts," as Rinehart's page was called, soon drove Mary to distraction. Part of the difficulty came from the fact that she worried constantly about deadlines. A more serious problem arose out of the difference of opinion between Rinehart and Schuler about what the editorials should contain. Mary had started off, in the May 1931 *Journal,* with some comparisons of women who were busy achieving goals with those who were simply busy from "activity." She went on to a discussion of the mystery story. In June she turned to bargain-counter divorces, some aspects of buying a house, and comments on the woman's responsibility to keep the home an interesting place for her husband and children to return to. In an attempt to bring more significance to the page, she wrote about the differences between premeditated crimes and "passionate" crimes, suggesting that the punishment for these should differ.

It was not long before Rinehart let Schuler know that she wanted to use the page for more serious topics than house-buying and homemaking. Schuler's reply presented "the magazine idea" with a vengeance: "Perhaps the subjects you have chosen so far have not been as big and internationally important as they might be, but the longer I stay in this business of editing the more I am impressed by the fact that what seem to you to be very unimportant details of life are tremendously important to the great mass of readers." Some readers, not many, will have an interest in international affairs, Schuler conceded. "But the interest will be greater if the information is camouflaged as gossip about men and things." In fact, a little coy name-dropping would be very effective: "If you can say, 'A famous diplomat said to me at dinner . . . .'" A few months later, he repeated this advice. He wanted anecdotes about famous people. "Work in more of your political and even your society friends—if you dare. Be indiscreet once in a while. It will make people talk."[22]

Mary labored on through the year, trying to find appropriate subjects.

She wrote about women who earned money and women who learned to be beautiful. She tried clothes several times, tactfully brought up the subject of "Birth Regulation," provided tips on holding a husband. Somewhat more topical were comments on cutting down expenses and, conversely, on spending money as an antidepression measure. In November, Schuler announced that the *Journal* would start a "great economic campaign" to "arouse women [to the] part they may play in ending the depression." He wanted Mary to use her page to participate in that campaign, especially to emphasize the need for living as usual, not hoarding, not succumbing to fear.[23] With that injunction, and with a presidential campaign in 1932, Rinehart was freer to turn her page to economic and political issues, but she was still unsatisfied.

Although Rinehart later judged her decision to assume the *Journal* responsibility a mistake, she kept on with the editorial page even when Schuler —citing economic conditions—reduced the price to $2,000. Finally, in April 1932, she did give it up, explaining that it left too little time for fiction, but in fact personal considerations were paramount—Stan was seriously ill.

Only a year before, Mary's recurrent ill health and pain had finally necessitated an operation to remove her gall bladder. When she heard her doctors' advice, Mary decided to undergo the operation almost immediately. Stan, Jr., wrote to tell Alan, adding, "I hate the prospect of it, though she was so very brave about it and pretends that it is nothing at all." Mary, too, wrote Alan: "I am not afraid, although I was a little shocked at first." She was sure that nothing would go wrong. "But anyhow I have had a grand life, and I am so rich in love that I am a multimillionaire!" She was not afraid of the outcome, though she added, "Frankly I do dread the pain later, and the long nausea."[24]

As it turned out, Mary was not to experience the long period of nausea that followed etherization. The doctors decided to give her a spinal anaesthetic, Stan reported to Alan and Gratia, even though they were aware of "the mental strain of an operation when a highly imaginative person knows exactly what's going on." Mary was conscious during the operation and Stan, as a doctor, was allowed in the operating room. At one point, when it appeared to him that the surgeon had made a critical error (he had not), his dangerous temper flared out. "I pretty nearly had a fit, having to go into the next room for a few minutes to get back my poise."[25]

Stan sent daily reports to all the children and, although there was considerable "discomfort," improvement continued. On June 10, ten days after the operation, Stan could report a comical incident. Mary had a new night nurse who was

a very solemn, matter-of-fact, big, fat woman, terribly impressed with her case and her responsibility, but pleasant withal. That night about one o'clock Mud was awakened by a slight explosive sound which it is altogether likely originated with her. All alert she called the nurse and insisted that there had been an explosion outside the room, that it was a signal from Scotland Yard, some deep mystery was afoot, the nurse must go and find out the cause.[26]

Until nearly five in the morning, Mary had her stolid night nurse playing Miss Pinkerton until she herself realized she had only been dreaming.

During her stay in the hospital, Mary received a visit from the staff psychiatrist, Dr. William A. White. He had noted the number of operations she had undergone and, when he came to her room, observed, "I've been wondering just what you are escaping from." Rinehart tells the story in the 1948 edition of her autobiography:

> "Escaping?" I said feebly.
> "Of course," he said. "All these operations. What do they mean? Do you dislike your work?"
> "Now look," I said, sitting up and glaring at him. "I *had* gallstones. I saw them myself. Don't tell me I could manufacture gallstones in order to stop."
> "Of course you could," he said placidly.
> I have often wondered if he was right.[27]

That summer in Massachusetts, while Mary recuperated from her operation, it became apparent that Stan's health was deteriorating rapidly. His arthritic condition had worsened and he was easily fatigued. By the end of the summer, Mary persuaded him to go to New York to see a specialist. The first reports were encouraging enough for Mary to leave Stan in New York with Stan, Jr., and Ted in order to go to the Homestead in Hot Springs, Virginia, to begin work on a new story.

Mary stayed at the Homestead, working on the new mystery, *Miss Pinkerton,* featuring nurse Hilda Adams, forgotten since "The Buckled Bag" and "Locked Doors" in 1914. She worked very successfully in what she described to Stan as "this loneliness and silence." She took a treatment of massages, bought her fall clothes, and wrote. She hoped that the *Post* would buy the serial for $30,000. "I think I can get forty elsewhere," she wrote Stan, "but I want the Post audience. It is good business and has largely put me where I am." In fact, the Boss paid Mary $50,000 but insisted that *Miss Pinkerton* be lengthened to six installments. By early October, Mary had written 60,000 words of the novel, spurred to that extraordinary energy by "the general situation," which, as she wrote to Alan, made her "depressed and anxious . . . and of course that sends me to my desk!" The work was better for Mary than the rest cure; she felt she "had taken a new lease on life." "But yesterday, going downstairs between pages, so to speak, I watched the market going down and down; so I rushed up and wrote the Forum article, not even going down again for dinner. It's funny, or it ought to be."[28]

Mary returned to Washington to find that Stan's health had not improved. Nevertheless, he had made up his mind to travel to the coast before Christmas to spend time with Alan, Gratia, and their two daughters, Topsy and Patsy. By now, Mary had become convinced that economic worries were contributing to her husband's ill health. Stan had insisted on covering his market losses with his own money, using none of Mary's. He returned from California "to a pretty tragic state of affairs" financially. "But," Mary wrote to Alan, "we have fixed it up once and for all." As her Christmas gift, Mary gave Stan the money to support his remaining stocks. "A little prosperity now," she observed, "will help his health as well."[29]

Christmas time was gay enough. The Rineharts attended the vice-president's annual dinner for the Hoovers and Mary assisted Mrs. Hoover one afternoon at tea. Stan and Mary gave their own party the day after Christmas, in Stan's terms a "boozle party, called by poetic license a tea." The family, save Alan's, was in Washington—Stan, Jr., with his children, Bab and George; Ted with his wife, the former Elizabeth Sherwood. Plans were made for a special surprise for Stan. Mary explained to Alan that she had bought a "folding bar with a brass rail. . . . When folded it looks like a small table." On Christmas morning, according to plans, "while we are at breakfast, the men are to place it, with pewter ice-bowl, pitcher, bottles and so on, behind the doors of the music room, in the library. Then when we go into the music room to look at the tree, the doors are to slide back, showing Reyes [the Rineharts' chef] in white coat mixing a drink behind the bar!" Stan, Mary was sure, had no idea of the surprise, "although he catches me chuckling now and then."[30]

At the end of the year, the family doctor advised Mary that Stan was improving, although he would need care and would have to avoid exertion. Reassured, Mary planned her own trip to California in January 1932, while Stan and Stan, Jr., went fishing together at Useppa. Then on the day she was to leave for the coast, Mary learned that Stan was "hopelessly ill."[31] The doctors did not want him told of his condition, and it was necessary that plans go on as arranged. When Mary returned from California, she thought Stan looked better, that the fishing had been good for him, so the two of them went almost directly back to Florida.

They stayed at Useppa until late in April, but even in Florida Mary could see that Stan was failing. The doctors now advised a trip to Germany, to try for some kind of cure in Baden-Baden. There were a few days of confusion and indecision. Mary was concerned about commitments she had made to magazines, particularly to the *Journal*. But Stan could not go alone. Briefly, they considered sending Alan with his father, for in the early part of the year Alan had lost his job at Paramount and was now thinking about coming back east. Within a day or two, Mary decided to go with Stan, and it was then she wrote to Schuler finally giving up the editorial page.

The crossing was dreadful. Writing from Heidelberg, Mary told the boys that Stan seemed to have "lost ground very fast." He was too weak even to sit up in bed and his weight had dropped from 175 pounds to 150. He had been so desperately sick on the ship that Mary feared he would die: "It has sure been hell, but what a blessing that he cannot remember it."[32] They remained in Heidelberg a little over a week until Stan was strong enough to be moved to Baden-Baden.

From Baden-Baden, Mary reported that the doctor was hopeful, not of a cure, but at least of "real relief." If Stan could spend his winters in a climate like that of Egypt, the doctor thought he might live many years. For several weeks Stan was pretty much confined to his bed; and even after he gained some strength, he continued to suffer attacks, some from arthritis, some Mary suspected from the medication.

Mary spent her time, she said, "sitting around . . . playing anagrams or doing cross-word puzzles" and getting "horribly fat." Stan, well enough to write one of his comical letters early in June, reported on Mary's German: "Mud does marvels and is a constant source of wonder to me. She has no verbs and ignores them utterly. A staccato word now and then uttered with smiling assurance brings results. How they know what she means is entirely beyond me, for even her occasional words bear no resemblance to those of any living language."[33]

Mary had some time as well to observe the condition of Germany. Brenner's Stephanie, the famous hotel-spa where they were staying, was nearly deserted. Unemployment was at a critical state: "Riding along the roads one saw groups of men and girls trudging from town to town hunting work or even food." These migrants slept at night in "roofed shelters without walls built by the wayside."[34]

Mary and Stan returned to the United States on July 6 and, after Stan made a brief visit to a Washington hospital to see his own doctors, the Rineharts went on to the Adirondacks, where Stan, Jr., and Ted had rented vacation cottages for the family. There Stan maintained a regimen of morning rest and expressed his impatience by firing the nurses hired to care for him. One lasted four days; the next, six. Although Mary thought Stan's general condition was improving, the attacks he was subject to continued, and each left him weaker.

On the last day of July, Stan collapsed and was taken to a hospital in Utica. To reporters asking about his condition, Mary at first spoke of improvement. The attending doctor, however, said his patient was "not so good," and by August 4 Mary called Stan's condition critical. By the eighth, he was strong enough to be taken back to Washington in a special car attached to a New York Central train. All three boys had been visiting with their parents, and the whole family returned together to Washington. The family doctor told reporters that Stan had stood the trip very well and was "well on the road to recovery."[35]

Nevertheless, once back in Washington, "it was over," as Mary wrote much later; "he knew it, and I knew it, but we never mentioned it." They both kept up the pretense: Mary washing her eyes to erase the evidence of tears; Stan pretending not to notice that they remained red and swollen. Occasionally, he was well enough to go downtown; then the weakness would return. For a long time he kept up his good spirits, at least for his sons. Alan was in Bermuda, and late in the summer Stan dictated a letter to him: "If you have any vision of my lying on a bed racked with pain and gasping . . . you've got me all wrong. I have just come back from an automobile ride through the smiling country and I am sitting here in my big chair with a book in my hand and have just had a cocktail of citrate of potash."[36]

Stan died on October 28, 1932; all the family was with him. As she had with her mother, Mary found his struggle for breath unendurable and wished for death to come. "Hours after it was all over I went into his room. He was alone, and after an old habit I sat down on the bed and took his hand. Only now there was no response, as there always had been before. I think it was then for the first time that I realized he had gone." The burial for Major Stanley M. Rinehart took place at Arlington National Cemetery, "the bugle sounding taps, and then the rifles firing."[37]

Mary had been married for thirty-six years when Stan died. Their marriage was not a conventional one, certainly not by the standards of the late nineteenth century. It had begun conventionally enough, but Mary never looked back with nostalgia to those days on Western Avenue—days consumed with housework and child care. After Mary Roberts Rinehart became a successful novelist and playwright, she and her husband both knew that the structure of their marriage had been permanently altered. Mary was a famous woman, a public person, and a highly paid professional writer.

The results of Mary's success altered almost every aspect of her relationship with Stan. When she earned thirty or forty dollars a story, the checks that arrived could be seen merely as extra pin money. But by the time her stories sold for thousands and her serials for tens of thousands of dollars, the pin-money fiction was exploded. It would be her income from then on that paid for the houses, cars, vacations, and luxuries the Rineharts enjoyed. Money is power and there were years when the sale of two of Mary's short stories more than equalled Stan's salary.

Nor was money the only issue. Mary was famous. She was interviewed; she was asked to speak at public functions; she was sent to report on significant events. For all Mary's insistence that her family came first, she had commitments that took her from her family, and she insisted on the freedom to come and go as her profession demanded.

Isolation, too, was essential for the writer. Sometimes that isolation was physical; the writer simply went away. At other times it was psychological. Mary entered her own world, engrossed, entirely preoccupied in her writing. Although she spoke frequently about the slamming of the door as the signal for work to stop, her family grew to understand that when mother was writing she was not to be disturbed—or more accurately, could not be disturbed. In an unpublished reminiscence, Alan described his mother at work:

> She concentrated. With doors open, children playing, phone ringing—and later, with servants and lawn mower rattling about their business, she could be lost in her fictional world. She was never unapproachable, anyone could at least try to interrupt her. I remember a couple of occasions when I wandered into her study while she was writing. One of these times I asked her if I could go out with some other boys and she smiled sweetly and said, "Four honors in my hand." So I went out, knowing I would not be missed.[38]

But in addition to freedom and privacy, Mary wanted her family, although the conflicting demands of her career and her marriage were not always resolvable—not even, as she frequently claimed, by harder and harder work. Occasionally, however, Mary did let it be known that she felt marriage to be an impediment and that she believed only the rare, exceptional woman could manage both roles. In 1931 *Forum* published "The Future of Marriage: A Socratic Dialogue," a discussion among four married women with professions. In the article Mary explained that there are three kinds of women. Most are marrying women, content with husband, home, and children. A few have no flair whatsoever for marriage; they have "masculine minds" and are happiest as career women. "A third type of woman, usually one of acute mentality, is a very extreme individualist, who would like to be the wife, the mother, and the individual at the same time." Mary went on to explain that the third type of woman "doesn't want to do without her chains, but resents them because she feels a capacity for doing something which marriage and its resultant factors have prevented."[39] The use of the word "chains" is remarkable, not only for the overtones of enslavement, but because the idea of marriage as a ball and chain has always been a masculine metaphor.

For Mary the chains were the natural result of marriage *for women,* the burdens and duties that prevent the expression of individualism. Mary went on in the article to explain that she did resent the chains of marriage but that she could not wish to be free of them. "I am saying this with a good deal of feeling, because undoubtedly I belong to the third group. I wouldn't give up my chains for anything in the world, but I would never fail to recognize that they are chains." At that point one of the other women interjected the comment that Mrs. Rinehart was "very clever." No, said Mary, "I am not clever at all. I have had a long time to live."[40]

Mary still had a long time to live ahead of her. She would live as a widow for a quarter of a century. It was a different kind of life, but Mary learned to live it. She wrote in the 1948 edition of *My Story:* "The shared life is gone. Hereafter you walk alone, but you do walk."[41] She had her grief to deal with, the shock of loss. For almost a year she traveled to one place or another about the country. Early in 1933 Ted took her to Florida. She spent the summer at Eaton's Ranch. At Christmas she was in Palm Springs, without the family for the first time, but awaiting the arrival—early in the new year—of old *Post* friends Lorimer and Sam Blythe.

And she worked. A mystery novel, *The Album,* began serialization in the *Post* in April 1933. In September the *Journal* published the first installment of *The State Vs. Elinor Norton.* It was work, after all, that she had come to believe in. It was her credo:

One worked and succeeded, one worked and got along, or perhaps one worked and failed. But always one worked.

12

The Writer

1933–1939

IN THE YEAR FOLLOWING STAN'S DEATH, Mary wrote almost obsessively, and she wrote well. In 1933 she published two novels, *The Album* and *The State Vs. Elinor Norton*. *The Album,* a mystery story, was well received, the critics generally reflecting the public's delight at another detective yarn from the hand of a master. Isaac Anderson, then the mystery-novel reviewer for the *Times* "Book Review," closed his piece with a pleasant compliment: "To paraphrase the Kentucky Colonel's dictum about whiskey, all Mary Roberts Rinehart mystery stories are good, but this one is better."[1]

The State Vs. Elinor Norton, despite its title, is not a mystery novel, although it does combine the story of an unsolved murder with the major plot elements of romance. It is a curious novel, almost a rewriting and combining of *Lost Ecstasy,* with its setting on a western ranch, and *This Strange Adventure,* with its unhappily married heroine driven to violence. Elinor Norton, from a wealthy society family, is pressured into marriage with a weak playboy, a man who disintegrates altogether after the war, perhaps even into sexual impotence. The Nortons try life on a ranch and it is not long before Blair Leighton, a brutal adventurer attracted to Elinor, buys into a partnership with Norton and joins them in the lonely farmhouse. Norton is shot—as we later learn, by Leighton, who subsequently lives on with Elinor at the ranch. Eventually Leighton seduces her and, sexually satisfied, postpones again and again the marriage he had promised. Then, like a retake of the scene in *This Strange Adventure,* Elinor, discovering her drunken lover embracing the house maid, recoils into violence.

> And it was then that he made his final, bungling error. He turned around and stumbled toward her. "Darling!" he said thickly, and held out his arms to her.
>
> He was not more than four feet from her when she raised the gun. "Don't come any closer! Don't touch me! . . . *Don't touch me!*" she screamed. And when he still came on she fired. She saw him sag to

his knees and drop. More, to begin that slow and terrible roll of his down the stairs. . . . Then she raised the gun to her own head, and the girl snatched it from her.[2]

Again the critics were enthusiastic, and the praise for the book must have pleased Rinehart greatly. The *Times* headline ran, "Mrs. Rinehart Writes a Realistic Novel," and the long review closed with the assertion that *The State Vs. Elinor Norton* "is a definite contribution to serious American literature." Fairly highbrow magazines, while making less extravagant claims, were also congratulatory. The *North American Review* called it "an exceedingly well-managed piece of story telling," and Willian Rose Benét, for the *Saturday Review of Literature,* noted that the novel has "its limitations," but Rinehart "tells a good story."[3]

Telling a good story had, by 1933, brought Mary Roberts Rinehart to a special position in the esteem of the public. To say that she was a best-selling author is to understate the case. She wrote more best-selling novels than any other American writer and wrote them over a longer period than almost any other American writer. In a study compiled by Irving Harlow Hart in the late 1940s, of the one hundred best-selling novelists from 1895 to 1944, Rinehart came out on the very top.[4]

But to the American public Mary Roberts Rinehart was a great deal more than a teller of good stories. She was admired and she was loved. Her opinions were sought in interviews and articles. Her life story, her life style, her values held significance. Public-opinion polls registered the admiration. Her fan mail, ranging from the laudatory to the confessional, reflected the love.[5]

What were the sources of that appeal? It is not difficult to see how Rinehart's life in the adventurous years of the war and in the world of high government and high society in the Washington of the 1920s could provide vicarious glamour for the public, certainly the female public. But the 1930s found many of Rinehart's readers caught in frightening social and economic changes. From a superficial viewpoint it seems incredible that they could maintain affection for and trust in a woman, by then near sixty, whose photographs in newspapers and magazines showed her untouched by the national calamity. In those pictures Rinehart remains exquisitely clothed and coiffed, invulnerably youthful and attractive.

It is possible, of course, that Rinehart's success and glamour—like those qualities in so many movies of the period—depended on the public's need to believe in the possibility of success, to escape from the grim daily life of depression America. But beyond that general symbolism Mary Roberts Rinehart had a direct and personal and unique appeal.

Fundamental to Rinehart's relationship with her public was her respect for it. Her novels and stories may seem at times evasive to contemporary readers or too easily resolved into satisfactorily moral happy endings, but very seldom does one have the impression that Rinehart saw them that way. For all the sophisticated experiences she had undergone, she probably kept a sense of moral values very close to that of her readers. She was not talking down to them, not even when she shaped her fiction to provide the escape she believed they needed. On the other hand, she had come to recognize the need to outflank her magazine editors, those guardians of public morality and corporate profits who stood between the writer and the reader, intercepting and distorting messages they did not approve of.

Stan had often said—and sometimes Mary had echoed him—that to write for the public was to write for the average twelve-year-old. Mary probably did not really think so, but for all her success, she—and her sons—continued to respect Stan as the family intellectual, and, if he said that about the public, his wife might sometimes have suspected that he was right, whatever the unspoken implications about her own success. Mary did not see herself as intellectual or clever. To echo the marriage discussion printed in *Forum,* she believed merely that she had lived a long time, earning some wisdom from experience.

Some combination of wisdom, moral conservatism, and a firm sense of reality—especially about women's lives—made itself felt in her serious fiction. Her novels and stories communicated a double message: Life is hard; there is some hope. Such a message, moreover, was not coldly conceived as a slogan to seduce the public; it was precisely what she believed. Like all profoundly successful, long-term masters of the popular culture—like George Horace Lorimer, for one—Rinehart was in her profoundest beliefs and values a part of that culture. That was what she and her readers shared.

The concluding lines of the 1948 edition of *My Story* touch on this sense of intimacy, even dialogue, between Rinehart and her readers. If, as she says, she knows she "must never fail them," it is because they have not failed her: "They are kind, even affectionate. Quite often in their letters they call me Mary, as though they had known me for a very long time." And then as a final paragraph, "As perhaps indeed they have."[6]

That sense of being admired and loved was a powerful stimulant and, along with work and travel, helped Mary over the difficult period of transition after Stan's death. She kept herself very busy for a time, but before long she returned to writing fiction that tested once again her hold over her public.

Early in 1933 she was looking around for some new excitement, even suggesting, fruitlessly, to Lorimer that he send her to Manchuria to report on the Japanese invasion. Then in the fall Mary suffered the first of a series of coronaries. She was back in Washington when she experienced violent chest pains and intense cold. She managed to get herself to her bed and then lost consciousness. Alan, who had moved his family back to Washington after his father's death, found her there, by circumstances mysterious enough to seem to substantiate Mary's own half-certain belief in the supernatural. As he tells the story, he felt a powerful compulsion, at one in the morning, to leave his home and walk to the house on Massachusetts Avenue. There he found his mother, nearly without a pulse, and it was he who called the doctor and, no doubt, saved her life.[7]

Mary was well enough the following spring to take a North Cape cruise. Her companion was a wealthy Washington friend, Evalyn Walsh McLean. Mrs. McLean owned the famous Hope Diamond and she wore it constantly, defying the curse associated with the stone. Mary was not entirely skeptical about the curse: Mrs. McLean had "lost her eldest son, killed by an automobile; and her husband, Ned McLean, was hopelessly insane." A decade after the cruise, "her only daughter committed suicide in her early twenties," and Mary wondered then if Mrs. McLean would put the diamond away. "But she did not. She wore it defiantly until her death."[8]

The family had welcomed the idea of the cruise as both a change and a rest for Mary, assuming, somewhat naïvely, that she would remain in her cabin whenever the ship stopped at port. Mary, those tamer expectations notwithstanding, saw the cruise as a chance to visit Russia. But at Stockholm secret Soviet police came on board to ask if she planned to write about their country, and, if so, whether she would let them see what she had written. Rinehart demurred; she had no definite plans about writing, and the interview ended with no assurances from the Soviet government that she would be permitted to land in Russia. But by the time the ship arrived there, the Soviets had decided to let Mary into the country and to accord her red-carpet treatment.

To Mary's eyes Russia was a police state pure and simple, where "there had been no communism . . . after the first sorry attempt." What appalled her was the poverty, in startling contrast to the Lincoln cars provided for her transportation and the hotel suite prepared for her in Moscow—"with a bath which did not work." The condition of the bath was matched, in Mary's view, with the condition of Russia as a whole: "Poverty and neglect were everywhere."[9]

No friend of socialism, let alone of communism, Mary did discover some meaning in the Revolution when she visited the Kremlin and saw the artifacts of czarism.

But when in the museum there I saw the diamond-covered Bibles, the jeweled capes and miters, and in the palaces the magnificence of such rooms as the one completely done in lapis lazuli; when in the royal stables I saw harness and even the wheels of carriages set with gems, I began to understand at least the Kerensky revolution about czarism.

Still, seventeen years had passed since the Revolution, and Mary wrote, "I had expected something better in Moscow than I found there."[10]

Interviewed on her return to the United States in August 1934, Rinehart told the press that three days in Russia had been "long enough to convince me that the present regime there is built up from peasant life. It may take generations for them to replace the intelligent people who once influenced and guided Russian life." A longer report came in a piece for *Cosmopolitan* in December, "Looking for the Magic Word." There was, Rinehart said, no magic word, not communism, nor fascism, nor Hitlerism, nor socialism. As for Russia itself, she wrote, "The experiment in pure Communism had come to an end. What is left is merely a harsh and brutal bureaucracy, a denial of all liberty, and a government running all business and doing it very badly." Staunchly maintaining her creed of work, she told the readers of *Cosmopolitan*, "One difference between ourselves and the rest of the world is that here the employed do *not* go hungry." Moreover, "the great majority of us are still employed."[11]

And the unemployed? Mary simply did not comprehend the extent of America's problem. She did not believe in the depth of poverty of millions of Americans in those years; she could not conceive it. In the 1948 *My Story* she admitted the existence of poverty in America. "But," she said, "we have no real rags, no naked children, no actual starvation." She was, of course, wrong; there was much of America she no longer understood. What she did understand, because she had lived it, was succeeding:

> I yield to no one in my desire to see men and women bettering their condition: that is America. But I do not see why being born below the tracks gives anyone the advantage or even privileges over those born on the other side. It has always been our great pride that people could cross the tracks without having any odium attached to them. In a non-social sense I had done precisely that myself.

Mary Roberts had been born in the year of Custer's Last Stand. In most ways she had grown and matured with the country. But she was the intellectual child of Herbert Spencer and she would remain a Social Darwinist all her life. "The only difference between success and failure," she wrote to Alan, "is industry."[12]

Mary was, by this time, at work on an ambitious new novel, but even hard work could not distract her from her loneliness. Alan and Gratia had returned to the West Coast, and in January, Mary wrote to them that she had just about decided to move to a small apartment in New York, where she could be with the family. Stan, Jr., had remarried, and he and his second wife Frances (Fay) Yeatman had a baby son, Stanley Marshall Rinehart III. There were also Bab and George, growing up now, and Ted and Betty's daughter, Cornelia (Connie).

Typically, Mary made her decision and acted on it with dispatch. By February 25, 1935, one moving van left Massachusetts Avenue with furniture to be distributed among the children, and on March 4 the large move of six vans took place. Those six vans took Mary's belongings to the not-so-small apartment at 630 Park Avenue, on the corner of Sixty-sixth Street. But, while the new apartment was large and elegant, it was difficult to break up the Washington house—"rather heart breaking,"[13] in Mary's words. But the move was right for her, establishing a new kind of world, surrounded by family, away from a house that had, like the one in Sewickley, become too empty.

In New York, Mary resumed work on her new novel *The Doctor.* In its way it was a memorial to Stan—the story of Dr. Chris Arden, of his professional and personal misadventures and sufferings that end, at last, in the achievement of his ambitions and desires. To some extent, and partly because of the medical background of the novel, *The Doctor* is reminiscent of *"K"*; nevertheless, there are important differences, especially in the absence of any spurious mystery and in the unwavering focus on the character of Chris.

The book opens when Chris enters private practice. A struggling young general practitioner, he takes rooms with the Walters family. The Walters are not at all like Sidney Page and her mother, with whom *"K"* had boarded. They are lazy, slatternly, and ignorant, a set of spongers for whom Chris grows to feel increasingly, if incomprehensibly, responsible. In that setting he meets Beverly Lewis, who brings her ailing dog to his dispensary—Rinehart's wry comment on the vicissitudes of general practice for the young doctor.

He and Beverly fall in love, but soon Chris finds himself the bitter opponent of her father, the local steel tycoon. Lewis refuses to improve the housing conditions of his workers, and as a result the annual typhoid epidemics devastate the working-class population, their homes seen here as Rinehart had found them in the Pittsburgh of the 1890s—crowded, filthy, without adequate sanitation. Doctoring the typhoid victims, Chris develops a profound disgust for Beverly's father, and that antagonism, reciprocated by Lewis, keeps the lovers apart.

Much of Stan's early career is rehearsed in Chris's story. Like Stan he becomes a county health officer, with a clinic for the poor. Like Stan he becomes a surgeon. Mary's own experiences as a nurse, however, are not—as they were in "*K*"—lent to a young woman of character and compassion, but to Katie Walters, and Katie cannot make the grade. She has, in fact, made her decision to enter the hospital only as a way of keeping close to Chris and, in the end, she is not allowed to complete her training. Eventually, both Chris and Beverly marry badly. He takes Katie out of pity and a free-floating sense of responsibility. Beverly marries a man of her own class, another of Rinehart's weak playboys. When war is declared, Beverly's husband joins up as an aviator, but after the war, unable to settle down, he becomes an alcoholic and kills himself doing stunts in a plane while drunk. Chris's own loveless marriage disintegrates at the same time, for Katie becomes a spender, running with the fast new crowd of the twenties, compelling Chris to ever more frantic work to support her excesses.

The crisis comes when Katie, driving recklessly fast, crashes. She is unhurt, but Chris suffers a broken arm, his nerves severed. Apparently no longer able to work as a surgeon, he goes to the country, living alone, brooding, drinking. In Rinehart's implacable morality, Chris must find his way back from despair to self-control and self-respect, and he must find it alone. Soon Katie obtains a divorce and Beverly feels free to come to him, but his trial by ordeal has not ended and he sends her away. Finally, and only after hundreds of pages, a phone call from the city informs him that Beverly is seriously ill with a perforated ulcer, about to undergo surgery, and he rushes to her side. On the final pages of the novel, resolution occurs and the long-awaited happy ending. Chris and Beverly will marry and Chris will operate again.

Reviews of *The Doctor* were mixed. The *New Republic*, hardly on the list of Rinehart fans, found it "not integrated," but remarked on the way in which it was written—"from a composure more interesting than the author's former assurance." *Time* thought it "a hearty moral tale," at least to "an uncritical eye"; however, it "shades almost imperceptibly away from real life." *Time* added that "by the standards of her school her sympathies are keen," and it is worth noting that Rinehart's "school," whatever that was, was clearly not the school of what *Time* considered to be "modern" American fiction. The *New York Times* was generous: "The book impresses the reader as having been written not as a matter of business but because Mrs. Rinehart wanted intensely to write it." A real snarl came from the *Saturday Review of Literature*, where Logan Clendening wrote that "there is simply nothing in this book to review"; he found it a "mess of cloying sentimentality."[14]

The reviewers were, overall, more favorable to *The Doctor* than they had been to *This Strange Adventure*, and the public shared that judgment. But *The Doctor* is a much less daring novel, and in too many ways it suffers from the qualities we have come to classify as those of soap operas—the "good"characters, those with self-control, compassion, dedication, made to suffer extraordinary deprivations for extraordinary periods of time. Rinehart speaks often in *The Doctor* of "decency," and she seems to be telling her audience that decency depends on the ability to endure—to take it. Other than endurance life offers work. When Chris has his work taken away from him, it seems nothing more than the irony of some sardonic fate. Again, there is only endurance. Curiously, the good characters, Chris and Beverly, do nothing to earn their bad fortune; nor do they do anything to struggle against it. And curiously, too, despite the happy ending, *The Doctor* does not seem to say that suffering endured will, someday, result in happiness achieved, for there is no cause-and-effect relationship between the suffering of the major characters and their final good fortune. The moral of *The Doctor* is grimmer than the happy ending indicates: Man is to work hard and to live decently, but he is not to do so with the expectation of earning happiness. The relationship between a moral life and a happy life remains oblique. What Rinehart says, after all, is not that her characters have earned their happiness, but that they have—through endurance—demonstrated their fitness for the inexplicable blessing of happiness.

Mary sold *The Doctor* to *Good Housekeeping*. Lorimer got wind of the new serial and Adelaide wrote in March of 1935 asking if Mary were "absolutely, irretrievably, unbreakably and fatally pledged to give the story elsewhere."[15] Apparently she was or, at any rate, must have known the Boss would not meet *Good Houskeeping*'s offer of $75,000, the largest amount Mary ever received for a serial. Moreover, although William F. Bigelow and Arthur McKeogh advanced some criticisms and suggestions, they were not prepared to insist on them, and Mary had her way.

The issue was Katie. Never before had Rinehart so carefully and realistically developed the psychology of a "bad" character. Nor had she ever placed one so fully center stage. McKeogh's job was to transmit to Rinehart Editor Bigelow's criticism, his distinct uneasiness about this bad woman, but the issue eventually grew significant enough for Bigelow himself to write, arguing that Katie "had in her great possibilities for development in a fine womanly way. . . . I feel that any person who develops strongly in wickedness—I mean who is adept at being bad—could have developed just as strongly in the other direction." Trying another tack, he argued that Chris looked weak in regard to Katie, for he demonstrated a lack of ability to take Katie and make a real woman of her. Mary stuck to her guns and the *Good Housekeeping* staff capitulated: "You have chosen not to develop her in that way, and I do not propose to quarrel with you." They wanted the story; the letter closed. How much?[16]

Lorimer was never so weak-kneed. The *Post* and its audience were his, and he maintained an iron hand over the materials that went into each weekly issue. In December 1934 he turned down "The Tall Tree," Mary's depression story of the woman writer and her out-of-work husband. Adelaide was given the job of reporting the news to Mary: "You have done a fine job of showing the mental workings of the unemployed husband, but it is just because you have made his despair so convincing and the wife's position so really hopeless that we feel it is not a depression time story for a publication that reaches the general public as we do."[17] *Good Housekeeping* printed "The Tall Tree" and paid $4,000 for it.

"The Tall Tree" was not the only piece of serious, even somber, short fiction that Rinehart wrote during these years. She did a number of such stories, all of them exploring the condition of marriage. They are strong and honest, certainly the finest of her serious short fiction. Collected by F&R as *Married People* (1937), they constitute Rinehart's mature and deeply considered ideas about men and women living their lives together, and at their darkest they reveal the deepening range of her imagination.

More than anything she wrote, with the exception of *This Strange Adventure*, the stories in *Married People* give credence to Rinehart's statement, "In my heart I had always been a realist." Of course, the "magazine idea" was still there. Rinehart knew what would and what would not be acceptable, and by the middle thirties she had found a method for saying what she believed and satisfying her editors at the same time. Her method consisted of developing realistic characters and placing them in unhappy, disruptive situations that threatened their marriages and, for the women, their self-esteem; but the sugar around the pill, in the favorite cliché of the *Journal*'s Schuler, came in the endings, nearly always conventional, affirming once again popular moral values. In the words of the *Times* reviewer, the stories "seem a little too sweet, a little unreal in their uniformly happy endings." Stephen Vincent and Rosemary Benét knew better. In an interview with Rinehart for the *New York Herald Tribune* in 1941, they closed with an evaluation of Rinehart's work and pointed out that among her writings were "occasionally, disquieting short stories, which show what her gifts might have been, under other stars, as a realist."[18] But Rinehart had worked out her compromise, the method by which she played the game.

The earliest of the marriage stories is "The Better Man," published in 1932. The protagonist, as in all the stories, is a middle-aged (fortyish) married woman. Here, she faces the problem of convincing her married daughter to return to her husband, and that is a particularly difficult problem for this mother since she had once run off herself. She tells her daughter that flight had been an error and her return the right choice. But the reader learns more about "the anguish of that final decision of hers to go back" to her husband, "of that last attempt at escape of a woman past her youth . . . [who] had loved only once, with all that was in her, and that the man was not Anita's father."[19]

"The Better Man" presents some hard truths about marriage as Rinehart understood it. The mother tells her daughter: "I suppose the real fact [about women] is that we all want different things at different ages. Even different husbands!" She adds, "You'll be attracted by a dozen men in the years to come." And she warns her: "We can't go on building up and then tearing down. There has to come a time when we can't build any more. We are too old, or too tired."[20] What she does not tell her daughter is that the punishment may also be too severe: The last words of the story let the reader know that for five years this woman's husband had refused to make love to her.

"Experiment in Youth" takes a lighter tone. Allison Bryce, forty-three, is seen first at her son's wedding. She looks young, though at one hundred forty pounds she is nothing like the young bride and bridesmaids who, with "thirty feet of intestines somewhere . . . looked as though a single hard-boiled egg would have made a bump in them." Her husband Harry begins to go youthful, dieting, dancing, and one night even kissing a young red-headed girl. In response Allison takes herself off to Europe for a "cure"—diet, massage, and exercise. Under that regime she loses weight, gains color, seems to drop some years, and attracts the attention of a Mr. Armstrong, thirty-eight, who asks her to divorce her husband and marry him. In terror Allison flees Europe. But Armstrong pursues her with a cable opened by Harry. "Darling," it reads, "I can't stand it any longer. Sailing next week." This is Harry's comeuppance and, in Rinehart's moralistic summation, "they had passed the inevitable milestone of middle age, and now were together again."[21]

Another tale of the married woman's revenge is "Lightning Never Strikes Twice," a strong story published in the *Post* in 1936, the last year of Lorimer's editorship. Camilla Rossiter, again a woman in her early forties, is married to a pompous bully who has dominated her all of her life. She eats onion soup because Jay likes it—and grows ill each time. She has the cook prepare the roast blood rare for him—though the sight of it nauseates her. As their son puts it, his father is "Complacent . . . Good-looking. Prosperous. Smug. Center of the world." Then he sees tears in his mother's eyes and understands that with these words he is "tearing down something she had built up over quite a number of years"—her image of her husband and their relationship.[22] So she continues, her own desires notwithstanding, to wear her hair long and buy only light blue dresses.

One evening Jay announces to Camilla that he wants a divorce, and he sets off for the country and a young widow, a member of the fast-riding, hard-drinking set. So much activity exhausts him, but he assumes a spurious youth and masculinity. In fact, he is an ass, and Rinehart enjoys telling us so. As for Camilla, she remains stunned for some time. Repeating an image from a letter to Stan a few years earlier when they had quarreled, Rinehart says that Camilla "could have lost a leg . . . and missed it less."[23] At last, with her children's urging and support, Camilla goes to Reno and gets a divorce. She even meets an attractive man there, who propositions her—unsuccessfully— but remains on the scene as a suitor for marriage.

When Camilla returns home, hair cut, in dresses other than blue, she finds that she is learning to lead a life of her own. Jay comes to see her one day and the effect is disturbing, but what she learns is that while the visit "brought an upsurge of memories . . . she did not love him any more." Yet, in another familiar Rinehart image, "the chains were still there." A second visit, made in his hope of reconciliation, follows. To a reader of Rinehart stories, the ending is a surprise, for Camilla drives Jay out of the house and out of her life. She has come to love "her dearly-bought peace, her small comforts." She sees Jay with clarity, as "pompous and arrogant and incredibly naive." "I thought I missed you," she tells him. "[But] I'm very happy without you. Happier than I ever was with you."[24]

Certainly, the story is vengeful: A woman learns to live without the man who has so badly bullied and mistreated her. But at the same time it is simply, oddly buoyant, with a resilience that comes from self-discovery and independence. To be sure, independence is headiest for a woman freeing herself from a pompous fool like Jay Rossiter. But what about independence altogether? What about life as a widow?

Mary remained a single woman. The closest she probably came to remarrying was to try it out imaginatively, by writing "The Second Marriage": "[Lilian] had had ten years of loneliness, ten years of frantic searching by the people she knew for an odd man to take her in to dinner, ten years of sitting down to lonely meals in her own house and of resisting the temptation to order a tray and eat in a comfortable dressing gown somewhere upstairs." Nevertheless, Lilian did not remarry in haste, insisting, "I'm so comfortable as I am."[25]

Lilian's acceptance of Warren comes in large part because he agrees to move into her house, a house she and her maid Matilda love and lovingly tend: "Each chair had its place, each vase." At the heart of the house is Lilian's bedroom and her bed with its apricot silk curtains. Each night she would (like Mary) read in bed till drowsy, "a soft protecting film of cream on her face and a clean towel over her pillow."[26] Warren's entry into the house is not unlike Sherman's march to the sea, with Matilda as Atlanta. His furniture has been moved into the bedroom; Lilian's things transferred to the guest room. And the very first night there is trouble with that bedroom.

Warren can't sleep with the light on; Lilian can't sleep without reading first. She ends up in the guest room, back with her apricot silk curtains, and stays there. The situation remains difficult, but amiable, until Warren brings a dog home. Matilda, defending the fortress, poisons the puppy and Warren leaves in a rage. Lilian fires Matilda and returns to her old ordered life—and finds it intolerable.

"The Second Marriage" moves on to a happy ending, but it also has a clear enough answer to any questions about a second marriage for Mary. Lilian eventually agrees to move to the country with Warren, and while joyful that their marriage will continue, she knows what the move means—"that the compromise was to be hers, that she was to live his life and not her own." For Lilian Barstow that compromise is well worth it: "She loved and was still loved. She was not alone."27 For Mary Roberts Rinehart life held other compensations.

Besides work and family some of those compensations lay in the life Mary was arranging for herself. By any standards she was making a great deal of money, but at the same time she was, as Stan had always noted, a spender. She was also a generous woman, especially with her family. Family, in this case, included not only her sons and their wives and children, but her aunts, especially Tish whom she helped out for years, and her sister Olive Roberts Barton, who wrote a syndicated column and published children's books with Houghton Mifflin.

With the money she earned, Mary wanted to surround herself with amenities and with luxuries. On the cruise to the North Cape, she had stopped in England, where she bought some fine antique furniture, notably a number of Chippendale and Sheraton chairs. Late in 1934 Mary bought herself a second-hand Rolls Royce, a gray ("pearl essence") cabriolet.28 She purchased some paintings, too, a Reynolds, a Lawrence, a Gainsborough, and had a portrait of herself done by the famous illustrator, Howard Chandler Christie. She liked jewelry, and those who met her late in life recall a woman wearing a rather astonishing amount of it. She continued to have many of her clothes made for her, and her working uniform, for those hours at her desk, was one of a number of tailored suits from Bergdorf-Goodman.

But what Mary liked best to buy was houses, and she would buy one more. In the summer of 1935, her damaged heart no longer able to tolerate the thin mountain air of Wyoming, she went to Bar Harbor, Maine, an elegant summer resort where she had a number of friends. She rented a cottage that summer and the following year leased a house. In 1937 Mary bought her own house at Bar Harbor. "Far View," in that depression year, was available at "an absurdly low price," but, like the Sewickley house, it turned out to need a good deal of rebuilding. "My early estimates doubled, then trebled." When the work was completed, Mary once more had a magnificent house of her own—seven acres, a view of the ocean, a stable "to hold any number of the horses I could no longer afford or even ride."[29] Built around an open court, the house was large, gracious, sun filled.

The summer population of Bar Harbor combined famous artists, like conductor Walter Damrosch, and equally famous millionaires, like Atwater Kent—whose income at that time was estimated at $20 million a year. Atwater Kent was a lavishly generous man himself. To Mary's astonishment, and some discomfort, he presented her with a Cadillac for one of her birthdays. At a dinner party one evening, he commented, "That old Rolls-Royce of yours is just about through, isn't it?" Mary said that the motor was fine, but he persisted: "I would like to give you a Cadillac," adding: "I have given several away. I like the car." Not long after, the Cadillac arrived.

Mary and the boys (Stan, Ted, and Alan) at the country club in Bar Harbor.

I was considerably embarrassed, but what was I to do? The car was beautiful, even to a rug with my monogram on it. There was no turning back a gift so lavish. . . .

I still have it [in 1948], but my ribald family has always called it My Sin, after—I hope—a perfume of that name![30]

Mary loved the life at Bar Harbor. It combined the social distinction of Washington with the opportunity to work. And if the cost had, as usual, exceeded her expectations and her pocketbook, there was the customary solution: "It had always been my policy to earn what I bought, and this meant going to work again." But, as Rinehart added, Far View meant more to her than an expensive house: "It meant a new interest in life, a new home."[31] Life had taken on a pattern once again. Part of each winter was spent at Useppa and the summer at Bar Harbor. For the rest of each year there was New York and the family and work.

Mary's health had appeared to stabilize, although she was forced to curtail some activities because of her heart condition. Then, suddenly, in 1936 she faced a new and more profound terror. She was at Useppa with Stan and Fay when she found that she had developed a lump on her breast. Mary had long feared cancer; she had at times believed that the suffering from her gall bladder was attributable to a malignancy. Now she acted with resolution and speed, returning immediately to New York and entering the hospital for a biopsy. The lump was malignant and a radical mastectomy was performed.

Nine years later Rinehart did a courageous thing that was, in its way, a tribute to her intimacy with her public. In those days breast cancer was not an open subject, nor were mastectomies. But Mary knew that women, from compounded fear and shame, died needlessly of cancers that, left too long, metastasized. In just such a way had Gratia Houghton Rinehart died in 1939, a little over a year after she and Alan had divorced. So, in 1946, the National Cancer Foundation learned that Rinehart would permit an interview with Gretta Palmer on the subject of her operation for breast cancer. The interview, "I Had Cancer," was published in *The Ladies' Home Journal* in July 1947. It is a review of Mary's life, familiar enough material, but it includes a plea for women to face up to the possibility of cancer, to have breast examinations, and to undergo a mastectomy if necessary. In the 1948 edition of *My Story*, Rinehart noted: "No other article or piece of fiction ever had so enormous a public reaction. So perhaps I have done some good, as I had hoped."[32]

Rinehart maintained her role as a public person even in these quieter years. In 1934 she was asked to be a member of the Conference on Crime—the only woman on a committee of twenty-one men. At least once, and possibly twice, she was offered an ambassadorship. Certainly one such offer had come before 1932, from her good friend Herbert Hoover. According to George H. Doran, in his autobiography, *Chronicles of Barrabas,* "in one [presidential] administration she declined ambassadorial appointment (the first tender of this rank to any American woman), feeling that she could be of greater service to her country outside of official position."[33]

As for real adventures, however, these remained only for Tish, and in 1936 and 1937 Rinehart wrote four more Tish stories for the *Post.* Two of these stories, "Strange Journey" and "Tish Marches On," take off from one of Mary's own, much tamer, experiences, her attendance at the coronation of George VI in May 1937.

The abdication of Edward VII had been the news story of the year and had been treated as the love story of the century. Mary had met Edward once, briefly, during the war. She found him "small and unimpressive." Now she was "outraged" by his abdication, by his decision to let sentimentality overcome responsibility in what was already clearly a chaotic world.[34] Even at the coronation, with all its splendor and pomp, Mary's feelings remained a curious mixture of resentment toward Edward and wonder at the British people who could summon up that pomp while the threat of Hitler spread over the continent. It was strange, too, for Mary to see the dowager queen and to remember the much younger woman she had met nearly a quarter of a century earlier, a queen who amused herself by trying on the gigantic slippers made by some patriotic English woman for a soldier in the trenches of France.

Preparing for her visit to England, Mary had written to an old friend, General Pershing. He too would attend the coronation, but only because the president had asked him to. Still, he acceded that the pageantry might be worth seeing even if, like all royal functions, it had its barbarous elements. The two planned to have lunch together at the Ritz, where Pershing was staying since, as he explained, King George was footing the bill.[35]

Mary sailed to England with her personal maid, Margaret Muckian, and the two found rooms in Berkeley Square. The accommodations were not ideal; in fact, Margaret had only a curved couch to sleep on. On coronation day, Mary arose at 4:00 A.M. in order to arrive by 5:00 at the stand set up at Westminster Abbey. Stan and Fay were there, too, and all were burdened by the day's essentials: "food, cameras, liquor, rugs, fur coats." The pageantry was indeed splendid, but the long day was cold and wet—and sometimes amusing. "Some of the nobility waited until seven [P.M.] for their cars, and the sight of them, sitting on the Abbey steps in their finery and holding their coronets, was pure comic opera."[36]

In London, Mary spent time visiting. Pershing did host a luncheon for twenty-four at the Ritz, and Mary "was pleased and surprised to be his honor guest!" "He's a dear old boy," she added. One day, with two American

An illustration for "Tish Goes to Jail" (1936), one of the last of the Tish stories published. The artist, May Wilson Preston, gave the original watercolor to Rinehart.

women, she visited Penshurst Castle and had tea "with a naughty old lord." The old lord, hearing that his visitor was a novelist, asked if her books were "*very* sexy." When Mary replied that she did not write about sex, he ignored her entirely. The castle was old and famous, with a minstrel's gallery and Queen Elizabeth's own clavier. American Mary wrote home that it must surely have "five hundred rooms. Queen Elizabeth lived there, and it has not been cleaned since." There was a chance as well to see the MacDonalds and recall the days they had spent together in Vienna, now twenty-seven years in the past. The MacDonalds had a "huge cocktail party" for Mary, with the chief commissioner of police, a former lord mayor of London, "a sprinkle of nobility, a soupcon of common people like ourselves."[37]

Tish goes to the coronation too, in "Strange Journey," although she travels via less conventional transport. Nephew Charlie Sands has his own plans to attend, as a journalist, and Tish is furious to be left behind. She nurses her wounded feelings and remarks in Mary's voice: "I begin to feel my age, Lizzie. . . . With life consisting only of taxes, and government a racket, I long for a desert island and peace." In that mood Tish talks her two pals into sailing off in a dirigible in pursuit of sharks! Eventually they lasso a torpedo which tows them along until they are conveniently dropped onto the ship carrying Charlie to England. From Southampton to London is a simple matter; Tish steals a car. "As to wrecking the car, who would have believed that the English drive on the left side of the road?"[38] Tish finally gets to the coronation. "Tish Marches On" continues the adventures of the lunatic threesome in London; and while the police search for them (in the interest of the owner of the dirigible), they pursue some young reporters they are convinced are thieves intent on stealing the crown jewels.

"Tish Marches On" was published in the *Post* on November 20, 1937, just a month before Lorimer's retirement. He wrote to Mary earlier that month expressing his delight in getting Tish in time for "one of the few remaining numbers that will appear under my name as editor of the The Saturday Evening Post." The *Post* would never be the same magazine without George Horace Lorimer. As Rinehart recalled him in the 1948 edition of *My Story*, "he was a reader's editor, rather than a writer's. He knew what his audience wanted and he gave it to them. He was kind, but he could also be ruthless. I once saw him turn down some stories by Rudyard Kipling with the brief comment: 'Not good enough!' "[39]

With an appropriate, if bitter, irony, "Tish Marches On" turned out to be the last Tish story ever published. Mary wrote another, but the new *Post*, at that time under the editorship of Wesley Winans Stout, turned it down. That was in 1941, and again it was Adelaide who was given the nasty job of writing to Mary. Mary was kind in her reply, for Adelaide was an old and very dear friend, but she was angry: "I am sure it hurt you to write me about Tish, and I more or less understand the situation. . . . It is possible too, in spite of the mail demand here, that as you say a new generation is coming along which would not understand her." The *Post* had decided that Tish was outdated, and perhaps she was. She had captivated audiences for almost thirty years, but when Tish first appeared women wore skirts to the floor, kept their hair uncut, and limited their lives to husband and children, their fantasies to fiction. Still, Adelaide's—or Stout's—criticism had wounded: "[it] struck me as a little biassed." The Lorimer days were over and Mary felt deeply that Stout was responsible for the turndown. "I suppose the difference lies between Lorimer's understanding of farce humor and Mr. Stout's." But Adelaide had reported that the editorial staff concurred with Stout's judgment; well then, Mary supposed, "It is because of the long hiatus and a young group who have not followed Tish." And no doubt, "the world is in so grave a mood that even humor seems out of place."[40]

No stronger signal could have sounded the end of the old days with the *Post*; it ominously suggested a rejection of Rinehart herself. This was a bitter realization, for as late as 1937 it had been said that Tish would remain her finest achievement: "Mrs. Rinehart has a large number of books to her credit," wrote a reviewer for the *Boston Evening Transcript*, "but it is to be doubted if, when the final judgment is made, her serious volumes, such as 'The Doctor,' will weigh as much as a straw against the not always so naive adventures of Tish." For Rinehart there was also the particularly irritating fact that *Arsenic and Old Lace* was a smash hit, and she was absolutely right in telling Adelaide that *Arsenic and Old Lace* was "definitely founded on the Tish idea, elderberry wine and all." And then, with her customary generosity of spirit, "Anyhow I understand fully, and this goes to you as always with my dearest love."[41]

The new *Post*, however, continued to want Rinehart's mysteries. In 1938 Stout paid $65,000 to serialize *The Wall*. The story is set at Sunset House, part of the summer colony of what is clearly Bar Harbor, and it is narrated by the typical Rinehart young woman, twenty-nine-year-old Marcia Lloyd, who provides the romantic interest as well. *The Wall* is an exemplary Rinehart mystery, one that fulfills absolutely the structure she had worked out and articulated for her mystery novels.

Mystery novels, Rinehart believed, depend upon "the buried story," a theory she explained a number of times, perhaps earliest in her first monthly page for *The Ladies' Home Journal*, in May 1931. There she said that, after she had written three mysteries, she discovered that she had a formula, one dependent upon the buried story, "the real tale of what has led to the crime." The buried story is never written, it is only worked out by Rinehart;

what the reader finds in the book is "the surface story." Rinehart diagrammed this formula as shown in figure 1. At every point where the buried

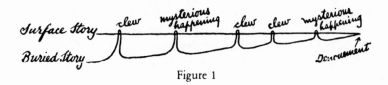

Figure 1

story emerges, "outcroppings" in Rinehart's term, there are two alternatives: The outcropping may provide a real clue, or it may simply be "a device for continuing the interest."[42]

The result of the two stories in a mystery novel, however, is a practically insoluble technical problem. As every reader of mystery novels knows, the solution must be held until the last possible moment. But with two stories, one solution must precede the other. Rinehart continually attempted to find a new method for the ending, but admitted that "it is rather difficult. . . . it consists in explaining as much as possible of the buried story before the discovery of the criminal's identity."[43] It was still a problem, however, to avoid an anticlimax, and it should be remembered that, since nearly all of Rinehart's mysteries also develop a love interest, a third ending was necessary as well.

What Rinehart never did point out, or perhaps did not consciously recognize, was that her buried story is almost always—after the very early years of her career—the story of a disastrous marriage. And in almost every case the marriage is disastrous because it crosses class lines. *The Wall* is an excellent example. The surface story deals with the murder of Juliette Ransom Lloyd, the ex-wife of Marcia's brother Arthur. Juliette, in her summers at Sunset House, had provoked affairs with all the married men in the novel. In the atmosphere of terror and mutual suspicion following the discovery of Juliette's body, Marcia mets Allen Pell, who appears to be a poor young painter; and he assists her in her sleuthing, although he too will fall under suspicion.

A recent addition to the summer colony is the Dean family; an older couple from Chicago, they have come east to help Mrs. Dean forget the suicide of her daughter. The hearty Manfred Dean is the soul of generosity and comfort to his neurotically dispirited wife, who, it is important to note, had been previously married.

As the novel reaches its denouement, we learn that Juliette Ransom, the young beauty Arthur Lloyd had married and learned to loathe, was born Julia Bates, a pretty, if vulgar, young thing, of no family and no quality. She ran off from a little midwestern town with a salesman of sporting goods. The salesman, in a coincidence that is less offensive in the novel than in this discussion, is the golf pro at the summer resort. But worse is to come. Allen Pell we discover is none other than (Allen) Langdon Page, another of Juliette's intoxicated lovers. He had been engaged to Emily Forrester but, at a country club dance on Long Island, had drunk too much, left Emily behind, and taken off with Juliette. She drove his car, drunk, and killed a man. Pell/Page took the blame and went to jail. Emily committed suicide—and Emily was the daughter of Agnes Dean's first marriage.

As Julia Bates's past emerges, motive piles on motive. There is virtually no one on the island who would not wish to see her dead. In that way, of course, the complexity of coincidence helped Rinehart in holding off to the very end the identity of the murderer.

In another mystery novel, *The Great Mistake* (1940), a young man is victimized by a bad marriage, and a buried story of marriages and liaisons emerges, so complicated that, unraveled, it provides strong implications of incest. Rinehart is no way emphasizes this, but the facts are clear: One major character has an affair with his daughter-in-law; a young woman begins a flirtation with a man who turns out to be her half brother. These undertones of incest are notable because, through the confusions of parenthood in the novel, we are returned to that universal childhood fantasy which so fascinated Rinehart in her earliest writing—Whose child am I?

Finally, both the buried and the surface stories of Rinehart's mystery novels reveal her continuing ambivalence toward the rich. At least as early as *Dangerous Days* she had shown her contempt for the idle women of the leisure class. By the late thirties and early forties, she had transferred that contempt to a new kind of parasitic woman, the female adventurer, the attractive nobody who makes her way by exploiting her sexuality. These women come from nowhere (usually the Middle West qualifies as a generalized "nowhere"); they are lazy and greedy; their tastes run to the glass-and-chromium modern of the thirties. Unscrupulous and vulgar, these young women baffle the more genteel ladies they come in contact with, but they get their way, take the men they want, and bleed other people for what they can.

Against the adventurers are set such young women as Patricia Abbott, the narrator of *The Great Mistake*; an orphan and poor, she must work for a living, although she comes from the finest of old families. According to the conventions of fiction, Pat will not (like Mary Roberts Rinehart) make her own way in life, but she will earn the love of a man wealthy enough to support her in fine style.

The married women of these novels fall into two categories. There are those who are too rich, too idle. Then there are those who, still well-off—or perhaps a little down at the heels due to the depression—continue to maintain propriety, duty, and fine houses. These are almost invariably older women—Mrs. Pendexter, salty, outspoken, aristocratic, of *The Wall,* or Maud Wainwright, independent, unpretentious, and courageous, of *The Great Mistake.*

Mary's own female friends, with an occasional exception like Adelaide Neall, were wealthy women, sometimes enormously wealthy women, whose style she admired, but who sometimes amused her. There is a story that one of these friends phoned Mary at Bar Harbor to ask advice on how to give a simple picnic. Mary proposed a menu—cold chicken, a macaroni salad—and tactfully suggested that butlers and footmen need not be in attendance. Fascinated by such arcane information, the other woman asked Mary to hold on while she got a pencil and wrote down the instructions. In *The Wall* one of the families in the colony gives an island picnic, "or what they called a picnic; that is, [they] ate on the ground, but there were men to serve the cocktails and the food."[44]

On the other hand, Mary was perfectly aware that social democracy would not wash at Bar Harbor. Very early one season, one of her grandsons came for a stay of some ten days. There was little to do, but one evening a bridge game was arranged at the home of one of "Granmary's" friends. The stakes were a quarter of a cent a point, but Granmary advised that there was no need to worry as her friends were dreadful bridge players. During the game someone rang for water, and a few minutes later Mary's grandson saw an astonishingly lovely girl carry in a tray. As soon as possible, he made himself the dummy and found his way to the kitchen where he arranged a date with the maid for her next night out.

On the way home Granmary was informed. "You cannot," she said coldly, "do this; you absolutely cannot." Growing, as she said, "a little excited," she went to her room, instructing her grandson to come see her later. At that time he was told, "Not only can you not do this, but if you insist on doing it, you are going to have to call the butler and ask his permission to take the parlormaid out on a date." Moreover, he would have to ask the girl's sister, also a maid for the summer, to accompany them as a chaperone. Not easily abashed, her grandson did as he was told and reported back to Granmary that it was all fixed up; what should he do now? Replied Granmary: "Get out of my sight."[45]

But if Mary now lived among the wealthy and shared their picnics and their bridge games, she was not of them. Idleness was an impossibility. Work remained what life was, essentially, all about. In 1939 the *Post* published an article of Rinehart's called "Writing Is Work." Like many of her articles, it reviews the by now well-known stories of her early career, stories that were firmly established as part of the Rinehart myth. But there is new material as well, especially about the way in which Rinehart worked at her novels.

In the earliest days, she recalled, "I could get an idea while making a cake, write it in the afternoon, get it typed—I had a little Jewish girl who lived around the corner for that—and send the story off the next day."[46] Now, writing *The Wall*, the pattern was quite different. She made notes for fourteen months, working out first the buried, then the surface story. After the notes, she wrote—in longhand—three versions of the novel; some parts, in fact, were written four or even five times. The writing itself took five months, working between seven and nine hours a day. There was, at last, a total of 375,000 words. Publication was planned for about 120,000, and Adelaide came to Bar Harbor to work with Mary on the cutting.

As Mary grew older, and suffered more from her bad heart, it was necessary to spend more and more time in bed. She preferred to write at her desk; if she had to return to bed in the afternoon, she would make her notes there. Her general routine, however, was simply to get to her desk as soon as possible in the morning. In "Writing Is Work," she explained that "from then until one o'clock there is a theory that I shall not be disturbed. It is largely theory." Lunch came on a tray at 1:00, and she continued at her desk during the afternoon. Learning from Arnold Bennett that he was up each day at 6:00 and wrote from then until 9:00 in the morning, at which point he was done for the day, Mary could comment only that it seemed to her "a miracle."[47]

Fiction writing was, though, something more than and other than work —and more than a rich mode of communication with the American public. In writing, Mary discovered "an almost complete detachment from the world I live in, a sort of armor against distraction. I talk to people, move about, appear on the surface much as usual. But later on I have only a confused memory of what has happened during that period." This detachment was not only armor against distraction; it could serve also as armor against life. "I do know that now and then I escape into writing, leaving a world I cannot face for a dream world of my own creating." The world she could not face was made up, as for all of us, of public and private horrors. It was, for example, an old trick of Mary's to arrive at the hospital, prepared to face a major operation— for gall bladder, for breast cancer—with a board and an unfinished manuscript. Just before her mastectomy, she sat in her hospital bed, "board on lap, writing the last third of a short story, *The Man Who Killed His Wife*. . . . This was not courage, however. I still hoped my trouble was not malignant, and work was as usual an escape from an unpleasant prospect."[48]

In "Writing Is Work," Rinehart also addressed the continuing problem of popularity versus critical success. "[Every writer] wants two things. He wants to be the fair-haired child of the critics and to be a best-seller at the same time. . . . It is no longer considered fatal to all literary craftsmanship to sell a lot of books, or to be a successful magazine writer." But it was, Rinehart confessed, difficult and often discouraging to try to be both. "My own personal discouragement, however, is so keen that it reaches the point of neurosis, and I have never failed to have it."[49]

Adding up her achievements—fifty books, stories and essays beyond her counting, seven plays—Rinehart confessed, "Every one of them has disappointed me; many bitterly, some less than others." As for her mysteries, she wanted her readers to know that they were the hardest of all to write, the most complex, the most demanding. A "ponderous tome" is easier. After all, she explained, "almost anyone with sufficient determination can make a roast beef. But it takes a light hand to make pastry. . . . The reader can be certain: the more easily anything reads, the harder it has been to write."[50]

13

The End of the Adventure
1940–1958

LIKE MANY OTHER AMERICANS of her age and class, Mary Roberts Rinehart was considerably shaken by Roosevelt's administration of the country. In many aspects of the New Deal, she saw the spectre of socialism or worse, and it was Stalin, not Hitler, whom she at first found more frightening in the increasing chaos and horror of Europe. In 1948, looking back at prewar Europe, Mary recalled with how little seriousness she, like most Americans, had taken the rise of Nazi Germany—and she had dreaded involvement in another European war. Early in 1938 she wrote for *Good Housekeeping* an antiwar plea, recalling the writing of "The Altar of Freedom" and the responsibility she had come to feel as the tide of letters from bereaved mothers washed up on her shore. War, she felt, was in itself evil, breeding more war and anarchy "and, eventually, revolution." "There is no humanity," she declared, "in killing to uphold an ideal of human society," and there was no reason for America to make itself "a sort of international police, setting up our own judgment of who is right and wrong."[1]

By 1940 Rinehart understood that America could not keep out of the war: "It took the shores of Dunkirk fully to rouse my fighting spirit." And if there would be war, Mary wanted to play the part she knew best—that of writer-reporter. Carefully keeping her plans secret from her sons, she set off for Philadelphia and an appointment with editor Stout of the *Post*. The proposition she laid before him was that she fly to England and report on the Blitz, "to tell people what the Germans are doing." "Probably [Stout] thought I was slightly irrational. Perhaps he was right, carried away as I was by fury at this new and brutal war against civilians. But in the end he yielded. He even gave me credentials for the State Department." Mary then went on to Washington. With charm and persistence she convinced the passport division of the State Department of the value of her idea, and they issued her a passport to London via Lisbon. But the family had got wind of Mother's activities, and Mary found a telegram awaiting her at her Washington hotel. "What are you doing? You are scaring the pants off us. You know you can't fly." It was, in the end, the flying that settled the matter. The heart specialist Mary was seeing explained to her that she could not survive the Lisbon to London flight, made in planes stripped of their oxygen equipment and forced by the war to fly at high altitudes. The doctor called it "a nice way to commit suicide."[2]

Mary was going to sit out the new war, but backing down was awkward, particularly on account of Rinehart's previous statements to the press about

The frontispiece for the new edition (1948) of *My Story*.

her plans to report on the Blitz. In December 1940 the *New York Times* "Book Review" carried a long interview with Rinehart, complete with a very glamorous photograph—furs, pearls, and youthfulness. Robert Van Gelder talked to her in her Park Avenue apartment, which, he noted, was "about as big as a park," where he found her restless at the remorseless comfort of her life: the apartment itself; Reyes, the Filipino cook, who was "a wizard with mashed potatoes and chicken"; and "the solicitous maid," who would say: "You have worked long enough, Madam. Your bed is turned down." According to Rinehart, such a life was perhaps not good for her.[3]

The problem, as Mary described it, was that a storyteller needs conflict; without change, the writer "must reach far back for material." But the war offered a solution: "If I could fly over bombed London . . . well, my imagination would flare up . . . my mind would again be filled with stories almost as it was during those years when I hardly could take time to write a story because there were so many more pressing for their turn to be written." She planned to go to England by the spring, or even earlier; it would be Belgium, 1915, all over again. She did, though, explain to Van Gelder: "There may be some small difficulties, as I am not allowed to walk upstairs. . . . My son Stanley made, I think, the most pointed comment: 'I'm sure you'd be magnificent, Mother, going down into a dugout, but how would you get up again?' But I'll worry about those stairs when I'm at the foot of them. I want to go to England."[4]

But it was not to be. With time, Mary learned to deal with this disappointment, and in the 1948 edition of *My Story* she evaluated her desire to fly to England as a gesture that, in its self-assertion, was like the incident of the diamond necklace so many years before. She wanted to prove that she "was still young enough, still brave enough, still strong enough, to go to a war."[5]

Mary was sixty-five when the Japanese attacked Pearl Harbor. Her war work was going to be done through committees, through agencies, through one kind of war board or another. Even Mary's sons were beyond the age of active service, and they too worked in civilian capacities: Stan and Ted as air raid wardens, Stan on the Council on Books in Wartime, and Alan in the War Shipping Administration. Of Mary's relatives only one would serve in the military, and that was Olive's daughter Virginia, who enlisted in the WACs and was sent to the South Pacific.

Most of Rinehart's war work consisted of writing, not the eye-witness journalism she had hoped to do, but exhortations—short pieces to be printed in newspapers or read over the radio, supporting the several war loan drives, urging people to give money to the Red Cross, and enjoining women to go to work for the war effort. She served on the Advisory Council of the Writers' War Board, a council made up of a number of the most eminent literary figures of the day: Louis Adamic, Franklin Pierce Adams, Stephen Vincent Benét, Louis Bromfield, Van Wyck Brooks, Henry S. Canby, Mary Ellen Chase, Edna Ferber, Paul Gallico, Langston Hughes, Edna St. Vincent Millay, Clifford Odets, Eugene O'Neill, Elmer Rice, Thornton Wilder, and Rinehart's old friend, William Lyon Phelps. The chairman of the board was mystery writer Rex Stout, working closely with Pearl Buck, J. P. Marquand, William Shirer, Clifton Fadiman, and Elmer Davis.

Rinehart produced mostly propaganda and inspirational pieces for the Writers' War Board. She wrote as well for the government—for the Treasury Department, with its own war loan drives, and for the Office of War Information. Occasionally, under the combined aegis of the Writers' War Board and the Office of War Information, she wrote longer articles (five to six thousand words) on some pressing topic. In October 1942, after she completed one that urged women to go to work, she was distressed to find that the boards and agencies expected her to place the piece herself. Marketing inspirational articles had not been one of her expectations.

The Red Cross War Fund had an Authors' Division of its own; chaired by Carl Van Doren, the committee had only six, very distinguished, members: Stephen Vincent Benét, Clifton Fadiman, Sinclair Lewis, Carl Sandburg, John Steinbeck, and Mary Roberts Rinehart. Like many other war boards, this one wanted both time and money, and in the Rinehart correspondence enough requests remain for contributions to one organization or another to recall the pace and passion of the war years. Rinehart made contributions to the Red Cross and to its Authors' Division, to the American Women's Committee for British War Relief, the United China Relief, the Friends of Democracy, the Council for Democracy, the New York Committee of the National War Fund, and to independent drives taken in Bar Harbor. She sent books of her own to the army and contributed her automobile tires to the Idle Tire Purchase Plan. In general, Mary was willing to contribute her money and her work but impatient at the triviality of much that was asked of her. She lamented to Stan in 1944, "Why doesn't Rex Stout give me something real to do? Such bosh!"[6]

Mary did find one thing to do for the war-effort other than writing propaganda pieces; she became an air raid warden.

In slacks, armed with a musette bag containing a police whistle, a screwdriver, a flashlight and a pencil, and later with a helmet from the First World War, at nine o'clock at night I would go to my post, there to sit by the telephone until midnight. I had two duties: one to call the other wardens in case of emergency; the other to extinguish the streetlights at my corner.

Wardens also attended lectures, learning how to put out fires set by incendiary bombs and to distinguish different kinds of poison gases. As Rinehart recalled, that information was merely academic: "As we never had any masks, the only advantage seemed to be that we could at least know by its smell what gas was killing us."[7]

Her experience as an air raid warden served as the background for a short story, "The Time Is Ten," published in 1942. The fiction is much more exciting than the reality proved to be, for the hero manages to avert an attempt at subversion and to save a troopship. The protagonist of the story, set against his vain, spoiled wife, also learns something about the American people. "He had never known anybody in the neighborhood. Now he found himself in a cross section of democracy." His new friends, his warden-colleagues, include a grocer, a local undertaker, and a group of women, ranging from young stenographers to "middle-aged widows, evidently well off."[8]

"The Temporary Death of Mrs. Ayres" is the most interesting of the short stories that Rinehart wrote during the war, because it is the most personal and analytic. In Mrs. Ayres, Rinehart drew a partial portrait of herself at sixty-six as a well-off widow with grown children. Mrs. Ayres worries about her taxes (the quarterly payment is due) and the war. She hates war. Her husband Herbert, dead for some years, had fought in the Spanish-American War (as Olive's husband had), and her oldest son, Joe, served in the First World War (as Stan, Jr., had). In short, decides Mrs. Ayres, she has done her bit already.

Mrs. Ayres also worries about her three children. Joe comes to see her in the middle of the day with a request for a loan, explaining, "It's these damned taxes." He promises that he will pay her back as soon as possible. "He would, she thought. He always had. She looked at him, at his tired face, his thinning hair. She would have lain down and let him trample her to death. Only now, with her own bank balance so low—" But she finds the money for him. One of the three children is a daughter, herself a mother complaining over marriage and children. But the major worry of all concerns her other son, Andy, "the handsomest of her children, and the most unpredictable."[9] Andy equals Alan as clearly as Joe represents Stan, Jr. Andy wants to go to war, and he wants to go with his mother's blessing. What Mrs. Ayres wants is to maintain maternal control over her now-adult children.

A combination of emotional exhaustion and frustration brings Mrs. Ayres to a decision, and that night at dinner she tells her family that, under doctor's orders, she is to have absolute rest. It will be, she explains, "rather drastic": no radio, no newspapers, no telephone, no visitors, and no family. She spends two weeks alone and in bed, "dead," as she insists on calling it, reviewing her own life, her childhood, her marriage. She thinks often and hard about Herbert, staring at his picture, rereading his old letters. It is through Herbert, his firmness, his steadfastness, that she comes to regain her courage and to see herself as a blind and selfish old woman. Staring at his picture, she feels "as if it asked her what she herself was doing, shut up in her room with a world afire."[10]

In her sabbatical from life, Mrs. Ayres learns to accept her lot, learns in particular that her family "did not need her. They hadn't really needed her for years."[11] She is, she decides, an anchor trying to run a ship. She bravely accepts her son in uniform and asks only to find something she can do to help win the war. And at the end she finds it in work as an air raid warden.

During the war years Rinehart continued to write mystery novels that received both popular and critical acclaim. Of *Haunted Lady* (1942), *Times* mystery reviewer Isaac Anderson commented that each murder mystery of Rinehart's "seems at the time to be better than those that have gone before. . . . How does she do it?" In 1945 Anderson reviewed *The Yellow Room;* and while he found the "unraveling" of the story somewhat strained, he commented, "Mrs. Rinehart has lost none of her skill in weaving an intricate web of mystery."[12] Rinehart was almost seventy when *The Yellow Room* was serialized in the *Post,* and she had been publishing in magazines for forty-one years.

Nevertheless, the world was changing, and changing faster than even Mary Roberts Rinehart could keep up with. Although the tastes (and ages) of book reviewers differ, it is worth comparing a 1941 and a 1944 review of Rinehart story collections. In 1941 the *Times* reviewer of *Familiar Faces* stressed Rinehart's versatility—romances, mysteries, Tish, travel, autobiography—and praised her for having "worked for the most part within the formulas imposed by the national magazines, but without any of the familiar symptoms of artistic strangulation." Rinehart not only worked without suffering the effects of formula, she also worked without repeating herself. "It would be difficult, perhaps impossible, to assemble from any other single source eleven short stories so various as these."[13]

Three war years later, in 1944, the *Times* reviewed *Alibi for Isabel,* seeing Rinehart primarily through the haze of nostalgia. Her world, the reviewer said, is "a vanished dream. . . . It is a dream of gilt-edged security, implicit in her snug brownstone fronts, wide shady verandas, country clubs, witty parents in dinner clothes, pert children straining slightly against the conventions of their elders." And for this reviewer Rinehart's fiction was formula fiction. "Within the limits of a formula too successful to make an argument very interesting, the author tells her stories warmly and skillfully." But it is a question of "souvenirs," all "reminiscent," all part of "the large, comfortable Rinehart world-with-a-watch-chain."[14]

After the war magazine editors too began to see Rinehart differently. The *Post* continued to publish Rinehart's stories but rather infrequently, and the majority of her fiction now appeared, after all those years of struggling against it, in women's magazines, in *Cosmopolitan* and *Good Housekeeping* predominantly. Moreover, some stories now failed to find any magazine market at all, making their first appearance in a collection. In 1952 *The Swimming Pool,* a full-length vintage-Rinehart mystery novel, was published by Rinehart and Company without any previous magazine serialization. The last of Rinehart's novels to appear only in book form had been *Where There's a Will* in 1912, forty years earlier.

Up to 1942 Mary kept up relations with the *Post* almost entirely through Adelaide Neall. In 1941 Adelaide wrote to Mary about her new mystery novel *(Haunted Lady),* expressing regret that the *Post* had not had a chance at it. Mary, who may still have been smarting from the Tish rejection, explained that the new novel had basic elements in it that the *Post* would not approve of—divorce, adultery, miscarriage (all aspects of the buried story). Adelaide agreed with that appraisal and hoped that Mary would do a serial for the *Post* soon and would "keep miscarriages and too, too compromising situations" out of it.[15]

Early in 1942 Ben Hibbs took over as editor of the *Post,* and Adelaide almost immediately resigned, explaining to Mary that she had to do so, that the Boss would approve. Changes were being made in the magazine that Adelaide strongly disliked, and the magazine would no longer be Lorimer's *Post* —"or mine," she wrote. After Stuart Rose took over Adelaide's professional correspondence with Rinehart, there were fewer acceptances and none of the old intimacy. When Rinehart tried to place a long piece done for the Writers' War Board, urging women to go to work, Rose turned it down. And early in 1943 he wrote to Stan, saying, "It would not be advisable for Mrs. Rinehart to submit the story [*Episode of the Wandering Knife*] formally to The Post as it did not impress me as being up to her high standards of performance."[16]

In 1945 the *Post* did publish the serialization of *The Yellow Room,* but nothing more of Rinehart's appeared there until 1949, when two stories were printed. She wrote to Hibbs that it was "like old times" to be back with the *Post* again, but in fact it was not at all like old times.[17] With Lorimer and in the heyday of Rinehart's popularity, her stories had been printed as quickly as possible after receipt. Now Hibbs was in no such hurry. He wrote to Mary in November 1948 that he would not be able to print "Unbreakable Alibi" until spring, and it did not appear until April 1949.

The second of the 1949 stories was "The Man Upstairs." Mary sent it to Rose in January, and early in April, Rose replied objecting to the title, which he wanted to change to "The Doctor Is Sick." The protagonist, a refugee psychoanalyst, also troubled Rose: "What use is all the physician's knowledge of broken minds? He himself is now a patient—and has to face a terrible truth." She waited, as she noted in a letter two days later, twenty-four hours "in order to reply to [his letter] like a lady and not like an infuriate shrew!" As for the title change, Mary explained that the doctor was not sick in the first place (Rose did not understand the story), and that the man upstairs was God. "In forty years with the Post my titles stood," Mary wrote with considerable asperity, and added, "I really think we have a comrade at work with the deliberate attempt to cheapen the magazine!"[18] Mary won that round.

But the situation worsened. Only one story of Rinehart's appeared in the *Post* in 1950 and none at all in 1951. In 1952 the *Post* turned down *The Swimming Pool.* Then, on February 16, 1952, Mary took direct action; she wrote to Rose suggesting that they see one another when he was next in New York. "The Post, in the last few years, has been worrying me. It turned down 'The Swimming Pool,' which is perhaps the best mystery novel I ever wrote. . . . I would like to feel that the Post is still friendly after my long years with it." Rose accepted a luncheon invitation from Mary and a week later wrote to say that the manuscript of *The Frightened Wife* looked promising. (He was never enthusiastic; what he said was, "We think there's a good chance for you to work up THE FRIGHTENED WIFE into a two or three-part serial.")[19]

By the time *The Frightened Wife* was ready for serialization in the *Post* early in 1953, the magazine requested information from Mary for "Keeping Posted," the weekly notes on contributors. She replied that she was proud to have another serial in the *Post* "after almost forty years of such distinction." Then, with old scores to settle and with an irresistible need to make a point, she added, "You might also say in Keeping Posted that my new novel, The Swimming Pool, is having an enormous success, and that for the first time, to my knowledge, a novel which is also a suspense story has appeared high up and for so long on the New York Times, New York Herald Tribune and other best seller lists."[20] H. Ralph Knight, who put "Keeping Posted" together, tactfully replied that he could use more personal information for the column, and Mary dutifully sent what was requested. She and Rose sent letters occasionally over the next few years, always on the occasion of business, but with *The Frightened Wife,* Mary Roberts Rinehart, at seventy-seven, ended her career with *The Saturday Evening Post.*

Significantly, the slow disintegration of Rinehart's association with the *Post* did not come about as a result of any failure on her part to remain at least relatively up-to-date. Exploiting the new freedom, Rinehart was able to construct plots for stories and novels that were considerably less sexually evasive than in the past. In no way, of course, were any of her books or stories overtly sexual, but it was possible now for her to acknowledge divorce or adultery or miscarriage. The *Post* did not make that acknowledgment.

On the other hand, even when Rinehart's stories take account of the more brutal side of human relations, there is at the same time a kind of insulation from it. Most of her realistic stories come to happy, and morally acceptable, resolutions. And in her mystery novels even the brutal fact of murder is softened, partly, of course, by the conventions of the genre but partly, too, from Rinehart's own predilections. No one is murdered in a Rinehart mystery who does not somehow deserve it. Seldom are the criminals themselves apprehended and sentenced; frequently suicide or natural death intervenes. As a result, no sense of vengeance permeates her mysteries. What emerges instead is the understanding that people make errors, very serious errors in their lives, errors typically arising out of sexual desire. The errors lie buried for a long time, festering, and when they erupt, they exact a grisly toll. Innocent people are involved—puzzled, frightened, even wounded by blunt instruments or guns. But in the end their placid world is restored and the heroine is rewarded with marriage.

To the extent that Rinehart's fiction existed in a world insulated from life's harshest realities, it continued to attract a large audience of readers who preferred their fiction that way. But, after World War II, her audience was primarily made up of older readers; few young readers of the late 1940s were avid Mary Roberts Rinehart fans.

People who met and talked with Mary Roberts Rinehart in those years came away most often with the impression of the grande dame. That image she projected through her clothing, her jewels, her environment, and her bearing. In 1946 *Life* magazine published a "Close-Up" of Rinehart: "For 35 years she has been America's best-selling lady author." The feature was written by Geoffrey T. Hellman, who interviewed Rinehart at her eighteen-room apartment on Park Avenue. The "Close-Up" emphasized wealth and success, describing Mary's apartment, cataloguing her sales, and altogether helping to maintain the institution of Mary Roberts Rinehart. Hellman was interested in discussing how Rinehart achieved the splendor he saw her living in—the paintings and antique furniture and Aubusson rugs. He talked of *The Bat,* with an estimated gross of over nine million dollars, and of her books, having reached a total sale (including translations into twelve languages) of nearly ten million copies.[21]

Two years later, in 1948, Dorothy Cameron Disney and Milton Mackaye wrote a combination retrospective and promotion of Rinehart, on the occasion of the publication of her new novel, *A Light in the Window.* Like the Hellman piece, this booklet dealt with Rinehart the institution, calling her "by all odds America's Number One career woman," and asserting,

"No other contemporary novelist—with the possible exception of W. Somerset Maugham—has had such a wide and lasting public appeal."[22]

Disney and Mackaye complemented the career woman with the family woman: "When Mrs. Rinehart is in New York she is always to be found at home and at her tea table at five o'clock. Her three sons and their families live within a few comfortable blocks of her apartment. Any member of the clan who cares to drop in of a late afternoon can be sure of a welcome." That was, of course, Mary's theme. She returned to it again and again, talking of the family and its significance. On the closing pages of the new edition of *My Story*, published that same year, Mary reiterated, "When I can have the family around me I ask for nothing more. It is still the center of my life, as it has been since my first baby was placed in my arms."[23]

Besides informal gatherings for tea or cocktails, the family enjoyed more ceremonial occasions as well—Thursday dinners and great parties at Thanksgiving and Christmas. On Christmas Eve, for example, Ted Falkenstrom, Mary's chauffeur, would drive her to her sons' apartments. She would stay for a while at each home, leaving off her Christmas presents; gifts from Mary were always wrapped in silver paper and tied with blue ribbons. Christmas night was always spent at Mary's; a black-tie party for the family, including children over twelve and perhaps an intimate friend or two. The guests, invited for six o'clock, gathered for cocktails. As hostess, Mary was very regal, very much the grande dame. Reyes prepared a traditional dinner, including sweet potatoes and marshmallows (from a recipe Stan, Jr., had brought home to Sewickley before the First World War); and guests were served at the large dinner table, with smaller tables for the children. There was champagne, and, after dinner, Reyes came in, accepting congratulations with a bow. With dinner over, there was bridge or canasta or poker for the card players and, of course, a game of pool. Every one played for chips representing fairly substantial amounts of money, and at the end of the evening—after the excitement of high stakes—the chips were cashed in at 10 percent of their value.[24]

Family parties could also be the occasion for elaborate jokes. Once, in the late thirties, the family secretly wrote a book for Mary, having ten copies printed and all bound by Stan's wife, Fay. They planned the presentation for a Thursday night family dinner, for which the Rinehart sons arrived, as Ted recalls, dressed to the teeth (white tie) and covered with medals, and after some complicated staging, "the book" made its appearance.[25]

It was divided into four parts, the first called "The Roots": "These roots go back, or down, to the year 1904, when a young matron with three of the best behaved children in the world took one on each knee and invited the poetic muse to climb aboard." The second section, "The Big Twig," contained Stan, Jr.'s Viennese diary, and "Branching Out" had poems and stories by the grandchildren. The fourth section, "Dear Family," was "A miscellany of Rinehartiana which shows both the root and the way the twigs inclined, the individual contributions having been removed from their authors either by force or without their knowledge."[26]

At the end is a parody of Eleanor Roosevelt's famous syndicated column, "My Day," signed, "Author Anonymous," but written in fact by Mary Roberts Rinehart. The parody is keen and there is a ribald cast to the piece, a side Mary carefully kept to herself and to her adult family. One example:

Luncheon was of fried eggs, and dear Mr. Farley was present. He had an excellent plan for expropriating Sunday School and Church collections for the election fund, stating that this was the only source as yet untapped. Also one for emasculating the members of the Supreme Court, but this last one my husband vetoed as they are too old anyway.[27]

Sometimes family humor was simpler in its execution. Mary never really appreciated the value of money; the things one bought with it seemed a good deal more real to her. She commented once to her sons that receiving checks for her work made it that much more difficult to understand money in any tangible way. The next time royalty payments from F&R were due, her sons filled a strongbox with small and large bills to the amount of her check—over $4,000. Mary opened the box, brimful of real money, and she loved it.[28]

One Mother's Day, Stan, Jr., surprised his mother with a poem, "To Mother, On the Occasion of Her Fifty-Third Murder." The final stanza of the poem reads:

> And so your offspring, on this Mother's Day,
> Do homage to your homicidal knowledge.
> Who says that bloody murder does not pay?
> It helped to put the lot of us through college![29]

Mary's life, by her seventieth birthday, seemed rich and gracious and fairly placid. Then, in the summer of 1947, it suddenly erupted into melodramatic horror. For over a quarter of a century, the Rineharts had employed one chef; Reyes had been very much a part of their elaborate world in Washington and later of Mary's household in New York. He married an Irish woman named Peggy and she, too, became a part of the Rinehart staff, in Washington and later in New York and Bar Harbor.

Trouble with Reyes first began when Mary hired a butler for the summer. Reyes resented having another man in a position traditionally superior

Mary in elegant summer attire at her home in Bar Harbor.

to that of the cook. Hearing his mistress' explanation of the situation, he responded with a simple and somehow ominous, "You are the madam." After a few weeks in Bar Harbor, Reyes gave notice, but since he had threatened to leave at other times, Mary did not take him seriously. The next morning, however, he "still maintained he was leaving."[30] What Mary did not then know was that he and Peggy had quarreled, for Peggy refused to leave with her husband.

After taking the morning orders and doing the marketing in town, Reyes returned to prepare lunch. Mary was sitting in her library, reading, when Reyes suddenly appeared in his shirt sleeves. Mary asked him where his coat was, and with the words "Here is my coat,"[31] he pulled a gun from his pocket. Standing about four feet away, Reyes pulled the trigger, but the gun was old and it misfired. Before he could try again, Mary jumped up and ran through the house, with Reyes in pursuit. When she reached the servants' wing she was rescued by Falkenstrom, the chauffeur, who threw Reyes to the floor. Margaret, Rinehart's personal maid, disarmed him.

The next few minutes were chaotic. Falkenstrom ran outside and threw the gun over the hedge, while Margaret ran to get the nitroglycerin Mary took for her heart condition. The butler, meanwhile, himself afraid of Reyes, had run to the road and hitched a ride into town. As Mary went to the telephone to call the police, Reyes tore loose and grabbed two long carving knives. Mary heard Margaret scream and, turning, faced Reyes and the knives. Again Mary was rescued. Falkenstrom and the gardener knocked Reyes down, and the police arrived to find him on the floor, wildly screaming, with Margaret, the chauffeur, and the gardener attempting to keep him subdued. The police took Reyes into custody, and that night he hanged himself in jail.[32]

The summer of Reyes's attack was the last summer for Mary's Bar Harbor house. That October a terrible fire ravaged Bar Harbor, destroying over seventy summer homes, including Mary's, a part of the village itself, and a number of farmhouses. The fire was ferocious, surrounding the town, setting whole hillsides aflame, driving the population to the harbor where small boats waited to evacuate them.

The month of the fire Rinehart's last serious novel began serialization in *The Ladies' Home Journal. A Light in the Window* tells the story of the Wayne family, publishers in New York. Beginning at the end of the First World War, the novel is Rinehart's attempt to write about the world she had known from the glamorous days in Washington, through the depression, and on to the next, once unimaginable, war. It is a story of cycle and change, especially of the breaking down of rigid social barriers and the erosion of false sexual morality. As Rinehart makes clear, any real hope for a society freed of prudery and snobbishness must lie in the future, with the generation that was coming to power after the Second World War. For Ricky, the central character of the novel, that future comes too late, and like many Rinehart heroines, she falls victim to old shibboleths and lives a life of stinted joy.

Because the Waynes own a publishing company, *A Light in the Window* offers Rinehart the chance to comment on literature in America. Among the minor characters, for example, is Anne Lockwood, a writer of old-fashioned romances now fast going out of date. Like Rinehart, Lockwood has worked hard all her life (supporting a tubercular husband) and has found in writing not only a means of support but a temporary "Never-Never Land of her own creation." But Lockwood is passé; she continues to write about "a static world, a peaceful world, safe and secure. Not one which vanished with the war."[33] No doubt, Rinehart saw some of Lockwood in herself, feared becoming dated, but *A Light in the Window* was to be testimony that, unlike Lockwood, she had survived the war.

At the same time Rinehart used the novel to question—once again—the value of the new writers; to that end she has her most sympathetic characters express their own strong reservations about current fiction. Old Matthew Wayne is not at all fond of the new "realism"; in fact, "he hardly recognized the world some of them wrote about; a world where the young drank to excess, where sex seemed the end of existence . . . and where new radical opinions were opposed to everything in which he believed." Ricky, a generation younger than Matthew, is old-fashioned too. She misses the beauty and elegance of the old world, and doesn't think much of modern painting or of Gertrude Stein, "who was either a poseur or a lunatic, and possibly both."[34]

The attack on Gertrude Stein seems gratuitous, particularly since Mary may have known for some time that Stein was a fan of her mystery novels. (Coincidentally, both women had been born in Allegheny, only two years apart.) Mary had a copy of *A Light in the Window* sent to Gertrude Stein in Paris, and in January 1948 Alice B. Toklas wrote to Rinehart and Company.

> It must have been before the 1914–1918 war that Gertrude discovered MRR. Anyway I can still see her coming into the room with a book at the rue de Fleurus and her saying she really writes very well—as if I knew what book she had under her arm. So thank you for the book [*A Light in the Window*] and the happy memory it revives.[35]

By her middle seventies, even Mary Roberts Rinehart began to slow down. Still, she continued to write, although more sporadically as her health dictated. After *My Story* and *A Light in the Window* appeared in 1948, she published only two short stories in 1949 and two more in 1950, three of them in the *Post*. Then, in 1951, Mary was hard at work again, completing *The Swimming Pool* for publication in 1952 and *The Frightened Wife* (a novella) for serialization early in 1953.

The Swimming Pool was Rinehart's last full-length work, and it is a first-class MRR mystery novel. Like many of the novels and stories of the later years, it provides a partial portrait of Mary herself, in this case, literally a portrait. At the center of the buried story is the dominating figure of Mrs. Maynard; although she has died before the novel begins, she still controls much of what occurs, just as she controlled her children's lives while she lived. She looms over the present from her portrait on the wall, grand in black velvet and her famous pearls, a precise echo of Mary Roberts Rinehart in her portrait by John Lavalle. In that painting Mary looks out at the viewer, gray haired, alert, poised, a slight smile on her face, her lovely long hands resting on a book in her lap. She is wearing black velvet and her own magnificent pearls.

In the last years of her life, as she became more and more of an institution, Mary Roberts Rinehart was frequently the subject of interviews and the recipient of awards. In 1950 Jinx Falkenberg and Tex McCrary interviewed her for their "Close-Up" column in the *Herald Tribune*. In the early fifties, Harvey Breit did two pieces on Rinehart for the *Times* "Book Review," the first an interview and the second a report on a social event: Breit attended a small luncheon Mary Roberts Rinehart gave for Agatha Christie and her husband, Dr. Mallowan. It was the first, and only, meeting of the reigning queens of mystery fiction.[36]

In 1952 Mary Margaret McBride interviewed Rinehart on her famous radio program. McBride was a bit fluttery and not a little overwhelmed at having on her program "an ideal of mine," a woman who had led "the best life of anyone I can think of." Are you, she asked Rinehart, "the happiest woman of all?" In a firm and somewhat husky voice, unrattled by the praise or the microphone, Mary responded simply that she was pleased at "the scope of the life I've lived." Most of the program consisted of questions and answers about highlights of that life, now well known. When McBride implied that it was the publication of *The Swimming Pool* that had made it possible for her to "get" Rinehart on the broadcast, Mary stated flatly, but pleasantly, that she was "not going to plug the book at all." She did, though, talk of her mystery novels—preferring the label, suspense novels—both in terms of the buried story and in terms of her contribution to the form. Without in the least knowing what she was doing, Rinehart said, she had altered the form of the mystery story by adding flesh and muscle to the skeleton of plot. With *The Circular Staircase* the mystery novel grew up.[37]

For that achievement, as well as for the great number of successful crime novels she had written, the Mystery Writers of America presented Rinehart with a special award in May 1954. Unfortunately, Mary was too ill to attend the presentation and dinner for 350 people. The same year illness forced her to turn down the offer of a second honorary degree, this one from the Uni-

The John Lavalle portrait of Rinehart. Compare the description of Mrs. Maynard in *The Swimming Pool.*

versity of Maine. Then, in 1956, when Mary was eighty years old, Edward R. Murrow asked her to appear on his "Person to Person" show. Unfortunately, Murrow was called away to report on the Arab-Israeli war, and Mary Roberts Rinehart was interviewed by comedian Jerry Lewis. Mary was generous, writing to tell Murrow that she "missed him very much on the program" but that "Jerry Lewis was fine and dignified." Perhaps, but the program has been described by a member of the family as a Mexican standoff. Lewis had little idea of who Rinehart was, and Rinehart had just as little idea of Lewis. *Variety* attacked Lewis, who "couldn't make up his mind whether to play straight-man or funny-man," and lamented the fact that Rinehart "had an interesting story to tell, but Lewis couldn't establish any kind of rapport with her."[38]

What Mary was most conscious of in the last years of her life was the absence in the postwar world of the sense of security she remembered from years before. Like most Americans she was uneasy over the atom bomb, and her uneasiness increased when the air raid sirens practiced their different emergency blasts in the city. She was appalled at the new rate of taxation. Having been born before there was an income tax, she often commented that it seemed absurd to write books at all since one only earned money for the government. She was apprehensive about Russia and about communism generally. On top of those anxieties, she deplored the United States' entry into Korea, writing to Sydney MacDonald's daughter in London: "I wonder why we ever took the risk of going into Korea. Perhaps Asia is only meant for the Asiatics. I do not know." Surprisingly, for she had never admired Truman's administration, she applauded his recall of MacArthur, an act that "showed a lot of courage."[39]

And Mary thought about her life, recalling her childhood, rehearsing in her mind the dramatic years, the First World War. Some of those memories she committed to paper, preparing a third autobiography. These very personal memoirs were intended only for circulation among the family, but as it turned out they were never read; of the nearly one hundred manuscript pages, only the first five were typed and distributed. The remaining pages, however, were written with the care Mary lavished on any serious work: yellow sheets of manuscript handed over to Bill Sladen for typing, those typed pages in turn cut and pinned in revision. And in the end, although she did not share this work with her family, Mary did, contrary to her common practice with notes and drafts, save these autobiographical pages, leaving them among her papers.

This autobiography provides the most honest and intimate of Rinehart's self-portraits, rich in details about her childhood, her family, her own early married life. Only here does she talk of Aunt Tish, the aunt with airs, deciding to become the fourth wife of a floor walker at a department store.

Poor Tish, she loved her Mr. Webb although he was notoriously unfaithful to her and once even gave her new sewing machine away to one of his lady friends. She recalls her father only dimly, and not with particular fondness, dwelling on his beautiful white hands, hands that never did any manual work, and recalling with revulsion his cuspidor, which it was sometimes her task to clean. Happier memories come with Aunt Tillie and the elegant party she once gave for Mary, white crash on the floor, a pianist and a violinist—the only party Mary Roberts ever had. Here, at last, Mary recalled the life on Western Avenue, her life as a young wife and mother. At close to eighty years of age, Mary finally wrote down her feelings of frustration and confusion from so many years before. The writing is intense but distant, as if Mary were looking at quite another person, at a wife and mother literally out of another century. Part of Mary had lived on, learning and changing with the world. Part of her, the domestic part, remained fixed in the mores of the nineteenth century.

The Mary Roberts Rinehart that grew up with the twentieth century was another story altogether. Even in her eighties she radiated energy, vitality, power. She was, recalls one who knew her in those years, a tycoon—a charming woman, but a tough woman, one who had made it in a man's world. She was proud of her social standing, for she loved the elite, but she remained remarkably unpretentious about her writing, continuing to call herself a storyteller. She maintained her curiosity about life and people. She

A favorite photograph depicts the serious writer.

always said she could see both sides of any issue, and what she meant was that she could understand the minds and feelings of persons on different sides of a problem or a quarrel. That understanding, supported by her curiosity, made her a writer.

Early in 1958 Mary suffered another heart attack and she never rallied from this one as she had from the others. She spent most of her time in bed, continuing, of course, to see the family. Apparently she knew that she was dying, but she faced it without self-pity or terror. Shortly before Mary's death, Alan's second wife, Ernestine, had to travel to New Orleans, and Mary promised her she would not die before her return. The promise cheered Ernestine, but Mary may have known she could not keep it. She died very peacefully shortly after, on September 22, 1958.

It had been a long life. She was born when Ulysses S. Grant was president, in the year when Alexander Graham Bell introduced the telephone to America. Civil War veterans were still young men. Reconstruction was coming to an end in the South as the nation made an effort at unification in celebration of the centennial anniversary of American independence. In that centennial year Custer made his last stand and Mark Twain published *Tom Sawyer*. For a girl born in Allegheny, Pennsylvania, in 1876, life patterns were clearly delineated, and expectations, just as clearly, limited; the great, perhaps the sole question was marriage—how fortunate would her choice prove to be? In her instance, the patterns were inadequate, the expectations far too narrow. Mary Roberts Rinehart constructed her own life drama. What still seems an improbable fiction became instead a great adventure.

Notes

Mary Roberts Rinehart:
A Chronological Bibliography

Index

Notes

These notes give shortened references for all Rinehart's books. The date in brackets is the date the work first appeared in any form and is given for ease in locating the full publication information in the chronological bibliography. All page numbers for her books refer to the first book publication.

Chapter 1: The Street, 1876–1895

1. Information about the Roberts family's households, addresses, and occupations comes from the City Directories of Pittsburgh and Allegheny from the 1860s to the 1890s.

2. *My Story* [October 1930–May 1931], p. 5. See introductory paragraph to notes.

3. Ibid., p. 9.

4. *"K"* [October 1914–October 1915], pp. 2–3.

5. *My Story*, p. 16.

6. *This Strange Adventure* [October 1928–February 1929], p. 2.

7. Unpublished autobiographical fragment, approximately one hundred holograph sheets, some fifty of these typed and edited, written about 1954, Rinehart collection, Hillman Library, University of Pittsburgh.

8. *My Story*, p. 6.

9. Unpublished autobiographical fragment.

10. Ibid.

11. Virginia Barton Wallace in interview with Jan Cohn.

12. Unpublished autobiographical fragment.

13. Ibid.

14. *My Story*, p. 7.

15. Unpublished autobiographical fragment; *My Story*, p. 30.

16. *My Story*, pp. 13–14.

17. Ibid., p. 90

18. Ibid., pp. 38, 41.

19. The academic record of Mary Ella Roberts, 1890–1893, at the Allegheny High School (now of Pittsburgh, Pa.).

20. *My Story*, p. 20.

21. Review essay of *When a Man Marries, Pittsburg* [*sic*] *Bulletin*, November 1909, p. 6.

22. *My Story*, p. 40; *Pittsburgh Press*, March 27 and April 17, 1892.

23. *My Story*, p. 40.

24. Ibid., p. 25; *"K,"* pp. 16–17.

25. Used as an illustration for *My Story*.

26. Ibid., p. 24. (Patterson is not named in *My Story*, but letters in the Rinehart collection provide the identification.)

27. Ibid., p. 24; Virginia Barton Wallace in interview with Jan Cohn.

28. *My Story*, pp. 24, 32.

29. Ibid., pp. 34–35.

30. Ibid., p. 35; unpublished autobiographical fragment.

31. *My Story*, pp. 21–22.

32. Stefan Lorant, *Pittsburgh: The Story of an American City* (New York: Doubleday, 1964), p. 196.

33. *Pittsburgh Press*, March 27, 1892.

34. *My Story*, p. 44.

35. Ibid., pp. 45, 48.

36. Ibid., p. 46; *"K,"* p. 59.

37. *"K,"* p. 102; *My Story*, p. 53.

38. *My Story*, p. 50; *The Doctor* [January–July 1936], p. 25.

39. *My Story*, pp. 58–59.

40. Ibid., pp. 66–68.

41. Ibid., pp. 72–73; *The Doctor*, p. 214.

42. *My Story*, p. 69.

43. Ibid., pp. 62, 63, 69.

44. Ibid., pp. 59, 64, 90.

45. Business card of W. & D. Rinehart, reproduced in Lorant, *Pittsburgh*, p. 105.

46. "Stanley M. Rinehart, M.D.," *History of Pittsburgh and Environs*, vol. 5 (New York: American Historical Society, 1922); unpublished, undated typescript, apparently a brief autobiography by Dr. Rinehart (however, on the first sheet, in Mary Roberts Rinehart's hand, is written "Stan's Story M.R.R."), Rinehart collection, University of Pittsburgh.

47. *My Story*, pp. 71, 72.

48. Ibid., p. 76.

49. Ibid., p. 48.

50. Certificate of death of Thomas B. Roberts, November 14, 1895 (Division of Vital Statistics, Buffalo, N.Y.); *Pittsburgh Press*, November 15, 1895, p. 3; *Pittsburgh Gazette*, November 16, 1895, p. 4; *Pittsburgh Daily Dispatch*, November 16, 1895, p. 5; *Pittsburgh Chronicle Telegraph*, November 16, 1895, p. 3.

51. *Pittsburgh Press*, November 15, 1895, p. 3.

52. *"K,"* p. 193.

Chapter 2: The Doctor's Wife, 1896–1907

1. *Pittsburg* [*sic*] *Dispatch*, April 22, 1896, p. 10.

2. Ibid.

3. Stanley M. Rinehart to Alan G. Rinehart, August 24, 1932.

4. *My Story* [October 1930–May 1931], p. 78.

5. Ibid., p. 79; Mary Roberts Rinehart to Alan G. Rinehart, June 16, 1927.

6. Mary Roberts Rinehart to Gratia Houghton Rinehart, August 7, 1927; *My*

Story, p. 79; unpublished autobiographical fragment, Rinehart collection, Hillman Library, University of Pittsburgh.

7. Information on Rinehart's medical history in these years comes from a resumé prepared by Dr. Stanley Nowak, Boston City Hospital, October 19, 1943, Rinehart Collection.

8. *My Story*, p. 80.

9. Ibid., pp. 82–83; Virginia Barton Wallace in interview with Jan Cohn.

10. *My Story*, p. 78.

11. Unpublished autobiographical fragment.

12. Ibid.

13. Ibid.

14. *My Story*, pp. 80, 89–90, 81, 82.

15. Publication information for early poems and stories can be found in the chronological bibliography.

16. "Signs of the Times," *Pittsburgh Sunday Gazette*, June 26, 1904; untitled poem, *Sanitation* (October 1904).

17. *My Story*, p. 84.

18. Ibid.

19. William M. Rimmel, "Advice" column, *Pittsburgh Post-Gazette*, March 7, 1964; according to Rimmel, Stan took his wife's manuscripts to Jack Wright, a reporter, and Erasmus Wilson, writer of the column "The Quiet Observer," both on the *Gazette Times* staff. Review essay of *When a Man Marries*, *Pittsburg* [*sic*] *Bulletin*, November 1909, p. 6.

20. *My Story*, p. 85.

21. The bankbook, the brown scrapbook, and a second, red, scrapbook are part of the Rinehart collection at Hillman Library, University of Pittsburgh. Information about payments for early stories and poems is taken from the bankbook.

22. *My Story*, p. 86.

23. See chapter 12, figure 1.

24. *The Man in Lower 10* [January–April 1906], pp. 286–87.

25. *My Story*, p. 93.

26. Ibid., p. 97.

27. Ibid., p. 99.

28. Unpublished autobiographical fragment; *My Story*, p. 103.

29. Unpublished autobiographical fragment.

30. "Up and Down with the Drama," *The Saturday Evening Post* (July 6, 1912); although Rinehart refers to "successful plays," in fact, at this time she had produced only one success, *Seven Days*.

31. Unpublished autobiographical fragment; *My Story*, p. 96.

32. Stanley M. Rinehart, Jr., "Boys Are like This," unpublished typescript, about 1940.

33. Ibid.

Chapter 3: Successes, 1908–1911

1. *My Story* [October 1930–May 1931], p. 94.

2. *My Story*, new ed. [1948], p. 446.

3. *My Story*, p. 94.

4. Ibid., pp. 94–96.

5. *The Circular Staircase* [November 1907–March 1908], p. 234.

6. Ibid., pp. 1, 361.

7. Ibid., pp. 3–4.

8. Ibid., p. 6.

9. "Saturday Review of Books," *New York Times*, August 22, 1908.

10. Typescript from the Bobbs-Merrill Mss. in the Lilly Library, Indiana University.

11. Ibid.

12. Unpublished autobiographical fragment, Rinehart collection, Hillman Library, University of Pittsburgh.

13. *My Story*, p. 96.

14. Alice Payne Hackett, *Seventy Years of Best Sellers: 1895–1965* (New York: R. R. Bowker, 1967), p. 105. According to Hackett, Rinehart's achievements included the largest number of best-selling titles (eleven) and the third longest time span for books on the list (twenty-seven years, 1909–1936).

These are Rinehart's best-selling books:

Year on List	Number	Title
1909	4	*The Man in Lower 10*
1910	8	*The Window at the White Cat*
1910	10	*When a Man Marries*
1915	5	*"K"*
1918	3	*The Amazing Interlude*
1919	4	*Dangerous Days*
1921	7	*A Poor Wise Man*
1922	6	*The Breaking Point*
1923	10	*The Breaking Point*
1927	6	*Lost Ecstasy*
1930	6	*The Door*
1936	9	*The Doctor*

15. "Saturday Review of Books," *New York Times*, April 3, 1909.

16. Hopwood's estate provided the money for the prestigious Hopwood awards at the University of Michigan.

17. *My Story*, p. 110.

18. *Theatre Magazine*, 10 (December 1909), xv, xvii.

19. *Pittsburgh Post*, February 25, 1913.

20. *My Story*, p. 109.

21. Ibid., pp. 111–12.

22. Ibid., p. 113.

23. Ibid.

24. Stanley M. Rinehart, Jr., to Stanley M. Rinehart, May 19, 1910.

25. *My Story*, pp. 114–15.

26. Mary Roberts Rinehart to Stanley M. Rinehart, May 19, 1910.

27. Stanley M. Rinehart, Jr., diary of European trip, 1910–1911; printed as part of the Rinehart family book, presented as a gift to Mary Roberts Rinehart in the late 1930s (see chapter 13). The diary provides a day-by-day record of the Rineharts' year abroad.

28. Stanley M. Rinehart, Jr., diary.

29. *My Story*, pp. 116–22; "The Medical Quick-Lunch Counter," *The Saturday Evening Post* (July 26, 1913).

30. Stanley M. Rinehart, Jr., diary.

31. "The Medical Quick-Lunch Counter."

32. *My Story*, p. 123.

33. *The Street of Seven Stars* [March 14–May 2, 1914], pp. 282–83.

34. Stanley M. Rinehart, Jr., diary.

35. *My Story*, p. 123.

Chapter 4: Sewickley, 1911–1914

1. *My Story* [October 1930–May 1931], p. 130.

2. Ibid.

3. Herbert N. Casson, "The Romance of Iron and Steel in America," *Munsey's Magazine*, 36 (1906–1907), 481.

4. *My Story*, pp. 124–25.

5. Ibid., p. 125.

6. Ibid., p. 130.

7. Ibid., p. 129.

8. Mrs. Robert W. McKnight in interview with Jan Cohn; Virginia Barton Wallace in interview with Jan Cohn.

9. *My Story*, p. 127.

10. Ibid., p. 125.

11. Ibid., p. 132.

12. Ibid., p. 134.

13. *The Case of Jennie Brice* [October 1912–January 1913], pp. 2, 226.

14. Mate Bram to Roger L. Scaife, January 19, 1914; *My Story*, p. 136.

15. *Pittsburgh Post*, February 25, 1913; *My Story*, p. 132.

16. *My Story*, p. 90.

17. *The Street of Seven Stars* [March 14–May 2, 1914], pp. 126, 95.

18. Ibid., pp. 372, 376.

19. Churchill Williams to Mary Roberts Rinehart, undated [early 1913?] and March 7, 1913; George H. Lorimer to Mary Roberts Rinehart, May 9, 1913.

20. *New York Times*, October 11, 1914; *Outlook*, 108 (November 4, 1914), 522; *Publishers Weekly*, 86 (October 17, 1914), 1283; *Springfield Republican*, October 29, 1914, p. 5.

21. *My Story*, p. 131.

22. *New York Times*, March 3, 1912.

23. Ibid.

24. Beatrice deMille to Mary Roberts Rinehart, October 5, 1913.

25. Fred H. Wagner, of Essanay Film Manufacturing Company, Chicago, to Mary Roberts Rinehart, February 6, 1914.

26. Fred H. Wagner to Mary Roberts Rinehart, February 6 and March 9, 1914.

27. Louella O. Parsons, of Essanay, to Mary Roberts Rinehart, July 7, 1914.

28. Rinehart correspondence with Winthrop Ames, 1913–1915; Beatrice de-Mille, 1914–1915; David Belasco, 1915; and Holbrook Blinn, 1915.

29. Roger Scaife to Mary Roberts Rinehart, 1915 (late spring).

30. *"K"* [October 1914–October 1915], pp. 16–17.

31. Ibid., p. 10.
32. Ibid., pp. 405, 408.
33. *My Story*, p. 144.
34. *My Story*, pp. 144–45.
35. *The Literary Digest*, 51 (September 11, 1915), 533; *Publishers Weekly*, 88 (September 18, 1915), 788; *Dial* (September 16, 1915), p. 222; *Boston Evening Transcript*, August 7, 1915, p. 8.
36. *New York Times*, August 8, 1915.

Chapter 5: The Great Adventure, Summer 1914–Spring 1915

1. *New York Times*, June 29, 1914; *Vienna Reichspost*, quoted in *New York Times*, June 29, 1914.
2. *My Story* [October 1930–May 1931], pp. 145, 146.
3. George H. Lorimer, editorial, *The Saturday Evening Post* (August 22, 1914).
4. *My Story*, p. 146.
5. Ibid., p. 147; "Salvage," *The Saturday Evening Post* (June 6, 1919).
6. George H. Lorimer to Mary Roberts Rinehart, August 18, 1914.
7. George H. Lorimer to Mary Roberts Rinehart, September 25, 1914.
8. Stanley M. Rinehart to Mary Roberts Rinehart, October 21, 23, December 5, 1914.
9. *My Story*, p. 148.
10. Telegram, George H. Lorimer to Mary Roberts Rinehart, December 29, 1914; George H. Lorimer to Mary Roberts Rinehart, December 31, 1914.
11. Mary Roberts Rinehart to Alan G. Rinehart and Frederick R. Rinehart, January 9, 1915.
12. Mary Roberts Rinehart war diary I, January 20, 1915, in Rinehart collection, Hillman Library, University of Pittsburgh.
13. Ibid., January 21, 1915.
14. Ibid., January 21, 22, 1915.
15. Ibid., January 24, 1915.
16. *Kings, Queens, and Pawns* [1915], p. 40; the articles in *Kings, Queens, and Pawns* were first published in *The Saturday Evening Post* between April 3 and July 31, 1915.
17. Mary Roberts Rinehart war diary II, January 27, 1915.
18. *Kings, Queens, and Pawns*, p. 82.
19. Ibid., p. 83; Mary Roberts Rinehart war diary II, January 29, 1915.
20. Mary Roberts Rinehart war diary II, January 30, 1915.
21. German postcard and translation, in strongbox of World War I memorabilia, in Rinehart collection, Hillman Library, University of Pittsburgh; printed in *Kings, Queens, and Pawns*, p. 160.
22. *My Story*, p. 157.
23. Comment in small maroon notebook, in strongbox of World War I memorabilia; *My Story*, p. 163.
24. Mary Roberts Rinehart war diary II, February 3, 1915.
25. Ibid.
26. Ibid., February 4, 1915.
27. *My Story*, p. 167.

28. Mary Roberts Rinehart war diary II, February 9, 1915.

29. Ibid.

30. Ibid., February 15, 1915.

31. Ibid., Feburary 18, 1915.

32. Mary Roberts Rinehart war diary III, February 18, 1915.

33. Ibid.

34. Official French pass, in strongbox of World War I memorabilia.

35. Mary Roberts Rinehart war diary II, February 18, 1915.

36. Mary Roberts Rinehart war diary III, February 20, 1915.

37. Alan G. Rinehart to Mary Roberts Rinehart, January 24, 1915; Frederick R. Rinehart to Mary Roberts Rinehart, January 31, 1915.

38. Mary Roberts Rinehart war diary III, February 23 and 24, 1915.

39. Ibid., February 24 and 25, 1915.

40. Mary Roberts Rinehart war diary III, n.d.

41. Ibid., February 26, 1915.

42. George H. Lorimer to Mary Roberts Rinehart, enclosing cable from Lord Northcliffe, May 4, 1915; George H. Lorimer to Mary Roberts Rinehart, June 17, 1915; Lord Northcliffe to Mary Roberts Rinehart, December 23, 1915.

43. *Kings, Queens, and Pawns,* p. 359.

44. Ibid., pp. 367–68.

Chapter 6: A Public Person, 1915–1917

1. By late 1915, Rinehart's views were considered significant enough to warrant a piece in the *New York Times* Sunday "Magazine Section" discussing them, particularly her belief that America needed to set up defense machinery in order to protect itself in the intense economic rivalry sure to follow the conclusion of the war (November 21, 1915).

2. *My Story* [October 1930–May 1931], p. 195; in fact, Rinehart ran into minor difficulties on this score. In April, George H. Lorimer received a letter from a reader asserting that one of the war articles unwittingly gave away an allied position. Lorimer sent the letter on to Rinehart who was considerably upset by it. Lorimer assured her that the matter was of no consequence: "There is nothing whatever to worry about. . . . recent developments have changed the whole line up in Belgium and the location of the rabbit trap is probably of no importance at this time" (George H. Lorimer to Mary Roberts Rinehart, April 28, May 3 and 6, 1915).

3. *My Story,* p. 194.

4. William Howard Taft, "The Military and Naval Defenses of the United States," *The Saturday Evening Post* (June 5, 1915); Owen Wister, "The Pentecost of Calamity," *The Saturday Evening Post* (July 3, 1915); George H. Lorimer, editorial, *The Saturday Evening Post* (June 5, 1915).

5. *My Story,* pp. 197, 198.

6. Ibid., p. 199.

7. *Through Glacier Park* [April 22 and 29, 1916], p. 22.

8. *My Story,* p. 200; *Through Glacier Park,* p. 30.

9. *My Story,* pp. 200–01.

10. *Through Glacier Park,* pp. 16–17, 55.

11. "My Country Tish of Thee," *The Saturday Evening Post* (April 1 and 8, 1916).

12. *My Story*, p. 203.

13. Telegram, Mary Roberts Rinehart to Roger Scaife, of Houghton Mifflin, July 22, 1915, Houghton Mifflin Archives, Houghton Library, Harvard University.

14. *My Story*, p. 205.

15. Ibid., p. 215.

16. *Tenting Tonight* [1918], p. 1.

17. Ibid., pp. 23, 64–65, 68.

18. Ibid., pp. 82, 86.

19. Ibid., p. 71.

20. Ibid., p. 150.

21. *My Story*, p. 197.

22. Ibid., p. 206.

23. Stanley M. Rinehart, Jr., to Mary Roberts Rinehart, November 28, 1915.

24. Ibid.

25. George H. Lorimer to Mary Roberts Rinehart, January 12, 1916.

26. "Her Diary," "The Sub-Deb," *The Saturday Evening Post* (February 17, 1917; March 4, 1916).

27. "The Sub-Deb," "Theme: The Celebrity," "The G.A.C." *The Saturday Evening Post* (March 4, November 25, 1916; June 2, 1917).

28. Mary Roberts Rinehart to George H. Lorimer, December 13, 1916; George H. Lorimer to Mary Roberts Rinehart, December 5 and 14, 1916.

29. The confession itself, along with the correspondence between D. A. Blakely and Detective Koehler, can be found in the Rinehart collection at Hillman Library, University of Pittsburgh.

30. Mary Roberts Rinehart to Stanley M. Rinehart, Jr., and Alan G. Rinehart, February 23, 1916.

31. "The Pirates of the Caribbean," *The Saturday Evening Post* (November 18, 1916); Mary Roberts Rinehart to George H. Lorimer, December 29, 1916. One "charming young gentleman" wrote to Rinehart, as she reported to Lorimer, "that if I were the last woman on earth he would not marry me—which is, of course, a matter of deep regret" (Ibid.).

32. *My Story*, p. 209.

33. Ibid., pp. 210–11.

34. Ibid., p. 212.

35. Mary Roberts Rinehart to Churchill Williams, September 18, 1916; Churchill Williams to Mary Roberts Rinehart, September 21 and 25, October 11, 1916. The story was "Theme: The Celebrity."

36. Montrose J. Moses, "Mary Roberts Rinehart—Author, Wife, and Mother," *Good Housekeeping*, 64 (April 1917), 30–31.

37. "My Creed," *American Magazine* (October 1917).

Chapter 7: The Rineharts at War, 1917–1918

1. "The Altar of Freedom," *The Saturday Evening Post* (April 21, 1917).

2. *My Story* [October 1930–May 1931], pp. 220–21.

3. "The Altar of Freedom."

4. Mary Roberts Rinehart to Curtis Brown, April 25, 1917.

5. Mary Roberts Rinehart to George H. Lorimer, April 6, 1917; George H. Lorimer to Mary Roberts Rinehart, April 9, 1917.

6. Stanley M. Rinehart, Jr., to Mary Roberts Rinehart, January 15, 1917.

7. Stanley M. Rinehart, Jr., to Mary Roberts Rinehart, March 9, 1917.

8. Mary Roberts Rinehart to Stanley M. Rinehart, Jr., April 5, 1917; Stanley M. Rinehart, Jr., to Mary Roberts Rinehart, [April 1917]; Newton D. Baker, secretary of war, to the Honorable Joseph P. Tumulty, secretary to the president, April 7, 1917.

9. Stanley M. Rinehart, Jr., to Mary Roberts Rinehart, March 4, 9, and 19, 1917; Stanley M. Rinehart, Jr., to Stanley M. Rinehart, March 23, 1917. The *Boston Evening Transcript* paid Stan, Jr., five dollars for his essay and "gave it the place of honor beside the editorials" (Stanley M. Rinehart, Jr., to Mary Roberts Rinehart, May 9). By May 23 the National Security League and the Special Aid for Preparedness Society were sending copies of his piece "all over the country" (Stanley M. Rinehart, Jr., to Mary Roberts Rinehart, May 23). Copey was pleased enough to award Stan, Jr., a B minus at midterm, but his other three grades (English, economics, and history) were all Ds.

10. Mary Roberts Rinehart to Alan G. Rinehart, June 16, 1917.

11. Josephus Daniels, secretary of the navy, to Adm. Henry T. Mayo, commander-in-chief, Atlantic Fleet, May 8, 1917.

12. George H. Lorimer to Mary Roberts Rinehart, May 25 and 29, 1917.

13. "The Gray Mailed Fist," *The Saturday Evening Post* (June 23, 1917).

14. *My Story*, p. 225; Mary Roberts Rinehart to Stanley M. Rinehart, [May 15, 1917].

15. *My Story*, p. 226.

16. Mary Roberts Rinehart to George H. Lorimer, June 1, 1917.

17. George H. Lorimer to Mary Roberts Rinehart, June 8, 1917.

18. Mary Roberts Rinehart, confidential report to Newton D. Baker, [summer 1917].

19. Mary Roberts Rinehart to Stanley M. Rinehart, Jr., August 3, 1917; Newton D. Baker to Mary Roberts Rinehart, July 11, 1917.

20. Mary Roberts Rinehart to William M. Ingraham, assistant secretary of war, April 23, 1917.

21. Mary Roberts Rinehart to Gen. Enoch H. Crowder, August 1, 1917.

22. *My Story*, p. 222.

23. Eric Fisher Wood, "The British Censorship," *The Saturday Evening Post* (April 28 and May 5, 1917).

24. *My Story*, p. 234.

25. Ibid., pp. 234–35.

26. Mary Roberts Rinehart to Lt. Col. R. H. Van Deman, Chief, Military Intelligence Section, Department of War, August 2, 1917.

27. R. H. Van Deman to Mary Roberts Rinehart, August 18, 1917.

28. *My Story*, p. 237; Helen Mayall to Mary Roberts Rinehart, September 10, 1917.

29. *My Story*, p. 238.

30. George H. Lorimer to Mary Roberts Rinehart, November 2, 1917.

31. Mary Roberts Rinehart to Stanley M. Rinehart, July 10, 1918.

32. *My Story*, p. 244.

33. Ibid., pp. 244–45.

34. Ibid., pp. 246, 248–49; Josephus Daniels to Mary Roberts Rinehart, May 3, 1918.

35. Frederick R. Rinehart to Mary Roberts Rinehart, April 14, 1918.

36. *My Story*, p. 251.

37. Mary Roberts Rinehart to Stanley M. Rinehart, June 15 and July 10, 1918.

38. Newton D. Baker to Mary Roberts Rinehart, July 8 and 16, 1918; Gen. John J. Pershing to Mary Roberts Rinehart, September 5, 1918.

39. Mary Roberts Rinehart to Stanley M. Rinehart, July 10, 1918.

40. Ibid.

41. Mary Roberts Rinehart to Stanley M. Rinehart, September 10, 1918.

42. Mary Roberts Rinehart to Stanley M. Rinehart, [late October, 1918].

43. Mary Roberts Rinehart to her family, November 8, 1918.

44. Ibid.

45. Mary Roberts Rinehart to her family, November 11–12, 1918.

46. Ibid.

47. Ibid.

48. Mary Roberts Rinehart to her family, November 23, 1918.

49. Discarded observation journal, in strongbox of World War I memorabilia, in Rinehart collection.

50. Mary Roberts Rinehart to her family, November 23, 1918.

51. Ibid.

52. Stanley M. Rinehart, Jr., to Mary Roberts Rinehart, December 2, 1918.

53. Mary Roberts Rinehart to her family, December 8, 1918.

54. Ibid.

55. *My Story*, pp. 276–77.

56. From typed list of hospitals available for Rinehart to visit in France, in strongbox of World War I memorabilia.

57. *My Story*, pp. 277–79.

58. Mary Roberts Rinehart to her family, December 8, 1918.

59. Stanley M. Rinehart to Alan G. Rinehart, November 16, 1918, and January 2, 1919.

60. Mary Roberts Rinehart to her family, December 8, 1918; *My Story*, p. 287.

Chapter 8: The Bat, 1919–1921

1. Cables, George H. Doran to Mary Roberts Rinehart, December [4 and 6?], 1918; Stanley M. Rinehart to Mary Roberts Rinehart, December [4 or 5], 1918.

2. Stanley M. Rinehart to Alan G. Rinehart, February 6, 1919; *My Story* [October 1930–May 1931], p. 286.

3. Stanley M. Rinehart to Alan G. Rinehart, February 12, 1919.

4. *My Story*, p. 288.

5. Ibid., p. 289.

6. Ibid. Among Rinehart's unpublished manuscripts is an incomplete draft from 1950 of an article, "The Little Red Book." No doubt responding to the Communist scare of the post–World War II years, Rinehart planned to add her experience with the Seattle man to the mounting evidence of Communist subversion. The informant from Seattle had given her a little red book, which she had subsequently shown to a man in the Department of the Interior, who called it "a handbook of bloody revolution." Rinehart warned her would-be readers that Communist takeover "will take a long time but they can afford to wait, with every year adding to the disaffection and general disruption of the country."

7. *Dangerous Days* [March 1919–(?)], p. 131. Compare "There were others

like him in that milling multitude . . . young men who had come to America with a dream in their hearts, and America had done this to them. Or had she? . . . Was it that America had made them her servants, but not her children?" (*A Poor Wise Man* [April–November 1920], p. 387).

8. *A Poor Wise Man*, p. 188.

9. *Dangerous Days*, p. 99.

10. The *New York Times*'s reviewer thought *Dangerous Days* "agreeably written" with convincing characters; however, he assessed it as "thoroughly conventional" and "stereotyped": "One reads [it] with a haunting sense of having done so before" (July 6, 1919). *A Poor Wise Man* suffered somewhat from flat characterizations, according to the *Times*, but the reviewer thought such shortcomings were more than compensated for by its political timeliness:"The book is intensely American," and its political "remedy" (vigilantism) "will certainly bear considering" (October 17, 1920).

11. Stanley M. Rinehart to Dr. Casey A. Wood, December 11, 1922.

12. *My Story*, pp. 320–21.

13. Ibid., pp. 291–92.

14. Mary Roberts Rinehart to Stanley M. Rinehart, [August 17], 1919.

15. *My Story*, p. 292.

16. Mary Roberts Rinehart to Stanley M. Rinehart, [August 19] and August 22, 1919.

17. Mary Roberts Rinehart to Stanley M. Rinehart, August 25, 1919.

18. Ibid.

19. *My Story*, p. 302.

20. "The Baby Blimp," *The Saturday Evening Post* (August 25, 1923).

21. *My Story*, p. 220.

22. Ibid., p. 249.

23. Ibid., p. 304.

24. Ibid.

25. Mary Roberts Rinehart to Stanley M. Rinehart, [March 31] and April 2, 1920.

26. Contracts for *The Bat*, in the Rinehart collection, Hillman Library, University of Pittsburgh.

27. Telegram, Wagenhals and Kemper to Mary Roberts Rinehart, August 18, 1920.

28. Telegrams, Avery Hopwood to Mary Roberts Rinehart, August 24, 1920; Wagenhals and Kemper to Mary Roberts Rinehart, August 24, 1920.

29. Mary Roberts Rinehart to Colin Kemper, September 15, 1920.

30. Lincoln Wagenhals to Mary Roberts Rinehart, October 20, 1921.

31. All figures on royalties and profits on *The Bat* come from financial statements in the Rinehart collection.

32. Geoffrey T. Hellman, "Close-up: Mary Roberts Rinehart," *Life*, 20 (February 25, 1946).

33. Mary Roberts Rinehart to Avery Hopwood, September 15, 1921.

34. *My Story*, p. 318.

35. Text of speech, "The College Woman and Life," sent to Adelaide Neall, spring 1920.

36. Stanley M. Rinehart to Adelaide Neall, October 16, 1920.

37. Cyrus Curtis to Mary Roberts Rinehart, November 7 and December 21, 1920.

38. George H. Lorimer to Mary Roberts Rinehart, August 19, 1919; Adelaide Neall to Mary Roberts Rinehart, [summer] 1920.

39. George H. Lorimer to Mary Roberts Rinehart, October 10 and 21, 1919; Mary Roberts Rinehart to George H. Lorimer, October 26, 1919.

40. George H. Lorimer to Mary Roberts Rinehart, May 20, 1920; Adelaide Neall to Mary Roberts Rinehart, May 22, 1920.

41. *My Story,* pp. 322, 327.

42. Ibid., p. 328.

43. Ibid., pp. 328–29.

44. Mary Roberts Rinehart to Stanley M. Rinehart, November 17, 1921.

45. Stanley M. Rinehart to Mary Roberts Rinehart, December 8, 1921.

46. *My Story,* p. 337.

47. Alan G. Rinehart in interview with Jan Cohn.

Chapter 9: The Public and the Critics, 1922–1927

1. Frederick Lewis Allen, *Only Yesterday* (New York: Harper, 1931; Perennial Library, 1964), pp. 124–25.

2. Stanley M. Rinehart to Mary Roberts Rinehart, [early fall 1922]; Mary Roberts Rinehart to Alan G. Rinehart, June 27, 1922.

3. *My Story* [October 1930–May 1931], p. 350.

4. *The Literary Review* (July 29, 1922), p. 835; *New York Times,* July 30, 1922; *New Republic,* 31 (August 23, 1922).

5. Stanley M. Rinehart to Mary Roberts Rinehart, August 7, 1922.

6. *My Story,* p. 358.

7. Mary Roberts Rinehart to Alan G. Rinehart, June 8, 1923.

8. Mary Roberts Rinehart to Alan G. Rinehart, June 20, 1923.

9. Stanley M. Rinehart to Alan G. Rinehart, June 24, 1923.

10. Telegram, Lincoln Wagenhals to Mary Roberts Rinehart, August 17, 1923; Lincoln Wagenhals to Mary Roberts Rinehart, [August 21? 1923].

11. Telegram, Lincoln Wagenhals to Mary Roberts Rinehart, August 21, 1923; cf. August 18 telegram: "RECEIPTS [$]937 HOUSE PACKED."

12. Mary Roberts Rinehart to Alan G. Rinehart, September 17, 1923.

13. Copy of promotional literature in Rinehart collection, Hillman Library, University of Pittsburgh; 15,000 copies were distributed to New York pedestrians.

14. Lincoln Wagenhals to Mary Roberts Rinehart, October 1, 1923.

15. *My Story,* p. 373; Mary Roberts Rinehart to Alan G. Rinehart, September 25, 1918.

16. "The Unreality of Modern Realism," *The Bookman* (December 1922).

17. Ibid.

18. "My Public," *The Bookman* (December 1920).

19. Mary Roberts Rinehart to Alan G. Rinehart, September 30, 1923.

20. Stanley M. Rinehart to Charles G. Norris, April 2, 1924.

21. Transcript of séance, Glen Osburne, Pennsylvania, March 17, 1921, Rinehart collection.

22. Transcript of séance, Washington, D.C., February 16 and 17, 1926, Rinehart collection.

23. Sir Arthur Conan Doyle to Mary Roberts Rinehart, May 19 and [undated], [1926].

24. Sir Arthur Conan Doyle to Mary Roberts Rinehart, [undated notes].

25. *The Red Lamp* [January 7 1925–(?)], p. 7.

26. Ibid., p. 9.

27. *My Story*, p. 383.

28. *New York Tribune*, August 16, 1925; *The Literary Review* (August 15, 1925), p. 2; *Boston Evening Transcript*, August 19, 1925.

29. *My Story*, p. 384.

30. Ibid., p. 388.

31. Mary Roberts Rinehart to Alan G. Rinehart, [summer 1925].

32. Eric Hodgins, *Trolley to the Moon* (New York: Simon & Schuster, 1973), pp. 260–67; Mary Roberts Rinehart's early bankbook, in the Rinehart collection, lists the forty-dollar sale to *Youth's Companion.*

33. Mary Roberts Rinehart to family, February 2 and 7, 1925.

34. *My Story*, p. 389.

35. Ibid., pp. 390–91.

36. Ibid., p. 394.

37. Ibid., p. 400.

38. Ibid., p. 398.

39. Mary Roberts Rinehart to Alan G. Rinehart, [summer 1925].

40. *New York Times*, September 20, 1925.

41. Mary Roberts Rinehart to Alan and Gratia Houghton, September 26, 1925.

42. George H. Lorimer to Stanley M. Rinehart, October 3, 1925. Dr. Rinehart published one article in *The Ladies' Home Journal* and one in *The American Mercury* in 1919; in 1920 he published one more in *The American Mercury* and eight in *The Saturday Evening Post.* His essays on health and medicine were directed to a popular audience, carrying such titles as "What Are You Afraid Of?" "How Hard Should We Work?" and "Symptoms and Symptom Hunting."

43. *My Story*, pp. 373–74; Mary Roberts Rinehart to Alan G. Rinehart, January 19, 1925.

44. Mary Roberts Rinehart to Alan G. Rinehart, January 19, 1925.

45. Adelaide Neall to Mary Roberts Rinehart, February 3, 1926.

46. Ibid.

47. Adelaide Neall to Mary Roberts Rinehart, February 11 and March 30, 1926; Mary Roberts Rinehart to Adelaide Neall, April 19, 1926.

48. Mary Roberts Rinehart to Adelaide Neall, April 19, 1926.

49. Stanley M. Rinehart to Mary Roberts Rinehart, [September 11], 1926; Mary Roberts Rinehart to Stanley M. Rinehart, September 17, 1926.

50. Mary Roberts Rinehart to Adelaide Neall, January 4, 1927; George H. Lorimer to Mary Roberts Rinehart, January 31, 1927.

51. William Sladen in interview with Jan Cohn.

52. Stanley M. Rinehart to George H. Lorimer, February 3 and 10, 1927.

53. Mary Roberts Rinehart to family, March 27, 1927.

54. Stanley M. Rinehart to family, June 22, 1927; Mary Roberts Rinehart to family, June 16, 1927.

55. Austin Corcoran to Mary Roberts Rinehart, May 17, 1927.

56. Stanley M. Rinehart to family, June 22, 1927; Mary Roberts Rinehart to Stanley M. Rinehart, July 6, 1927.

57. "Book Review," *New York Times*, June 19, 1927.

Chapter 10: "Gesture Toward Truth," 1927–1928 and Beyond

1. Mary Roberts Rinehart to Alan and Gratia Rinehart, August 7 and September 4, 1927; Mary Roberts Rinehart to family, August 26, 1927; Mary Roberts Rinehart to Alan and Gratia Rinehart, July 27, 1927.

2. Jean West Maury, "An Afternoon with Mary Roberts Rinehart," *Boston Evening Transcript,* June 14, 1926.

3. "Just a Touch of Celebrity," *The Saturday Evening Post* (January 14, 1928).

4. "I Buy Clothes Twice a Year," *Ladies' Home Journal* (March 14, 1928).

5. Ibid.

6. "Companionate Marriage," *McCall's* (March 13, 1928).

7. *My Story* [October 1930–May 1931], p. 424.

8. *This Strange Adventure* [October 1928–February 1929], p. 181.

9. Ibid., pp. 143–45.

10. Ibid., pp. 183, 185, 187.

11. Ibid., p. 213.

12. Ibid., p. 214.

13. Ibid., p. 227.

14. Ibid., p. 333.

15. Stanley M. Rinehart to family, March 28, 1928; Mary Roberts Rinehart to Gratia Rinehart, May [4?], 1928.

16. Mary Roberts Rinehart to Alan G. Rinehart, May 26 and 30, 1928.

17. Mary Roberts Rinehart to Gratia Rinehart, June [2?], 1928; Mary Roberts Rinehart to Alan G. Rinehart, May 30, 1928.

18. *New York Herald Tribune,* April 7, 1919, and *The Nation,* 28 (July 31, 1929). *Boston Evening Transcript,* February 23, 1919: "It is hardly a pretty story"; *Springfield Republican,* June 16, 1929: "an interesting but far from cheerful narrative." Mary Roberts Rinehart to Alan and Gratia Rinehart, August 12, 1928.

19. Mary Roberts Rinehart to Alan G. Rinehart, August 30, 1929.

20. "Live a saintly life," says a character in *The Man in Lower 10.* "Prayers and matins and all that, and the subconscious mind hikes you out of bed at night to steal under-muslins. Subliminal theft, so to speak" (p. 234). It is reasonable to suppose that Mary learned something about Freudian thought from Stan whose professional reading may well have introduced him to this subject. (See Claudia Morrison, *Freud and the Critics* [Chapel Hill: University of North Carolina Press, 1968] for a discussion of turn-of-the-century articles on Freudian ideas in medical and psychic research journals.)

In Vienna, in 1910–1911, Stan attended at least one of Freud's lectures on infant sexuality, which left him offended and incredulous (see chapter 3; Alan G. Rinehart in interview with Jan Cohn).

21. Mary Roberts Rinehart to Alan G. Rinehart, June 21, 1929.

22. *My Story,* pp. 418–19.

23. Arthur McKeogh to Mary Roberts Rinehart, December 27, 1930; unpublished autobiographical fragment, Rinehart collection, Hillman Library, University of Pittsburgh.

24. *My Story,* p. 3.

25. Unpublished autobiographical fragment.

26. Ibid.

27. *My Story,* new ed. [1948], pp. 532–33.

28. Ibid., p. 476.

29. *My Story*, p. 429.

30. *My Story*, new ed., p. 470.

31. *My Story*, p. 3.

32. Arthur McKeogh to Mary Roberts Rinehart, [fall 1930]; William S. Hart to Mary Roberts Rinehart, March 19, 1932.

33. Stanley M. Rinehart to Gratia Rinehart, June 21, 1928; *My Story*, pp. 422.

34. Arthur McKeogh to Stanley M. Rinehart, January 7, 1931.

35. *My Story*, pp. 427–28.

36. Ibid., pp. 406–07.

37. William Lyon Phelps to Mary Roberts Rinehart, May 1, 1926; June 24, 1927; and [March?] 13, 1929.

38. *My Story*, p. 406.

39. Ibid., pp. 430–31.

40. William Lyon Phelps, *Autobiography with Letters* (New York: Oxford University Press, 1939), p. 782; Howard Mumford Jones to Mary Roberts Rinehart, February 19, 1949.

41. *My Story*, pp. 431–32.

Chapter 11: Endings, 1929–1932

1. *My Story* [October 1930–May 1931], p. 425.

2. Mary Roberts Rinehart to Frederick R. Rinehart, July 11, 1929.

3. A copy of the flyer remains in the Rinehart collection at the Hillman Library, University of Pittsburgh.

4. Stanley M. Rinehart to Alan G. Rinehart, March 7, 1929.

5. All these items are now part of the Rinehart collection.

6. Kenneth Parker to Mary Roberts Rinehart, November 26, 1930; Stanley M. Rinehart to Kenneth Parker, December 3 and 18, 1930; Mary Roberts Rinehart to Kenneth Parker, February 23, 1933; Kenneth Parker to Mary Roberts Rinehart, April 4, 1939.

In the April 1939 letter, Parker asked, tactfully, whether Rinehart would consider a "delicate" request for a "dignified" endorsement. Rinehart, who carefully avoided endorsements, replied that only twice had she lent her name for advertising purposes: "once for a car I did not want or need and again when I wanted to buy a boat." She regretted both but had come to feel she owed Parker Pen a favor: "no full page spread . . . but possibly my name in a list of Parker Pen users" (April 13, 1939). Parker then wrote telling Rinehart to forget the whole thing: "I do not want to embarrass you in the least about it" (April 17, 1939). But Mary's conscience bothered her and five years later she sent a written statement to Parker to use as he saw fit (January 29, 1944). Parker wrote immediately to express his appreciation—and to request a rewrite, something more personal (February 3, 1944). Rinehart graciously complied: "I am writing out of a purely spontaneous feeling that this pen deserves recognition, and that after several million words and during storm, stress, sickness and travel, it has remained, like Rebecca's parasol at Sunnybrook Farm, a great joy but also a great responsibility" (February 5, 1944).

7. George H. Lorimer to Mary Roberts Rinehart, October 31, 1929; *My Story*, new ed. [1948], pp. 442, 460; Stan told Adelaide Neall in December that, should the *Post* pay Mary the full amount due her, it would cost them $10,000 in additional in-

come taxes (Stanley M. Rinehart to Adelaide Neall, December 10, 1929). The amount in question was presumably the $40,000 for the second payment on *The Door;* the *Post* sent that check on January 1, 1930.

8. *My Story,* new ed., p. 442.

9. "The Chaotic Decade," *Ladies' Home Journal* (May 1930).

10. Ibid.

11. Loring Schuler to Mary Roberts Rinehart, March 11, 1932.

12. Loring Schuler to Mary Roberts Rinehart, March 27, 1930.

13. Mary Roberts Rinehart to Loring Schuler, May 5, 1930; "The Effect of Fashion on Manners," *Ladies' Home Journal* (October 1930).

14. "A Woman Goes to Market," *The Saturday Evening Post* (January 31, 1931).

15. Ibid.

16. *My Story,* new ed., p. 466; Mary Roberts Rinehart to Alan G. Rinehart, December 10, 1931.

17. Adelaide Neall to Mary Roberts Rinehart, March 6, 1936; *My Story,* new ed., p. 488.

18. "The Tall Tree," *Good Housekeeping* (May 1935).

19. *My Story,* new ed., p. 468.

20. Mary Roberts Rinehart to Alan G. Rinehart, August 30, 1929.

21. Stanley M. Rinehart to Alan G. Rinehart, January 16, 1931; Mary Roberts Rinehart to Alan G. Rinehart, February 14, 1931.

22. Loring Schuler to Mary Roberts Rinehart, May 7 and October 28, 1931.

23. Loring Schuler to Mary Roberts Rinehart, November 4, 1931.

24. Stanley M. Rinehart, Jr., to Alan G. Rinehart, May 18, 1931; Mary Roberts Rinehart to Alan G. Rinehart, May 29, 1931.

25. Stanley M. Rinehart to Alan and Gratia Rinehart, June 2, 1931.

26. Stanley M. Rinehart to Alan G. Rinehart, June 10, 1931.

27. *My Story,* new ed., p. 470.

28. Mary Roberts Rinehart to Stanley M. Rinehart, September 25, 26, and October 4, 1931; Mary Roberts Rinehart to Alan G. Rinehart, October 6, 1931.

29. Mary Roberts Rinehart to Alan G. Rinehart, December 10, 1931.

30. Stanley M. Rinehart to Alan G. Rinehart, December 21, 1931; Mary Roberts Rinehart to Alan G. Rinehart, December 22, 1931.

31. *My Story,* new ed., p. 474.

32. Mary Roberts Rinehart to family, May 16, 1932.

33. Mary Roberts Rinehart to family, May 21, 1932; Stanley M. Rinehart to family, June 5, 1932.

34. *My Story,* new ed., p. 485.

35. *New York Times,* August 2, 4, 5, 9, and 10, 1932.

36. *My Story,* new ed., p. 474; Stanley M. Rinehart to Alan G. Rinehart, August 24, 1932.

37. *My Story,* new ed., pp. 476, 437.

38. Alan G. Rinehart, "How to Write a Story," unpublished typescript.

39. "The Future of Marriage: A Socratic Dialogue," *Forum* (August 1931); the three other women participating in the discussion were writers Margaret Culkin Banning and Alice Beal Parsons and *Golden Book* editor Frederica Field.

40. Ibid.

41. *My Story,* new ed., p. 437.

Chapter 12: The Writer, 1933–1939

1. Isaac Anderson, review of *The Album, New York Times,* May 28, 1933.
2. *The State Vs. Elinor Norton* [September 1933–January 1934], p. 280.
3. Reviews of *The State Vs. Elinor Norton*: J. S. Southron, *New York Times,* January 28, 1934; Herschel Brickell, *North American Review,* 237 (April 1934), 378; William Rose Benét, *Saturday Review of Literature,* 10 (February 3, 1934), 453.
4. According to a complicated point system that figured numbers of best-selling books and numbers of years on best-seller lists (from monthly lists issued by *The Bookman* and figures from lending libraries and other sources), Rinehart achieved the highest number of total points (595) of all best-selling English and American writers from 1895 to 1944; see Irving Harlow Hart, "The One Hundred Leading Authors of Fiction from 1895 to 1944," *Publishers Weekly,* 149 (January 1946), 285–90. See also chapter 3, n.14.
5. Rinehart received a vast amount of fan mail. Some unusual letters, among the very few that have been saved, suggest how strong an emotional pull she exerted. Many wrote asking for help with their writing, among them a thirty-two year old cerebral palsy victim, whom Mary could not refuse, "although I practically never do this" (Mary Roberts Rinehart to Guy Epling, November 24, 1956). More striking was her compassion, as early as 1921, for a Wyoming physician who wrote that he had lived for twenty-seven years as a woman before discovering, in a medical examination, that he suffered from "complete, congenital and incurable Homosexuality." For the previous four years he had lived as a man, but had been discovered, hounded. He wondered if Mrs. Rinehart would read and critique his autobiography. She would and did. (Wyoming physician to Mary Roberts Rinehart, August 3, 1921; Rinehart to physician, August 12, 1921).
6. *My Story,* new ed. [1948], p. 570.
7. Alan G. Rinehart in interview with Jan Cohn.
8. *My Story,* new ed., p. 495.
9. Ibid., p. 496.
10. Ibid., p. 498.
11. Associated Press interview with Mary Roberts Rinehart, August 25, 1934; "Looking for the Magic Word," *Cosmopolitan* (December 1934).
12. *My Story,* new ed., pp. 501, 503; Mary Roberts Rinehart to Alan G. Rinehart, August 5, 1933.
13. *My Story,* new ed., p. 503.
14. Reviews of *The Doctor:* S. J. Roof, *New Republic,* 87 (June 24, 1936), 220; *Time,* 27 (June 8, 1936), 84; L. M. Field, *New York Times,* May 24, 1936; Logan Clendening, *Saturday Review of Literature,* 14 (June 6, 1936), 6.
15. Adelaide Neall to Mary Roberts Rinehart, March 1, 1935.
16. W. F. Bigelow to Mary Roberts Rinehart, June 24, 1935.
17. Adelaide Neall to Mary Roberts Rinehart, December 11, 1934.
18. Review of *Married People, New York Times,* February 28, 1937; Stephen Vincent and Rosemary Benét, "Mrs. Rinehart's Bread and Butter," *New York Herald-Tribune,* October 19, 1941.
19. "The Better Man," *Good Housekeeping* (December 1932).
20. Ibid.
21. "Experiment in Youth," *Cosmopolitan* (December 1936).
22. "Lightning Never Strikes Twice," *The Saturday Evening Post* (June 6, 1936).

23. Ibid.
24. Ibid.
25. "The Second Marriage," *Ladies' Home Journal* (June 1935).
26. Ibid.
27. Ibid.
28. William Sladen in correspondence with Jan Cohn.
29. *My Story*, new ed., p. 530.
30. Ibid., p. 549.
31. Ibid., pp. 530–31.
32. Ibid., p. 522.
33. George H. Doran, *Chronicles of Barrabas* (New York: Harcourt Brace, 1935), pp. 187–94.
34. *My Story*, new ed., p. 526.
35. Gen. John J. Pershing to Mary Roberts Rinehart, April 21, 1937.
36. Mary Roberts Rinehart to family, May 19, 1937.
37. Ibid.
38. "Strange Journey," *The Saturday Evening Post* (October 16, 1937).
39. George H. Lorimer to Mary Roberts Rinehart, November 5, 1937; *My Story*, new ed., p. 509.
40. Mary Roberts Rinehart to Adelaide Neall, February 8, 1941.
41. W. H. Clark, review of *Tish Marches On, Boston Evening Transcript* (December 4, 1937), p. 1; Mary Roberts Rinehart to Adelaide Neall, February 8, 1941.
42. "Thoughts," *Ladies' Home Journal* (May 1931).
43. Ibid.
44. William Sladen in interview with Jan Cohn; *The Wall* [May–July 1938], p. 240.
45. George H. D. Rinehart in interview with Jan Cohn.
46. "Writing Is Work," *The Saturday Evening Post* (March 11, 1939).
47. Ibid.
48. *My Story*, new ed., p. 521.
49. Ibid.
50. Ibid.

Chapter 13: The End of the Adventure, 1940–1958

1. "Before the Drums Beat," *Good Housekeeping* (January 1938).
2. *My Story*, new ed. [1948], pp. 541, 546–47.
3. Robert Van Gelder, "An Interview with Mary Roberts Rinehart," *New York Times*, December 15, 1940, "Book Review" section.
4. Ibid.
5. *My Story*, new ed., p. 546.
6. Mary Roberts Rinehart to Stanley M. Rinehart, Jr., June 21, 1944.
7. *My Story*, new ed., p. 555.
8. "The Time Is Ten," *Good Housekeeping* (July 1942).
9. "The Temporary Death of Mrs. Ayres," *Good Housekeeping* (October 1942).
10. Ibid.
11. Ibid.
12. Isaac Anderson, review of *Haunted Lady, New York Times*, May 3, 1942; Isaac Anderson, review of *The Yellow Room, New York Times*, October 28, 1945.

13. Margaret Wallace, review of *Familiar Faces, New York Times,* July 20, 1941.

14. Isabelle Mallett, review of *Alibi for Isabel, New York Times,* August 20, 1944.

15. Mary Roberts Rinehart to Adelaide Neall, November 15, 1941; Adelaide Neall to Mary Roberts Rinehart, November 17, 1941.

16. Adelaide Neall to Mary Roberts Rinehart, [March 1942]; Stuart Rose to Stanley M. Rinehart, Jr., February 3, 1943.

17. Mary Roberts Rinehart to Ben Hibbs, November 27, 1948.

18. Stuart Rose to Mary Roberts Rinehart, April 7, 1949; Mary Roberts Rinehart to Stuart Rose, April 9, 1949.

19. Mary Roberts Rinehart to Stuart Rose, February 16, 1952; Stuart Rose to Mary Roberts Rinehart, February 29, 1952.

20. Mary Roberts Rinehart to H. Ralph Knight, May 17, 1952.

21. Geoffrey T. Hellman, "Close-Up: Mary Roberts Rinehart," *Life* (February 25, 1946).

22. Dorothy Cameron Disney and Milton Mackaye, *Mary Roberts Rinehart* (New York: Rinehart and Company, [1948]).

23. Ibid.; *My Story,* new ed., p. 567.

24. Stanley M. Rinehart III in interview with Jan Cohn.

25. Frederick R. Rinehart in interview with Jan Cohn.

26. *Family Book,* quoted from original galleys belonging to Frederick R. Rinehart.

27. Ibid.

28. Frederick R. Rinehart in interview with Jan Cohn.

29. Quoted in *My Story,* new ed., p. 568.

30. *My Story,* new ed., pp. 560–64; *Time* (June 30, 1947), pp. 41–42.

31. Ibid.

32. Ibid.

33. *A Light in the Window* [October 1947–February 1948], pp. 142–43.

34. Ibid., pp. 163, 268.

35. Alice B. Toklas to "Editor," Rinehart and Company, January 1948.

36. Tex McCrary and Jinx Falkenberg, "Close-Up," *New York Herald-Tribune,* November 6, 1950; Harvey Breit, "Talk with Mary Roberts Rinehart," *New York Times,* February 3, 1952; Harvey Breit, "In and Out of Books," undated clipping from *New York Times* "Book Review" in Rinehart collection, Hillman Library, University of Pittsburgh; William Sladen in interview with Jan Cohn.

37. Tape of Mary Margaret McBride's radio interview with Mary Roberts Rinehart, February 4, 1952.

38. Elizabeth S. Rinehart in interview with Jan Cohn; Mary Roberts Rinehart to Edward R. Murrow, November 17, 1956; undated clipping from *Variety,* in Rinehart collection.

39. Mary Roberts Rinehart to Ruby MacDonald, June 3 and December 16, 1950, and April 17, 1952.

Mary Roberts Rinehart:

A Chronological Bibliography

This bibliography includes stories, articles, poems, novellas, and full-length novels published in magazines, as well as first book publications of novels and of collections of stories and articles. Plays, movies, and radio and television performances are also listed. Not included are newspaper syndications, second serial rights, English and Canadian publications, or translations.

If an entry is incomplete, the omitted information is unknown. A question mark occurs in an entry when information has not been verified but appears to be accurate. Alternative titles are given in parentheses only when they are important.

When a film entry gives the date of a review, the review was used to verify the existence of the film; the date may not be the year the film was actually released. When an entry gives a copyright date, e.g., "C. 1909," the evidence comes from a film bibliography. When the entry gives a questioned date in parentheses, e.g. "(1909?)," no other information but the date is available; in such cases the information has usually come from the Rinehart files, which may have indicated a payment received.

1904–1909

"Farmer Jones on Medicine." *National Press Association.* (1904?).
      Poem.
"Housekeeping." *Pittsburgh Gazette.* (1904?).
      Article; $25.
"The Toy Railroad." *Pittsburgh Sunday Gazette.* (1904?).
      Poem; $2.
"The Detective Story." *Munsey's.* May 1904.
      Poem; $10.
"Modern Drama." *Munsey's.* June 1904.
      Poem; $12.
"Signs of the Times." *Pittsburgh Sunday Gazette.* June 26, 1904.
      Poem; $4.
"La Grippe: A Tale of Conspiracy." *Sanitation.* August 1904.
      Poem.
"Harmony in the House." *Associated Sunday Magazines.* October 1904.
      Story; $9.
Untitled. *Sanitation.* October 1904.
      Poem.

267

"The Worm Turned." *Munsey's*. November 1904.
  Poem; $10 (anonymous).
"When Ma Baked a Cake." *Sunday Magazine*. November 27, 1904.
  Poem; $7.
"His Other Self" ("The Alter Ego"). *Munsey's*. December 1904.
  Story; $34.
"His Honor's Psychic Experiment." *All-Story*. 1905.
  Story; $25.
"The Mystery of the Clay Balls." *All-Story*. 1905.
  Story; $20.
"The Cow of Destiny." *American Boy*. (1905?).
"A Heart Convention." *Smith's Magazine*. (1905?).
  Story; $25.
"The Mother Tree." *Munsey's*. (1905?).
  Poem; $6.
"The Poisoning of Michael." *Youth's Companion*. (1905?).
  Story; $30.
"The Rain." (1905?).
  Poem; $5.
"A Type-Writer Idyl." (1905?).
  Poem; $4.
"An Imaginary Inebriate." *Munsey's*. February 1905.
  Story; $25.
"The Misadventures of a Pearl Necklace." *Argosy*. February 1905.
  Story; $30.
"The Prize Pumpkin Pie." *Munsey's*. February 1905.
  Story; $40.
"A Transgression." *Era*. February 1905.
  Story; $6.
"A Gasoline Road Agent." *All-Story*. April 1905.
  Story; $20.
"An Anonymous Guest." *Munsey's*. May 1905.
  Story; $60.
"The Doctor's Visitor." *Munsey's*. August 1905.
  Story; $40 (pseud.: Elliott Roberts).
"An Episode of the City." *Woman's Home Companion*. August 1905.
  Story; $50.
"The Old Maid's Boy." *Munsey's*. August 1905.
  Story; $40.
"Through the Gap." *Munsey's*. October 1905.
  Story; $40.
"An Experiment in Poverty." *American (Illustrated) Magazine*. November 1905.
  Story; $80.
"The Artist and the Elephant." *Munsey's*. (1905–1906?).
  Story; $33.
"Clearwater Bridge." *Everybody's*. (1905–1906?).
  Story; $66.
"The Girl Across the Street." *Home Magazine*. (1905–1906?).
  Story; $50.

"The Housekeeper's Story: Tale of an Ancient House." *Short Stories*. (1906?).
Story; $20.
"The Man in Lower Ten." *All-Story*. January–April 1906.
Serial, mystery; $400.
BOOK: *The Man in Lower 10*. Indianapolis: Bobbs-Merrill, 1909.
FILM SALE: Selig, (1909?). (Rights forfeited.)
"A Call to Battle." *All-Story*. May 1906.
Story; $15.
"The Night of the Play." *Argosy*. May 1906.
Autobiographical story; $25.
"A Trolley Car Mutiny." *All-Story*. May 1906.
Story; $20.
"The Broken Quarantine." *Munsey's*. June 1906.
Story; $100.
"The Love Affair of a Freak." *Scrap Book*. June 1906.
Story; $15.
"The Way of the Transgressor." *All-Story*. June 1906.
Story; $30.
"Two Criminals." *Ladies' World*. July 1906.
Story; $10.
"Accessory After the Fact." *All-Story*. August 1906.
Story; $35.
"At the Foot of the Hill." *Munsey's*. August 1906.
Story; $50.
"The Doctor's Story." *Watson's Magazine*. August–November 1906.
Serial; $225.
"Poverty and Petulance." *All-Story*. September 1906.
Story.
A Double Life. 1906.
Play; opened December 24, 1906, Bijou; 12 performances (pseud.: Roberts
Rinehart).
"The Elixir of Benevolence." *Chicago Magazine*. (1906–1908?).
Story; $35.
"The Ex-Urbanites." *New Idea Magazine*. (1906–1908?).
Story; $30.
"Janet and the Poor." *All-Story*. (1906–1908?).
Story; $35.
"Out on the Hills." *Munsey's*. (1906–1908?).
Story; $65.
"The Sanitorians." (1906–1908?).
Story; $25.
"Sidney Easton's Wife." *Blue Book*. (1906–1908?).
Story; $40.
"Striking Storks." *Munsey's*. (1906–1908?).
Poem; $16.
"The Sutherland Tragedy." *All-Story*. (1906–1908?).
Story; $75.
"Pittie's Professional Pride." *All-Story*. January 1907.
Story; $50.

"Acquitted." *Pearson's.* February 1907.
   Story; $40.
   FILM: Triangle. C. 1916.
"After the Play." *Argosy.* April 1907.
   Story; $40.
"The Adoption of Eliza." *The Story-Teller.* May 1907.
   Story; $20.
"The Little Tin Bear." *Ladies' Work.* June 1907.
   Story; $10.
"The Salvage of the Madigan Baby." *Woman's Home Companion.* June 1907.
   Story; $75.
"The Shelter of the Fold." *Munsey's.* June 1907.
   Story.
"The Fault of the Fog." *Broadway Magazine.* September 1907.
   Story; $25.
"The Dismembering of Henry Simmons." *Blue Book.* October 1907.
   Story; $25.
"A Triangular Elopement." *Munsey's.* October 1907.
   Story.
"The Circular Staircase." *All-Story.* November 1907–March 1908.
   Serial, mystery; $500.
   BOOK: *The Circular Staircase.* Indianapolis: Bobbs-Merrill, 1908.
   FILM: *The Circular Staircase.* Selig-Polyscope. C. 1915.
   TELEVISION PLAY: *Climax.* June 21, 1956. (Judith Anderson starred.)
"A Conflict of Authorities." *Munsey's.* November 1907.
   Story; $52.50.
"Christmas in Town." *Munsey's.* December 1907.
   Poem; $12.
"The Diary of an Ambulance Doctor." *Delineator.* (1908–1909?).
   Story; $50.
"Sic Transit." (1908–1909?).
   Poem.
"For Auld Lang Syne." *Red Book.* February 1908.
   Story.
"His Father's Son." *Munsey's.* February 1908.
   Story; $75.
"The Mystery of 1122" (*The Window at the White Cat*). *Live Wire.* February 1908–(?).
   Serial, mystery; $500.
   BOOK: *The Window at the White Cat.* Indianapolis: Bobbs-Merrill, 1910.
   FILM SALE: Selig, 1911. (Rights forfeited.)
"The Valley of Oblivion." *New Broadway Magazine.* February 1908.
   Story; $50.
"The Room Beyond." *Munsey's.* March 1908.
   Story; $125.
"A Family Affair." *All-Story.* April 1908.
   Story; $22.
"Her Uncle-in-Law." *All-Story.* May 1908.
   Story; $33.75.
"Down Happy Valley." *Short Story.* June 1908.
   Story.

"A Question of Advertising." *All-Story*. June 1908.
>   Story; $35.

"The Sabine Woman." *Young's*. August 1908.
>   Story; $20.

"The Upper Room." *Success*. October 1908.
>   Poem; $12.

"Seven Days." *Lippincott's*. December 1908.
>   Novella; $300.
>   BOOK: *When a Man Marries*. Indianapolis: Bobbs-Merrill, 1909.
>   PLAY: *Seven Days* (with Avery Hopwood). Opened November 10, 1909, Astor; 397 performances.
>   MUSICAL PLAY: *Tumble In*. Opened March 24, 1919, Selwyn; 128 performances.
>   FILM: *Seven Days*. Christie. Review 1925. C. 1925. MRR's share: $5,000.

"A Lion Rampant." *Munsey's*. January 1909.
>   Story; $150.

"I Go a Playing." *Munsey's*. January 1909.
>   Story.

"Lady Godiva at the Springs." *Lippincott's*. May 1909.
>   Story.

"The Borrowed House." *The Saturday Evening Post*. August 14 and 21, 1909.
>   Story.

"What Happened to Father." *Lippincott's*. September 1909.
>   Story.
>   FILMS: *What Happened to Father*. Vitagraph. C. 1915. *What Happened to Father*. Warner Bros. C. 1927.

1910–1919

"Those That Wait." *Scribner's*. January 1910.
>   Story; $80.

"That Awful Night." *The Saturday Evening Post*. March 5, 1910.
>   Tish story.

"Grandfather Bixby, Nurse." *Lippincott's*. July 1910.
>   Story.

"Your Explanation, Gentlemen." *Munsey's*. July 1910.
>   Story.

"Three Pirates of Penzance." *The Saturday Evening Post*. August 20, 1910.
>   Tish story.

"A Cup of Water to the Thirsty." *The Saturday Evening Post*. October 24, 1910.
>   Story; $100(?).

"The Amazing Adventures of Letitia Carberry." *The Saturday Evening Post*. November 18–December 2, 1911.
>   Serial, Tish story.
>   BOOK: *The Amazing Adventures of Letitia Carberry*. Indianapolis: Bobbs-Merrill, 1911.
>   >   Contents:
>   >   "The Amazing Adventures of Letitia Carberry"
>   >   "That Awful Night"
>   >   "Three Pirates of Penzance"
>   FILM SALE: Selig, (1911?). (Rights forfeited.)

Where There's a Will. Indianapolis: Bobbs-Merrill, 1912.
    Fictionalized version of Rinehart's unproduced play, *The Water Wooers.*
"The Checkerboard Table." *The Saturday Evening Post.* February 3, 1912.
    Tish story.
"Jane." *The Saturday Evening Post.* May 25, 1912.
    Story.
    FILM: Essanay, (1912?).
"The Miracle." *McClure's.* June 1912.
    Hospital story.
"Up and Down with the Drama." *The Saturday Evening Post.* July 6, 1912.
    Article (anonymous).
"The Cave on Thundercloud." *The Saturday Evening Post.* July 22, 1912.
    Tish story.
"The Darkest Hour." *Harper's Bazaar.* August 1912.
    Story.
"The Case of Jennie Brice." *Everybody's.* October 1912–January 1913.
    Serial, mystery.
    BOOK: *The Case of Jennie Brice.* Indianapolis: Bobbs-Merrill, 1913.
"Mind Over Motor." *The Saturday Evening Post.* October 5, 1912.
    Tish story.
    FILM: Essanay, (1912?). $200.
"In the Pavilion." *The Saturday Evening Post.* November 9, 1912.
    Hospital story.
    FILM: *The Glorious Fool.* Goldwyn. Review 1922. C. 1922. Combines "In the
        Pavilion" and "Twenty-Two" (1917?).
"The Dancer at the Tabarin." *Collier's.* December 14, 1912.
    Story.
Cheer Up. 1912.
    Play; opened December 30, 1912, Harris; 24 performances.
"A Doctor's Diary." *Smart Set.* January 1913.
    Story.
"Like a Wolf on the Fold." *The Saturday Evening Post.* April 26, 1913.
    Tish story.
    FILM: Essanay, (1913?). $200.
"The After House." *McClure's.* June–October 1913.
    Serial, mystery.
    BOOK: *The After House.* Boston: Houghton Mifflin, 1914.
    TELEVISION PLAY: "Telephone Time" (ABC), 1957. Combines "The After
        House" and the story of Rinehart's solving the mystery. (Claudette
        Colbert played Rinehart.)
"The Little Lamp." *Woman's World.* June 1913.
    Story.
"The Medical Quick-Lunch Counter." *The Saturday Evening Post.* July 26, 1913.
    Article.
"The Game." *The Saturday Evening Post.* October 18, 1913.
    Story; $1,250.
"The Simple Lifers." *The Saturday Evening Post.* October 25, 1913.
    Tish story.
    FILM: Essanay, (1913?). $200.

"Affinities." *The Saturday Evening Post*. November 29, 1913.
    Story.
    FILM: Essanay, (1914?).
"God's Fool." *The Saturday Evening Post*. December 6, 1913.
    Hospital story.
"Sauce for the Gander." *The Saturday Evening Post*. (1914?).
    Story.
"The Buckled Bag." *The Saturday Evening Post*. January 10 and 17, 1914.
    Two-part Miss Pinkerton story.
"The Street of Seven Stars." *The Saturday Evening Post*. March 14–May 2, 1914.
    Serial, romance.
    BOOK: *The Street of Seven Stars*. Boston: Houghton Mifflin, 1914.
    FILM: De Luxe Pictures, (1918?). $2,500.
"The Papered Door." *Collier's*. March 21, 1914.
    Story.
    FILM: Essanay, (1915?). $125.
"The Little General." *The Saturday Evening Post*. April 11, 1914.
    Story.
"The Secret House." *Metropolitan*. May 1914.
    Story.
"Locked Doors." *The Saturday Evening Post*. August 22 and 29, 1914.
    Two-part Miss Pinkerton story.
"The Girl Who Had No God." *Delineator*. September 1914–January 1915.
    Serial.
"Lily." *Cosmopolitan*. September 1914.
    Story.
" 'K.' " *McClure's*. October 1914–October 1915.
    Serial, romance.
    BOOK: *"K."* Boston: Houghton Mifflin, 1915.
    FILMS: *The Doctor and the Woman*. Jewel Productions. Review 1918. C. 1918.
        K—the Unknown. Universal. C. 1924.
"The Truce of God." *Collier's*. December 12, 1914.
    Story; $1,200.
    BOOK: *The Truce of God*. New York: Doran, 1920.
Kings, Queens, and Pawns. New York: Doran, 1915.
    Collected war articles.
"Tish's Spy." *The Saturday Evening Post*. February 20 and 27, 1915.
    Two-part Tish story.
    FILM: Essanay, (1915?). $200.
"A Talk with the King of the Belgians." *The Saturday Evening Post*. April 3, 1915.
    War article; $1,000.
" 'Twas a Famous Victory." *The Saturday Evening Post*. April 10, 1915.
    War article; $1,000.
"For King and Country." *The Saturday Evening Post*. April 17, 1915.
    War article, $1,000.
"No Man's Land." *The Saturday Evening Post*. May 8, 1915.
    War article; $1,000.
"Wipers." *The Saturday Evening Post*. May 15, 1915.
    War article; $1,000.

"The Man of Ypres." *The Saturday Evening Post*. May 22, 1915.
 War article; $1,000.
"The Sick and Sorry House." *The Saturday Evening Post*. June 12, 1915.
 War article; $1,000.
"Queen Mary of England." *The Saturday Evening Post*. June 19, 1915.
 War article; $1,000.
"Volunteers and Patriots." *The Saturday Evening Post*. June 26, 1915.
 War article; $1,000.
"The Queen of the Belgians." *The Saturday Evening Post*. July 3, 1915.
 War article; $1,000.
"Clara's Little Escapade." *The Saturday Evening Post*. July 17, 1915.
 Story; $1,500.
"The Red Badge of Mercy." *The Saturday Evening Post*. July 31, 1915.
 War article; $1,000.
"The Family Friend." *The Saturday Evening Post*. December 15, 1915.
 Story; $1,500.
Tish. Boston: Houghton Mifflin, 1916.
 Contents:
 "Mind Over Motor"
 "Like a Wolf on the Fold"
 "The Simple Lifers"
 "Tish's Spy"
 "My Country Tish of Thee"
"Are We Downhearted? No!" *The Saturday Evening Post*. January 8, 1916.
 Story; $1,750.
"The Sub-Deb." *The Saturday Evening Post*. March 4, 1916.
 Bab story.
"My Country Tish of Thee." *The Saturday Evening Post*. April 1 and 8, 1916.
 Two-part Tish story.
"Through Glacier Park with Howard Eaton." *Collier's*. April 22 and 29, 1916.
 Two-part travel article.
 BOOK:*Through Glacier Park*. Boston: Houghton Mifflin, 1916.
"The Empire Builders." *The Saturday Evening Post*. May 20, 1916.
 Story; $1,750.
 FILM: *It's a Great Life*. Goldwyn. Review 1920. C. 1920.
"The Curve of the Catenary." *Pictorial Review*. June –August 1916.
 Serial, mystery.
"Sight Unseen." *Everybody's*. June–August 1916.
 Serial, mystery.
 BOOK: *Sight Unseen and the Confession*. New·York: Doran, 1921.
"The Pirates of the Caribbean." *The Saturday Evening Post*. November 18, 1916.
 Travel article.
"Theme: The Celebrity." *The Saturday Evening Post*. November 25, 1916.
 Bab story; $1,750.
"On the Trail in Wonderland." *Wide World*. December 1916.
 Travel article.
"Twenty-Two." *Metropolitan*. (1917?).
 Story.

Bab: A Sub-Deb. New York: Doran, 1917.
Contents:
"The Sub-Deb"
"Theme: The Celebrity"
"Her Diary"
"Bab's Burglar"
"The G.A.C."
FILMS: *Bab's Burglar. Bab's Diary. Bab's Matinee Idol.* C. 1917. *Bab's Candidate.* C. 1920. Famous Players-Lasky. $10,000.
"Long Live the King" ("Otto the Ninth"). *Everybody's.* February–October 1917.
Serial, romance.
BOOK: *Long Live the King.* Boston: Houghton Mifflin, 1917.
FILM: *Long Live the King.* Jackie Coogan Prod. Metro, 1923. $20,000.
"Her Diary." *The Saturday Evening Post.* February 17, 1917.
Bab story; $1,750.
"The Raging Canal." *Cosmopolitan.* April 1917.
Travel article.
"The Altar of Freedom." *The Saturday Evening Post.* April 21, 1917.
War article; $1,000.
BOOK: *The Altar of Freedom.* Boston: Houghton Mifflin, 1917.
"The Confession." *Good Housekeeping.* May–August 1917.
Serial, mystery; $5,000.
BOOK: *Sight Unseen and the Confession.* New York: Doran, 1921.
"Bab's Burglar." *The Saturday Evening Post.* May 12, 1917.
Bab story; $2,000.
"The G.A.C." *The Saturday Evening Post.* June 2, 1917.
Bab story; $2,000.
"The Gray Mailed Fist." *The Saturday Evening Post.* June 23, 1917.
Navy article; $1,750.
"Tish Does Her Bit." *The Saturday Evening Post.* July 17, 1917.
Tish story; $2,000.
"One Woman's View of War." *Current Opinion.* August 1917.
War article.
"The Boys Are Marching." *The Saturday Evening Post.* August 18, 1917.
Army camp article; $2,000.
"For the Great Adventure." *The Saturday Evening Post.* August 25, 1917.
Army camp article (continuation of "The Boys Are Marching").
"My Creed." *American Magazine.* October 1917.
Article.
Tenting Tonight. Boston: Houghton Mifflin, 1918.
Travel book.
"From My Camp Window." *The Saturday Evening Post.* February 16, 1918.
War article.
"The Amazing Interlude." *The Saturday Evening Post.* February 23–March 30, 1918.
Serial, war story and romance; $10,000.
BOOK: *The Amazing Interlude.* New York: Doran, 1918.
"The Woman Behind the Soldier." *McClure's.* March 1918.
War article.

"The Family Goes a-Gypsying." *Outlook.* June 12, 1918.
   Travel article; $150.
"Going to the Sun." *The Saturday Evening Post.* July 20, 1918.
   War article.
"Twenty Three and a Half Hours Leave." *The Saturday Evening Post.* August 24, 1918.
   Story; $2,000.
   BOOK: *Twenty Three and a Half Hours Leave.* New York: Doran, 1918.
   FILMS: *Twenty Three and a Half Hours Leave.* Thomas H. Ince. Review 1919.
      C. 1919. *Twenty Three and a Half Hours Leave.* Grand National Films.
      Review 1937. C. 1937. $4,000.
"His Letters." *McClure's.* September 1918.
   Story; $1,000.
"The Gains of War." *McClure's.* October 1918.
   War article; $500.
"On the Trail in Mexico." *McCall's.* December 1918.
   Travel article; $1,900.
Love Stories. New York: Doran, 1919.
      Contents:
      "Twenty-Two"
      "Jane"
      "In the Pavilion"
      "God's Fool"
      "The Miracle"
      "Are We Downhearted? No!"
      "The Game"
"Dangerous Days." *Pictorial Review.* March 1919–(?).
   Serial, romance; $25,000.
   BOOK: *Dangerous Days.* New York: Doran, 1919.
   FILM: *Dangerous Days.* Eminent Authors (Goldwyn). C. 1920.
"Salvage." *The Saturday Evening Post.* June 6, 1919.
   Tish story.
"Ça ne fait rien." *The Saturday Evening Post.* July 19, 1919.
   Story.
"Isn't That Just like a Man?" *American Magazine.* October 1919.
   Article.
   BOOK: *Isn't That Just like a Man?* New York: Doran, 1920.
      (Combined with Irwin S. Cobb, *Well! You Know How Women Are!*)
"Finders Keepers." *The Saturday Evening Post.* October 4, 1919.
   Bab story.
   FILM: *Finders Keepers.* Universal. Review 1928. C. 1928. $14,500.
"The Sky's the Limit." *The Saturday Evening Post.* November 1919.
   Article; $1,000.

1920–1929

Affinities. New York: Doran, 1920.
      Contents:
      "Affinities"
      "The Family Friend"

"Clara's Little Escapade"
"The Borrowed House"
"Sauce for the Gander"
"A Poor Wise Man." *Ladies' Home Journal*. April–November 1920.
  Serial, romance.
  BOOK: *A Poor Wise Man*. New York: Doran, 1920.
"Waiting for the Stork." *Ladies' Home Journal*. August 1920.
  Article; $1,000.
Spanish Love. 1920.
  Play (with Avery Hopwood); opened August 17, 1920, Maxine Elliott;
    307 performances.
The Bat. 1920.
  Play (with Avery Hopwood); opened August 23, 1920, Morosco;
    878 performances.
  BOOK: *The Bat*. New York: Doran, 1926. (Fictionalized anonymously
    by Stephen Vincent Benét.)
  FILMS: *The Bat*. Feature Productions. Review 1926. C. 1926. *Bat Whispers*. Art
    Cinema Corporation. Review 1931. C. 1931. MRR's share: $11,875.
    (Una Merkle starred.)
"My Experience in the Movies." *American Magazine*. October 1920.
  Autobiographical article.
"My Public." *Bookman*. December 1920.
  Autobiographical article.
More Tish. New York: Doran, 1921.
    Contents:
    "The Cave on Thundercloud"
    "Tish Does Her Bit"
    "Salvage"
"The Year's Big Business." *Good Housekeeping*. January 1921.
  Article.
"A New Citizen in the White House." *Ladies' Home Journal*. March 1921.
  Editorial.
"Home or a Career?" *Ladies' Home Journal*. April 1921.
  Editorial.
"The Sleeping Giant." *Ladies' Home Journal*. May 1921.
  Editorial.
"How About the Movies?" *Ladies' Home Journal*. June 1921.
  Editorial.
"The Breaking Point." *McClure's*. June-July 1921–August 1922.
  Serial, romance; $30,000.
  BOOK: *The Breaking Point*. New York: Doran, 1921.
  PLAY: *The Breaking Point*. Opened August 16, 1923, Klaw; 68 performances.
  FILM: *The Breaking Point*. Famous Players. C. 1924. $18,000.
"The Magnet of Success." *Ladies' Home Journal*. July 1921.
  Editorial.
"Two Billions Waste." *Ladies' Home Journal*. August 1921.
  Editorial.
"Freedom and Our Changing Standards." *Ladies' Home Journal*. September 1921.
  Editorial.

"A Midsummer's Knight's Dream." *The Saturday Evening Post*. December 17, 1921.
    Story: $4,000.
The Out Trail. New York: Doran, 1922.
    Travel book.
"The Great Success." *McCall's*. 1922.
    Story; $2,475.
"Tish Plays the Game." *The Saturday Evening Post*. March 4, 1922.
    Tish story; $2,200.
"Roughing It with the Men." *American Magazine*. December 1922.
    Article.
"The Unreality of Modern Realism." *Bookman*. December 1922.
    Article.
"A Houseboat on the Keys." *Good Housekeeping*. July 1923.
    Travel article.
"The Baby Blimp." *The Saturday Evening Post*. August 25, 1923.
    Tish story; $3,000.
Temperamental People. New York: Doran, 1924.
        Contents:
            "Her Majesty"
            "The Altar on the Hill"
            "Cynara"
            "The Great Success"
            "The Secret House"
            "A Midsummer's Knight's Dream"
            "Lily"
            "Ça ne fait rien"
"Imagination and the String Bean." *Collier's*. 1924.
    Story; $3,500.
"Cynara." *Collier's*. March 1924.
    Story: $3,500.
"Adventures Into the Unknown." *Cosmopolitan*. April–May 1924.
    Two-part spiritualism article; $3,500.
"The Altar on the Hill." *The Saturday Evening Post*. June 14, 1924.
    Story; $2,500.
    FILM: *The Silent Watcher*. First National. C. 1924. $20,000.
"Butler, the Trouble Shooter." *Collier's*. July 1924.
    Article.
"Her Majesty—The Queen." *Cosmopolitan*. July 1924.
    Story.
    FILM: *Her Love Story*. Famous Players-Lasky. Review 1924. C. 1924. $21,000.
        (Gloria Swanson starred.)
"These Girls of Ours." *Delineator*. December 1924.
    Article.
"The Red Lamp." *Cosmopolitan*. January 7, 1925–(?).
    Serial, mystery; $40,000.
    BOOK: *The Red Lamp*. New York: Doran, 1925.
"Hijack and the Game." *The Saturday Evening Post*. January 31, 1925.
    Tish story.

"The Surgeon Explodes a Bomb. *The Saturday Evening Post*. February 7, 1925.
 Story; $3,500.
"Summer Comes to the Ranch." *The Saturday Evening Post*. July 4, 1925.
 Travel article; $2,000.
"Little Goldilocks." *The Saturday Evening Post*. October 3, 1925.
 Story; $3,500.
"Riding the Circle on Hanging Woman." *The Saturday Evening Post*. October 17, 1925.
 Travel article; $2,500.
Tish Plays the Game. New York: Doran, 1926.
  Contents:
  "Tish Plays the Game"
  "The Baby Blimp"
  "Hijack and the Game"
  "The Treasure Hunt"
  "The Gray Goose"
"After Twenty Years." *The Republican Woman*. 1926.
 Article.
"The Lark." 1926.
 Film Script; $3,000.
"My America." *Metropolitan News Service*. January 20, 1926.
 Article.
"The Treasure Hunt." *The Saturday Evening Post*. February 13, 1926.
 Tish story; $4,000.
"Willie Cheatham Looks at the Senate." *The Saturday Evening Post*. March 20, 1926.
 Article.
"Two Flights Up." *Redbook*. April–July 1926.
 Serial, mystery and romance; $20,000.
 BOOK: *Two Flights Up*. New York: Doran, 1926.
 FILM SALE: Famous Players-Lasky, 1926. $2,000. (Option lapsed.)
"Nomad's Land." *Cosmopolitan*. April–July 1926.
 Travel articles; $10,000.
 BOOK: *Nomad's Land*. New York: Doran, 1926.
  Contents:
  "Nomad's Land"
  "Hunting Trouble"
  "Summer Comes to the Ranch"
  "Riding the Circle on Hanging Woman"
  "The Sky's the Limit"
"The Trumpet Sounds." *Collier's*. April 24, 1926.
 Story; $4,000.
 BOOK: *The Trumpet Sounds*. New York: Doran, 1927.
"The Gray Goose." *The Saturday Evening Post*. August 14, 1926.
 Tish story; $4,000.
"The Cavvy." *The Saturday Evening Post*. September 25, 1926.
 First part of travel article; $4,000 (for two parts).
"To Wyoming." *The Saturday Evening Post*. October 2, 1926.
 Second part of travel article.
"A Rock River Fugitive." *Youth's Companion*. November 11, 1926.
 Story; $40.00 (sold twenty years earlier).

"Lost Ecstasy." *The Saturday Evening Post.* April 16 –June 17, 1927.
    Serial, romance; $50,000.
    BOOK: *Lost Ecstasy.* New York: Doran, 1927.
    FILM: *I Take This Woman.* Paramount. C. 1931. $15,000. (Gary Cooper and
      Carole Lombard starred.)
"What Is a Dude Ranch?" *Harper's Bazaar.* August 1927.
    Article; $1,500.
"Just a Touch of Celebrity." *The Saturday Evening Post.* January 14, 1928.
    Autobiographical article; $2,500.
"Companionate Marriage." *McCall's.* March 13, 1928.
    Article.
"I Buy Clothes Twice a Year." *Ladies' Home Journal.* March 14, 1928.
    Article.
"This Strange Adventure." *Pictorial Review.* October 1928–February 1929.
    Serial, romance; $60,000.
    BOOK: *This Strange Adventure.* New York: Doubleday Doran, 1929.
The Romantics. New York: Farrar and Rinehart, 1929.
        Contents:
        "The Old Man Cleans His Revolver"
        "The Second Honeymoon"
        "The Papered Door"
        "Red Rides It Out"
        "An Error in Treatment"
        "The Trumpet Sounds"
        "His Letters"
        "The String Bean"
"Writing as a Career." *Bookman.* February 1929.
    Article.
"A New First Lady Becomes Hostess for the Nation." *World's Work.* March 1929.
    Article; $1,250.
"Dude West." *Ladies' Home Journal.* April 1929.
    Article; $2,500.
"The Dipper." *The Saturday Evening Post.* April 13, 1929.
    Tish story; $4,000.
"A Lodge in Some Vast Wilderness." *American Home.* May 1929.
    Article; $250.
"Etiquette in Washington." *Woman's World.* June 1929.
    Article.
"Passing the Theatrical Buck." *Theatre Magazine.* June 1929.
    Article.
"The Second Honeymoon." *Ladies' Home Journal.* July 1929.
    Story; $4,000.
"If Only It Were Yesterday." *Ladies' Home Journal.* August 1929.
    Story; $2,500.
"The Old Man Cleans His Revolver." *Cosmopolitan.* August 1929.
    Story; $2,500.
"In Praise of Discontent." *Ladies' Home Journal.* December 1929.
    Article; $2,500.

1930–1939

Mary Roberts Rinehart's Mystery Book. New York: Farrar and Rinehart, 1930.
> Contents:
> *The Circular Staircase*
> *The Man in Lower 10*
> *The Case of Jennie Brice*
> *The Confession*

"The Door." *The Saturday Evening Post*. February 1–March 22, 1930.
> Serial, mystery; $60,000.
> BOOK: *The Door*. New York: Farrar and Rinehart, 1930.

"The Increasing Repute of the Crime Story." *Publishers Weekly*. February 1930.
> Article.

"The Chaotic Decade." *Ladies' Home Journal*. May 1930.
> Article; $2,500.

"The Oyster Has a Mouth." *The Saturday Evening Post*. June 28, 1930.
> Tish story (two parts?); $7,500.

"The Cruise of the Greyhound." *The Saturday Evening Post*. August 30, 1930.
> Travel article; $3,000.

"The Effect of Fashion on Manners." *Ladies' Home Journal*. October 1930.
> Article; $2,500.

"My Story." *Good Housekeeping*. October 1930–May 1931.
> Autobiography; $45,000.
> BOOK: *My Story*. New York: Farrar and Rinehart, 1931.

"Why Crime Stories Are Popular." *True Detective Mysteries*. November 1930.
> Article.

The Book of Tish. New York: Farrar and Rinehart, 1931.
> Contents:
> *Tish*
> *More Tish*
> *Tish Plays the Game*
> "The Amazing Adventures of Letitia Carberry"
> "Three Pirates of Penzance"

Mary Roberts Rinehart's Romance Book. New York: Farrar and Rinehart, 1931.
> Contents:
> *"K"*
> *The Amazing Interlude*
> *The Street of Seven Stars*

"A Woman Goes to Market." *The Saturday Evening Post*, January 31, 1931.
> Autobiographical article.

"Your Child and the Movies." *Ladies' Home Journal*. April 1931.
> Article; $2,500.

"Thoughts." *Ladies' Home Journal*. May 1931–June 1932.
> Editorials; $2,500 each until April 1932; then $2,000.

"The Worst Job in the World." *American Magazine*. July 1931.
> Article.

"The Future of Marriage: A Socratic Dialogue." *Forum*. August 1931.
> Discussion.

"Miss Pinkerton." *The Saturday Evening Post.* January 2–February 13, 1932.
 Serial, mystery; $50,000.
 BOOK: *Miss Pinkerton.* New York: Farrar and Rinehart, 1932.
 FILM: *Miss Pinkerton.* Warner Bros. Review 1932. C. 1932. $30,000. (Joan
  Blondell and George Brent starred.)
"If I Had a Daughter." *Forum.* March 1932.
 Article; $500.
"Our House." *Home and Field.* April 1932.
 Article.
"Women on a Dude Ranch." *Harper's Bazaar.* April 9, 1932.
 Article.
"That Is All." *The Saturday Evening Post.* April 16, 1932.
 Story; $4,000.
"Who Will Be Nominated?" *Ladies' Home Journal.* June 1932.
 Article.
"Sounds in Silence." *Ladies' Home Journal.* July 1932.
 Article.
"Your America and Mine." *Cosmopolitan.* July 1932.
 Article; $1,750.
"Tish." July 12–September 8, 1932.
 Radio plays: July 12, 1932, $1,200; July 27, 1932, $800; August 12, 1932,
  $800; August 20, 1932, $400; September 8, 1932, $800.
"The Gold-Button Fish." *Good Housekeeping.* August 1932.
 Story; $2,500.
"Why Don't You Use Your Vote?" *Ladies' Home Journal.* August 1932.
 Article.
"Taking the Cure in Europe." *The Saturday Evening Post.* October 1, 1932.
 Article; $1,500.
"Code No. 31." *The Saturday Evening Post.* October 15, 1932.
 Story; $3,500.
"The Better Man." *Good Housekeeping.* December 1932.
 Story; $4,000.
The Crime Book. New York: Farrar and Rinehart, 1933.
    Contents:
    The After House
    "The Buckled Bag"
    "Locked Doors"
    The Red Lamp
    The Window at the White Cat
"*The Tinsel Star.*" *Cosmopolitan.* January 1933.
 Story; $5,000.
"Mr. Cohen Takes a Walk." *Good Housekeeping.* February 1933.
 Story; $5,000.
 BOOK: *Mr. Cohen Takes a Walk.* New York: Farrar and Rinehart, 1934.
 FILM: *Mr. Cohen Takes a Walk.* Warner Bros. Review 1936. $7,000.
"The Album." *The Saturday Evening Post.* April 8–May 27, 1933.
 Serial, mystery; $60,000.
 BOOK: *The Album.* New York: Farrar and Rinehart, 1933.

"The State Vs. Elinor Norton." *Ladies' Home Journal.* September 1933–January 1934.
Serial, romance; $45,000.
BOOK: *The State Vs. Elinor Norton.* New York: Farrar and Rinehart, 1933.
FILM: *The State Vs. Elinor Norton.* Fox Films. C. 1934. $20,000.
"Can Women Stop Crime?" *The Saturday Evening Post.* November 18, 1933.
Article; $1,500.
"The Fallacy of Freedom." *Good Housekeeping.* December 1934.
Article; $1,500.
"Looking for the Magic Word." *Cosmopolitan.* December 1934.
Article; $2,000.
"The Inside Story." *The Saturday Evening Post.* December 22, 1934.
Story; $4,000.
"The Lighted Candle." *Cosmopolitan.* January 1935.
Article; $1,000.
"Women of the Year as Seen by Mary Roberts Rinehart." *Pictorial Review.* January
1935.
Article.
"The Family Pays the Bill." *Ladies' Home Journal.* March 1935.
Article.
"The Tall Tree." *Good Housekeeping.* May 1935.
Story; $4,000.
"The Second Marriage." *Ladies' Home Journal.* June 1935.
Story; $4,000.
"The Uselessness of Fear." *Cosmopolitan.* June 6, 1935.
Article; $1,000.
"Spreading Christmas Throughout the Year." *Reader's Digest.* December 1935.
Article; $500.
"The Doctor." *Good Housekeeping.* January–July 1936.
Serial, romance; $75,000.
BOOK: *The Doctor.* New York: Farrar and Rinehart, 1936.
"Lightning Never Strikes Twice." *The Saturday Evening Post.* June 6, 1936.
Story; $5,000.
TELEVISION PLAY: Screen Gems, June 1955. $1,000.
"The Man Who Killed His Wife." *Cosmopolitan.* August 1936.
Story; $4,000.
"Valiant Picture for a Valiant Star." *Woman's Home Companion.* October 1936.
Article.
"The Sanctuary." *Good Housekeeping.* November 1936.
Story; $5,000.
"Experiment in Youth." *Cosmopolitan.* December 1936.
Story; $5,000.
"Tish Goes to Jail." *The Saturday Evening Post.* December 19, 1936.
Tish story; $4,000.
Married People. New York: Farrar and Rinehart, 1937.
Contents:
"An Experiment in Youth"
"The Inside Story"
"The Tall Tree"

"Sanctuary"
"That Is All"
"Code No. 31"
"The Second Marriage"
"The Man Who Killed His Wife"
"Lightning Never Strikes Twice"
"The Better Man"
"The Tinsel Star"

Tish Marches On. New York: Farrar and Rinehart, 1937.

Contents:
"Strange Journey"
"Tish Marches On"
"The Mouse"
"Tish Goes to Jail"
"The Oyster"
"The Dipper"

"I Speak for Wives." *Ladies' Home Journal.* February 1937.
Article; $2,000.

"The Mouse." *The Saturday Evening Post.* June 12, 1937.
Tish story; $4,000.

"The Young Visitor." *The Saturday Evening Post.* July 3, 1937.
Story; $4,000.

"Strange Journey." *The Saturday Evening Post.* October 16, 1937.
Tish story; $4,000.

"Tish Marches On." *The Saturday Evening Post.* November 20, 1937.
Tish story.

"Before the Drums Beat." *Good Housekeeping.* January 1938.
Article.

"The Philanderer's Wife." *Cosmopolitan.* February 1938.
Story; $5,000.
RADIO PLAY: September 1938 (San Francisco). $200.

"The Wall." *The Saturday Evening Post.* May 14–July 9, 1938.
Serial, mystery; $65,000.
BOOK: *The Wall.* New York: Farrar and Rinehart, 1938.

"Writing Is Work." *The Saturday Evening Post.* March 11, 1939.
Article; $1,500.
BOOK: *Writing Is Work.* Boston: The Writer, Inc. 1939.

1940–1949

"Dorothy Dresses for Dinner." *Cosmopolitan.* January 1940.
Story; $4,000.

"Lily Comes Home at Last." *Cosmopolitan.* April 1940.
Story; $5,000.

"One Hour of Glory." *Good Housekeeping.* May 1940.
Story; $5,000.
FILM SALE: Warner Bros., (1940–1941?). $5,500. (Never produced.)

"The Dog in the Orchard." *Cosmopolitan.* September 1940.
Story; $4,000.

FILM: *The Dog in the Orchard.* Warner Bros. C. 1941. $500. (Howard da Silva
 starred.)
"The Great Mistake." *The Saturday Evening Post.* September 7–November 2, 1940.
 Serial, mystery; $55,000.
 BOOK: *The Great Mistake.* New York: Farrar and Rinehart, 1940.
Familiar Faces. New York: Farrar and Rinehart, 1941.
 Contents:
 "One Hour of Glory"
 "The Young Visitor"
 "The Dog in the Orchard"
 "The Philanderer's Wife"
 "One Night in Spring"
 "The Door That Would Not Stay Closed"
 "The Empire Builders"
 "Lily Comes Home at Last"
 "Dorothy Dresses for Dinner"
 "Mr. Caswell Looks out the Window"
 "Mr. Cohen Takes a Walk"
The Nurse's Secret. Warner Bros. Review 1941. C. 1941.
 Film.
"Mr. Caswell Looks out the Window." *Cosmopolitan.* February 1941.
 Story; $5,000.
"The Door That Would Not Stay Closed." *Good Housekeeping.* June 1941.
 Story; $5,000.
 TELEVISION PLAY: Screen Gems, December 18, 1953. $1,500.
"America." *Cosmopolitan.* August 1941.
 Article; $2,000.
"One Night in Spring." *Redbook.* August 1941.
 Story; $2,000.
"The Fishing Fool." *Cosmopolitan.* September 1941.
 Story; $5,000.
"The Pattern." *Good Housekeeping.* December 1941.
 Article; $750?
Tish. Review 1942. C. 1942.
 Film. (Majorie Main starred.)
"Haunted Lady." *Cosmopolitan.* March–May 1942.
 Serial, mystery; $35,000.
 BOOK: *Haunted Lady.* New York: Farrar and Rinehart, 1942.
"Building a Marriage." *Cosmopolitan.* June 1942.
 Article.
"The Lipstick." *Cosmopolitan.* July 1942.
 Story; $5,000.
"The Time Is Ten." *Good Housekeeping.* July 1942.
 Story; $4,000.
"The Temporary Death of Mrs. Ayres." *Good Housekeeping.* October 1942.
 Story; $5,000.
"The Battered Angel." *Cosmopolitan.* January 1943.
 Story; $5,000.

"Episode of the Wandering Knife." *Good Housekeeping.* June and July 1943.
    Serial, mystery; $20,000.
        BOOK: *Episode of the Wandering Knife.* New York: Rinehart, 1950.
           Contents:
           "Episode of the Wandering Knife"
           "The Man Who Hid His Breakfast"
           "The Secret"
Alibi for Isabel and Other Stories. New York: Farrar and Rinehart, 1944.
           Contents:
           "Once to Every Man"
           "The Fishing Fool"
           "The Clue in the Closet"
           "Test Blackout"
           "The Portrait"
           "Alibi for Isabel"
           "The Temporary Death of Mrs. Ayres"
           "The Butler's Christmas Eve"
           "The Lipstick"
"The Clue in the Closet." *Cosmopolitan.* March 1944.
    Story; $5,000.
"Once to Every Man." *Woman's Home Companion.* June 1944.
    Story; $4,000.
"The Portrait." *Cosmopolitan.* June 1944.
    Story; $5,000.
"Alibi for Isabel." *Good Housekeeping.* August 1944.
    Story; $5,000.
"Edwin and the Hospital Shirt." *The Saturday Evening Post.* November 4, 1944.
    Story; $2,500.
        RADIO PLAY: "Saturday Evening Post Program" (WJZ), October 1944.
"The Dowager and the Milkman." *Woman's Home Companion.* April 1945.
    Story; $4,000.
"Murder and the South Wind." *Good Housekeeping.* June 1945.
    Story; $5,000.
"The Yellow Room." *The Saturday Evening Post.* September 8–October 27, 1945.
    Serial, mystery.
        BOOK: *The Yellow Room.* New York: Farrar and Rinehart, 1945.
"I Had Cancer." With Gretta Palmer. *Ladies' Home Journal.* July 1947.
    Article.
"A Light in the Window." *Ladies' Home Journal.* October 1947–February 1948.
    Serial, romance; $50,000.
        BOOK: *A Light in the Window.* New York: Rinehart, 1948.
My Story: A New Edition and Seventeen New Years. New York: Rinehart, 1948.
    Autobiography.
"Four A.M." *Cosmopolitan.* September 1948.
    Story; $5,000.
"The Unbreakable Alibi." *The Saturday Evening Post.* April 9, 1949.
    Story; $10,000?
"The Man Upstairs." *The Saturday Evening Post.* June 18, 1949.
    Story; $3,500

"Phoenix in New England." *Town and Country*. July 1949.
     Article; $300.

1950–1957

"Hazard." *Good Housekeeping*. January 1950.
     Story; $2,250.
"Things I Can't Explain." *Reader's Digest*. April 1950.
     Article.
"The Scandal." *The Saturday Evening Post*. July 15, 1950.
     Story; $3,500.
"The Case Is Closed." *This Week*. March 10–24, 1951.
     Serial; $5,000.
The Swimming Pool. New York: Rinehart, 1952.
"The Frightened Wife." *The Saturday Evening Post*. February 14–March 7, 1953.
     Serial, mystery; $30,000.
     BOOK: *The Frightened Wife and Other Murder Stories*. New York: Rinehart,
          1953.
          Contents:
          "The Frightened Wife"
          "If Only It Were Yesterday"
          "The Scandal"
          "Murder and the South Wind"
          "The Burned Chair"
"Welcome Home." *Collier's*. June 26, 1953.
     Story; $3,500.
"Please Come Home for Christmas." *Collier's*. December 25, 1953.
     Story.
"The Splinter." *Ellery Queen's Mystery Magazine*. May 1954.
     Story; $400.
The Best of Tish. New York: Rinehart, 1955.
          Contents:
          "Mind Over Motor"
          "The Cave on Thundercloud"
          "The Simple Lifers"
          "Tish Does Her Bit"
          "Salvage"
          "Tish Plays the Game"
          "The Baby Blimp"
          "Hijack and the Game"
          "The Dipper"
          "Tish Goes to Jail"
          "Strange Journey"
          "Tish Marches On"
The Mary Roberts Rinehart Crime Book. New York: Rinehart, 1957.
          Contents:
          The Door
          The Confession
          The Red Lamp

Index

The titles of Rinehart works cited in the text are listed alphabetically here; the first publication date of each is noted in parentheses following the title, for convenience in locating it in the chronological bibliography.